D1337287

LITIGATING RIGHTS

THE LIBRARY

University of Ulster at Magee

Due Back (subject to recall)

0 8 DEC 2005		
0 6 JAN 2010		
2 8 NOV 2013		
1 1 MAY 2016		

Fines will apply to items returned after due date

1312/1199/12/99

Litigating Rights

*Perspectives from Domestic
and International Law*

Edited by
GRANT HUSCROFT
The University of Western Ontario

and

PAUL RISHWORTH
The University of Auckland

·H A R T·
PUBLISHING

OXFORD – PORTLAND OREGON
2002

Hart Publishing
Oxford and Portland, Oregon

Published in North America (US and Canada) by
Hart Publishing c/o
International Specialized Book Services
5804 NE Hassalo Street
Portland, Oregon
97213-3644
USA

Distributed in the Netherlands, Belgium and Luxembourg by
Intersentia, Churchillaan 108
B2900 Schoten
Antwerpen
Belgium

Hart Publishing is a specialist legal publisher based in Oxford, England.
To order further copies of this book or to request a list of other
publications please write to:

Hart Publishing, Salter's Boatyard, Folly Bridge,
Abingdon Road, Oxford OX1 4LB
Telephone: +44 (0)1865 245533 or Fax: +44 (0)1865 794882
e-mail: mail@hartpub.co.uk
WEBSITE: http//www.hartpub.co.uk

British Library Cataloguing in Publication Data
Data Available
ISBN 1–84113–194–6 (hardback)

Typeset by Hope Services (Abingdon) Ltd.
Printed and bound in Great Britain on acid-free paper by
Biddles Ltd, www.biddles.co.uk

Preface

This book has its origins in New Zealand, a country that considered but rejected the adoption of a supreme-law bill of rights in the 1980s. A statutory bill of rights—The New Zealand Bill of Rights Act—was enacted in 1990, and its constitutional status remains a matter of debate. By the late 1990s, however, the call for human rights in New Zealand seemed to capture the egalitarian spirit of New Zealanders in a way that the 1980s liberal conception of a Bill of Rights had not. Some pointed to New Zealand's anti-discrimination statute—entitled the "Human Rights Act", despite its limited scope—and asked whether Parliament should be free to enact laws overriding it. Override "human rights"? It was one thing not to have a written constitution, but could Parliament really override *human rights*?

Of course, it is not all that simple, as jurists know. The question is not *whether* human rights should be protected, but *how* they should be protected, and what their protection means. To explore these questions, we assembled a group of leading jurists from New Zealand and abroad. The idea was to debate the subject of rights and the desirability of protecting them in constitutions enforced by judges. The result was a lively and enjoyable conference that we called "Liberty, Equality, Community: Constitutional Rights in Conflict". Some of the flavour of the conference can be appreciated from a transcript of part of the proceedings published in the *New Zealand Law Review* ("A Dialogue on Rights" [1999] *NZ Law Review* 547).

We are grateful to those who participated in the conference, but in particular want to single out the keynote speakers: Justice Ian Binnie of the Supreme Court of Canada; Justice Antonin Scalia of the United States Supreme Court; Elizabeth Evatt, then a member of the United Nations Human Rights Committee; Professor Hilary Charlesworth of the Australian National University; Professor Nadine Strossen, President of the American Civil Liberties Union; and Professor Jeremy Waldron of Columbia University, all of whom came a long way to attend, and gave generously of their time to staff and students at The University of Auckland Faculty of Law during their visits.

The conference could not have happened without the support of the former President of the Legal Research Foundation, Justice Bruce Robertson (now President of the New Zealand Law Commission), the Foundation's Director, Bruce Gray, and the Foundation's Secretary, Jane Kilgour. We thank them, and all those who attended and contributed to the success of the conference.

Following the conference there was an opportunity to revise papers, and we sought additional contributions. We are grateful to Murray Hunt and Ian Leigh, both of whom contributed papers addressing the Human Rights Act 1998 (UK), and to Tim Dare, who contributed a paper introducing the group rights discussion.

The result is a collection of essays that examines the nature of rights and constitutional adjudication not only in New Zealand but also the United States, Canada, and the United Kingdom. The experience with international adjudicative bodies like the United Nations Human Rights Committee is also considered, along with the challenge of integrating the concerns of indigenous peoples and conceptions of group rights into the framework of constitutional adjudication.

Thanks to Lucy Barker (LLB (Hons), Auckland, 2001), who provided research and editorial assistance of exceptional quality.

Finally, thanks to Richard Hart for his support of this book, and his patience with us in completing it. We hope that it contributes to further discussion and debate about human rights and judicial review.

Grant Huscroft and Paul Rishworth

Contents

Part IV—Internationalism

List of Contributors

James Allan is Associate Professor of Law at the University of Otago.

The Hon Justice Ian Binnie is a Justice of the Supreme Court of Canada.

Andrew Butler is counsel at the Crown Law Office in Wellington, New Zealand.

Hilary Charlesworth is Professor of Law and Director of the Centre for International and Public Law at the Australian National University.

Tim Dare is Senior Lecturer in Philosophy at The University of Auckland.

Scott Davidson is Professor of Law at the University of Hull.

Justice Eddie Durie is a member of the High Court of New Zealand and President of the Waitangi Tribunal.

Elizabeth Evatt was a member of the United Nations Human Rights Committee from 1993 to 2000.

Murray Hunt is a Barrister and member of Matrix Chambers in London.

Grant Huscroft is Associate Professor of Law at The University of Western Ontario.

Ian Leigh is Professor of Law at Durham University.

Paul Rishworth is Associate Professor of Law at The University of Auckland.

Justice Antonin Scalia is an Associate Justice of the United States Supreme Court.

Andrew Sharp is Professor of Political Studies at The University of Auckland.

Nadine Strossen is Professor of Law at the New York Law School and President of the American Civil Liberties Union.

Jeremy Waldron is the Maurice and Hilda Friedman Professor of Law and Director of the Center for Law and Philosophy at Columbia University.

PART I

Judicial Review and Bills of Rights

1

Rights, Bills of Rights, and the Role of Courts and Legislatures

GRANT HUSCROFT★

I

It is not long since the United States was one of the few western democracies to have a bill of rights. Now, it seems, countries without bills of rights are in a minority, and they are criticised for not having them. Countries like New Zealand and the United Kingdom, which have recently adopted bills of rights, do not escape criticism; they are criticised because their bills of rights preclude the judiciary from overturning legislation. This, it is said, offers inadequate protection for rights. The fact that these countries have human rights records that are enviable by international standards—including those countries with entrenched, supreme-law bills of rights—counts for little:[1] the United Nations Human Rights Committee has on several occasions expressed "regret" that countries like New Zealand do not have supreme-law bills of rights, even though it is clear that nothing in the International Covenant on Civil and Political Rights requires the adoption of a bill of rights, let alone a supreme-law model.[2]

If it is difficult to argue against the idea of bills of rights, it is even more difficult to argue against expansive interpretations of the rights they protect. Outside the United States, it appears to be well settled that bills of rights are to be interpreted "generously". As Lord Wilberforce put it in an oft-cited dictum, bills of rights:[3]

> "call for a generous interpretation avoiding what has been called 'the austerity of tabulated legalism,' suitable to give to individuals the full measure of the fundamental rights and freedoms referred to".

The willingness of the courts to adopt "generous interpretations" often negates the intention to limit the scope of rights at the drafting stage. For example, having studied American constitutional law, the drafters of the Canadian Charter of Rights and

---

★ Thanks to Jim Allan, Neil Campbell, Janet McLean, and Mike Taggart for comments on an earlier draft.

[1] Indeed, having an entrenched bill of rights *and* an enviable human rights record may count for little; Canada is more likely to be required to defend itself before the United Nations Human Rights Committee than most other countries.

[2] Cf Butler's and Evatt's contributions to this volume, discussing the criticism of the United Nations Human Rights Committee.

[3] *Minister of Home Affairs* v. *Fisher* [1980] AC 319, 328 (PC).

Freedoms (the "Charter") sought to avoid interference with substantive law by using the term "fundamental justice" instead of "due process". That due *process* ought never to have been interpreted to include a substantive component in the first place—"substantive due process",[4] as it is called—apparently persuaded no one in Canada of the futility of their enterprise. Predictably, shortly following passage of the Charter the Supreme Court of Canada held that fundamental justice did in fact have a substantive component, regardless of clear evidence indicating a contrary intention.[5] The Court noted that had procedural protections been intended the narrower term "natural justice" could have been used.[6] That term was in fact adopted by those who drafted the New Zealand Bill of Rights, again in an attempt to limit the right to procedural protection,[7] but it would be naive to suppose that this term will be any more successful than its predecessors. Nothing prevents natural justice or any other term with a well-understood meaning from being interpreted more expansively if the courts are disposed to doing so. Indeed, arguments that a bill of rights means what it says, or what it was intended to mean, have become the stuff of parody—"ancestor worship", according to some.[8]

What are we to make of all this? The lesson to be learned, I think, is that the manner in which rights disputes are resolved is much more important than the particular rights that a bill of rights protects, or the manner in which those rights are expressed. Far from being a mere corollary of the importance of protecting rights, judicial review is the raison d'être for modern bills of rights.

II

This is not the ostensible purpose of bills of rights. On the contrary, the argument for bills of rights has usually depended upon the appeal of the individual rights and freedoms they protect. What is more, the argument has usually been based upon the sorts of examples that make opposition to their protection seem churlish.[9]

---

[4] See generally, L Tribe, *American Constitutional Law* 3rd edn. (New York, Foundation Press, 2000) 1332–81.

[5] *Re BC Motor Vehicle Act* [1985] 2 SCR 486, 504–5.

[6] *Ibid*, 503–4.

[7] The White Paper describes natural justice as of central importance in ensuring that the powers of public authorities are exercised "in a fair way", and contemplates compliance with "procedures" varying in relation to the seriousness of the substantive matter, with courts determining the rights and interests which would be accorded "this degree of procedural protection". Where substantive as well as procedural protection was intended (eg, the right to life in s 8), the term "fundamental justice" was used. See *A Bill of Rights for New Zealand* (1985) AJHR A6, 87–8 (right to life), 109–10 (right to natural justice).

[8] M Kirby, "Constitutional Interpretation and Original Intent: A Form of Ancestor Worship?" (2000) 24 *Melbourne University Law Review* 1.

[9] Indeed, the same is true of the argument for an implied bill of rights. It is no accident that those who asserted judicial power to refuse to enforce legislation seized upon examples like torture—a right unlikely to be infringed in a modern democracy. Lord Cooke's assertion that "[s]ome common law rights presumably lie so deep that even Parliament could not override them" (*Taylor* v. *New Zealand Poultry Board* [1984] 1 NZLR 394, 398) could not otherwise be taken seriously. The development of Cooke's assertion is chronicled (and criticized) in M Kirby, "Lord Cooke and Fundamental Rights" in P Rishworth (ed.), *The Struggle for Simplicity in the Law* (Wellington, Butterworths, 1997) 331, 334–9.

Judicial review is proffered as a means to the end of protecting rights, rather than the end itself. This is unsurprising: no one would be heard to suggest that democratic decision-making should be replaced by judicial rule.

But rights violations are seldom of the sort that give rise to the decision to adopt a bill of rights in the first place. Limitations on rights are bound to be established, but these will usually be thoughtful, rather than arbitrary; and they are bound to be controversial. The question is not whether a bill of rights is required in order to prevent cruel or unusual punishment, slavery, or the taking of life—matters on which everyone may be expected to agree, so long as the meaning of the terms is not explored in any detail. The question is whether such things as life sentences without parole, work-for-welfare legislation, and legislation regulating abortion are permissible or precluded. The answer to these sorts of questions is not obvious and, as Jeremy Waldron has argued, there is no obvious reason why we should privilege the views of judges in resolving them.[10]

III

The White Paper that proposed the entrenchment of a bill of rights in New Zealand makes interesting reading in retrospect. Written in 1984, it raised the spectre of an out-of-control state:[11]

> "Parliament has supreme law-making powers . . . Furthermore, the powers can be exercised overnight: the law requires no particular notice to be given or a period of time to pass before legislation, even of the most drastic kind, is approved by the House.
>
> That is to say, the law and convention of the constitution gives the Executive, through Parliament, very wide powers, possibly unrestrained by law, to take away our most precious rights and freedoms, rights and freedoms which have been won, enlarged, and affirmed over long centuries."

The political processes, both formal and informal, were said to offer inadequate protection. Elections were described as "blunt instruments", unable to deliver judgments on particular issues. Less formal political processes were potentially part of the problem: "they can ride roughshod over minority interests" and, as with elections, they were "subject to possible threat from the great powers of the State" in any event.[12] The solution, according to the White Paper, was judicial review, with courts empowered to strike down laws found to be inconsistent with the Bill of Rights.

The White Paper conceded that "[n]o Government and no Parliament we are likely to have in New Zealand in the foreseeable future are going to attempt to sweep away basic rights", but said that was not the real point. "What is in point is the continual danger—the constant temptation for a zealous Executive—of

---

[10] See generally J Waldron, *Law and Disagreement* (Oxford, Clarendon Press, 1999).
[11] *A Bill of Rights for New Zealand* (1985) AJHR A6, 25.
[12] *Ibid*, 27.

making small erosions of these rights. . . . [E]ach small step makes the next small step easier and more seductive."[13]

This is, in essence, a slippery slope argument, and it does not support the proposition that a supreme-law bill of rights is required. It would be one thing if the parameters of the protected rights were well known and accepted, but in fact the opposite is true: there is, and always will be, disagreement about the nature and extent of even the most basic rights. So it is not simply a matter of empowering the courts to protect rights; it is about empowering the courts to determine what rights we have.

The White Paper answered the objection that a bill of rights was unnecessary with an aphorism: "It is much better not to wait for a flood before we build the dam."[14] At the same time, the White Paper sought to minimise the force of objections to the transfer of power to the judiciary that entrenchment would entail by maintaining that the scope of judicial review under the Bill of Rights would be limited: "[W]ith a very few quite basic exceptions the Bill of Rights would not control matters of substance", it declared—only to undermine this assurance with a question-begging qualification: "It is another matter if [policies] are pursued beyond necessity and beyond their proper importance at the expense of individual rights and freedoms."[15]

There is something disquieting about advocating judicial review while promising to limit its scope. But there is a larger objection. As we noted earlier, rights are usually given generous interpretations by courts, thus precluding attempts to limit the scope of judicial review in any event. Ronald Dworkin has sought to justify this, arguing that bills of rights call for a "moral reading":[16]

> "Most contemporary constitutions declare individual rights against the government in very broad and abstract language . . . The moral reading proposes that we all—judges, lawyers, citizens—interpret and apply these abstract clauses on the understanding that they invoke moral principles about political decency and justice. . . . So when some novel or controversial constitutional issue arises . . . [we] must decide how an abstract moral principle is best understood."

Dworkin denies the charge that his moral reading theory gives judges "absolute power to impose their own moral convictions on the rest of us", describing it as "exaggerated":[17] judges, he says, are bound by restraints established by history, practice, and integrity.

But Dworkin exaggerates the extent of these constraints, and his own fealty to them.[18] The moral reading inevitably results in conflict with the idea that various

---

[13] *A Bill of Rights for New Zealand* (1985) AJHR A6, 27.

[14] *Ibid*, 31.

[15] *Ibid*, 28.

[16] R Dworkin, *Freedom's Law: The Moral Reading of the American Constitution* (Cambridge, Mass. Harvard University Press, 1996) 2.

[17] *Ibid*, 11.

[18] See especially M McConnell, "The Importance of Humility in Judicial Review: A Comment on Ronald Dworkin's 'Moral Reading' of the Constitution" (1997) 65 *Fordham L Rev* 1269.

areas of the law can be kept beyond the reach of a bill of rights. One of the two approaches must yield and, as history shows, it is usually the latter. Not only is it impossible to limit the scope of judicial review but, as I have suggested, it is contrary to the purpose of modern bills of rights in any event.

How is it, then, that the White Paper could assert that the Bill of Rights would not control "matters of substance"? It is worth setting out the assertion in full:[19]

> "[T]he Bill would in large measure promote the accountability of government and the quality of democracy. *For the most part it would not control the substance of the law and of the policy which would continue to be elaborated in, and administered by, present and future parliaments and governments.* Thus the Bill would reaffirm and strengthen the fundamental procedural rights in the political and social spheres—rights such as the vote, the right to regular elections, freedom of speech, freedom of peaceful assembly, and freedom of association."

Here, as elsewhere, the influence of John Hart Ely is apparent.[20] But if Ely's process-based theory is unsatisfactory as an explanation of the US Bill of Rights,[21] it is simply inadequate as an explanation for the detailed and specific substantive rights found in the New Zealand Bill of Rights, and there was no reason to suppose that courts would adopt so limited a conception of their judicial review authority. Throughout the White Paper, however, it was asserted that entrenchment of the Bill of Rights would have a minimal effect on New Zealand law. A scant two pages was devoted to the right to freedom of expression, for example, there being "no doubt" that for the most part existing law would not constitute an unreasonable limitation of the right.

This suggests that there was little understanding about the nature of rights and the possible impact of judicial review. But the decision not to include a right to equality demonstrates that the Government knew all too well the risks of judicializing public policy, and wanted to avoid them:[22]

> "The phrase 'equality before the law' as a right is not used in this Article, or anywhere in the Bill of Rights. Although commonly appearing in national and international instruments (including the Canadian Charter), its meaning is elusive and its significance difficult to discern. . . .
>
> Nor is the phrase 'the equal protection of the law' included. This is because of its openness and the uncertainty of its application. In particular, on the basis of American experience under the Fourteenth Amendment, it would enable the courts to enter into many areas which would be seen in New Zealand as ones of substantive policy."

---

[19] *A Bill of Rights for New Zealand* (1985) AJHR A6, 28 (emphasis added).

[20] See P Rishworth, "The Birth and Rebirth of the Bill of Rights" in G Huscroft and P Rishworth (eds.), *Rights and Freedoms* (Wellington, Brookers, 1995) 1, 13–14, and M Taggart, "Tugging on Superman's Cape: Lessons from Experience with the New Zealand Bill of Rights Act" [1998] *PL* 266, 268, discussing the legal process views of those involved in drafting the NZ Bill of Rights. See also K J Keith, "A Bill of Rights for New Zealand? Judicial Review Versus Democracy" (1985) 11 *NZULR* 307.

[21] See eg, L Tribe, "The Puzzling Persistence of Process-Based Constitutional Theories" (1980) 89 *Yale LJ* 1063.

[22] *A Bill of Rights for New Zealand* (1985) AJHR A6, 86–7.

This makes its endorsement of judicial review in other contexts appear disingenuous. Against this, the proposal to include the Treaty of Waitangi in the Bill of Rights defies explanation. This was a proposal fundamentally at odds with the purpose of the enterprise—the protection of universal, individual rights—and the Government had no idea what the incorporation of Treaty-based group rights would mean. Yet the Government was content to leave things to the courts. The paragraph guaranteeing the "rights of the Maori under the Treaty of Waitangi" was described in the White Paper as "recognis[ing] and affirm[ing] the rights of the Maori under the Treaty *without attempting the inherently impossible task of defining precisely what they are*".[23] It is one thing to adopt a bill of rights acknowledging that there is room for disagreement about the interpretation and application of the relevant rights; it is quite another to propose that a bill of rights include an uncertain number of innominate rights, and that the judiciary be empowered to enforce them.

IV

Is judicial review the best means of protecting rights in any event? Ronald Dworkin has said that rights enjoy greater protection in the United States as a result of judicial review,[24] but the truth of his claim is difficult to assess.[25]

It is clear, however, that unlike the US Bill of Rights, the most noteworthy feature of modern bills of rights is the *limitations upon* rights that they permit—the power, in other words, that they confer upon courts to decide how important rights will turn out to be, regardless of how generously they are interpreted. The Canadian Charter of Rights and Freedoms, the New Zealand Bill of Rights, and the South African Constitution all include a provision that permits the establishment of reasonable limitations on rights. Applying these provisions courts may permit many limitations or few, and a wide variety of results is possible across the enumerated rights.

The concept of reasonable limitations on rights is well known internationally. Both the European Convention on Human Rights and the International Covenant on Civil and Political Rights enumerate permissible limitations following particular protected rights. The use of a single, general limitations provision ostensibly covering all of the protected rights is a Canadian innovation, and is the cornerstone of the Canadian Charter of Rights and Freedoms. The very first provision of the Charter provides that rights are guaranteed "subject only to such reasonable limits prescribed by law as can be demonstrably justified in a free and democratic society".

---

[23]   *A Bill of Rights for New Zealand* (1985) AJHR A6, 75 (emphasis added).

[24]   R Dworkin, *Law's Empire* (Cambridge, Belknap Press, 1986) 356: "The United States is a more just society than it would have been had its constitututional rights been left to the conscience of majoritarian institutions." Dworkin offers no argument for this claim, noting that "a further book would be necessary to do so" (n. 2).

[25]   Jeremy Waldron comments on the claim in "Judicial Review and the Conditions of Democracy" (1998) 6 *Journal of Political Philosophy* 335, 337–8.

The separation of definition and justification envisaged by this sort of provision sometimes results in a game of "give and take". Lord Wilberforce's advocacy of "generous" interpretations was adopted by the Supreme Court of Canada,[26] for example, and expansive interpretation of Charter rights is common. This is the "give", and it is supposed to demonstrate the judiciary's commitment to the protection of rights. Certainly, generous conceptions of rights facilitate challenges to state action: the more broadly a right is defined, the more likely it is that the state can be held to account in judicial review proceedings. But generous interpretations do not necessarily result in greater rights protection. The broadly defined right loses any claim to coherence and becomes a grab bag of things, all of them important to some, but none having any greater claim to protection than any other. This is where the "take" comes in: the more broadly a right is defined, the less protection it is likely to offer in practice. The judges will see to that with their interpretation of the reasonable limitations provision.[27]

On this sort of approach, the broadest of rights may turn out to be nothing more than *prima facie* rights, and whether or not they turn out to have any real force in particular circumstances depends upon whether or not the courts think that they should.

v

Writing extrajudicially, the current President of the New Zealand Court of Appeal, Sir Ivor Richardson, has described the reasonable limits provision in the New Zealand Bill of Rights (section 5) as requiring:[28]

"a utilitarian assessment of the public welfare in determining whether setting reasonable limits on a protected right is justified. On its face, that involves a Brandeis brief inquiry where the Court undertakes an extensive empirical examination supported by economic, statistical, and sociological data, makes a cost-benefit analysis of the effects of various policy choices and chooses the solution which best reflects a balancing of the values involved."

Leaving aside the casual assertion of judicial expertise on matters of social science, it is striking to see how little rights mean on this approach. As Jeremy Waldron says,[29]

---

[26] *Minister of Home Affairs* v. *Fisher* [1980] AC 319, 328, referred to with approval in *Hunter* v. *Southam Inc* [1984] 2 SCR 145, 156, per Dickson J. In New Zealand see *Flickinger* v. *Crown Colony of Hong Kong* [1991] 1 NZLR 439, 440, and *MOT* v. *Noort* [1992] 3 NZLR 260, 268 per Cooke P (describing Lord Wilberforce's words as "destined for judicial immortality") and 277 per Richardson J.

[27] P Hogg, "Interpreting the Charter of Rights: Generosity and Justification" (1990) 28 *Osgoode Hall LJ* 817; "Section 1 Revisited" (1991) 1 *NJCL* 1. See also F Schauer, *Free Speech: A Philosophical Enquiry* (New York, Cambridge University Press, 1982) 134–6. The Canadian freedom of expression cases are the best example in this regard. See the discussion in the text below.

[28] I Richardson, "Rights Jurisprudence—Justice for All?" in P Joseph (ed.), *Essays on the Constitution* (Wellington, Brooker's, 1995) 61, 82. (Cooke P was President at the time; Richardson J succeeded him.)

[29] J Waldron, "A Right-Based Critique of Constitutional Rights" (1993) 13 *OJLS* 18, 30.

"[t]o believe in rights is to believe that certain key interests of individuals, in liberty and well-being, deserve special protection, and that they should not be sacrificed for the sake of greater efficiency or prosperity or for any aggregate of lesser interests under the heading of the public good".

Rights involve costs, and any serious commitment to them will inevitably compromise the pursuit of the public good from time to time. Richardson suggests, however, that these costs can and should be avoided by the courts. He stresses, in particular, the need to avoid an "overly broad application" of the Bill of Rights:[30]

"If the courts fail to develop a balanced interpretation approach, a Bill which is meant to protect individual liberty may soon be producing very undesirable outcomes with serious consequences for continuing community acceptance of the rule of law."

Of course, as long as Parliament can override the decisions of the courts, there is no need for the courts to seek to avoid the "very undesirable outcomes" that concern Richardson. His concerns make more sense in a system in which the decisions of the courts are final.

The decisions of the courts under the Canadian Charter are, in effect,[31] final, and similar concerns have been raised by Canadian judges. In *R* v. *Edwards Books and Art Ltd*, Dickson CJ cautioned courts not to allow rights to undermine progressive social policies:[32]

"In interpreting and applying the *Charter* I believe that the courts must be cautious to ensure that it does not simply become an instrument of better situated individuals to roll back legislation which has as its object the improvement of the condition of less advantaged persons."

The sentiment underlying Dickson CJ's concern is easy to understand,[33] but his caution is problematic. How is it, after all, that *rights* have less force when they are exercised by the "better situated"? How are we to determine who the "better situated" are, and the circumstances in which they may exercise their rights when doing so would involve cost to the "less advantaged"?

Dickson CJ's caution is sometimes invoked in cases in which the justification proffered for limiting a right appears weak, as support for a less stringent application of the reasonable limits test.[34] The Canadian freedom of expression cases are

---

[30] Richardson, above n. 28 at 73.

[31] See the discussion of s. 33 in the text accompanying note 39, below.

[32] [1986] 2 SCR 713, 779.

[33] Especially, for example, in the South African context, where the very purpose of the Constitution is to roll back the legacies of apartheid. The South African Constitution is largely *amendatory* rather than confirmatory, to borrow terminology suggested by Justice Antonin Scalia in his contribution to this volume.

[34] As set out in *R* v. *Oakes* [1986] 1 SCR 103. Dickson CJ's caution has been cited in a number of cases. See eg, *Irwin Toy Ltd* v. *Quebec (Attorney-General)* [1989] 1 SCR 927 (vulnerability of young children to advertising) and *Slaight Communications Inc* v. *Davidson* [1989] 1 SCR 1038 (inequality of power between employees and employers).

a good example in this regard.[35] Like its American counterpart, the Supreme Court of Canada has purported to adopt a broad conception of the right to freedom of expression, holding that expression is protected regardless of its content: "[T]he content of a statement cannot deprive it of the protection accorded by [the right], no matter how offensive it may be".[36] In practice, however, this is a pale imitation of the American concept of content neutrality, the "bedrock principle" underlying the First Amendment.[37] Content neutrality in Canada is relevant only at the definitional stage of the inquiry, when the *prima facie* scope of the right is determined. It is not relevant at the limitation stage.[38] At this stage, the content of the expression *is* relevant and may be held to justify the establishment of extensive limitations, especially where the court considers that the interests of the vulnerable or less advantaged are at stake.

VI

The difference between Canadian and American conceptions of freedom of expression raises a fundamental question: what is to be done when courts' conceptions of rights do not accord with those of the legislature? In the United States, nothing short of constitutional amendment can overcome a judicial interpretation to which the Supreme Court is committed: that is what the decision to constitutionalise rights means. The situation in other countries is not so severe, in theory; in practice, however, judicial interpretations are hard to overcome even where the legislature has the last word.

[35] In *Ross* v. *School District No. 15* [1996] 1 SCR 825, for example, Dickson CJ's caution was invoked in answer to the assertion of freedom of expression and freedom of religion by a schoolteacher who expressed neo-nazi beliefs in his private capacity. He was challenging the decision of a provincial human rights tribunal, which had concluded that his continued employment constituted an act of illegal discrimination by the school board against Jewish students. The Court stated (at 875): "The respondent must not be permitted to use the *Charter* as an instrument to 'roll back' advances made by Jewish persons against discrimination." In *R* v. *Sharpe* [2001] 1 SCR 45, 120, L'Heureux-Dubé J commented on the right to freedom of expression in the context of a prosecution for possession of child pornography as follows: "Given our democratic values, it is clear that the Charter must not be used to reverse advances made by vulnerable groups or to defeat measures intended to protect the disadvantaged and comparatively powerless members of society. The constitutional protection of a form of expression that undermines our fundamental values must be carefully scrutinised."
[36] *R* v. *Keegstra* [1990] 3 SCR 697, 828.
[37] *Texas* v. *Johnson* 491 US 397, 414 (1989) per Brennan J. See generally G Stone, "Content Regulation and the First Amendment" (1983) 25 *Wm & Mary L Rev* 189 and J Weinstein, *Hate Speech, Pornography, and the Radical Attack on Free Speech Doctrine* (Boulder, Westview Press, 1999) 34–49.
[38] A similar result has obtained under the European Convention on Human Rights. Although the European Court of Human Rights has held that the right to freedom of expression protects expression that might "shock or disturb the State or any sector of the population", the Court has afforded states an extensive "margin of appreciation" in establishing limitations on the right that routinely go to content. See *Handyside* v. *United Kingdom* (1976) 1 EHRR 737. See A Lester, "Freedom of Expression" in R St J Macdonald, F Matscher and H Petzold (eds.), *The European System for the Protection of Human Rights* (The Hague, Kluwer, 1993) 465, and D J Harris, M O'Boyle and C Warbrick, *Law of the European Convention on Human Rights* (London, Butterworths, 1995) 372.

Consider the Canadian Charter of Rights. An important condition of its passage was the inclusion of section 33, the "notwithstanding" clause, which allows a province or the federal government to legislate in a manner contrary to most of its provisions.[39] The "notwithstanding" clause is often proffered as evidence of the Charter's democratic credentials. Within a short time, however, it has become anathema to contemplate its use.[40] But while section 33 allows government to override the Charter itself, it was never likely that any government would do so; far more likely was a decision to override a *decision of the courts interpreting the Charter*, in circumstances in which there was room for disagreement as to the justification for a particular limitation on a right.

Yet even legislation in these circumstances is considered illegitimate. Interpretation of the Constitution has long been viewed as the province of the judiciary, and passage of the Charter and resulting changes in the scope and nature of constitutional litigation have not altered this view. The idea that the Constitution depends upon judicial interpretation is clear from the Canadian practice of advisory opinions. The Supreme Court of Canada often issues advisory opinions at the request of the federal government, on questions as profound as the durability of the Canadian federation itself,[41] and the opinions provided by the Court are invariably accepted as correct. Extensive obiter dicta are a prominent feature of Canadian Charter cases, and another example of the way in which the Court perceives its role. By contrast, the United States Supreme Court cannot issue advisory opinions, and often strives to avoid deciding constitutional questions unless absolutely necessary.[42] Even where a dispute is properly before the Court, and its decision is final for the purposes of the particular dispute, that decision may be opposed by successive governments, which are free to

---

[39] S. 33 provides as follows:

"Exception where express declaration

33 (1) Parliament or the legislature of a province may expressly declare in an Act of Parliament or of the legislature, as the case may be, that the Act or a provision thereof shall operate notwithstanding a provision included in section 2 or sections 7 to 15 of this Charter.

Operation of exception

(2) An Act or a provision of an Act in respect of which a declaration made under this section is in effect shall have such operation as it would have but for the provision of this Charter referred to in the declaration.

Five year limitation

(3) A declaration made under subsection (1) shall cease to have effect five years after it comes into force or on such earlier date as may be specified in the declaration.

Re-enactment

(4) Parliament or the legislature of a province may re-enact a declaration made under subsection (1).

Five year limitation

(5) Subsection (3) applies in respect of a re-enactment made under subsection (4)."

[40] The override has been invoked just once outside Quebec, which must be regarded as a special case. See P Hogg, *Constitutional Law of Canada* (Scarborough, Carswell, 1997, updated) ch. 36.

[41] *Reference re Secession of Quebec* [1998] 2 SCR 217.

[42] See generally, Tribe, above note 4 at 311–85, and L Fisher, *Constitutional Dialogues: Interpretation as a Political Process* (Princeton, Princeton University Press, 1988) 85–116, describing the constitutional "case or controversy" requirement, along with "ripeness", "mootness", and the "political questions" doctrines.

pursue a number of strategies to undermine its viability or limit its precedential effect.[43]

This is possible because it is generally understood that the US Bill of Rights stands apart from the decisions of the Court that interpret it.[44] In Canada, by contrast, there is a tendency to conflate the decisions of the Supreme Court of Canada with the Charter itself. The terms of the override provision further this suggestion. Far from simply reserving the authority to decide some questions pursuant to the democratic process, invocation of the "notwithstanding" clause suggests a decision to violate the Charter itself.[45]

The New Zealand Bill of Rights contains no override provision; none was needed because it is not supreme law. Legislation that the courts consider inconsistent with the Bill of Rights governs by virtue of section 4, which precludes the courts from striking down or rendering inoperative legislation that it finds to be inconsistent with the Bill of Rights.[46] The New Zealand Court of Appeal has, however, recently announced that it may issue declarations of inconsistency in such cases. In *Moonen* v. *Film and Literature Board of Review*,[47] the Court commented that it has "the power, and on occasions the duty" to issue declarations (referred to as "indications") that legislation establishes an unreasonable and unjustified limitation on a right. The declaration jurisdiction inferred from the Bill of Rights borrows from a procedure specified in section 4 of the UK Human Rights Act 1998, which in fact borrowed from the New Zealand Bill of Rights in denying courts the power to strike down legislation.[48]

---

[43] The Supreme Court's controversial decision in *Roe* v. *Wade* 410 US 113 (1973) is the best example in this regard. The series of cases heard by the Court following that landmark decision constitutionalising the law of abortion arose because so many state governments opposed the Court's decision and sought to limit its effect: over 300 legislative measures were passed by 48 states from 1973–1989. See N Devins, *Shaping Constitutional Values* (Baltimore, Johns Hopkins University Press, 1996) 60–3.

[44] Cf L Alexander and F Schauer, "On Extrajudicial Constitutonal Interpretation" (1997) 110 *Harv L Rev* 1359, arguing in support of judicial supremacy on constitutional interpretation. See N Devins and L Fisher, "Judicial Exclusivity and Political Instability" (1998) 84 *Va L Rev* 83 and M Tushnet, *Taking the Constitution Away from the Courts* (Princeton, Princeton University Press, 1999) 6–32, critiquing Alexander and Schauer and rejecting judicial supremacy. From time to time the Court asserts supremacy on constitutional interpretation. See eg, *City of Boerne* v. *Flores* 521 US 507 (1997), in which the Court asserts supremacy on the meaning of the Constitution in striking down legislation designed to overturn its earlier decision in *Employment Division* v. *Smith* 494 US 872 (1990). The Court has also asserted the constitutional nature of its decisions. See *Dickerson* v. *US* 530 US 428 (2000), striking down legislation undermining the Court's earlier decision in *Miranda* v. *Arizona* 385 US 436 (1966). Cf the dissenting opinion of Justice Scalia.

[45] S. 33 contemplates that legislation may be declared to operate "notwithstanding a provision included in . . . this Charter". See above n. 39.

[46] S. 4 provides as follows:

"No court shall, in relation to any enactment (whether passed or made before or after the commencement of this Bill of Rights),—
a) Hold any provision of the enactment to be impliedly repealed or revoked, or to be in any way invalid or ineffective; or
b) Decline to apply any provision of the enactment—
by reason only that the provision is inconsistent with any provision of this Bill of Rights."

[47] [2000] 2 NZLR 9, 17.

[48] See the discussion in Butler, Rishworth, and Leigh's contributions to this volume.

VII

The power of courts to make declarations seems to offer the best of both worlds: consideration by judges in the forum of principle that Dworkin values, on one hand, and the determination in the democratic forum favoured by Waldron, on the other. Declarations may even facilitate the dialogue between courts and legislatures that so many seem to value.[49]

But dialogue is meaningful only if disagreement with the decisions of the courts is not only possible but *legitimate*, and there is little reason to suppose that it will be perceived as such: legislators are usually perceived as the enemy of rights, while courts are their champions.[50] The argument for bills of rights, after all, presupposes that judicial review is required as a check on the legislature in order to protect rights. Disagreement with the decisions of the courts is therefore difficult, to say the least, and it is reasonable to expect that governments in the United Kingdom and New Zealand will accept judicial declarations and legislate in accordance with them. To be sure, there may well be delays in doing so, and for this reason declarations may be thought ineffective to vindicate rights. In general, however, judicial declarations increase the cost of political disagreement considerably, no matter how controversial or contestable the courts' decisions may be.

Tradition also militates against government disagreement with the courts' decisions. The convention that governments and Ministers refrain from so much as commenting upon the decisions of courts is strong, and while there is no reason for that convention to continue in the context of judicial review of legislation, political considerations suggest that it is likely to persist: in countries like Canada, New Zealand, and the United Kingdom, the courts enjoy a preferred position in respect of the public's trust. We can argue about *why* this is so, but undoubtedly it is so, even after years of dealing with rights-based, public policy litigation.[51]

---

[49] The dialogue concept originates with Louis Fisher's *Constitutional Dialogues: Interpretation as a Political Process*, above n. 42. In the Canadian context see P Hogg and A Bushell, "The *Charter* Dialogue Between Courts and Legislatures (Or Perhaps the *Charter of Rights* Isn't Such a Bad Thing After All)" (1997) 35 *Osgoode Hall LJ* 75; the critique of C Manfredi & J Kelly,"Six Degrees of Dialogue: A Response to Hogg and Bushell" (1999) 37 Osgoode Hall LJ 513, and the reply of Hogg and Thornton (1999) 37 *Osgoode Hall LJ* 529. See also C Manfredi, *Judicial Power and the Charter* (Toronto, Oxford University Press, 2001) 176–181. The dialogue concept has made it to Australian shores. See R G Atkinson, "The Constitutional Conversation between the Courts and Parliament" (2000) 21 *University of Queensland LJ* 1, commenting with approval on J Hiebert, "Why Must a Bill of Rights be a Contest of Political and Judicial Wills?" (1999) 10 *PLR* 22.

[50] Antipathy towards legislators is often apparent in academic critique, if not specifically addressed. Andrew Butler's praise for the decision of the NZ Court of Appeal in *Moonen* creating the declaration jurisdiction is a good example here. The Court, he says, has "potentially added a new politically powerful *weapon* to the [Bill of Rights] armoury", as though the branches of government are at war over rights. See "Judicial Indications of Inconsistency—A New Weapon in the Bill of Rights Armoury?" [2000] *NZ Law Review* 43, 59 (emphasis added).

[51] A National Post/COMPAS poll in Canada found that "Majorities in every region of the country believe that the courts should be taking away more, not less, power from elected politicians". See "The Power of Judges", Report to National Post, 18 February 2000 (www.compas.ca/html/archives/powerjudges_surv.html (viewed 12 April 2001)).

Acceptance of the courts' decisions is therefore likely, and is expected by the courts themselves.

In *Moonen*, for example, although the New Zealand Court of Appeal said simply that its declarations "may . . . be of *assistance* to Parliament if the subject arises in that forum",[52] it also made a veiled threat: its declarations "will be of value should the matter come to be examined by the Human Rights Committee".[53] In other words, the Court is assuming a role as rights watchdog; its decisions will be invoked to embarrass the government, should the government not legislate in accordance with them. The willingness of the Court to assume this sort of role comes only ten years after the decision not to entrench the New Zealand Bill of Rights as a supreme-law constitution—predominantly because of a mistrust of the judiciary—and reflects the extent to which the stature of the courts has increased as respect for the political process has diminished. By contrast, the power to issue declarations was deliberately conferred upon the UK judiciary under the Human Rights Act 1998, and while that Act also preserves the sovereignty of Parliament, it establishes a fast-track process that allows Parliament to be circumvented, at least temporarily: in "compelling" circumstances a *Minister* can amend legislation to address an inconsistency identified by the courts.[54]

If it turns out that governments invariably legislate in accordance with the declarations of the courts, then the preservation of Parliamentary sovereignty in New Zealand and the United Kingdom will prove meaningless—a matter of form rather than substance. That will suit those who would have preferred judicial supremacy, but something important will be lost. Rights remain contestable even in a constitutional order in which the courts have the last word. Where final authority over rights questions has deliberately been left with the elected branch, its duty is to develop and articulate coherent conceptions of rights—not simply to legislate under the direction of the courts.

VIII

These are just some of the issues discussed by the contributors to this book, which is in four parts. Part I concerns the role of judicial review and the nature of rights litigation, and addresses American, Canadian, New Zealand, and UK perspectives on the constitutionalisation of rights, and the role and scope of judicial review. Part II focuses on the litigation of equality rights in Canada and internationally, and considers the relationship of equality and liberty rights from an American perspective. The essays in part III address questions about group rights in general and the rights of indigenous peoples in particular, focusing on the New Zealand Maori. Part IV discusses the role of international human rights adjudicative bodies and the impact of

---

[52] *Moonen v. Film and Literature Board of Review* [2000] 2 NZLR 9, 17 (emphasis added).
[53] *Ibid.*
[54] Human Rights Act 1998, s. 10 and sched. 2.

the decisions of the United Nations Human Rights Committee and the European Court of Human Rights from Australian, New Zealand, and UK perspectives.

In the essays that follow in this part, Justice Antonin Scalia of the United States Supreme Court discusses what constitutionalising rights in the United States has meant, drawing a distinction between bills of rights that are confirmatory and those that are amendatory. The US Bill of Rights is largely an example of the former, but it is increasingly interpreted as the latter, as the concept of the "Living Constitution" has taken hold. With every expansion of rights the Court removes some items from the realm of democratic debate and decision-making. But the Living Constitution may also operate to contract existing rights that prove unpopular. The result, he concludes, is that the Bill of Rights may come to reflect majoritarian preferences, the very thing it was designed to protect against. He warns that bills of rights that are not "ruthlessly specific" should limit the ability of the courts to alter them by clearly tying the liberties they guarantee to what is reflected in the laws and practices of the current society.

James Allan discusses the link between rights and paternalism. So long as consideration is limited to the effect of rights, given their orientation to individual interests, the linkage is not obvious. But, he argues, if one looks to the motive for according rights to others, the link becomes clear: by constitutionalising rights, the present generation does the thinking for future generations, disabling their ability to make decisions for themselves by limiting the power of their legislature. This is paternalistic, in that it imposes rights upon others for their benefit. From here, he considers whether there are grounds to conclude that judges exercise social policy-making power better than elected lawmakers—paternalistic power they exercise on an ongoing basis. However one measures the capabilities of unelected judges and elected politicians when it comes to rights, the argument favouring judicial review is, in essence, a utilitarian, consequentialist case—the very sort of case that was rejected in establishing a bill of rights in the first place.

Andrew Butler argues that bills of rights must empower the judiciary to overturn legislation. The New Zealand Bill of Rights Act 1990 is flawed, he suggests, because in terms of the obligation established under the International Covenant on Civil and Political Rights, it does not provide an effective remedy. The UK Human Rights Act 1998 is not a good alternative, because although it encourages challenges to inconsistent legislation, declarations of inconsistency provided by the courts may ultimately prove meaningless, and a complainant may be required to go to Strasbourg to get a remedy. The Canadian Charter of Rights and Freedoms provides the preferred model, in his view, because it renders the majority of statutes susceptible to review for Charter compliance and empowers the courts to strike down inconsistent legislation. Although it allows a legislature to override the Charter in specific cases by invoking the "notwithstanding" clause, the starting point is that human rights trump inconsistent legislation, rather than the other way around, as in New Zealand and the UK.

Murray Hunt argues that while constitutional theory has usually been concerned with justifying the role played by courts in policing the democratic process, modern debate must take account of the shift in the locus of power from the public to the private. Privatisation and globalisation have altered the political and legal landscapes, and the power to interfere with human rights is increasingly concentrated in private hands. Meanwhile, the ability of governments to control private actors is diminished by a range of overlapping international, supranational and intergovernmental obligations and agreements. As a result, any account of the justification for constitutional judicial review must consider the justification for a judicial role in reviewing the law governing "private" relations for compatibility with human rights norms. He addresses questions about the "horizontality" of human rights protections in the United Kingdom and New Zealand.

2

The Bill of Rights:
Confirmation of Extant Freedoms or
Invitation to Judicial Creation?

JUSTICE ANTONIN SCALIA

Should New Zealand have a so-called "entrenched" bill of rights—that is to say, one that can not be amended by the legislature itself, and hence one that can be applied not only against the actions of the executive but also against the enactments of the legislature?

This question confronted—and was considered by—the framers of the United States Constitution 210 years ago; and they decided *not* to have a Bill of Rights. The principal protection of the people's liberty, they thought, was the dispersal and equilibration of power achieved by the carefully crafted structural provisions of the Constitution. They split the most powerful (and hence the most dangerous) branch, the legislature, into two equally powerful chambers—dividing it against itself—and prohibited its members from occupying any executive offices. They further weakened the legislature—and strengthened the executive—by giving the President an active role in the legislative process through his exercise, or threatened exercise, of the power to kill all measures that cannot muster the support of a two-thirds majority in each house. And finally, of course, power was also dispersed by reason of our federal system, under which the vast majority, indeed almost the totality, of domestic subjects are the exclusive responsibility of the States, and no business of the federal government. (That is why federal law enforcement officers number less than 85,000, compared to almost 700,000 state and local officers.)

Now as a matter of fact I think our framers were correct that the separation and equilibration of power—setting ambition against ambition, as Madison put it—is the key to preserving liberty. If you doubt that, ask yourself whether, twenty years ago, you would have preferred to live in New Zealand, which had a fairly good system of separated powers but no bill of rights (not even an "unentrenched" one) or rather in the former Evil Empire, the Union of Soviet Socialist Republics, whose constitution contained a bill of rights that made the American one look stingy by comparison. Of course you would have picked New Zealand, and the reason is that a bill of rights is just a piece of paper *unless* what I call the *real* constitution—that is, the portion of the document that establishes the structure (the *constitution*) of the government—succeeds in preventing the centralisation of power.

Once power is centralised, the bill of rights can be ignored at will, as it is in many of the one-man dictatorships around the world that hold meaningless elections and boast marvellous bills of rights.

Even so, to say that a bill of rights is not crucial is not to say that a bill of rights is not helpful. And that is why Americans in effect overruled the judgement of the framers. Two years after its ratification, our Constitution was amended by adoption of the first ten Amendments, the first eight of which comprise our Bill of Rights. (In point of fact, the ratification of the original Constitution by several of the States was conditional upon the prompt adoption of a bill of rights—which was accordingly proposed by the very first Congress.) We are fond of our Bill of Rights. We would not think of eliminating it. On the whole it has worked very well.

But I am not sure that the American Bill of Rights—or at least the American Bill of Rights during most of our history—was the same kind of animal as most bills of rights that have been adopted nationally, and even internationally, in the last half of the twentieth century. The American Bill of Rights was meant to preserve a state of liberty that was believed already to exist—to confirm the rights of Englishmen that the former colonists believed they already possessed. "The free exercise of religion," for example, was not some abstract concept that had to be given content by philosopher-judges. It referred to that freedom to practice religion that was recognised in all the States—which did not include the right to violate valid, generally applicable, nondiscriminatory laws. Thus when, in the 1870s, my Court had its first case involving an alleged violation of this provision—a claim that Mormons had a free-exercise right to ignore the federal law applicable in the Utah Territory prohibiting bigamy[1]—the Justices did not have to consult Aristotle, or natural law, or what is now called the "sense of the international community". It had simply never been part of religious freedom in the United States to violate non-discriminatory, generally applicable laws when God tells you to do so. Whether a religious-practice exception from this or that law is reasonable and desirable is to be determined, not by some philosophical inquiry conducted by lawyers ill suited to the task, but by the people's representatives, who could (and often did) make exceptions as they saw fit. Easy question. Next case.

But how is the guarantee of religious freedom to be interpreted when it appears in the bill of rights of a newly formed Federal Republic of Germany, or Republic of Italy, or Russian Republic, or in the bill of rights of an international organisation that includes those countries? Surely it is not meant to refer to the pre-existing freedom of religion in Nazi Germany, or Mussolini's Italy, or the Soviet Union. Unlike the American Bill of Rights, these modern bills of rights are *amendatory*; they are not meant to confirm and preserve the past, but to *repudiate* it. There is no way to interpret them except as an appeal—not to traditional national or international legal concepts—but to some Platonic ideal of freedom of religion that judges will ultimately have to invent. And maybe—who knows?—that Platonic

---

[1] See *Reynolds* v. *United States* 98 US 145 (1878).

ideal *does* include the right to have multiple wives if one believes God has so ordained.

That the individual guarantees of the American Constitution have traditionally been regarded as confirmatory rather than amendatory is strikingly demonstrated by the fact that we adopted a constitutional amendment, in 1920, to compel all States to give women the vote—even though the Constitution already contained (in the Fourteenth Amendment, adopted after the Civil War) a requirement that the States accord all persons equal protection of the laws. Surely as a philosophical matter it can be said that equal protection of the laws is incompatible with denial of the franchise on the basis of sex. But the issue was not regarded as a philosophical one. Equal protection of the laws could mean a *lot* of things insofar as equality of the sexes is concerned. It could mean, for example, that wives are responsible for supporting their husbands, just as husbands were responsible for supporting their wives; it could mean that women must be subject to the military draft and sent into combat; it could even mean (and I am sure there are some who believe so) that all public buildings must have unisex bathrooms. Why did our Fourteenth Amendment mean none of those things? Simply because it was not understood to mean any of those things when it was ratified, as innumerable state and federal laws on the books in 1867—and unchanged and unchallenged after ratification in 1868—amply demonstrated. And it was also not understood to mean that women had to be accorded the vote. States could discriminate in the franchise on many grounds that we would today not consider appropriate—not only on the basis of sex, but on the basis of property ownership and even literacy. Thus, when American society came to believe that denying the vote to women was unfair, the constitutional change was made, not by the Supreme Court's revisionist reading of the Fourteenth Amendment, but in the manner the Constitution provided: adoption by the people, in 1920, of the Nineteenth Amendment, which reads "The right of the citizens of the United States to vote shall not be denied or abridged by the United States or by any State on account of sex."

Another, more recent, example of the confirmatory nature of the American Bill of Rights is a case decided a few terms after I joined the Supreme Court involving the constitutionality of personal-service jurisdiction—so-called "gotcha" jurisdiction, under which you may be required to defend a civil suit in (for example) Los Angeles if, while you are changing planes at Los Angeles Airport, a process server comes up to you with a summons, places it in your hand, and says (ideally) "gotcha!"[2] The plaintiff in the case before us, who had been subjected to "gotcha" jurisdiction in a state that had no other connection with the cause of action that was the subject of the suit, argued that he had been deprived of his constitutional right to due process of law (the Fourteenth Amendment). Now most jurisdictions in the world do not recognise transitory presence in the jurisdiction as a valid basis for the exercise of judicial power. Germany, for example, would not recognise an American judgment resting only upon service of a summons in the United States

---

[2] See *Burnham v. Superior Court of California* 495 US 604 (1990).

as the jurisdictional contact. But my Court had little trouble with the case. However unfair, as an abstract matter, "gotcha" jurisdiction may appear to be, it was unquestionably considered a valid basis of jurisdiction at the time our Due Process Clause was adopted. Indeed, at that time it was the *only* valid basis of jurisdiction recognised by the common-law courts. (So-called long-arm jurisdiction, based upon the connection of the jurisdiction with the subject of the suit, is a Johnny-come-lately.) And so, while some of the Justices of my Court wrung their hands at how unfair it all was, we held *unanimously* that "gotcha" jurisdiction was constitutional.

Those familiar with the jurisprudence of my Court—especially that of the past few decades—will be aware that my asserted proposition that the Bill of Rights was confirmatory rather than amendatory may be historically correct, but has been honoured as much in the breach as in the observance during recent years. The Court under Chief Justice Warren, for example, held that the guarantee of equal protection of the laws required an electoral regime of one man, one vote—thereby rendering unlawful the system of bicameral state legislatures, with one House apportioned by region rather than by population, which existed in almost all the States when the Equal Protection Clause was adopted, and which still exists in the federal Congress itself![3] And the Court under Chief Justice Burger, for example, held that State laws prohibiting abortion are unconstitutional—even though most States had such laws at the time the provision allegedly producing their unconstitutionality (the Due Process Clause) was adopted.[4] And the Court under Chief Justice Rehnquist has held, for example, that single-sex military academies operated by the State are unconstitutional—even though West Point as an all-male institution was almost as old as the country itself, and several States (such as Virginia and South Carolina) had maintained men's military academies (with no thought that they were unconstitutional) from the first half of the 1800s.[5]

The fact that my Court sometimes applies an amendatory concept of the Bill of Rights is reflected most clearly in our recent jurisprudence concerning the Eighth Amendment, which prohibits cruel and unusual punishments. We have said, in several of our opinions, that what constitutes cruel and unusual punishment *changes* from age to age, to comport with "the evolving standards of decency that mark the progress of a maturing society".[6] And it is up to the Court, of course, to intuit what those evolving standards of decency might be. Applying that approach, the Court has invalidated, in all States, the death penalty for all crimes except murder[7]—and three of the Justices with whom I have sat during my time on the bench would have invalidated it for murder as well.

Now I am fully aware that much of the world has admired my Court for its wonderful ability to do good things through an amendatory Bill of Rights. Before you

---

[3] See *Baker* v. *Carr* 369 US 186 (1962).
[4] See *Roe* v. *Wade* 410 US 113 (1973).
[5] See *United States* v. *Virginia* 518 US 515 (1996).
[6] *Trop* v. *Dulles* 356 US 86, 101 (1958).
[7] See *Enmund* v. *Florida* 458 US 782 (1982).

decide to emulate the practice, however, you should be aware that this has been neither the traditional practice of the United States Supreme Court, nor is even its uniform practice today. The evolving Bill of Rights, which means from age to age whatever it *ought* to mean, is a relatively new phenomenon. We have not lasted the past 210-odd years with that philosophy, and I do not believe we could survive with it for the next 200.

There is no difficulty, of course, with an amendatory bill of rights that is, in all of its provisions, precise and specific: If it says, for example, that all criminal defendants shall be entitled to grand jury indictment, or that all persons in custody shall be warned of their right to remain silent and to receive assistance of counsel, it is quite possible for judges, without departing from their traditional roles or their distinctive field of competence, to apply those provisions in the face of traditional practice to the contrary. The traditional practice of omitting grand jury indictment in some cases, or of failing to warn prisoners of their rights, has simply been overruled. The problem arises when the bill of rights sets forth general principles, such as a guarantee of due process of law, or of freedom of religion, or of equal protection of the laws, or a prohibition of discrimination on the basis of sex. Unless the judge is bound to give content to these generalities by referring to pre-existing practice, he is left to govern society on the basis of his own philosophy, his own biases, or his own worldview. Apart from traditional practice, there is simply no answer as to what due process of law requires—whether it includes, for example, a right to grand jury indictment or a warning of the right to counsel. The judge is left to make up those details as he sees fit. And the same is true of the other magnificent guarantees, such as equal protection of the laws (does it mean that minors must be allowed to manage their own affairs in general, or more specifically must be allowed to have an abortion without parental consent?). Or freedom of religion (does it mean that polygamy, or animal sacrifice, or for that matter human sacrifice, must be tolerated?). Or freedom of speech (does it mean that libel laws are void?). Or a guarantee against discrimination on the basis of sex (does it mean that women must be subject to the military draft and sent into combat?).

There are no answers to these questions—or at least no answers that courts (that is to say, committees of lawyers) can figure out through their accustomed analytical processes. The specific questions at issue are *matters of policy*, which in a democratic society must be resolved by the people. The point is best demonstrated by reference to one of the more controversial amendatory Bill of Rights decisions of my Court, *Roe* v. *Wade*—the case that held it was a denial of due process of law to prohibit abortion.[8] In a later elaboration—or in fact revision—of that opinion, a case called *Casey*, we laid down as the governing principle that a State cannot place an "undue burden" upon a woman's right to an abortion.[9] I ask you to imagine, if you will, the discussion that is likely to take place at the next Supreme Court post-argument conference applying this standard. Suppose,

[8] 410 US 113 (1973).
[9] See *Planned Parenthood* v. *Casey* 505 US 833 (1992).

for example, that the case at hand involves a state law requiring parental notification and a one-day waiting period before a minor can be given an abortion. What possible *legal* arguments can be summoned forth to decide whether or not this constitutes an "undue" burden? If one consults the case law and legislative practice pre-*Roe* v. *Wade*, one would have to conclude that *no* burden is an "undue" burden, since it is clear that abortion could constitutionally be entirely proscribed. The law books, in other words, are no help. How, then, is the Court to decide? The discussion will have to go something like this: "I don't think it's an *undue* burden. Do *you* think it's an undue burden? How many think it's an undue burden?" Five hands and the state law will be invalidated; four and it will stand. This is not law but policy-making.

The same is true of the other new, amendatory rights my Court has discovered—or has expressed its willingness to discover—under the Due Process Clause, or the Equal Protection Clause, or any of the other grand general provisions of our Bill of Rights. We intimated in our last opinion on the subject that there may be a "right to die" ensconced somewhere in our Constitution—at least a right to decline needed medical treatment, and perhaps even a right to assisted suicide.[10] Now how am I to decide this last question when it is squarely presented? If we have a confirmatory Bill of Rights, the answer is easy: the right to have someone help you kill yourself did not exist when the Bill of Rights was adopted, and has existed in only one State I am aware of since then. But if past practice does not matter, how am I to decide the point? Has Harvard Law School prepared me for this? Of course not. It is not a legal question but a question of policy, and however much I may trick up my opinion with learned citations of law review articles and United Nations committee reports, I will essentially be applying my own policy preferences rather than, in any meaningful sense, interpreting the law.

It might not be so bad if the policy preferences of the judges were likely to be the policy preferences of the people. But on many issues, of course, they are not. As one of our more prominent Founding Fathers recognised in the Federalist Papers, the judiciary is a sort of natural aristocracy, remote from the people. (That is one of the reasons he considered it the Least Dangerous Branch.) On many issues, the predominant view within the circle of highly educated intellectuals in which we judges live and move is quite different from the predominant view in the society at large. I am sure that my Court was astounded by the extensive and vehement opposition—which shows no sign of abating—to our decision in *Roe* v. *Wade*. In the circles we frequent abortion was regrettable but okay. Or the issue of homosexual rights: the federal Congress, like the vast majority of the States, has refused to add sexual preference to the list of beliefs or conditions protected against private discrimination in our civil rights laws. But the legal community from which judges are drawn is so overwhelmingly and ardently in favour of homosexual rights that a school will be dropped from membership in the American Association of Law Schools if it permits on-campus hiring interviews by law firms that refuse to hire

---

[10] See *Washington* v. *Glucksberg* 521 US 702 (1997).

open homosexuals. The policy views of the judges are not likely to be the policy views of the people.

You should not gather from my last remarks, however, that judicial policy-making will always differ from democratic policymaking in the direction of being more liberal. Not necessarily. Historically, in fact, judges have usually been more conservative. And the decisions of my Court that have abandoned an originalist approach to the Constitution—ie, an approach which makes it confirmatory of the rights extant when it was adopted—sometimes go in a conservative direction. That this is *not* a conservative-versus-liberal issue is nicely exemplified by two decisions announced on the same day a few terms ago. In the first of them the Court invalidated, on the basis of no constitutional authority in either text or precedent, an amendment to the state constitution that had been adopted by plebiscite by the people of Colorado, prohibiting the State or any political subdivision of the State from adding homosexuality to the list of grounds (race, religion, sex, age, disability) on which it is unlawful to discriminate.[11] The liberals loved that non-originalist innovation, and the conservatives criticised it bitterly. In the second case, announced immediately thereafter, the Court—again on the basis of no constitutional authority in either text or precedent—held that a jury award of punitive damages against an automobile manufacturer was unconstitutional because it was (in the Court's view) excessive.[12] The conservatives loved that non-originalist innovation, and the liberals criticised it bitterly.

Nor should you think that an amendatory bill of rights will always produce the creation of new rights (whether rights favoured by liberals or rights favoured by conservatives). Sometimes it will produce the *elimination* of pre-existing rights—it can "amend" in *that* direction as well. Two of my Court's cases demonstrate that reality. In the first, a criminal defendant accused of sexual abuse of a little girl was tried pursuant to a state law that permitted the child, if she was found to be too nervous to testify in the defendant's presence, to testify in a separate room with only counsel present—the judge, the jury, and the defendant watching the examination over closed-circuit TV.[13] This may seem entirely reasonable to the modern mind, but it could not be more plainly opposed to the Sixth Amendment of our Bill of Rights, which says that "[i]n all criminal prosecutions, the accused shall enjoy the right . . . to be confronted with the witnesses against him." There is little doubt what the right to "confront" consisted of, and what it was intended to achieve. From its Latin roots (*contra* means "against" and *frons* means "forehead") the word connotes face-to-face encounter. And one of the principal purposes of confrontation was, of course, to produce *precisely* that nervousness which the little girl found it difficult to endure. It is, the framers thought, difficult to accuse a person falsely *to his face*, and imposing that difficulty was thought to be conducive to truth-telling. Nonetheless, my Court, in a non-originalist judgment, held that the state law was

---

[11] See *Romer* v. *Evans* 517 US 620 (1996).
[12] See *BMW of North America, Inc.* v. *Gore* 517 US 559 (1996).
[13] See *Maryland* v. *Craig* 497 US 836 (1990).

constitutional. The right of confrontation, in child-abuse cases, has been eliminated.

Last term another valued constitutional right barely escaped elimination. The Sixth Amendment guarantees trial by jury in criminal cases. In recent years, Congress and state legislatures have taken to enacting so-called "sentencing enhancements", whereby the penalties specified for certain crimes will be increased if a particular factor is present—for example, the addition of five years to the allowable sentence for robbery if a firearm is used. Since these add-ons are *called* sentencing enhancements, rather than elements of the crime, many courts—indeed, most courts—have allowed the presence of the aggravating factor to be determined by the sentencing judge rather than the jury, and to be found (as sentencing factors traditionally are) by a preponderance of the evidence rather than beyond a reasonable doubt. Last term, my Court found this to violate the jury-trial guarantee.[14] Any factor, we said, that increases the severity of the sentence to which the defendant is exposed is an element of the crime and must be determined by the jury beyond reasonable doubt. I voted with the majority in that case—as did the only other originalist on the current Court, Justice Thomas—since that represents the traditional understanding of what the right to a jury verdict consists of. But the vote in the case was 5–4; replace one of the originalists with a nonoriginalist law-and-order judge, and the right to trial by jury would be significantly impaired.

The argument often made in defence of a bill of rights untethered to original understandings and susceptible of judicial evolution is that a constitution, after all, is meant to endure for many years and hence must be flexible. It is a "living organism" that must "grow" with the society that it governs; otherwise, it will become brittle and snap. This argument always reminds me of the similar anthropomorphism of some stock-market analysts, who advise us that "the market is resting for an assault on the 11,000 level". (One pictures the stock market panting at some base-camp for the final assault.) Of course the stock market is not Sir Edmund Hillary, and a constitution is not an organism. It is a democratically adopted law, and should be interpreted, like all laws, to mean what it meant when it was adopted—not to commit the future of the society to management by an unelected judiciary. And if you believe that the enthusiasts of a "living constitution" are seeking to bring us flexibility, you are wrong. My Constitution is a flexible one: it says nothing, for example, about abortion. Do you think there should be a right to abortion? Then create it the way most rights are created in a democratic society: persuade your fellow citizens that it is desirable and enact a law. Do you think there should not be such a right? Then persuade your fellow citizens that abortion should be banned. *That* is flexibility. The same with the death penalty. Constitutional evolutionists, on the other hand, would bind the entire society to one or another disposition on these and many other questions—remove them entirely from the realm of democratic debate and decision-making—now and forever. They seek, of

---

[14] See *Apprendi* v. *New Jersey* 530 US 446 (2000).

course, not flexibility but rigidity—which is unsurprising, since that is precisely what the constitutionalization of rights is designed to achieve.

If I may revert to a thought that I suggested near the outset of these remarks: you should not think that the evolutionary constitutionalism of the modern Supreme Court of the United States reflects a time-honoured and time-tested tradition. To the contrary, it is quite new, and its consequences for our system of government are only beginning to be apparent. The people are not fools. Once it has become apparent to them—as it now has—that the Constitution does not have a fixed meaning determinable by lawyers through the use of analytical tools; that it means, rather, whatever it *ought* to mean in light of modern needs and modern desires; then they will begin selecting their Justices not for legal ability, but for agreement with them, the majority, as to what the Constitution *ought* to mean. And you have seen that new criterion for selecting Justices being played out in confirmation hearings, in which Senators, representing the majority, quiz nominees regarding one right after another that they would like, or would not like, to be written into the living Constitution. We conduct, in effect, a mini-Constitutional Convention whenever a new Justice is to be named: the consequence of which is the delicious irony that the meaning of our Bill of Rights has been committed to the charge of precisely that entity that it was meant to protect the individual against: the majority.

What this suggests to those who are contemplating an "entrenched" bill of rights, is that the document should either be ruthlessly specific, eschewing all evolution-prone generalities such as "due process" and "equal protection"; or else, if such generalities are employed, the document should clearly state that the liberties thereby guaranteed are no more and no less than what is reflected in the laws and practices of the current society. Otherwise—if I may resort to a perhaps untranslatable Americanism—you will be buying a pig in a poke.

3

Rights, Paternalism, Constitutions and Judges

"The pity is that there is not more judge-made law. For most of His Majesty's judges are much better fitted for the making of laws than the queer and cowardly rabble who are elected to parliament for that purpose by the fantastic machinery of universal suffrage. . . . My Lords, we are venerable, dignified, and wise, superior in almost every respect to the elected legislators in the House of Commons."[1]

Life imitates art. The mooted satire of 1935 seems an all too plausible description of many persons' thinking and motivation throughout the common law world at the end of the millennium—those of ordinary citizens, social activists, lawyers, legal academics, even (dare one suggest it) of the odd judge. Or so I will argue.

This paper travels the well-trodden path that considers questions about rights, judges, constitutionalism and political philosophy. The only excuses I can offer for travelling that path yet again are that it accepts less than is customary, and it veers down somewhat unusual byways coming to conclusions not currently favoured by the majority. This being the era of concern and respect for minorities, perhaps that is excuse enough.

I RIGHTS

No examination of political philosophy at the end of the twentieth century could long ignore rights. They are now the dominant currency of political and indeed moral philosophy. In a book such as this, plenty will be said about rights. Plenty, that is, about who may claim these rights (that is, only individuals, or groups too, or even bodies corporate?); their extent (that is, just what is the complete set of claimable rights); their overriding character (for example, that they have an international and universal quality which often outweighs the legislative, domestic and parochial); and even the relation of rights to notions of equality and liberty. These

* The author is grateful to Jeff Goldsworthy, Wojciech Sadurski, Richard Kay, Richard Cullen, Grant Huscroft, Janet McLean and Michael Robertson for their helpful comments on and criticisms of an earlier draft.

[1] A P Herbert, *Uncommon Law* (reprinted in Methuen, London, 1984—first published in book form in 1935 and before that in the pages of *Punch*) 153 at 156, 158. The author wishes to thank D F Dugdale for this reference.

are all realms, after all, in which the rights movement's true believers can debate, argue and disagree about rights.

But what about more heretical concerns to do with rights, questions raised not by the rights-believing faithful but by atheists, apostates or even agnostics? To start, there is a widespread tendency to ignore or gloss over the foundational issue of what, precisely, rights are. This omission may be understandable in the company of the converted, but it takes for granted something (viz, the primacy and over-riding nature of rights) that is notably difficult to substantiate or validate. Even such a devotee of rights as Ronald Dworkin recognises this difficulty:[2]

> "But what are rights and goals and what is the difference? It is hard to supply any defin-ition that does not beg the question."

Dworkin can be taken to mean that attempts to provide a theory of rights that does not fall back on some sort of utilitarian, consequentialist thinking are by no means easy to defend. Were we all Benthamite utilitarians, then rights could more or less be understood as enforceable rules (say, protecting free speech or foreclosing tor-ture) that tended to increase social happiness, well-being, or pleasure. Rights in this view would be much like utilitarian notions of justice, liberty, or equality—short-hand generalisations for traits, conduct, or qualities that tend to increase human happiness.

Of course, as in all utilitarian calculations the only *ultimate* good is human happi-ness. It follows that such utilitarian determinations would be contingent in so far as the people doing the calculating might, and sometimes would, disagree both about likely future consequences and about what will increase that happiness and to whom. Utilitarianism provides only an approach, after all, *not* transcendent answers. Thus it also follows that a point would eventually be reached when short-hand generalisations of what *tends* to increase human happiness (say, freedom, choice, justice, equality or certain rights) will have to give way to more direct consequentialist calculations in the case at hand. This seems true even of highly sophisticated rule utilitarian[3] theories of rights. Hence, even for the rule utilitarian it is true that rights against (or rules[4] prohibiting), say, torture are no more absolute or robust than the underlying claims (a) that state utilisation of torture has bad long-term consequences (everything considered) in terms of citizens' apprehensions, police officers' uncontrollable conduct, etc and (b) that it is wiser and more pro-ductive of social happiness to lay this down as a hard and fast rule of conduct rather than to try to calculate competing utilities about the desirability of torture on a case-by-case basis.

---

[2] R Dworkin, *Taking Rights Seriously* (London, Duckworth, 1977) 90.

[3] See "Introduction" in J Waldron (ed.), *Theories of Rights* (New York, Oxford University Press, 1984) 18.

[4] On a purely analytical level, as we learn from Wesley Hohfeld, a right ("others must") is the con-verse of a duty ("I must") and both are linked to some rule; in other words a right is a rule: W W Cook (ed.), *Fundamental Legal Conceptions as Applied in Judicial Reasoning* (Westport, Greenwood Press, 1919, reprinted 1978).

However, the point about utilitarian versions, explanations, and justifications of rights—even the highly sophisticated, modern, rule-utilitarian versions[5]—is that (b) appears never to generate an absolute bar on *any* conduct. At some point, if the facts are pushed far enough,[6] torture *will* be justified on utilitarian grounds.

Consequently, utilitarian conceptions of rights (and utilitarianism itself) are very much out of fashion in contemporary liberal discussions of political, moral and legal philosophy. Rights adherents overwhelmingly reject utilitarianism (and its ultimate willingness to trade off the interests of a few against a greater total of lesser interests of the many) as a basis for their faith and adherence.

Unfortunately, non-utilitarian theories of rights—what precisely rights are, together with defences of their claimed basic and fundamental status—tend to be very thin indeed. Here's what Jeremy Waldron says:[7]

> "Non-utilitarian theories [of rights] tend to be technically less sophisticated; often they contain little more than a bare assertion that certain rights are intuitively evident or are at any rate to be taken as first principles."

Certainly any attempt to put forward a non-utilitarian, non-subjective[8] theory of rights—and of course I mean of *moral* or *non-legal* rights, not those obviously man-made creations, legal rights, which have been legislated for or constitutionalised in some particular jurisdiction and so are consequently clearly justiciable—involves recourse to some sort of moral theory that asserts there in fact *are* non-contingent, universal moral answers that are *not* just relative to culture, epoch or a society's level of material development and well-being.

A moral theory making these sort of claims about the ultimately mind-independent status of moral evaluations falls into what is described as the moral realist or moral objectivist camp. Here, at least some moral questions have answers that transcend the subjective, the local, the cultural and the established. Hence, for example, slavery and torture will be asserted now to be, and indeed always to have been, objectively wrong and evil, whatever their long-standing pedigree and common usage in history and in fact.

---

[5] For an entry into discussions of Rule Utilitarianism see G Postema, *Bentham and the Common Law Tradition* (Oxford, Clarendon Press, 1986); R M Hare, *Moral Thinking* (New York, Oxford University Press, 1981) and D Lyons' chapter "Utility and Rights" in J Waldron, *Theories of Rights*, above note 3.

[6] I support this claim at greater length in *A Sceptical Theory of Morality and Law* (New York, Peter Lang, 1998) at 218ff and in "Scepticism, Rights and Utility" (1988) 11 *Ratio Juris* 413. Of course, it is not just utilitarian theories of rights that fail to generate an absolute bar on any conduct. Most other theories of rights acknowledge that rights can at least sometimes be overridden in order to protect other rights. The gravamen against utilitarian theories is presumably that they countenance this possibility too easily and too often. Arguing strongly that this is not so, however, see M Bagaric, "In Defence of a Utilitarian Theory of Punishment: Punishing the Innocent and the Compatibility of Utilitarianism and Rights" (1999) 24 *Australian Journal of Legal Philosophy* 95.

[7] J Waldron, *Theories of Rights*, above n. 3 at 19 (internal footnote omitted).

[8] I emphasise here that a non-utilitarian theory of rights does not have to be wedded to moral realism. One could certainly support rights on a purely subjective basis (what Bentham called "sympathy and antipathy" and which seems in part to lie beneath the citation at fn 48 below). A sort of "useful fiction" theory of rights might also, arguably, fall outside utilitarianism.

It is fairly clear, I take it, that the human rights movement[9] of the last half-century rests overwhelmingly on such moral realist or moral objectivist foundations. Oddly enough, while the last few decades have seen a geometric growth in the importance and usage of rights, not least so-called human rights, there has been a more or less concurrent explosion in such notions as cultural relativism, postmodernism and deconstructionism. The former tends to emphasise the universal, the transcendent and the shared, while the latter accentuates indeterminacy, ambiguity and uncertainty. Perspective and vantage are everything to one, and nothing (or next to nothing) to the other.

Remarkably, a fair number of people seem to want it both ways; they want to have their universal rights protections and their inherent dignity and equality at the same time as they rubbish claims to the value neutrality of liberalism, or point out that "truth" and "right" vary according to the prevailing hierarchy and dominant ideology, or even endorse an extreme, radical scepticism embracing not just values but the external, causal world too.[10] The feat of reconciliation required to hold fast to both these basic positions, however, seems to me far beyond the abilities of even a Dworkinian Hercules.

Be that as it may, my focus in this paper is just with rights and the universalising, non-relativistic branch of the two post-war trends in political, social and legal thought. For that focus it suffices here simply to note the transcendent, vaguely Kantian flavour and underpinnings to so much of the rights discourse we hear. I will take it as granted that behind almost all of the aspirational, emotively powerful rights talk that today seems to surround us there are moral realist pre-suppositions (explicit or implicit) about the status of moral evaluations and of rights themselves. The true believer may go on to ground his faith in rights in some sort of old-fashioned intuitionism or in born-again natural law thinking,[11] or in its related Dworkinian cousin,[12] or in purportedly logical connections between purposive human action and rights,[13] or, perhaps most likely of all, may think such groundings unnecessary, even distasteful. Whichever, the moral realism behind the rights claims is rarely hard

---

[9] Again, I here refer in particular to claims about rights that are not grounded in the legally or constitutionally enacted rights of a particular municipal legal system. Although such legal rights are obviously a concern and interest of the human rights movement, so too are rights claims in places where there is no legal basis for the claim. (Eg, any such claims as that person X has a right to free speech in China or to have an abortion in 1980s Ireland or to housing and tertiary education in the United States.) These sorts of moral or non-legal rights claims, lacking enforceable, domestic legal bases, have to be based on something.

[10] For an interesting and enjoyable documentation of the burgeoning of the latter, indeterminacy-emphasising trend in American universities see P Gross and N Levitt, *Higher Superstition* (Baltimore, Johns Hopkins University Press, 1994).

[11] See J Finnis, *Natural Law and Natural Rights* (Oxford, Clarendon Press, 1980).

[12] See R Dworkin, *Taking Rights Seriously*, above n. 2 and *Law's Empire* (Cambridge, Mass. Harvard University Press, 1986). I list Dworkin as a moral realist though he once seemed to deny it. (See my *A Sceptical Theory of Morality and Law*, above n. 6, ch. 7.) More recently, in "Objectivity and Truth: You'd Better Believe It" (1996) 25 *Philosophy & Public Affairs* 87, Dworkin, who is best seen as a neo-Kantian, revealed his true colours.

[13] See T Nagel, *The Possibility of Altruism* (Oxford, Clarendon Press, 1970) and A Gewirth, "The Epistemology of Human Rights" (1984) 1 *Social Philosophy & Policy* 1.

to find. Indeed, a barely qualified absolutism is part of the attraction to many adherents. It is almost as though the reverse of Hume's Law[14] were being infringed, and the "is" derived from the "ought": hence human rights *do* exist and *are* universally held just because they are good, desirable things all of us *should* have.[15]

However, rather than go on next to chart or retrace the arguments for and against moral realism's persuasiveness,[16] or the concomitant likely success or otherwise of establishing a non-utilitarian foundation for rights, I would like instead to take a road less travelled. I would like in the next section to consider paternalism and its relation to rights, especially in the context of judicially enforced, constitutionalised rights. I finish this section simply by declaring my own atheism about the existence of non-legal, moral rights understood in any non-subjective, non-consequentialist, moral realist way.[17] Mine is a view of rights from beyond the stockade; where most others today seem to see them as non-derivative, I lack the faith to sustain such a view. I am emotionally on the outside of the imperial rights adventure. For those like me, rights will lack that characteristically conclusive quality they hold for true believers.

II PATERNALISM AND RIGHTS

At first glance many might think rights and paternalism have little to do with one another. Start with rights. Roughly speaking, "legal rights are protections—protections against interference or uncooperativeness—conferred by legal norms".[18] Similarly, moral rights are protections conferred by moral norms or rules.[19] And in the realm of political morality, the realm in which rights are normally situated, those

[14] "Hume's Law" is the name commonly given to David Hume's assertion that copula "ought" relations cannot be derived from copula "is" relations. Attempts to do so are also referred to as the "Naturalistic Fallacy" because natural law claims often rest on such a shift from the way things happen to be to the way they ought to be. See V C Chappell (ed.), *Hume* (New York, Anchor Books, 1966), in particular the chapter by A C MacIntyre, "Hume on 'Is' and 'Ought'".

[15] In Bentham-like terms, "We all do have bread because hunger is bad."

[16] For what it is worth, my view is that moral realism fails to convince. Moral evaluations ultimately are subjective and relative, tied to the evaluator's contingent sentiments and so in part to her culture and era. I make this argument at length in *A Sceptical Theory of Morality and Law*, above n. 6. For an American judge's argument that comes to much the same conclusion see R Posner, "The Problematics of Moral and Legal Theory" (1997) 111 *Harv L R* 1637.

[17] In other words, I find persuasive the case for seeing rights in derivative terms, deriving from goals and subjective preferences. Just how far into the future one is prepared to look, and so how much weight one gives to the indirect, rule utilitarian considerations helping support such derivative rights, is obviously open to great disagreement and debate. Wherever the derivatist chooses to draw the line, though, the fact remains that for him rights have lost that conclusiveness and urgency which they hold for the true believer. For my full account of how rights can be understood from the moral sceptic's vantage see *A Sceptical Theory of Morality and Law*, above n. 6, ch. 9.

[18] M Kramer, "Also Among the Prophets: Some Rejoinders to Ronald Dworkin's Attacks on Legal Positivism" (1999) 12 *Can JL & Juris* 76 (internal footnote omitted).

[19] Obvious differences between the two then are (i) the greater ease with which legal rules generally can be identified; (ii) the fact there is rarely if ever consensus about what the moral rules are or should be; and (iii) the fact there is no way, mutually, to resolve this moral dissensus. Of course, these three points are inter-related.

protections are overwhelmingly conferred on the individual. As even a perfunctory consideration of national bills of rights, international human rights documents or the concerns of groups such as Amnesty International or Human Rights Watch makes abundantly clear, group rights are the equivalent of a minor galaxy (albeit one expanding hyperbolicly) in a universe dominated by concern for individual rights. It is the claims *of individuals* that rights overwhelmingly protect. It is *the individual* who is owed a duty (because of rights) not to have the free expression of his opinions interfered with, or not to have the free practice of her religion constrained, or not to be tortured, or—more contentiously—to be provided with fair wages, safe working conditions, and an adequate standard of living. Rights everywhere are associated with the protection and claims *of individuals*, be they against the state, against persons or bodies acting in a public function, or just against other individuals.

This emphasis on the individual betrays the close connection rights have to liberalism, both historically and theoretically. At its starkest, in the liberal world-view the individual is the basic, core currency, the starting point of political philosophy.[20] Each separate person is an irreducible unit of society. The stark liberal presents a rather atomistic view of society, stressing not only the individual's separateness from others but also the notions of autonomy, choice, self-determination, and liberty. A good liberal society, according to this extreme formulation, requires protections to be put in place to safeguard such separateness, scope for autonomy, and liberty.

That is where rights come in. For such protections today often take the form of rights, frequently constitutionally not just legislatively protected. So we see throughout the liberal democratic world[21] hosts of civil and political rights (and less often and less numerously, social and economic rights), the most fundamental of which are in most such countries constitutionally entrenched in a manner aping, or at least not too dissimilar to, the American constitutional model.[22]

In other words, today's liberal world is predominantly—though not quite yet exclusively—one in which rights have been constitutionalised; their protections of

---

[20] Or so says Bikhu Parekh in "The Cultural Particularity of Liberal Democracy" in D Held (ed.), *Prospects for Democracy: North, South, East, West* (Cambridge, Polity Press, 1993) 156. See too C B Macpherson, *The Life and Times of Liberal Democracy* (Oxford, Oxford University Press, 1977).

[21] I have argued elsewhere that in liberal democracies, liberal features and values (viz, protections of the individual) generally prevail over raw democratic features that 'let the numbers count'. In other words, when liberal values clash with the beliefs and sentiments of the majority of voters, as expressed in democratic elections and through democratically elected legislators, the cards are everywhere—in varying degrees—stacked on the side of liberalism. See my "Liberalism, Democracy and Hong Kong" (1998) 28 *Hong Kong L J* 156.

[22] This mimicry of the American constitutional model is a relatively recent phenomenon, mostly post-dating World War II. Before then, the American and French models were the exceptions in the democratic world. Leaving aside the trend towards constitutionalising rights for a moment, the other distinctive feature of the American model, a strict separation of powers, has not proved itself easy to transplant successfully. See The Economist, 8 May 1999, Lexington column (page 35 in the Asian edition) where the weaknesses and disappointments of countries having adopted strict separation of powers regimes are detailed. "Between 1973 and 1989 . . . democratic institutions were introduced in 53 countries outside the OECD: parliamentary systems proved more than twice as likely to survive as presidential ones. Bruce Ackerman . . . reckons that all in all about 30 countries have adopted American-style systems. 'All of them, without exception, have succumbed to the nightmare [of breakdown] one time or another, often repeatedly' " (*ibid*).

the individual have been entrenched against mere legislative change and handed over to the judiciary to be interpreted, expanded, narrowed and applied—even altered and created *de novo*—as particular cases arise.

Now turn to paternalism. Something is described as paternalistic when it is imposed on others *for their benefit* (rather than the benefit of those doing the imposing). In the political context, then, when someone's (or some body's) liberty or scope for action is restricted on the basis of an argument about *this agent's own good*, we say the restriction was paternalistic. The defining test and characteristic is whether the action, restriction, limit or rule is motivated by a belief that it would be to the benefit of those so affected and limited.[23]

Take the example of a government imposing speech restrictions on its citizens. Regulations that limited or foreclosed so-called "hate speech" or which banned (only) pro-abortion expression would be unlikely to proceed from paternalistic motives. It is hard to see how in normal circumstances such restrictions can be based upon a genuine concern *for the speakers*, rather than the listeners.[24] On the other hand, regulations disallowing the publication of how to make atomic weapons or limiting the amount of spending in election campaigns may plausibly be seen as paternalistic; these restrictions limit individuals' freedom of expression in pursuit of (what is thought to be) their own—and admittedly others'—good. Genuine concern *for the speakers* is one plausible motivation for such bans.

What motivates a paternalistic concern for others can vary though, as these last two examples illustrate. One inducement to enacting paternalistic limits on people's freedom of action may be the realisation that individuals sometimes find themselves in a Prisoner's Dilemma-type situation. The predicament may be such that ". . . a foreclosure of certain individual actions which, if taken generally, would make everybody or nearly everybody worse-off, but which people have an incentive to take unless assured that others will also abstain"[25] is beneficial to almost all those upon whom it is imposed. Choices open to people are therefore restricted for their own good. Campaign finance limits can arguably be understood (at least partially) in this first paternalistic way.

Notice that this first sort of paternalistic motive does *not* require those doing the imposing and restricting necessarily to believe the people governed by the restrictions cannot recognise what is good for them. It is in the nature of a Prisoner's Dilemma-type situation that in fact one *does* realise that uniform compliance with course A (which would be the result of an external rule limiting everyone's actions)

---

[23] This discussion of paternalism owes much to correspondence with, and papers written by, Professor Wojciech Sadurski of the University of Sydney. The author wishes to express his thanks. It should not be assumed that Professor Sadurski would agree with everything that follows.

[24] One obviously abnormal circumstance might be where the speaker's words were quite likely to lead to her inflaming the audience so much that she was, say, assaulted or killed. Banning her words then could be genuinely done on paternalistic grounds. For a full, and interesting, elaboration of the relation between speech restrictions and paternalism in the context of US First Amendment jurisprudence see W Sadurski, "Does the Subject Matter? Viewpoint-Neutrality and Freedom of Speech" (1997) 15 *Cardozo Arts & Ent L J* 315.

[25] *Ibid*, 368.

would be preferable to uniform opting for course B (which is in everyone's self-interest in the absence of external constraints guaranteeing compliance). One realises it but cannot effect it oneself. So paternalism in these sort of situations does not really spring from a belief that the person or group imposing the limit knows what is good for some group of others better than they themselves do.

However, this first sort of paternalistic motive, where I impose something on you that I know you too think is for your benefit, is rather rare. Much more common is the out and out belief that we (the imposers of the restriction) know better than you (the group who will be so restricted) what is good *for you*. It is just as much in *your* long-term interest to be prevented from publishing the details of how to make an atomic bomb—even if you think otherwise. Paternalism generally origin-ates in a belief about others' deficiencies: their incapacities to evaluate arguments; their lack of measured calmness and too great emotionalism; their susceptibility to demagogues and populist appeals; and so on. It is this second sort of paternalism, by far the most common variety, that involves an attitude essentially hostile to the idea that each person knows what is best for himself (at the personal level), or that each generation knows what is best for itself (at the constitutional level).

Depending upon the particular factual circumstances and other people under consideration, we are all paternalists in this second, condescending sense. At some point each of us, even the most deferential-to-others liberal, is prepared to say she knows better than another what is good for that other. Sometimes we are even pre-pared to enforce that paternalistic assessment. It is all a question of where each of us draws the line. Jeremy Bentham thought[26] the vast preponderance of individu-als were, each one themselves, the best judges of their own happiness.[27] However, he did *not* think *everyone* was the best such judge. Children and insane people are obvious counter-examples. Certainly when it comes to diet, television watching, wearing of seat-belts and myriad other matters, I, for one, think I know what is better for my six-year-old son than he himself does. I am overtly paternalistic, in other words, and I enforce my views over his.

So paternalism, whatever the connotations of the word itself, is certainly not an indefensible notion in all circumstances, as applied to all others. Sometimes person X *will* know what is best for person Y better than person Y himself.

That said, the range of situations in which such paternalistic claims hold true (on average, over time) is, in my view, very limited indeed. Yes, they generally hold as regards children,[28] the insane, possibly too the severely inebriated. But when it comes to the ordinary situation of normal adult and normal adult, Bentham was

---

[26] See Jeremy Bentham's *An Introduction to the Principles of Morals and Legislation* (with an introduc-tion by Hart and Burns) (Oxford, Clarendon, 1996, first published in 1787). For an excellent compari-son of Bentham's views to those of J S Mill, and to later economic, purely preference-based theories, see Robin West, "The Other Utilitarians" in Brian Brix (ed.), *Analyzing Law* (New York, Clarendon, 1998).

[27] The claim, of course, is that over time, on average, most individuals will do better at achieving happiness for themselves than some other person would for them.

[28] Though the validity of paternalistic claims about knowing what is best for children may more or less vary inversely with the child's age.

correct. Each of us is more likely to know what is best for ourselves better than any other person who could be identified in advance by some easily applicable rule— however intelligent, sensitive, socially attuned, psychologically perceptive, or well-read up on social studies that other may be. Or put in political and social terms, even if I am not the best judge of what is optimal for me, the costs of the imposition by a paternalist who (for the sake of argument) *does* know what is best for me, will in most cases (save easily identifiable cases like children and the insane) more than cancel out the overall optimality of the paternalistic imposition. Jim wants to do X. There are experts out there who know Y is better for Jim. But the costs of imposing Y on Jim and preventing him from doing X are so high (in terms which include finding reliable experts with enough regularity, guarding against bureaucratic over-reach, allowing for Jim's anger and frustration in not having it his own way and in being treated this way, paying to administer the imposition process, and much more) that the imposition will be sub-optimal. This is because while Y is more than X (*ex hypothesi*), Y minus Z (the costs) is less than X. So in most instances the best or most efficient rule is just to leave people to decide what is best for themselves.

The essence of paternalism then—that I know better than you what will further your welfare—is not always false nor indefensible. Rather, experience shows that as a rule it is *usually* false. Each adult (and each generation) *generally* knows what is best for herself (or itself) better than any practicable alternative. The burden lies on the paternalist to show some particular situation is out of the ordinary.

We are in a position now to finish this section the way it started, by considering the relation between rights and paternalism. As I hinted above, the individualistic emphasis of the former is not obviously compatible with the imperiousness of the latter. Indeed, as long as one considers the *effects* of rights, their affording protections and entitlements to the individual to protect his interests,[29] one is unlikely to link them to paternalism. However, if instead one asks about the *motives* for according rights to others, the link to paternalism is immediately more obvious. The link between rights and paternalism becomes even stronger still if one narrows her focus further to constitutionally entrenched, justiciable rights of the sort found in the American Bill of Rights or Canadian Charter of Rights. One way of understanding such constitutionalised rights is in terms of the generation doing the entrenching thinking it knows what is best for later generations[30]—that is why the rights have to be entrenched and made more or less immune from legislative (that is,

---

[29] This paper takes no position on whether the so-called Benefit or Interest Theory of Rights or the so-called Choice or Will Theory of Rights is the more compelling. Interested readers can start with Waldron, 9ff and for a full-length discussion see M Kramer, N E Simmonds and H Steiner, *A Debate over Rights* (New York, Clarendon Press, 1998).

[30] The constitutionalisation of rights, and so the possibility of judicial invalidation of democratically adopted statutes, is, as I made clear at the start, a subject with a vast literature. This paper has deliberately approached the subject from a somewhat unusual direction, namely in terms of paternalism. No doubt defenders of strong judicial review can also understand the practice in largely non-paternalistic terms. On either understanding though, Part 4 below is applicable and, in my view, the practice is undesirable and undemocratic.

ordinary democratic) revision. If later generations were as much, or more, to be trusted, such entrenchment would make little sense; in fact it would be counter-productive. Some form or other of parliamentary supremacy would be the choice of those favouring democratic government.

That such parliamentary supremacies are nearing extinction is a sign of the close relationship between constitutionalised rights and paternalism.

III CONSTITUTIONS, PATERNALISM AND RIGHTS

"As the twentieth century comes to a close, the triumph of constitutionalism appears almost complete. Just about every state in the world has a written constitution. The great majority of these declare the constitution to be law controlling the organs of the state. And, in at least many states, that constitution is, in fact, successfully invoked by courts holding acts of the state invalid because inconsistent with the constitution."[31]

In particular then, democratic countries around the world overwhelmingly have written constitutions. The only exceptions are Israel, the United Kingdom and New Zealand, and even these three are not totally free of constitution-like elements or restraints. Israel has a series of Basic Laws that purport to be beyond ordinary legislative modification; the United Kingdom has the recently enacted Human Rights Act which, though just a statute and not allowing judges to strike down other Acts, does allow judges to make declarations of incompatibility with the European Convention on Human Rights (itself more or less enforceable by the European Court of Human Rights in Strasbourg); and New Zealand too has a statutory bill of rights which, though explicitly forbidding judicial invalidation of statutes also asks courts to interpret other enactments, so far as possible, as consist-ent with the rights listed.[32] But these three are evidently exceptions, or partial exceptions, to the prevailing rule of constitutionalism (understood in the sense in which there exists an overarching, written constitution specifying what the state may and may not do and who or what may do it).

The motives for adopting one form or other of constitutionalism are patently many and include the need to divide up powers in a federal state, the attraction of articulating in entrenched form certain aspirations and goals for the state, the desire for stability and rigidly bound state action by means of fixed rules, and the wish to recognise some moral pre-eminence of the individual even, perhaps, while giving special protections to minority groups. These and many other not always mutually compatible grounds can be, and are, given in defence of constitutionalism. That said, one rationale seems to me to be at the forefront when a person desires a writ-ten constitution, namely, a desire to lock in one particular set of rules, rights and division of powers so that later revision is more than usually difficult, indeed often

---

[31] R Kay, "American Constitutionalism" in L Alexander (ed), *Constitutionalism, Philosophical Foundations* (New York, Cambridge University Press, 1998) 16.
[32] *Ibid*, 50 n. 1.

near impossible. As Justice Antonin Scalia of the United States Supreme Court rightly notes:[33]

> "It certainly cannot be said that a constitution naturally suggests changeability; to the contrary, its whole purpose is to prevent change—to embed certain rights in such a manner that future generations cannot readily take them away. . . . [This is] the whole anti-evolutionary purpose of a constitution."

Such an anti-evolutionary purpose clearly applies to all components of a written constitution, from its specific provisions dividing powers between centre and region to its general enunciation of individual freedoms and liberties in the form of an entrenched charter or bill of rights.[34] However, my focus in this paper is solely on the latter, on such constitutionalised—and so immunised against ordinary democratic alteration or repeal—rights. What is the basis for thinking such rights should and must be constitutionally locked in? Why does the generation doing the locking in think itself wiser, calmer, less susceptible to demagogues and emotional over-reactions than later generations? In short, what justification is there for donning the paternalist's robes and thinking we (viz, the generation locking in these constitutionalised rights) know more about rights than you (viz, all the later generations whose views about rights will, in effect, count for less than ours)? If, as I argued above, the burden lies on the paternalist to show some other person or generation is not best placed to further his or its own welfare or interests, can that burden plausibly be met here, when it comes to constitutionalised rights?

My own view is that the paternalistic defender of constitutionalised rights (and notice that *all* defenders of constitutionalised rights are paternalistic to some degree—if others were to be trusted with weighing and ranking rights as much as or more than they themselves, then entrenching and constitutionalising such rights would be counter-productive and make no sense)[35] will fail to meet that burden.

---

[33] A Scalia, *A Matter of Interpretation* (Princeton, Princeton University Press, 1997) 40 and 44. See too R Kay, "American Constitutionalism", above n. 31 at 17–27. Having noted the anti-evolutionary purpose of many who favour adopting a constitution, it should also be mentioned that some later users of that constitution will look for ways to slip out of the straight-jacket. For instance, later judges may talk of this constitution as a "living tree" and say its provisions need to be interpreted "charitably", "generously", "so as to avoid the austerity of tabulated legalism", etc. Such metaphors and prescriptions are, of course, devices to limit the constitutional constraints and so afford themselves more power.

[34] I emphasise here that a written constitution need not include such an enunciation of individual rights. However, written constitutions lacking some sort of bill of rights are in fact extremely rare. As far as I am aware Australia is the only developed country that today has a written constitution that unequivocally lacks a bill of rights. One of Australia's written constitution's main functions is to divide up powers between the states and the centre. Canada's pre-1982 written constitution was the same.

[35] One might say in response that this is to understand a "generation" in misleadingly unitary terms. From the point of view of the individual citizen, a majority of citizens at the time of adopting the constitution is imposing its views on later majorities who might disagree. This might be because today's majority thinks it would benefit the later majority (hence paternalistic) or it might not be. One obvious counter-example would be where today's majority seeks to protect tomorrow's minority (possibly because it fears being that minority). This is not, then, an example of telling the later majority to do what is good for it and so is not paternalism in any straightforward sense. However, in an odd sort of way—one combining moral superiority and *noblesse oblige*—today's majority still purports to be doing what is best for later societies as a whole and in that enervated sense is being paternalistic.

She will be unable to show that *her view* of what is good for others when it comes to the set of rights they should have, their relative ranking, their relation to general welfare claims, etc, is any better or more likely to benefit others than the views of *all those others*. Of course the paternalistic defender of constitutionalised rights will *believe* that locking these rights in and immunising them against ordinary democratic (that is, legislative) revision is for the benefit of all of us so affected, including all later generations. She will believe she knows best; but her belief, in my view, will be unfounded. There is no persuasive reason for thinking the rest of us are somehow deficient and less able to weigh, rank, and legislate for rights than she. Our incapacities to evaluate arguments, to stay calm and reflective, to see through demagogues and short-sighted populist appeals, are no greater than hers. For her to know what is best for us *better than we do ourselves*, is to assume a situation analogous to the one in which the paternalistic defender of constitutional rights is the normal adult and all the rest of us are, or will be, children, insane or severely inebriated. I do not believe that analogy can be sustained.

Many others, it must be confessed, disagree. Common are the defences of constitutionalised rights that appeal to analogies of Ulysses bound to the mast so that he can resist the otherwise irresistible allure of the sirens or of the people drunk and the people sober. Let us call this the "sirens defence" of entrenching some set of constitutional rights. Its gist amounts to this: we should lock in rights now, today, while we are sober and cannot hear the sirens. The temptation to violate rights tomorrow—a temptation all too easy when rights are simply in statutory form and at the mercy of the legislature—may prove irresistible. Give your host your car keys *before* you start drinking. Afterwards you may not know what is in your own best interests. This sirens defence is neatly set out, and ultimately rejected, by Jeremy Waldron:[36]

> "The analogy is an interesting one, but it is not ultimately persuasive. In the cases of individual pre-commitment, the person is imagined to be quite certain, in her lucid moments, about the actions she wants to avoid and the basis of their undesirability. . . . The drinker knows at the beginning of the evening that her judgment at midnight about her own ability to drive safely will be seriously impaired. But the case we are dealing with is that of a society whose members disagree, even in their 'lucid' moments, about what rights they have, how they are to be conceived, and what weight they are to be given in relation to other values. They need not appeal to aberrations in rationality to explain these disagreements; they are . . . sufficiently explained by the subject-matter itself. A pre-commitment in these circumstances, then, is not the triumph of pre-emptive rationality that it appears to be [in Ulysses'] or in the drinker's case. It is rather the artificially sustained ascendancy of one view in the polity over other views whilst the philosophical issue between them remains unresolved."[37]

Quite so. Lashing oneself to the mast before one's mind becomes over-awed or taking away the drunk's keys before he becomes drunk is one thing. The eventual

---

[36] See J Waldron, "A Right-Based Critique of Constitutional Rights" (1993) 13 *OJLS* 18, 46–9. See too R Kay, "American Constitutionalism", above n. 31, ch. 1, n. 47 and the accompanying text.

[37] *Ibid*, 47–8 (italics in original).

paternalism, when the ropes are not untied or the keys not given back, can be justified and defended. The other party will be deficient, will not know his own best interests. However, unlike in those cases, I can see no basis for thinking others and later generations will be more deficient in assessing rights and resisting their infringement than those who seek, now, to have them entrenched and constitutionalised. The implicit paternalistic claim—that drunkenness looms so that we had better protect you for your own sake—is unconvincing. Statutory rights that can be altered, repealed and enacted anew through the ordinary legislative and democratic process are, to my mind, preferable.

It follows, obviously, that I hope New Zealand retains some version of parliamentary supremacy as a main feature of its form of government. I want democratically elected legislators—yes, politicians who have to face the voters on a regular basis—to have the last word *even about what rights we are to enjoy and how they are to be balanced.*

To say that, though, lets slip the fact that a strong desire to avoid constitutionalising rights rests on more than just a rejection of inter-generational paternalism. So far, and quite artificially, I have deliberately avoided all mention of the judiciary. Now it is time to descend back to earth and bring judges into the equation. There will inevitably be greater judicial law making, and so less scope and range for more democratic,[38] legislative law making, once a set of constitutionalised rights are entrenched. Such rights are always, perhaps unavoidably, expressed in general, amorphous—if also stirring, emotively charged—terms. Whatever the catalogue of individual, constitutionalised rights in a particular jurisdiction, later judicial intervention to interpret, apply, stretch and limit them in the specific cases that arise will be necessary.

In practice then, the paternalism of the founding fathers who seek to adopt a written constitution with an entrenched bill of rights is a one-off. Once successful, it is not they who will be called on to interpret those rights but rather unelected judges. Judges, though they have not asked for the job, will have the power to override the will of the legislature (and so, however indirectly, of the people). To find ongoing rather than one-off paternalism, one must look here.

IV JUDGES, CONSTITUTIONS, PATERNALISM, AND RIGHTS

"The most familiar example of the operation of constitutional rules is the judicial invalidation of unconstitutional acts of the legislature. It should be stated immediately that the

---

[38] I do not claim legislative law making is somehow perfectly democratic or that there is some canonical version of democracy. My claim is strictly a relative or comparative one: whatever judicial review on the basis of constitutionalised rights is, it is assuredly less democratic than legislative law making. "To provide a democratic justification for the judges' prevailing, one has to show not only that they have democratic credentials but that they have a better democratic claim than that asserted in the legislative action in question. I don't know of any jurist who can maintain that (with a straight face)." J Waldron, "A Right-Based Critique of Constitutional Rights", above n. 36 at 44 (italics in the original and internal footnote omitted).

preference for a constitutional regime depends on an implicit or explicit judgment that self-government, immediate or long-term, is not a pre-emptive value".[39]

That refreshingly candid observation, from a writer who approves of constitutionalism it should be noted, is a good place to start this last section. Rather than tie ourselves in scholastic knots or devise casuistical arguments trying to show how systems with strong judicial review somehow are no less democratic than those parliamentary supremacies without it, let us cut through such endeavours. Let us concede that constitutionalising rights and making them justiciable hands much power—social policy-making power that *would have otherwise* rested with elected lawmakers—to unelected judges. Instead, let us finish by considering two questions:

i)   Are there grounds to think judges use this power better than elected legislators? (That is, do judges—who, under a constitutionalised rights regime, have to decide which laws conflict with those rights and so, at least sometimes and indirectly,[40] what they think is in the best interests of us others—deliver the goods? Is the on-going paternalism justified, in other words?)

ii) How reticent do judges appear to be to assume this power? (Differently put, how deferential are they to elected politicians given that the scope of the constitutionalised rights is necessarily vague and amorphous?)

Start with the latter query first. The careful, nuanced answer would be that "it depends on the particular jurisdiction, its legal culture, and indeed on the individual judge herself". Some judges are much more reticent to override legislative enactments than others. So much is obvious.

Still, there is some room for generalising about judges' relative willingness to defer to elected politicians. For a start, and not surprisingly, judges in jurisdictions still today lacking constitutionalised rights seem generally more deferential. Consider the United Kingdom. Even a judge as associated with the human rights movement as Lord Hoffmann, while endorsing the enactment of the Human Rights Act 1998, can say:[41]

> "I must admit that I like it that way and I feel particularly comfortable with the fact that, for example, the law on abortion has been made by the elected representatives of the people rather than being deduced from some very general statements in the Bill of Rights. I do not relish the role of a Platonic guardian and I am pleased to live in a society that does not thrust it upon me."

[39] R Kay, "American Constitutionalism", above n. 31 at 25.

[40] Judges who take an evolutionary or "living" approach to the interpretation of constitutionalised rights have to be pre-supposing that their own view of what those rights should today mean is, in some sense, the best one. Nor is this interpretive approach imposed on them. Judges are perfectly free to adopt a more textualist approach to interpreting the constitutionalised rights, one that looked to enactors' original intentions or to what the constitutionalised rights were understood to mean when adopted. But even a textualist approach, which in my view clearly imposes more constraints on the judge, will sometimes leave the judge with discretion, in the penumbra of doubt as it were, because no answer seems clearly dictated. In such cases it would be odd if the judge did not opt for what he or she thought to be, in some sense, the best answer.

[41] Rt Hon Lord Hoffmann, "Human Rights and the House of Lords" (1999) 62 *MLR* 159, 161.

In the United States, by way of contrast, judicial reticence to assume this power would appear to be somewhat less marked, to put it mildly. Professor Gordon Wood of Brown University, commenting on Justice Scalia's 1996 Tanner Lectures at Princeton replied:[42]

"I have a good deal of sympathy with the complaint that modern judges have tended to run amok, have become makers rather than simply interpreters of the law, and have come to exercise a degree of authority over our lives that is unparalleled among modern Western nations. . . . I do not know of any country in the world where judges wield as much power in shaping the contours of life as they do in the United States."

Leaving aside the plausible retort that Professor Wood has overlooked the judicial activism in Canada, it must be said again that of course each individual judge is different. In relative terms, some American judges are more deferential to elected legislators, and some are less so. Justice Scalia, himself one of the more deferential of American judges, sees the key divide being between those who interpret the constitution on the basis of original meaning, like him, and those who interpret on the basis of current or evolving or living meaning.[43] The latter, he thinks (and with good cause in my opinion), not only has become the ascendant school of American constitutional interpretation in the United States, it provides virtually no constraints on the interpreting judge. A living constitution:

"means . . . what it ought to mean. . . . If it is good, it is so . . . [till we have arrived at the stage] when it is publicly proclaimed, and taught in the law schools, that judges *ought* to make the statutes and the constitution say what they think best."[44]

Even an American judge as hard-headed and attracted to the notion of utility maximisation as Richard Posner is prepared sometimes to use the position granted judges in the American political system to override the democratic political process. Mind you, I suspect Chief Judge Posner would be more reticent to do this than many American judges. Still, after telling us in the course of delivering the 1997 Oliver Wendell Holmes Lectures[45] at Harvard Law School that morality is local, in a sense subjective, and certainly relative to the particular culture in which a claim is advanced; that moral theory lacks the necessary resources for resolving moral controversies; that academic moralism is sterile and cannot succeed in its aim of improving human behaviour; that moral beliefs are contingent and not the emanations of some universal law or set of universal rights; in short that "there is nothing good or bad, but thinking makes it so"[46] (all of which, by the way, I more or less fully agree with[47])—Posner concludes Part II of his lecture thus:[48]

---

[42] G Wood, "Comment" in A Scalia, *A Matter of Interpretation*, above n. 33 at 49.

[43] See A Scalia, *A Matter of Interpretation*, above n. 33 at 38ff.

[44] *Ibid*, 47, 39, 132 (italics in the original).

[45] See R Posner, "The Problematics of Moral and Legal Theory", above n. 16.

[46] Hamlet, Act II, scene II, lines 259–61.

[47] See J Allan, *A Sceptical Theory of Morality and Law*, above n. 6.

[48] R Posner, "The Problematics of Moral and Legal Theory", above n. 16 at 1708. On the next page, it must be noted, Posner does go on to say "one's moral intuitions or (in Holmes's) phrase 'can't helps' don't seem to be very heavy counterweights to democratic preference as reflected in the actions of the political branches" (p 1709, internal footnote omitted).

"Some constitutional and other legal issues cannot be resolved [on the facts or in terms of institutional competence], and then the judge has two choices. One is to say that if public opinion is divided on a moral issue, judges should refuse to intervene, should leave resolution to the political process. The other is to say, with Holmes, that while this is ordinarily the right way to go, every once in a while an issue on which public opinion is divided will so excite the judge's moral emotions that he simply will not be able to stomach the political resolution that has been challenged on constitutional grounds. . . . I prefer the second route."

Even the judicial world's Posners, to the extent that their subjective "can't helps" are also thought to benefit others, do not completely forswear paternalism.

At least, though, they are honest and forthright about their paternalism, even somewhat abashed. From the perspective of this particular ex-patriate Canadian, the same cannot be said of Canada's highest judges. From them we hear continuously of how they are engaged in a "dialogue" with the elected legislators.[49] They say this all the while they are striking down statutes that restrict the advertising of tobacco products (free speech)[50] and put spending limits on referendum campaigns (again, free speech and also freedom of association);[51] that limit the salaries of provincially appointed judges (infringement of judicial independence);[52] that require certain children born abroad to undergo security checks before becoming Canadian citizens (equality);[53] that impose support obligations only on opposite-sex couples, not same-sex couples (equality again, and even though the legislature had a few years earlier considered and deliberately rejected imposing the obligations on same-sex couples);[54] that are held to need rewriting and indeed a new ground is added by the judges to a province's human rights legislation (equality again, but seemingly compromising the division of powers by requiring funding);[55] and so on, and so on, and so on. Apparently the fact that the Canadian constitution has a "notwithstanding" clause that allows politicians to override the judiciary somehow turns the judges' paternalistic pronouncements into a dialogue. Unfortunately it is no such thing. The "notwithstanding" clause has only ever been used twice in the 18 years of the Charter of Rights' existence—both times at the

---

[49] See, for example, the 27 March 1999 *National Post* report of a speech by Canadian Supreme Court Justice Frank Iacobucci to University of Ottawa law students. ("Supreme Court decisions that strike down or rewrite legislation should be viewed as a 'dialogue' with parliamentarians, not an attempt to trample over elected officials.") Or again, see *MacLean's*, 8 March 1999, pp. 23ff. For an extremely unconvincing defence (in my view) of the 'dialogue' relationship, one which the judges themselves like to cite (see eg n. 54 below), see P Hogg and A Bushell, "The Charter Dialogue Between Courts and Legislatures" (1997) 35 *Osgoode Hall L J* 75: "Accordingly, the 'dialogue' to which this article refers consists of those cases in which a judicial decision striking down a law on Charter grounds is followed by some action by the competent legislative body" (p 82, second italics mine). Can one imagine a less stringent definition of "dialogue"?

[50] *RJR MacDonald Inc v. Canada* [1995] 3 SCR 199.

[51] *Libman and Equality Party v. Attorney General of Quebec* [1997] 3 SCR 569.

[52] *Reference Re Remuneration of Provincial Court Judges* [1997] 3 SCR 3.

[53] *Benner v. Canada (Secretary of State)* [1997] 1 SCR 358.

[54] *M v. H* [1999] 2 SCR 3.

[55] *Vriend v. Alberta* [1998] 1 SCR 493.

provincial level.[56] Worse, many of the people (judges and legal academics included) who hold the "notwithstanding" clause up to vouchsafe the democratic credentials of the whole strong judicial review process would howl if it were ever used.[57] The climate of absolutism surrounding the rights' guarantees in the Charter has been built up to such a degree that overriding the judges is practically impossible. And I suspect the Canadian judges know it. They are not engaged in a dialogue with the politicians; it is more like an example of class dictation. The students do what they are told. Their only recourse is to claim the teacher is drunk on the job or physically abusive. But the benefits of such a course hardly ever outweigh the costs.

Enough of my native country and its Charter and enough about the relative reticence or otherwise of judges to assume social policy-making power. Instead, let us return to the question posed several pages ago. When it comes to the social policy-making power implicit in being the final determiners of what content, scope, and relative weight rights are to have, do unelected judges handle this power better than elected politicians? Are we better off letting judges decide rights questions for us, and trusting their paternalistic exercise of this power?

My own view is that judges are no better at determining, shaping and protecting rights than elected legislators responsible to voters. That may be a somewhat heretical assessment. Nevertheless, I do not intend to defend it here.[58] For present purposes I simply point to the UK, Australia, and New Zealand, parliamentary supremacies all, and assert that in so far as these things are open to comparison, citizens' relative freedoms and overall social egalitarianism have fared no worse there than in the United States or in post-1982 Canada.[59]

But however one measures the competing abilities of unelected judges and elected politicians when it comes to shaping the scope, content and relative weight of rights, it is crucial that one realises what one is doing in making this sort of "Trust Judges More" argument. Quite simply, one is making the utilitarian, consequentialist case that judges deliver the goods. Nothing more. If a set of high priests and clerics or of South American caudillos were as capable as judges, then they too should be entrusted with this power. It is results that count. So the very people who made rights-based appeals focusing on the individual both fundamental and determinative before, now ignore *rights-based* appeals to individuals' right of participation

---

[56] Saskatchewan in 1986 on a labour law matter, and Quebec in 1982 on a French language matter.

[57] For an example of pre-emptive howling, see J Whyte, "On Not Standing for Notwithstanding" (1990) 28 *Alberta L Rev* 347. For a less hostile view of the use of the legislative override, but one that still argues that in some circumstances even this override can and should be reviewed by the courts, see D Greschner and K Norman, "The Courts and Section 33" (1987) 12 *Queen's L J* 155. This hostility to the override exists despite the fact that the Charter would never have been adopted without the inclusion of the "notwithstanding" clause. Indeed, were one inclined to indulge in pseudo-psychology, it is not implausible to suggest that the existence of a "notwithstanding" clause—even one used but twice in 19 years—frees the judges to be even more active than they would be without the "cover" of such an override.

[58] However, I do argue the case against judicial paternalism when it comes to rights in "Bills of Rights and Judicial Power" (1996) 16 *OJLS* 337, especially pages 347–51.

[59] Lord Hoffmann appears to agree in so far as UK–US comparisons are concerned. See Hoffmann, "Human Rights and the House of Lords" above n. 41 at 161.

(even in formulating and shaping rights themselves) or to the dignity, autonomy and self-governing nature of the individual. When it comes to rights, they *now* say, we are to restrict political participation to the select few who qualify as judges—we must opt for a full-blooded bill of rights that ensures the vast majority's unvarying and continual exclusion from deliberation about so many rights—*because judges are better at it than the rest of us.*

The irony of defending a non-utilitarian, non-subjective, non-contingent version of rights while at the same time, on purely utilitarian grounds, leaving those same rights to be interpreted and shaped overwhelmingly by unelected judges, should be all too apparent. Those of us who take a more consequentialist, utilitarian view of rights can enjoy the incongruous spectacle; we can watch as democratic institutions are by-passed and diminished so that tobacco and gun-control reforms in America and gay-marriage reforms in Canada and extensions to the role of the military in Germany and much else besides can be sought (and frequently achieved) through the courts. We can watch this heightened trust so many social activists, ordinary citizens and legal academics place in the judiciary and we can laugh or we can cry. Most utilitarians prefer to laugh.

4

Judicial Review, Human Rights and Democracy

ANDREW S BUTLER*

My modest proposal is that the importance of human rights, coupled with our international human rights obligations, requires us to rethink the current arrangements in place with respect to judicial review of legislation. In particular, section 4 of the New Zealand Bill of Rights Act 1990 needs to be replaced with a mechanism resembling the "notwithstanding" clause in the Canadian Charter of Rights and Freedoms 1982, which allows for judicial review of all legislation, except those statutes specifically immunised from review by express parliamentary declaration.

I THE CURRENT POSITION

At the beginning, it is important to outline the current position in respect of the interaction between judicial review, human rights and democracy in New Zealand. I start with a number of generalities that I hope are not too controversial.

First, human rights have a high value in the New Zealand polity[1] and a prominent position in the New Zealand legal system. Respect for, and practical enjoyment of, human rights is at a relatively high level. There is a substantial body of statute and case law that gives legal effect to human rights and applies them across a wide range of activities both public and private.[2] I do not intend to engage in a debate about the acceptability of human rights as legally recognised concepts in the New Zealand legal system—in light of statutory developments (such as the Human Rights Act 1993, the New Zealand Bill of Rights Act 1990 and the Privacy Act

---

* The opinions expressed in this paper are personal to the author and do not represent the views of the Crown Law Office.

[1] That is not to say that there have been no serious human rights violations: see for example, Report of the Justice and Electoral Committee, *Inquiry into Matters Relating to the Visit of the President of China to New Zealand in 1999* (1999–2000) AJHR I 7A and the *Ministerial Inquiry into Management Practices at Mangaroa Prison*.

[2] See eg, the Human Rights Act 1993 (subsuming the earlier Race Relations Act 1971 and the Human Rights Commission Act 1977), the New Zealand Bill of Rights Act 1990 and the Privacy Act 1993. In addition to the large body of jurisprudence interpreting those statutes, see also the use of international human rights law to interpret other New Zealand statutes recorded in A S Butler and P Butler, "The Judicial Use of International Human Rights Law in New Zealand" (1999) 29 *VUWLR* 173.

1993), it is clear that there is sufficiently widespread community support for such measures in certain forms.

Second, in the New Zealand context, the debate has not been concerned with *whether* we should recognise human rights (although this is not to say that there has not been debate on which human rights to recognise).[3] Rather, the focus in New Zealand has been upon (1) how human rights should be expressed; and (2) the appropriate mechanisms through which effect can be given to the rights recognised by the legal system.

As regards manner of expression, New Zealand has adopted a mixed system. The Human Rights Act, following the models of its predecessors, is quite detailed—it prohibits discrimination only on certain grounds (each individual ground being separately defined with some precision), and only in respect of certain activities (employment, provision of services/goods, etc) and contains reasonably specific and limited exceptions or qualifications to the non-discrimination rules. In the Human Rights Act, therefore, Parliament has attempted to anticipate a large number of scenarios and legislate a solution in respect of each of them. In contrast, the New Zealand Bill of Rights follows the classical bill of rights mould—generally-worded, open-ended concepts delegating a large measure of interpretative freedom to those who must apply its provisions.

Enforcement of New Zealand human rights legislation is also mixed. The Human Rights Act and Privacy Act involve a number of enforcement procedures. For example, complaints may be made to the Complaints Division of the Human Rights Commission or to the Privacy Commissioner respectively. Following investigation, conciliation may be attempted. If conciliation is unsuccessful there are possibilities for formalised proceedings to occur before the statutorily created Complaints Review Tribunal, with possibilities of appeal to the High Court on questions of law. For the complainant, activating investigation is free. If there is substance to the complaint, and it proceeds to a hearing, it will be free if the Proceedings Commissioner pursues the matter on the complainant's behalf. It is also possible to obtain a declaration from the High Court in respect of conduct that is thought to be in breach of the Human Rights Act.[4] Both Acts permit complaints and proceedings to be taken in respect of the conduct of both public and private bodies. However, these Acts cannot be relied upon to override legislation or regulations which are inconsistent with their provisions. For example,[5] section 151(1)

---

[3] Thus, for example, current human rights legislation does not explicitly protect rights accruing under the Treaty of Waitangi (although there is obvious potential for developing a Treaty of Waitangi jurisprudence under s. 20 of the New Zealand Bill of Rights Act 1990); nor property rights (a deliberate omission from the 1990 Act and subsequently rejected by Parliament in refusing to allow the New Zealand Bill of Rights Amendment Bill 1998 a second reading); nor social and economic rights (notwithstanding a suggestion in favour of this by the Justice and Law Reform Select Committee in its final report on the White Paper: (1988) *AJHR* I 8C at 10); nor a general equality (as opposed to a general anti-discrimination) provision. Indeed, our human rights legislation is, in comparison with modern constitutional bills of rights, much narrower in focus. Little is contained on family rights, for example, nor is there a programmatic "manifesto" feel to the relevant documents.

[4] See eg, *Coburn* v. *Human Rights Commission* [1994] 3 NZLR 323.

[5] See also s. 7 of the Privacy Act.

of the Human Rights Act 1993 provides that the 1993 Act does not "limit or affect" other legislation.[6]

The Bill of Rights does not establish a complaints framework nor does it contain an explicit remedial regime. However, across the ten years of its life, the Bill of Rights has been the subject of substantial litigation (mainly criminal) and displayed significant enforcement potential. A strong exclusionary rule has been developed to vindicate various criminal procedure rights; compensation may be awarded for breach of rights guaranteed by the Bill of Rights.[7] The Bill of Rights has been relied upon to overturn a gagging order on press reporting of a notorious Family Court proceeding;[8] to effectively vindicate the rights of student protestors on Parliament grounds;[9] to check the exercise of Customs forfeiture procedures;[10] to vindicate an accused's right to make submissions on sentencing,[11] and so on.

However, as with the Human Rights Act, in legislating for human rights in the Bill of Rights, Parliament has explicitly forestalled the possibility that judges can rely on the Bill of Rights to override inconsistent legislation. Section 4 provides:

> **"Other enactments not affected**—No court shall, in relation to any enactment (whether passed or made before or after the commencement of this Bill of Rights),—
> (a) Hold any provision of the enactment to be impliedly repealed or revoked, or to be in any way invalid or ineffective; or
> (b) Decline to apply any provision of the enactment—
> by reason only that the provision is inconsistent with any provision of this Bill of Rights."

Thus, the obvious common element to both the 1990 legislation and the two 1993 statutes is a Parliamentary decision not to empower judges to set aside or refuse to apply inconsistent legislation.

Before moving on, a recent development in respect of section 4 of the Bill of Rights must be noted. The Court of Appeal in *Moonen* v. *Film and Literature Board of Review*[12] has suggested that the New Zealand courts may have the power ("and on occasions the duty") to give an "indication" of inconsistency between a statute and the Bill of Rights.[13] In *R* v. *Poumako*[14] Thomas J made a formal declaration

---

[6] See eg, *Gilmour* v. *Accident Rehabilitation and Compensation Insurance Corporation* (DC Hamilton, 104/95, 23 August 1995, Middleton DCJ) ("spouse" confined to member of opposite-sex couple; sexual orientation discrimination explicitly provided for by s. 3 Accident Rehabilitation, Compensation and Insurance Act 1992; s. 151(1) protected); *Quinn* v. *ARCIC* [1997] NZAR 289 (DC) (cessation of earnings-related compensation on attaining 65 years of age; age discrimination provided for in s. 142 Accident Rehabilitation, Compensation and Insurance Act 1992; s. 151(1) protected).

[7] See generally R Mahoney, "Vindicating Rights: Excluding Evidence Obtained in Violation of the Bill of Rights" and R Harrison, "The Remedial Jurisdiction for Breach of the Bill of Rights", in G Huscroft and P Rishworth (eds.), *Rights and Freedoms* (Wellington, Brookers, 1995) chs. 10 and 11.

[8] *Newspaper Publishers Association of New Zealand* v. *Family Court* [1999] 2 NZLR 344.

[9] *Police* v. *Beggs* [1999] 3 NZLR 615.

[10] *Wilson* v. *New Zealand Customs Service* (1999) 5 HRNZ 134.

[11] *Attorney-General* v. *Upton* (1998) 5 HRNZ 54 (CA).

[12] [2000] 2 NZLR 9, 17.

[13] For comment on this aspect of *Moonen*, see A S Butler, "Judicial Indications of Inconsistency—A New Weapon in the Bill of Rights Armoury?" [2000] *NZ Law Review* 43. See also for a helpful discussion on the possibility of declarations of inconsistency under the New Zealand Bill of Rights, P Rishworth, "Reflections on the Bill of Rights after *Quilter* v. *Attorney-General*" [1998] *NZ Law Review* 683, 689–95.

[14] [2000] 2 NZLR 695.

that section 2(4) of the Criminal Justice Amendment Act (No 2) 1999 violated section 25(g) of the Bill of Rights and could not be justified under section 5. The other members of the Court declined to express views on the question of whether there is a jurisdiction to make such orders, the Crown having put such a jurisdiction in issue. However, more recently, in *R* v. *Pora*,[15] a bench of seven declined to deal with the declaration of incompatibility issue, notwithstanding substantial written submissions on the point from the appellant and the Crown.

Returning to general propositions about human rights law in New Zealand, third, and in turn, it must be noted that the decision to deny judicial power to invalidate or refuse to apply legislation that is inconsistent with either the Bill of Rights or the Human Rights Act does not mean that Parliament intends to assign no significance to these human rights statutes when it comes to shaping legislation. Far from it.

First, all legislative proposals which go to Cabinet must be certified as complying with the Bill of Rights, the Human Rights Act and New Zealand's international human rights obligations.[16] Thus, there is an internal governmental procedure designed to ensure that significant effect is given to human rights norms in the shaping of Government policy and legislation.

Second, additional formal procedures are in place to check legislation for compatibility with the Bill of Rights. The Attorney-General reporting procedure established by section 7 of the Bill of Rights is well known. The purpose of that section is to ensure that Bills introduced into the House of Representatives undergo a screening process for compliance with the Bill of Rights. By this means, significant pressure is placed on officials and politicians who advance legislative proposals to ensure that they comply with human rights standards. After all, the legislative process is fraught enough (particularly now in a Mixed Member Proportional environment) without adding to the danger of unnecessarily creating a self-inflicted blow to progress while Parliament considers submissions on the Bill from concerned citizens and lobbying groups claiming breaches of the Bill of Rights.

The section 7 procedure ensures that where Government or a private member is determined to push ahead with a proposal that interferes with human rights norms, those voting on the proposal are fully aware of the proposal's human rights implications and are prepared to live with the political fallout which support for the measure involves. In other words, the procedure creates a more fully informed Parliament. While there have not been a large number of section 7 reports made by the Attorney-General,[17] this is not a sign of the weakness of the procedure. Even after a short period "on the inside", it has become obvious to me from my work at the Crown Law Office that the section 7 procedure works well in eliminating a large number of proposals that, if enacted, may have resulted in unjustified intrusions upon human rights. Most departments, once informed of the human

---

[15] [2001] 2 NZLR 37 (CA).

[16] *Cabinet Office Manual* (Wellington, Cabinet Office, 1996) paras. 5.26–5.29.

[17] As at 2 March 2001, s. 7 reports had been made by the Attorney-General in respect of 7 Government bills and 14 member's, local and private bills.

rights implications, are more than happy to alter the proposals in such a way as to accommodate those concerns.

Finally, the formalised Bill of Rights procedures have raised awareness among lobby groups and submitters of the importance of human rights norms as part of the political process. Bill of Rights claims are now a relatively frequent feature of the select committee process, and on occasion select committees have quizzed departmental officials on issues of Bill of Rights consistency.[18] In addition, the Bill of Rights is slowly entering public discussion of topical issues and bringing a new dimension to the shaping of public policy choices (and at a much earlier stage of that process than previously).[19]

Turning from the Bill of Rights, more extensive in their ambit but more politically sensitive were the procedures established pursuant to sections 5(i)–(k) of the Human Rights Act to survey the entire statute book for compatibility with the non-discrimination principles—the "Consistency 2000" review process. The then Government effectively brought that project to a halt by a press release in late 1997[20] and the project was only partially completed.[21] Nonetheless, significant statutory inconsistencies were identified, important generic discrimination issues were revealed, and a departmental review of statutes[22] is currently underway.

II IS THE CURRENT SITUATION SATISFACTORY?

Is the current situation satisfactory? In my view the answer must be no. On the positive side of the ledger, the Privacy and Human Rights Acts provide usefully detailed guidance on the application of human rights norms in their particular fields.[23] An examination of the legislation indicates that a fair balance has been reached in terms of respecting individual rights, yet (1) allowing society to function in a reasonable manner and (2) accommodating the competing rights of individuals. Somewhat

[18] See eg, Report of the Government Select Administration Committee on the Crimes (Criminal Appeals) Amendment Bill 2000.

[19] See eg, A Gregory, "Rights Warning on Travel Block" *NZ Herald* 14 February 2001; A Young, "Backbench Threat to Party-Hop Legislation" *NZ Herald* 1 March 2001, p. 46; and New Zealand Press Council, "Press Council on Proposed Opinion Poll Legislation" Media release 26 March 2001 (noting that ban on opinion polling 4 weeks prior to election a breach of s. 14 Bill of Rights).

[20] In June 1997, Cabinet announced that the project was being reviewed and that it intended to abandon Consistency 2000. In October 1997, Cabinet instructed officials to develop legislation to give effect to this decision. In response the Human Rights Commission scaled back the project. In the end, however, government was unable to have its proposals pushed through Parliament.

[21] See *Consistency 2000: Report of the Human Rights Commission* (Wellington, Human Rights Commission, 1998).

[22] This process has now been put on a statutory footing and involves six-monthly reporting to Parliament by the Minister of Justice on the progress made by or on behalf of the government in remedying significant inconsistencies between existing legislation and Part II of the Human Rights Act: see Human Rights Amendment Act 1999, ss. 4–6.

[23] There are, of course, problems. For example, the Human Rights Act fails to provide any definition of key terms such as "services" or "facilities" in s. 44, nor is there a properly worded bona fide justification provision to allow for exceptions to anti-discrimination norms that have not been provided for in the 1993 Act (although see s. 97).

differently, the Bill of Rights Act protects many important rights against violation through parliamentary procedures and officers,[24] judicial acts,[25] acts of the executive or acts of private persons performing public functions, powers or duties.[26] There are, of course, a number of significant rights that have been omitted from the Bill of Rights and to this extent the coverage of the Bill of Rights is probably not wholly satisfactory.[27]

This point aside, the obvious major deficiency is that each of the human rights statutes can be overridden by any other ordinary Act of Parliament. Moreover, they can be overridden by a statute that, although not necessarily intentionally designed to undermine particular human rights norms, nonetheless through its language or underlying concepts has this effect. In examining this particular deficiency, I concentrate hereafter on the example of the New Zealand Bill of Rights Act 1990.[28]

III PROBLEMS ASSOCIATED WITH LACK OF POWER OF JUDICIAL
INVALIDATION OR DISAPPLICATION

There are a number of problems associated with the absence from the Bill of Rights of a judicial power to invalidate, or refuse to apply, statutes (hereafter "invalidation").

A Lack of an Effective Remedy

Primarily, the absence of such a power leaves a citizen without an effective remedy in the case of a breach of his or her rights occasioned by an Act of Parliament. Conversely, unless an affected citizen has sufficient cash and time to demonstrate that section 4 applies to his or her factual situation (and why would you spend your time and money in this manner?), the likelihood of early discovery of, and prompt

---

[24] See *Police* v. *Beggs* [1999] 3 NZLR 615 (Speaker bound by Bill of Rights).

[25] *Lewis* v. *Wilson & Horton Ltd* [2000] 3 NZLR 546 (CA) and *Lange* v. *Atkinson and Australian Consolidated Press NZ Ltd* [1997] 2 NZLR 22, 32.

[26] On the application of the Bill of Rights see A S Butler, "Is This a Public Law Case?" (2000) 31 *VUWLR* 747.

[27] For example, privacy, honour and reputation, family rights, children's rights and equality before the law are just some of the rights guaranteed by the International Covenant on Civil and Political Rights that are omitted from the Bill of Rights.

[28] The position in respect of the overriding effect of the Human Rights Act 1993 in the future is uncertain. At present it is envisaged that the specific clause subjugating the 1993 Act to all other legislation (s. 151) will expire on 31 December 2001 (s. 152, as amended by s. 3 of the Human Rights Amendment Act 1999). What the legal position will be upon the expiry of this clause has been the subject of some debate: see eg P Rishworth, "Affirming the Fundamental Values of the Nation: How the Bill of Rights and the Human Rights Act affect New Zealand Law" in *Rights and Freedoms*, above n. 7 at 107–18; P Rishworth, "Human Rights" [1999] *NZ Law Review* 457, 462–3; G Palmer, "Human Rights and the New Zealand Government's Treaty Obligations" (1999) 29 *VUWLR* 57, 69; *Re-evaluation of the Human Rights Protections in New Zealand: Report for the Associate Minister of Justice & Attorney-General Hon Margaret Wilson* (Wellington, Ministry of Justice, 2000) paras 36–46 ("Re-evaluation Report").

parliamentary rectification of, an inconsistency between legislation and a right or freedom guaranteed by the Bill of Rights is low. Simply put, the incentives for such an early discovery are low.

Re Bennett [29] demonstrates the point. There, the plaintiff prisoner unsuccessfully challenged provisions of the Electoral Act 1956 that denied the right to vote at elections to those persons detained at a penal institution pursuant to a sentence of imprisonment.[30] Canadian authorities under the Canadian Charter would indicate that imprisonment per se does not justify loss of voting rights.[31] In the High Court, Greig J held that since the terms of the statute were quite specific there was no possibility of interpreting the legislation in a manner that was compatible with the Bill of Rights. Section 4 required the judge to uphold the provisions of the Electoral Act, and any "remedy" that the prisoner might seek to reverse the situation would have to be pursued before international human rights tribunals and not domestically.[32]

B   Obligation to Interpret Consistently With Bill Of Rights: Section 6

Alternatively, it might be argued that the risk of a citizen being exposed to a statute that is incompatible with the Bill of Rights is minimal. First, section 6 of the Bill of Rights requires the courts to give a meaning to an enactment that is consistent with the rights and freedoms contained in the Bill of Rights if that enactment "can be given" such a meaning. Assuming that the courts act in good faith and give it such fair, large and liberal construction as best ensures the attainment of the purpose of the Bill of Rights[33] (to affirm, protect and promote human rights and fundamental freedoms and to affirm New Zealand's commitment to the International Covenant on Civil and Political Rights),[34] section 6 should reduce the chances of a person being exposed to a rights violation.[35] To some extent, of course, section 6 does minimise the risk; but as Mr Bennett can well attest, it does not come anywhere near to eliminating that risk. Moreover, there is only so much that section 6 can do. The Court of Appeal has been at pains to emphasise that section 6 cannot be relied upon to support a "strained interpretation" of another enactment;[36]

---

[29]   (1993) 2 HRNZ 358.

[30]   Ironically, however, this case has a "happy ending". The impugned provisions were replaced by the Electoral Act 1993 s. 80(1)(d), which only deprives those prisoners serving a sentence of three years or more of their right to vote.

[31]   See *Sauve* v. *Canada (AG)* [1993] 2 SCR 438. For a discussion of the Canadian case law see G-A Beaudoin, "Des droits démocratiques" in G-A Beaudoin and E Mendes (eds.), *The Canadian Charter of Rights and Freedoms*, 3rd edn. (Toronto, Carswell, 1996) ch. 7.

[32]   (1993) 2 HRNZ 358, 361.

[33]   Interpretation Act 1999, s. 5(1), with a nod of abiding respect for the words of the recently repealed Acts Interpretation Act 1924, s. 5(j).

[34]   Long Title to the New Zealand Bill of Rights Act 1990.

[35]   For a description of the case law on s. 6 see A S Butler, "Interface between the Human Rights Act 1998 and Other Enactments: Pointers from New Zealand" [2000] *EHRLR* 249.

[36]   *Ministry of Transport* v. *Noort* [1992] 3 NZLR 260, 272 (CA) per Cooke P; see also *R* v. *Phillips* [1991] 3 NZLR 175, 177 (CA).

it can only be relied upon where the Bill of Rights-consistent meaning is properly open and reasonably capable of being given effect.[37]

C Section 7 Reporting Mechanism

Second, it might be submitted that risk of exposure to Bill of Rights-incompatible laws is reduced by the section 7 reporting procedure. By requiring all legislative proposals to undergo a screening process for compliance with the Bill of Rights, many potential breaches of the Bill of Rights will be detected and eliminated without a report having to be made; while in the case of those proposals which still proceed to Parliament notwithstanding a negative section 7 report, the chances of passage are substantially reduced because of that report.

Again, one can concede that the mechanism will have a significant impact without conceding that it provides for effective protection of human rights nor an effective remedy in case of violation. First, it is asking an awful lot of those undertaking the Bill of Rights screening process to anticipate all possible applications of the proposed measure and assess them for Bill of Rights compliance.[38] It is also asking a lot of those screeners to anticipate how Bill of Rights jurisprudence will develop over time. Thus, what might not occur to a screener today to involve a breach of the Bill of Rights could well appear to be so tomorrow when a new judgment comes out which indicates the direction the jurisprudence is taking. Yet, in either situation if the Bill has been passed, the screener cannot "recall" the legislation on the basis that his or her approval was based on imperfect information.

Second, the section 7 process is prospective not retrospective. So even if the process were effective in eliminating almost all Bill of Rights infirmities from proposals before Parliament, it does nothing to address pre-1990 legislative breaches until the provisions in which those breaches occur are before Parliament for consolidation, re-enactment and so on.[39] Indeed, where an amendment is proposed to a pre-Bill of Rights provision, as a general rule only the amendment itself is scrutinised for Bill of Rights compatibility not the parent provision which is being amended (although in a number of instances the screener has noted the incompatibility of the pre-1990 parent provision, if there is one).

---

[37] See the general discussion in J F Burrows, *Statute Law in New Zealand*, 2nd edn. (Wellington, Butterworths, 1999) 428–30 and *Quilter* v. *Attorney-General* [1998] 1 NZLR 523, 581 (CA) per Tipping J. On occasions, however, this self-constraint has not been followed: see the criticisms of *R* v. *Poumako* [2000] 2 NZLR 695 in A S Butler, "Declaration of Incompatibility or Interpretation Consistent with Human Rights in New Zealand" [2001] PL 28.

[38] Similar criticisms have been made in reference to judicial abstract review of bills for constitutional compatibility in Ireland: see G Hogan and G F Whyte, *Kelly's Irish Constitution*, 3rd edn. (Dublin, Butterworths, 1992) 494, referring to the pre-promulgation referral procedure in Art. 26 of the Irish Constitution.

[39] The *Consistency 2000* Project identified a significant number of pre-1993 statutes which violated the freedom from discrimination, just one of the many rights guaranteed by the Bill of Rights Act: see above n. 21 at Appendix B.

Third, the section 7 reporting process only applies at the introduction stage of a Bill. Hence, any provisions adopted thereafter are likely to escape Bill of Rights scrutiny,[40] with the real possibility of a Bill of Rights-inconsistent provision being enacted.[41] Because of this a good many provisions are on the statute book that cannot be guaranteed to be Bill of Rights compatible.

Fourth, section 7 provides no effective *remedy*. Certainly, section 7 provides a hearing on Bill of Rights issues, because if there is a negative report the result will be that a significant amount of discussion will be addressed to the human rights implications of the legislative proposal.[42] Indeed, even where a *positive* Bill of Rights vet has occurred, section 7 has contributed to creating an atmosphere in which Bill of Rights issues can be debated between Members of Parliament in the House,[43] and be the subject-matter of submissions before Select Committees.[44] But the procedure is only a "safeguard designed to alert members of Parliament" and provides no remedies: if the Bill of Rights has not been properly addressed or considered in undertaking a section 7 report, the High Court has established that there is no legal remedy available against the resulting statute for that failure.[45]

D Optional Protocol Communication

Third, it might be suggested that the absence of a judicial power of invalidation does not leave citizens without a remedy—they can always take a case to the Human Rights Committee under the Optional Protocol to the International

[40] On occasion, however, the Ministry of Justice and the Crown Law Office have been asked to review Supplementary Order Papers for Bill of Rights consistency.

[41] See P Fitzgerald, "Section 7 of the New Zealand Bill of Rights Act 1990: A Very Practical Power or a Well-Intentioned Nonsense" (1992) 22 *VUWLR* 135, 142 and 154; J McGrath, "The Bill of Rights and the Legislative Process" in *The New Zealand Bill of Rights Act 1990* (Auckland, Legal Research Foundation, 1992) 98, 104 and the comments of the members of the Court of Appeal in *R v. Poumako* [2000] 2 NZLR 695, 700, 709 and 717 (CA) on the retrospectivity of s. 80(2A) of the Criminal Justice Act 1985 (minimum non-parole period of imprisonment for "home invasion" murder) created by s. 2(4) of the Criminal Justice Amendment Act (No 2) 1999, which was added at the Committee stage of the latter piece of legislation.

[42] See eg, the report of the Government Administration Select Committee on the Films, Videos and Publications Classifications (Prohibition of Child Pornography) Amendment Bill 2000, 15 February 2001, where discussion on the Attorney-General's negative report on that bill takes place.

[43] See eg, the many references to the Bill of Rights in the Second Reading debate on the De Facto Relationships (Property) Bill, with a number of Members of Parliament querying the absence of a s. 7 report in light of the exclusion of same-sex relationships from the ambit of the proposed legislation. The debate surrounding the Second Reading of the Bill may be found at 567 NZPD 7916–25; 8228–39; 8267–87.

[44] See eg, the various submissions made on the Transport Safety Bill 1992 which provided for random stopping of motorists for the purposes of breath-alcohol testing. Bill of Rights concerns are a reasonably regular feature of the submissions of the New Zealand Law Society Legislation Committee to parliamentary Select Committees hearing submissions on Bills: see eg submissions on the Transport Safety Bill (*LawTalk*, 3 August 1992, 1); Fisheries Bill 1995 (*LawTalk*, 1 May 1995, 6); the Harassment and Criminal Associations Bill 1997 (*LawTalk*, 9 June 1997, 5–6); Crimes (Criminal Appeals) Amendment Bill 2000 (*LawTalk*, 29 January 2001, 10).

[45] *Mangawaro Enterprises v. Attorney-General* [1994] 2 NZLR 451, 457 and *Westco Lagan v. Attorney-General* (HC Wellington, CP142/00, 15 August 2000, McGechan J).

Covenant on Civil and Political Rights ("the Covenant"). This reasoning is unconvincing for a number of reasons.

At the legal level, under Article 2 of the Covenant New Zealand has accepted the obligation to provide for measures that will ensure effective *domestic* remedies where a right guaranteed by the Covenant has been violated (see in particular Articles 2.2 and 2.3). Delegating this remedial task to an international body does not represent proper fulfilment of this obligation. We shall return to this aspect of the Covenant again shortly.

At a practical level, the Optional Protocol communication procedure, while serving a useful purpose, suffers from a number of defects, principally (from the complainant's point of view) excessive delays in handling communications. The Human Rights Committee is dreadfully under-resourced and understaffed and there is a massive backlog in dealing with communications, to the point that even a simple acknowledgement of receipt of a communication and on-sending to the defendant State Party requires a year.[46] A five year delay between the lodging of a communication and vindication through the adoption of favourable views by the Committee hardly amounts to an effective remedy, particularly if there have also been previous domestic proceedings which themselves have taken some time.[47]

Finally, even if views favourable to a complainant are rendered by the Committee, the views do not in themselves create an enforceable remedy. While the Committee invariably suggests remedies that the State Party should grant to the victim of a violation, it is not established that these views are binding in international law (although there seems to be growing opinion that the views may have binding effect),[48] and certainly it has not yet been held that a New Zealand court can give effect to the views of the Committee through subsequent domestic enforcement proceedings.[49] And, of course, where the suggested remedy is repeal,

---

[46] See eg, *Report on the Effective Functioning of Bodies Established Pursuant to United Nations Human Rights Instruments* (UN Doc E/CN4/1997/74 27 March 1997) prepared by well-known Australian professor of international law, Phillip Alston, chairman of the Committee on Economic Social and Cultural Rights ("The Alston Report") and D MacKay, "The UN Covenants and the Human Rights Committee" (1999) 29 *VUWLR* 11, 16. The writer can confirm that his experience of the system reflects the views expressed by these authors. See more generally, A Alston and J Crawford (eds.), *The Future of UN Human Rights Treaty Monitoring* (Cambridge, Cambridge University Press, 2000) especially chs. 1, 21 and 22.

[47] The problems associated with the tardiness of international human rights procedures are apparent in *Fisher* v. *Minister of Public Safety and Immigration (No 2)* [2000] 1 AC 434 (PC) (petition to Inter-American Commission on Human Rights challenging imposition of death penalty outstanding for twenty months; Government of The Bahamas indicating intention to implement death sentence if no response received from IACHR within seven weeks; no response received; Privy Council holding that legitimate for Government to proceed with reading of warrant for execution in absence of such a response). See now, however, *Lewis* v. *Attorney-General (Jamaica)* [2000] 3 WLR 1785 (PC) where the Privy Council appears to have undertaken a *volte-face* on the question of suspending execution pending the outcome of international human rights procedures.

[48] See eg, Evatt and Davidson contributions to this volume, chs. 15 and 16.

[49] Such a domestic follow-up procedure exists in Switzerland (see *La loi federale d'organisation judiciaire*, art 139a, *La loi federale sur la procedure penale* art 229(4) and *La loi federale sur le droit penal administratif*, Art. 89), and a limited number of other European jurisdictions allow domestic proceedings to be reopened where there has been a ruling from the European Court of Human Rights which affects the resolution of decided domestic proceedings: see Committee of Experts, *The European Convention on*

disallowance or non-application of a domestic statute, the New Zealand courts cannot give effect to the Committee's views.[50] Moreover, the New Zealand Government has specifically reserved to itself the right to determine on a case-by-case basis whether to give effect to views adopted by the Human Rights Committee in individual communications—they are certainly not regarded as self-executing.[51] Thus, there is no guarantee of respect for the Committee's views and the practical impact of the international procedure lies in the discretion of the executive—surely the antithesis of an effective remedy.

Overall, then, Don MacKay may well be right to point out that the various resource deficiencies and procedural handicaps under which the Human Rights Committee operates "may suggest a need for caution in any elevation of the Human Rights Committee as part of our quasi domestic legal structure, and the status to be accorded its views".[52] But if that is the case, it is even more incumbent upon us to secure *domestic* procedures which guarantee that a New Zealand court can grant effective redress for a violation of rights, including remedies in relation to threats posed by legislation.

E High Standard of Human Rights

Finally, it might be suggested that in light of our generally high standard of human rights, it is unlikely that many violations of human rights are protected by section 4 immunity. I disagree.

Although Sir Kenneth Keith has expressed the view that section 4 has "rarely been invoked successfully",[53] in fact there are a considerable number of cases in which it has been deployed, including:[54]

Human Rights: Institution of Review Proceedings at the National Level to Facilitate Compliance with Strasbourg Decisions reproduced at (1992) 13 HRLJ 71, 73–6. It has, of course, been held that the Committee's jurisprudence can be drawn upon in interpreting relevant provisions of New Zealand legislation and that the Committee's jurisprudence "must be of considerable persuasive authority": see *R* v. *Goodwin (No 2)* [1993] 2 NZLR 390, 393 (CA). And see the significance attached to the Committee's jurisprudence in *Simpson* v. *Attorney-General [Baigent's case]* [1994] 3 NZLR 667 (CA) detailed in Butler and Butler, above n. 2 at 186–9.

[50] *Re Bennett* (1993) 2 HRNZ 358, 361. See also *Tangiora* v. *Wellington District Legal Services Committee* [2000] 1 NZLR 17, 21 (PC).

[51] See Response of New Zealand's Permanent Representative to the United Nations, Colin Keating, on the presentation of New Zealand's Third Periodic Report under Art. 40 of the International Covenant, 23 March 1995, recorded at UN Doc HR/CT/393, pp. 11–12. In a similar vein see *Response of the Australian Government to the Views of the Human Rights Committee in Communication No. 560/1993 (A* v. *Australia)*, recorded in (1997) 9 Int J Ref L 674 (Australian government refusing to give compensation to refugee claimant detained for four years as recommended by Human Rights Committee).

[52] MacKay, above n. 46 at 17.

[53] "'Considering Change': The Adoption and Implementation of the New Zealand Bill of Rights Act 1990" (2000) 31 *VUWLR* 721, 728.

[54] See also Butler, above n. 35. It should be noted that in some cases the statutes that were enforced on the basis of s. 4 of the Bill of Rights could equally have been upheld if a s. 5 ("justified limitation") analysis had been undertaken. However, in most of the cases detailed below the Court either accepted or assumed an unjustifiable breach of the Bill of Rights had occurred. On this problem see A S Butler, "The Bill of Rights Debate: Why the New Zealand Bill of Rights Act 1990 is a Bad Model for Britain" (1997) 17 *OxJLS* 323, 324.

—*TV3 Network Services Ltd* v. *R*[55] (automatic name suppression of person accused of sexual offences);

—*R* v. *Phillips*[56] (possession of 28 grams of cannabis deemed to be possessed for supply "unless proved to the contrary");

—*Re Bennett*[57] (prisoners deprived of right to vote);

—*Menzies* v. *Police*[58] (criminalisation of cannabis possession and reverse onus provision);

—*R* v. *Pora*[59] and *R* v. *Poumako*[60] (retrospective increase in imprisonment).

—*Quilter* v. *Attorney-General*[61] (same-sex marriage);

—*Nicholls* v. *Registrar of the Court of Appeal*[62] (criteria for legal aid for criminal appeals; no explicit reliance on section 4 Bill of Rights, but implicit in analysis of Court);

—*New Zealand Apple & Pear Marketing Board* v. *Apple Fields Ltd*[63] (statutory corporation permitted to sue for defamation by Defamation Act 1992; overriding any Bill of Rights free expression argument to the contrary);

—*Birch* v. *Ministry of Transport*[64] and *Reille* v. *Ministry of Transport*[65] (no jury trial for certain public disorder offences even though carrying penalty of more than three months);

—*R* v. *Waddel*[66] (Misuse of Drugs Act 1975 search powers);

—*Freeborn* v. *Accident Rehabilitation and Compensation Insurance Corporation*[67] (impact of statutory obligation to make a declaration on right against self-incrimination);

—*Hasmeer* v. *Removal Review Authority*[68] (natural justice negated by section 35A Immigration Act 1987, concerning power of Minister to grant permits in special circumstances at his/her discretion);

—*B* v. *District Court Hamilton*[69] (ex parte non-molestation order in Domestic Protection Act section 37A overrides natural justice rights);

---

[55] [1993] 3 NZLR 421 (CA).

[56] [1991] 3 NZLR 175 (CA).

[57] (1993) 2 HRNZ 358.

[58] HC Dunedin, AP 66/94, 19 July 1994, Williamson J.

[59] [2001] 2 NZLR 37 (CA).

[60] [2000] 2 NZLR 695 (CA).

[61] [1998] 1 NZLR 523 (CA). Note that in this case, a majority of the Judges (3–2) concluded that, in any event, there was no discrimination contrary to s. 19 of the Bill of Rights.

[62] [1998] 2 NZLR 385 (CA) (applied *sub silentio*—explicit language of Legal Services Act 1991 excluding possibility of meaning consistent with International Covenant on Civil and Political Rights being given; relevant Bill of Rights right in same terms as Covenant right). The decision has been effectively reversed by the Legal Services Act 2000, s. 8(2).

[63] HC Wellington, CP 211/96, 24 July 1997, M Thomson.

[64] (1992) 9 CRNZ 83.

[65] [1993] 1 NZLR 587.

[66] HC Auckland, T119/91, 25 October 1991, Thomas J.

[67] [1998] 2 NZLR 371, 383–384. S. 4 relied upon; but also concluded that reasonable limit for s. 5 purposes.

[68] HC Auckland, HC134/98 and M1733/98, 15 March 2000, Nicholson J.

[69] (1995) 13 FRNZ 413. See also *M* v. *M* (1995) 14 FRNZ 102 (DC).

—*Fullers Group Ltd* v. *Auckland Regional Council*[70] (provisions in the Resource Management Act 1991 relating to making of rules and non-notification of consent applications overriding natural justice); and

—*MAF* v. *Yamada*[71] (right to silence overridden by section 79 Fisheries Act 1983).

Even if there had not been so many cases, to adapt the words of Sir Kenneth, "[t]he [relative paucity] of such cases might be explained in significant part by the very existence of section 4."[72] Who would waste their money (and what Legal Aid Committee would authorise funding for proceedings) "challenging" a provision that was clearly protected by section 4 of the Bill of Rights?

Moreover, it is to be doubted that section 4 clothes very few offending statutes. If the results of the Human Rights Commission's partially completed *Consistency 2000* project are anything to go by, there is likely to be a large number of Bill of Rights-inconsistent provisions on the statute roll. And in my own practice I have come across provisions that clearly oust the Bill of Rights and are protected by section 4 of the Bill of Rights.[73]

IV INTERNATIONAL OBLIGATIONS

I have already referred to the international procedures that are potentially available to deal with complaints of rights violations, including those posed by legislation. I have also referred to the obligations accepted by New Zealand under Article 2 of the Covenant. Those provisions bear closer examination.

A Article 2, International Covenant on Civil and Political Rights

Article 2.1 requires New Zealand to "ensure" to all persons within New Zealand the rights guaranteed by the Covenant. Article 2.2 requires New Zealand to "take the necessary steps . . . to adopt such legislative or other measures as may be necessary to give effect to the rights recognised" in the Covenant. Article 2.3(a) requires New Zealand to "ensure" that anyone who has suffered a violation of his or her Covenant rights "shall have an effective remedy"; Article 2.3(b) requires New Zealand "to develop the possibilities of judicial remedy"; while by Article 2.3(c) those remedies must be enforced by the competent authorities.

In light of the preceding discussion it will be clear that there is no effective remedy where a violation of Covenant rights has been occasioned pursuant to an Act

---

[70] HC Auckland, M1077/98, 21 August 1998, Laurenson J.

[71] [1993] DCR 241, 247.

[72] Above n. 53 at 728, n. 18. The word "rarely" in Sir Kenneth's original has been replaced by "relative paucity".

[73] See eg s. 10(3) of the Immigration Act 1987, which excludes any possibility of judicial review of decisions related to visas (except returning residents' visas) contrary to s. 27(2) of the Bill of Rights. It may be, of course, that this provision is justifiable in terms of the Bill of Rights, s. 5.

of Parliament. In our constitutional system it is not possible for the courts to generally question the validity of legislation;[74] nor to order an official to (1) ignore a statute or (2) not to apply a statute; nor can compensation be awarded where a statutory power has been validly applied.[75] Section 4 of the Bill of Rights re-enacts that fundamental principle and gives statutory force to the notion that a court, when faced with a clash between legislation and human rights, must decide in favour of the former. It therefore explicitly denies the only effective judicial remedy for such a rights violation—invalidation or non-application of the statutory provision. Moreover, there are no other remedies of a non-judicial nature which can effectively prevent or redress a violation of Covenant rights. While it is possible that an aggrieved citizen could petition Parliament for a law change, this is not a legal remedy—there is no guarantee that any significant heed will be paid to the petition, never mind appropriate legislative response made on foot of it.

B Comments of the Human Rights Committee

This has been a matter of deep concern to the Human Rights Committee. On the occasion of the presentation of New Zealand's last Periodic Report in March 1995,[76] a number of Committee members (including Messrs Prado Vallejo, El-Shafei, Lallah, Klein and Mrs Evatt) expressed concern at the fact that the Bill of Rights had been enacted as an ordinary statute and subject to all other enactments.[77] In its Final Comments on the Periodic Report, the Committee expressed regret at the fact that the Bill of Rights:[78]

"does not repeal earlier inconsistent legislation, and has no higher status than ordinary legislation. The Committee notes that it is expressly possible, under the terms of the Bill of Rights, to enact legislation contrary to its provisions and regrets that this appears to have been done in a few cases."

Further, in its Suggestions and Recommendations, the Committee recommended that:[79]

"the Bill of Rights be revised in order to [inter alia] . . . give the courts power as soon as possible to strike down or decline to give effect to legislation on the ground of inconsistency with Covenant rights and freedoms as affirmed in the Bill of Rights".

---

[74] Recently reaffirmed in *Shaw* v. *Commissioner of Inland Revenue* [1999] 3 NZLR 154, 157 (CA).

[75] I note, however, the interesting, if radical, suggestion of Hammond J in *Manga* v. *Attorney-General* [2000] 2 NZLR 65, 83 that it may be possible to award extra compensation to a person whose rights under the Bill of Rights have been violated due, in part, to poorly drafted legislation.

[76] Third Periodic Report of New Zealand under Art. 40 of the International Covenant on Civil and Political Rights, CCPR/C/64/Add 10 and HRI/CORE/1/Add 33. The Third Periodic Report has been helpfully reproduced in *Human Rights in New Zealand* MFAT Information Bulletin No 54 (June 1995).

[77] See HR/CT/393, p. 9 and p. 11 and HR/CT/395 p. 8, p. 9 and p. 8 respectively.

[78] A/50/40, para. 176.

[79] *Ibid*, para. 185.

It should be noted that the Committee's concern at the absence of a judicial power of invalidation of statutes that trench unjustifiably upon Covenant rights is not confined to New Zealand.[80] In considering the Fourth Periodic Report of the United Kingdom,[81] Committee members criticised the absence of a power of judicial invalidation of statutes for breach of Covenant rights. Mrs Evatt invited the United Kingdom Government to consider [82]

> "whether it would not better fulfil its obligations under the Covenant if the courts were empowered to determine whether laws and policies met international standards".

Mr Buergenthal pointed out that the unavailability of domestic procedures to ensure respect for human rights violations caused by legislation meant that many persons were unable to obtain proper remedies, and that even where legislation was finally repealed due to a negative judgment before the European Court of Human Rights in Strasbourg, many previous victims of that legislation were without remedy.[83] In its Final Comments on the United Kingdom Periodic Report,[84] the Committee expressed as its first principal subject of concern "the absence of a constitutional Bill of Rights".[85] In its Suggestions and Recommendations, the Committee "strongly recommend[ed]" reconsideration of the United Kingdom's human rights protection mechanisms, specifically urging the Government to:[86]

> "examine the need to . . . introduce a bill of rights under which legislative or executive encroachment on Covenant rights could be reviewed by the courts".

C *Ballantyne* v. *Canada*

These comments are consistent with the views adopted by the Human Rights Committee in *Ballantyne* v. *Canada*.[87] In that case, a communication was made concerning Quebec's French-only outdoor signage laws. In an attempt to protect Quebec's *visage linguistique*, the Quebec National Assembly prohibited the use of English in outdoor signs. The laws had been prospectively immunised from challenge for breach of the Canadian Charter of Rights and Freedoms through Quebec's use of the "notwithstanding" clause provided for in section 33 of the Canadian Charter (discussed in detail below).

The Canadian Government sought to have the communication declared inadmissible on the ground that the complainants had failed to exhaust all available

---

[80] See also the Committee's concluding observations on the Third Periodic Report of Norway: CCPR/C/79/Add 27, para. 8 (29 October 1993).
[81] CCPR/C/95/Add 3; HRI/CORE/1/Add 5/Rev 1.
[82] CCPR/C/SR.1432 (20 July 1995) para 61. See also the concerns of Mrs Medina Quiroga at para. 82.
[83] *Ibid*, para. 90.
[84] A/50/40, paras. 408–35.
[85] *Ibid*, para. 416.
[86] *Ibid*, para. 427.
[87] Comm Nos 359/1989 and 385/1989, UN Doc CCPR/C/47/D/359/1989 and 385/1989/Rev 1 (31 March 1993).

domestic remedies. More particularly, the Government claimed that the victims could have applied to the Quebec courts for a declaration that the laws violated their right to free expression. The Committee rejected this argument. In particular, the Committee pointed out that, in light of the "notwithstanding" clause, the relevant provisions of the Quebec law would still be left "operative and intact" *even if* a declaration of inconsistency with the Charter were obtained; the Quebec courts would be required through the combined effect of the sign law and the "notwithstanding" provision to uphold an interference with free expression.[88] The net result was that no effective remedy was available before the domestic courts.

In my view, the principle of *Ballantyne* is equally applicable to the New Zealand Bill of Rights. By virtue of the structure of that Act, New Zealand courts operate in a permanent and complete "notwithstanding" environment—with the result that in respect of unjustifiable statutory incursions upon Covenant rights there can be no effective remedy available.

D *Matadeen v. Pointu*

In light of the above, the recent judgment of the Privy Council in *Matadeen* v. *Pointu* is of interest.[89] There it had been submitted that the non-discrimination principle enshrined in section 3 of the Constitution of Mauritius should be interpreted as conferring a wide-ranging substantive equality guarantee in line with Article 26 of the Covenant. The Privy Council rejected this submission on the basis, inter alia, that the terms of Article 2.2 did not require a *justiciable* substantive equality right—all that was required was that the legal and political system by whatever appropriate mechanisms (judicial and/or non-judicial) complied with that principle. This judgment would mean that a supreme law bill of rights is not required by the Covenant.

A number of observations are appropriate. First, in coming to its conclusion, the Privy Council did not refer to the relevant views of the Committee (discussed above), which is charged with expounding the meaning of the Covenant, and has much greater familiarity with its requirements than the Privy Council. This lessens the persuasiveness of *Matadeen*. Second, the Privy Council failed to pay any regard to the terms of Article 2.3, which requires the availability of *effective* remedies and the development of *judicial* remedies. This is a significant flaw. Third, even if *Matadeen* is correct, it makes only a narrow point—that *constitutionalisation* (in the sense of supreme law justiciability) is not required by Article 2.2, but only if other mechanisms would secure the particular right.[90] Conversely, there is an obligation to secure appropriate mechanisms. In New Zealand we have not done so in relation to many rights, which are vulnerable to our substantial statute book.

---

[88] Comm Nos 359/1989 and 385/1989, UN Doc CCPR/C/47/D/359/1989 and 385/1989/Rev 1 (31 March 1993), para. 10.3.

[89] [1999] AC 98, 116 (PC).

[90] See, in particular, the discussion at 116 D–G.

V WHY IS THERE NO POWER OF JUDICIAL INVALIDATION IN THE BILL OF RIGHTS?

While the absence of a judicial power of invalidation of legislation which is incompatible with human rights norms is not unique to New Zealand,[91] it is certainly unusual. The modern trend in constitutionalism has been to establish a supreme law Bill of Rights coupled with a power of judicial enforcement extending even to the power of invalidation of legislation. Why does New Zealand not have such a power?

As is well known, the draft Bill of Rights contained in the 1985 White Paper[92] proposed to establish the Bill of Rights as an entrenched supreme law document with power being given to the judiciary to enforce even to the extent of invalidating inconsistent legislation (see Articles 1, 25 and 27). In the commentary accompanying the White Paper, the Minister of Justice, Geoffrey Palmer, attempted to dispel concerns about the impact upon the location of political power which might occur by vesting a judicial review power in the judiciary. However, the Justice and Law Reform Committee to which the White Paper was referred received many public submissions questioning the proposed judicial role.[93] Prominent among these critics was the New Zealand Law Society, which opposed the supreme law White Paper document on the basis that it transferred political power to non-elected Judges who might well be out of touch with community values.[94] Indeed, many other submissions focussed on this feature, either at the general level or in the context of criticising the broad language and phraseology of some of the rights guaranteed by the Bill of Rights, suggesting that such language would delegate a large discretion to the unelected judges. The Justice and Law Reform Committee recorded that the proposed power of the judiciary to invalidate legislation "was clearly the principal reason" for the overwhelming opposition to the Bill of Rights proposal.[95] In its final report on the White Paper proposal tabled in October 1988, the Select Committee noted the substantial opposition to any power of judicial invalidation of legislation to the extent that Parliament would be subject to the judges, and proposed that the Bill of Rights proceed as an ordinary, unentrenched statute.[96] Ultimately, this view prevailed.

---

[91] See eg, the United Kingdom (notwithstanding the enactment of the Human Rights Act 1998) and various European jurisdictions which deny the possibility of judicial invalidation of statute law.

[92] *A Bill of Rights for New Zealand* (1985) AJHR A6.

[93] Interim Report of the Justice and Law Reform Committee, *Inquiry into the White Paper—A Bill of Rights for New Zealand* (tabled in Parliament on 9 July 1987) 8.

[94] *Ibid*, 9.

[95] *Ibid*, 8.

[96] *Final Report of the Justice and Law Reform Committee on a White Paper on a Bill of Rights for New Zealand* (1987–90) AJHR I 8C.

VI RECONCILING THE NEED FOR MORE EFFECTIVE REMEDIES
AND CONCERNS OVER JUDICIAL POWER

In light of the analysis to date it is clear that in a New Zealand context there is a tension between the need to provide more effective remedies for persons suffering violations of their rights, on one hand, and public concern over a redistribution of power between Parliament and the courts in favour of the latter, on the other. Is there a means to reconcile this tension? A number of overseas models provide guidance as to how this situation can best be reconciled. I shall consider the models provided for in the Human Rights Act 1998 (UK) ("the UK Act") and the Canadian Charter of Rights and Freedoms 1982, and I shall refer to evolving notions of parliamentary sovereignty in that regard. Ultimately, I reject the United Kingdom approach as being too weak, and prefer the Canadian approach.

A Human Rights Act 1998 (UK)

When considering the inadequacies of section 4 of the Bill of Rights, the point was made that there are few incentives for taking a case to court to demonstrate that a particular statute violates rights and freedoms guaranteed by the Bill of Rights. Such a process is time-consuming, financially-consuming, and it is unlikely (unless a formalised declaration mechanism is recognised) that hard-pressed civil legal aid funds are going to be given to a lawyer to mount a Bill of Rights "challenge" to a statute that, if successful, will provide no tangible legal benefit to the client!

It might be argued that the structure of the UK Act[97] points to a possible way forward. The UK Act incorporates a number of the articles of the European Convention on Human Rights into United Kingdom law.[98] It permits those articles to be invoked in domestic proceedings. The Convention rights can form the basis of challenges to the legality of executive and judicial conduct and outputs.[99] Like section 6 of the New Zealand Bill of Rights, section 3 of the UK Act requires the courts to read enactments consistently with Convention rights. While the UK Act does not contain a provision similar to section 4 of the New Zealand Bill of Rights, it is apparent from a reading of the Act as a whole that Westminster[100] enactments that irreconcilably conflict with the Convention rights take precedence over those rights.[101] However, the United Kingdom's measure departs from the New Zealand model by providing two mechanisms to encourage Convention rights-based attacks on statute law.

---

[97] 1998, c 42.

[98] The Convention rights incorporated by the 1998 Act are set out in its schedule 1.

[99] S. 6 of the 1998 Act sets out those acts to which it applies.

[100] It should be noted that legislation passed by the devolved legislatures of Scotland and Northern Ireland can be invalidated for violation of Convention rights, unless the purpose of that legislation is to give effect to Westminster legislation.

[101] See, in particular, s. 4(6) of the UK Act discussed below shortly.

First, section 4 of the UK Act provides a procedure under which a person can ask a competent court to declare that an Act of (the Westminster) Parliament is incompatible with a Convention right.[102] Thus, a litigant can squarely require a United Kingdom court to determine whether or not his or her rights have been violated by statute. Legal aid will be available, as the procedure is one properly sanctioned by Parliament. Furthermore, securing a "declaration of incompatibility" will also presumably protect a citizen against an award of costs for the same reason. However, there are clear limits on the effectiveness of a declaration of incompatibility. In particular, section 4(6) of the UK Act provides that a declaration of incompatibility "does not affect the validity, continuing operation or enforcement of the provision in respect of which it is given" (section 4(6)(a)), nor is it binding on the parties to the proceedings in which it is made (section 4(6)(b)).

That is not the end of the story, however. A second mechanism is provided for in section 10 of the UK Act. That section allows a Minister of the Crown to take so-called "remedial action" in respect of legislation that, inter alia, has been declared to be incompatible with Convention rights in section 4 proceedings. Section 10(2) of the UK Act authorises a Minister of the Crown to make, by order, "such amendments to the legislation as he considers necessary to remove the incompatibility" if he or she considers that there are "compelling reasons" for such action.[103] (Interestingly, no definition of "compelling reasons" is provided for in the Act, and presumably relevant criteria and practices will evolve over time.) A remedial order can operate retrospectively[104] and make different provision for different cases.[105]

The point, for present purposes, is that the combined effect of sections 4 and 10 of the UK Act is to (1) explicitly permit judicial declarations of incompatibility; and (2) make such declarations the gateway or springboard to accessing a potentially valuable and speedy parliamentary device. This is certainly an improvement on the New Zealand Bill of Rights model. But is it enough? In my view it is not.

First, a declaration of incompatibility provides no immediate tangible remedy to a successful litigant. The whole section 4 procedure is premised on the notion that, notwithstanding its incompatibility with a Convention right, the offending statutory provision stays in place. Moreover, there is no guarantee that a remedial order will follow a declaration of incompatibility. Section 10 is entirely discretionary; the Minister is not required to act as a result of a declaration of incompatibility, nor is

---

[102] Three such declarations have been made. See the discussion in Ian Leigh's contribution to this volume, ch. 17.

[103] The Second Schedule to the 1998 Act, "Remedial Orders", specifies the scope of, and establishes detailed procedures for the making of, such orders.

[104] Second Sched., para. 1(1)(b) (except that by para. 1(4) no person is to be guilty of an offence solely as a result of the retrospective effect of a remedial order).

[105] Second Sched., para. 1(1)(d). Presumably this power is intended to give a Minister suitable flexibility to give a successful litigant the benefit of a declaration of incompatibility while not giving the order general retrospective effect. For an example of such an approach by judges see *Murphy* v. *Attorney-General* [1982] IR 241 (Ir SC) (unconstitutional tax law not giving rise to right of recovery for unconstitutionally collected tax except to litigants in instant proceedings and all others who had taken out proceedings before date of judgment).

there any statutory "follow-up" procedure requiring the Government to report what it intends to do in respect of a declaration of incompatibility. And the threshold established by the UK Act is very high—"compelling reasons" are necessary as a pre-condition to invoking the section 10 procedure. In short, neither section 4 nor section 10, individually or in combination, secures an effective remedy in terms of Article 2 of the Covenant.[106]

Second, even if a section 10 remedial order is made, there is no guarantee that it will operate retrospectively and inure to the benefit of the original litigant who brought the proceedings. This may well prove to be a significant disincentive for a private litigant who needs the legislation set aside in respect of his or her case in order to obtain something of value.

Third, if a section 10 order is not made that is no obstacle to seeking to have the issue addressed through Parliament. But it is unlikely that that route will provide more satisfactory resolution of the issues, bearing in mind the pressures of parliamentary business, the likelihood of Parliament following the Minister's inaction, and so on.

Finally, the United Kingdom procedures create the same unfortunate impression as the New Zealand Bill of Rights—that all other legislation is to be accorded prima facie precedence over human rights law and a compelling case has to be made out that human rights should trump legislation, rather than the other way around.

B Canadian Charter of Rights and Freedoms 1982

Another model is provided by section 33 of the Canadian Charter of Rights and Freedoms, the so-called "notwithstanding clause". Section 33 reads:[107]

> **33.** (1) Parliament or the legislature of a province may expressly declare in an Act of Parliament or of the legislature, as the case may be, that the Act or a provision thereof shall operate notwithstanding a provision included in section 2 or sections 7 to 15 of this Charter.
>
> (2) An Act or a provision of an Act in respect of which a declaration made under this section is in effect shall have such operation as it would have but for the provision of this Charter referred to in the declaration.

---

[106] The same view has recently been expressed about s. 4 HRA in terms of the requirement in Art. 13 of the European Convention that Contracting States provide effective remedies for Convention violations: C Neenan, "Is a Declaration of Incompatibility an Effective Remedy?" [2000] JR 247.

[107] There is an extensive literature on s. 33. For general discussions (although there is much more), see eg P Hogg, *Constitutional Law of Canada*, 3rd edn. (Scarborough, Carswell, 1992) ch. 36; T Macklem, "Engaging the Override" (1991) 1 *NJCL* 274; J Hiebert, "Why Must a Bill of Rights be a Contest of Political and Judicial Wills? The Canadian Alternative" (1999) 10 *PLR* 22; P Hogg and A Bushell, "The Charter Dialogue Between Courts and Legislatures" (1997) 35 *Osgoode Hall LJ* 75, 83–4; P Russell, "Standing Up for Notwithstanding" (1991) 29 *Alta L Rev* 293; P Weiler, "Rights and Judges in a Democracy: A New Canadian Version" (1984) 18 *J of Law Reform* 51 and J Whyte, "On Not Standing for Notwithstanding" (1990) 28 *Alta L Rev* 347. For the political debate over the override clause (there have been suggestions in some quarters that the override clause be dropped altogether or at least that a special majority be required before it can be invoked) see M Mandel, *The Charter of Rights and the Legalization of Politics in Canada*, rev'd edn. (Toronto, Thompson, 1994) 85.

(3) A declaration made under subsection (1) shall cease to have effect five years after it comes into force or on such earlier date as may be specified in the declaration.

(4) Parliament or a legislature of a province may re-enact a declaration made under subsection (1).

(5) Subsection (3) applies in respect of a re-enactment made under subsection (4).

A principal advantage of the section 33 procedure is that, assuming Parliament does not pass a blanket "notwithstanding" clause,[108] it renders almost the entire statute book open to scrutiny for human rights compatibility. It allows Parliament to deliberately determine which statutes it would prefer to immunise from judicial invalidation, yet leaves the remainder open to judicial testing. In practice, this means that a large bulk of the statute book is susceptible to an effective remedy should it be discovered to violate human rights norms.

Second, if the "notwithstanding" clause is used in a targeted fashion the likelihood of unintentional and unwitting breaches of rights and freedoms is much reduced.

Third, there will usually be clear incentives for persons who feel that their rights and freedoms have been violated to do something about it through the litigation process. The prospect of invalidation exists as a tangible reward.

Of course, in light of our earlier discussion of the Human Rights Committee's views in *Ballantyne* v. *Canada*,[109] it must be accepted that invocation of a "notwithstanding" clause in respect of any particular statute will have the result that an effective remedy for any violation of rights caused by that statute will be unavailable. In turn this means that a breach of Article 2 may occur.

However, the advantage of the "notwithstanding" mechanism is that (again assuming no blanket reliance on such a clause) it renders the vast majority of statutes susceptible to domestic review for Charter compliance. If transplanted to New Zealand this would represent a significant advance in terms of securing the effective enjoyment of rights. Moreover, it is surely worthy of interest that, when considering Canada's most recent Periodic Report in 1999,[110] the Human Rights Committee made no enquiries in relation to section 33 of the Charter and made no critical comments on its existence.[111]

At the same time, in my view, the "notwithstanding" procedure preserves in a meaningful, but targeted, way the sovereignty of Parliament.

What is the sovereignty of Parliament? For some, parliamentary sovereignty seems to equiparate to the operation of implied repeal of earlier statutes. The reasoning is that in order to retain parliamentary sovereignty, (1) a later Parliament

---

[108] The Quebec Government used s. 33 to immunise all of its statutes for the first five years of the Charter's operation and as a matter of course each subsequent statute until late 1985 (this being done as a protest against the entrenchment of the Canadian Charter in the face of Quebec's objection). This practice was only discontinued due to the election of a more pro-federal provincial government in December 1985.

[109] See the discussion above.

[110] Canada's Fourth Periodic Report, CCPR/C/103/Add 5 considered at the Committee's 1737th and 1738th meetings (CPPR/SR 1737–1738) (26 March 1999).

[111] See the concluding observations of the Committee, CCPR/C/79/Add 105 (7 April 1999).

must be able to trump the enactments of an earlier Parliament; (2) no statute can purport to prevent Parliament from enacting a later statute inconsistent with the earlier one; and (3) therefore, a later statute that is inconsistent with an earlier one *must* impliedly repeal the latter.[112] To my mind this is a bizarre conceptualisation of parliamentary sovereignty, primarily because statement (3) is not the proper deduction from statements (1) and (2). In my view, Parliament is only truly sovereign when it can indicate in advance how it wants a conflict between two inconsistent statutes, regardless of their antiquity, to be resolved yet retains the power for a later Parliament to deliberately alter that conflict-resolution decision. How can Parliament be considered sovereign if, when it comes to deciding how to resolve a conflict between *its* statutes, it is hamstrung in its choice by a pre-packaged decision of the courts favouring implied repeal? So long as it does not deny the possibility of later alteration of the basic rule of choice by a later Parliament (that is, so long as there is no entrenchment), where is the danger to sovereignty? Moreover, presumably many of the difficulties would be resolved if it were recalled that this basic rule of choice can be readily recast as a rule of interpretation directed primarily at the courts, telling the judges how they should proceed in the case of irreconcilable conflict—both statutes are "valid" (in the sense that both have been lawfully enacted) but, in light of a pro-Bill of Rights precedence rule, only one can be given operative effect.[113]

Precisely this approach appears to have been adopted by the United Kingdom courts in relation to the domestic application of European Community law. In the well-known *Factortame (No 2)* case,[114] the House of Lords granted an interim injunction to prevent the enforcement of the Merchant Shipping Act 1988 (UK) on the ground that the Act was inconsistent with the United Kingdom's obligations under the Treaty of Rome. The authority for this approach was found in section 2 of the European Communities Act 1972, which provides that certain types of Community law are directly enforceable in domestic law, and that the courts are to construe British law (whether passed before or after the 1972 Act) consistently

---

[112] See eg, *Vauxhall Estates* v. *Liverpool Corporation* [1932] 1 KB 733 and *Ellen Street Estates* v. *Minister of Health* [1934] 1 KB 590.

[113] In my view, however, the possibility of the earlier statute "overriding" the later statute can only be entertained when it is clear that the purpose of the "overriding" clause in that earlier statute is, indeed, to allow for an override. If not, the usual rules of statutory interpretation apply and the later statute will generally prevail. To my mind, therefore, the decision of three (Elias CJ, Tipping and Thomas JJ) of the seven judges in *R* v. *Pora* [2001] 2 NZLR 37 (CA) that s. 4(2) of the Criminal Justice Act 1985 (enacting a rule against retrospective punishments "notwithstanding any other enactment or rule of law to the contrary") overrides s. 2(4) of the Criminal Justice Amendment (No 2) Act 1999 (enacting that various alterations to the circumstances in which a judge could impose, and the length of, minimum non-parole eligibility periods applied retrospectively) was wrong, because it was not clear that s. 4(2), on a fair reading, was intended to override later statutes. See Butler, above n. 37.

[114] *R* v. *Secretary of State for Transport; Ex parte Factortame Ltd* [No 2] [1991] 1 AC 603 (HL). For comments on the case and its implications, see especially T R S Allan, "Parliamentary Sovereignty: Law, Politics and Revolution" (1997) 113 *LQR* 443; P P Craig, "Sovereignty of the United Kingdom Parliament after *Factortame*" (1991) 11 *YEL* 221; B V Harris, "Parliamentary Sovereignty and Interim Injunctions: *Factortame* and New Zealand" (1992) 15 *NZULR* 55; H W R Wade, "Sovereignty—Revolution or Evolution?" (1996) 112 *LQR* 568.

with the requirements of Community law. If this required the courts to ignore/ disapply a post-1972 statute, *Factortame* has established that must be done—there is to be no *implied* repeal of European Community law by post-1972 Acts. The *Factortame* principle was subsequently applied by the House of Lords in *R v. Employment Secretary, ex parte Equal Opportunities Commission*,[115] where several United Kingdom provisions which conferred lesser employment rights on part-time workers than full-time workers were declared to be "incompatible" with relevant provisions of European law.[116]

While Professor Wade has attempted to argue that *Factortame* effected a revolution in terms of the legal sovereignty enjoyed by the Westminster Parliament, by effectively transferring a significant chunk of that sovereignty *irrevocably* to Europe,[117] my own view[118] and, more importantly, that of other more eminent commentators is that in fact *Factortame* has not deprived the Westminster Parliament of the legal possibility (as opposed to the political possibility) of legislating contrary to European law where it does so *by an enactment which specifically expresses that to be its purpose* or by repeal of section 2 of the 1972 Act itself.[119] In the meantime, however, the rules in the 1972 Act are to be treated as guiding the courts as to how to resolve an irreconcilable conflict of laws.

Returning to section 33 of the Canadian Charter, it will be seen that it is perfectly compatible with notions of parliamentary sovereignty. Through the "notwithstanding" clause the federal and provincial parliaments can choose to (prospectively)[120] override judicial pronouncements on statutes or anticipate negative judicial views and preclude the possibility of review. Thus, the clause gives parliamentarians the power to override human rights.

But the attraction of section 33 is that it also forces politicians to accept the responsibility that goes with that power. A decision to invoke the "notwithstanding" clause requires explicit action and means that the politicians must accept the public relations consequences of their actions. Surely this is how it should be—a responsible exercise of parliamentary sovereignty designed to trump or forestall judicial assessment on human rights grounds should be *defensible and defended*. It should engender public debate on the reasonableness of the measure at stake and the importance of the rights under threat. Only under such conditions could depriving someone of an effective remedy become acceptable (if at all).

Recent Canadian experience suggests that this is exactly how the "notwithstanding" clause works. For example, in March 1998 the Alberta provincial

---

[115] [1995] 1 AC 1 (HL).

[116] *Ibid*, 31 per Lord Keith of Kinkel.

[117] Wade, above n. 114 at 573–4.

[118] Butler, above n. 54 at 340.

[119] See eg, Allan, above n. 114 at 444–6; A Bradley, "Sovereignty of Parliament—In Perpetuity?" in J Jowell and D Oliver (eds.), *The Changing Constitution*, 3rd edn. (Oxford, Clarendon Press, 1994) 97–8; S Kentridge, "Bills of Rights—The South African Experiment" (1996) 112 *LQR* 237, 256.

[120] The Supreme Court of Canada held in *Ford* v. *Quebec* [1988] 2 SCR 712, 744 that s. 33 only had prospective derogative effect, and hence could not be used to retrospectively overrule a judicial decision in a particular case in respect of the parties to that case. Legislation could of course be passed which contradicted the judgment and be clothed with immunity from challenge through s. 33.

government introduced legislation (Bill 26) that would have set a cap on the damages payable to victims of the province's eugenics programme in the first half of the twentieth century. Included in the Bill was a "notwithstanding" clause designed to protect the law from Charter challenge. Within a day public reaction to the use of the "notwithstanding" clause persuaded the Government to withdraw the Bill.[121] Equally, the same Government in the same year flagged the possibility of invoking the "notwithstanding" clause to reverse the anticipated result of the judgment of the Supreme Court of Canada on gay rights (the *Vriend* case),[122] but did not proceed with such legislation after public debate.[123]

1999 also witnessed public discussion of the "notwithstanding" power. When the Supreme Court of Canada ruled that the definition of "spouse" in Ontario's Family Law Act was unconstitutional because it amounted to discrimination on the ground of sexual orientation,[124] some public debate ensued during which opponents of the decision unsuccessfully pressed for use of the "notwithstanding" clause.[125] Then there was the *Sharpe* case. Public outrage[126] greeted the decision of first the British Columbia Supreme Court[127] and then the Court of Appeal in *R* v. *Sharpe*,[128] where it was held that the Criminal Code offence of possessing child pornography unjustifiably interfered with freedom of expression because of, inter alia, overbreadth. Rather than being hamstrung by a supreme law bill of rights, the federal Parliament was able to consider what its reaction to the judgment might be. After a debate in Parliament a motion to invoke the override clause and thus to protect the Criminal Code provision was defeated.[129] On appeal to the Supreme Court of Canada,[130] the child pornography law was, in almost all respects, upheld by the Court, but a majority carved out two exceptions to the law to protect freedom of expression. Reacting to the decision, Federal Justice Minister, Anne McLellan, ruled out the potential use of the "notwithstanding: clause to reverse these two exceptions.[131]

---

[121] "Public's Reaction a 'Perception Problem'—MLAs" *Edmonton Journal* 12 March 1998. See also Hiebert, above n. 107 at 34.

[122] *Vriend* v. *Alberta* [1998] 1 SCR 493 (reading sexual orientation as a ground of proscribed discrimination into the Alberta human rights legislation).

[123] "Klein Won't Rule Out Use of Clause in Vriend case" *Edmonton Journal*, 12 March 1998. See also Hiebert, above n. 107 at 30.

[124] *M* v. *H* [1999] 2 SCR 3.

[125] "Same Sex Ruling to Rewrite Many Laws" *Toronto Star*, 21 May 1999; "Ontario's 3 leaders will honour new ruling" *Toronto Star*, 21 May 1999.

[126] See eg G Kent, "Nation Anxiously Awaits Court's Decision on Child Porn" *Edmonton Journal*, 26 January 2001 (referring to call by Hermina Dykxhoorn, president of Alberta Federation of Women United for Families that s. 33 of Charter be used to protect relevant Criminal Code provisions).

[127] (1999) 169 DLR (4th) 536.

[128] (1999) 175 DLR (4th) 1.

[129] T MacCharles, "Reform Fails to Override B.C." *Toronto Star*, 3 February 1999; D Girard, "Porn Ruling Goes to Top Court" *Toronto Star*, 1 July 1999; E Stewart, "Ottawa Cautious About B.C. Porn Ruling" *Toronto Star*, 3 July 1999.

[130] *R* v. *Sharpe* 2001 1 SCR 45.

[131] T Bennett and A Jeffs, "Court Creates Loopholes in Child Porn Law" *Edmonton Journal*, 27 January 2001.

I conclude this section by noting that there is some irony in advocating adoption of the Canadian Charter mechanism in New Zealand. In the 1985 White Paper, passing reference was made to the Canadian Charter model of entrenchment of fundamental rights, but it was dismissed as providing insufficient protection to such rights due to the very presence of section 33.[132] Unfortunately, once it had been decided to abandon the entrenched supreme law model advocated in the White Paper, the allegedly weak Canadian model did not feature in the public discussion documents of the Justice and Law Reform Committee nor Justice Department advice. In many ways, a better response to the concerns felt by many submitters on the White Paper proposal would have been adoption of the "weak" Canadian Charter model.

VII CONCLUSION

This paper has adopted a modest focus in considering the issues raised by judicial review, attempting to apply aspects of those issues to the contemporary New Zealand debate on rights protection. While human rights enjoy a high level of enjoyment and a good measure of protection, there is a significant deficiency in the current New Zealand system: the inability to obtain an effective remedy where human rights have been interfered with by statute. Close examination of the position under the Bill of Rights demonstrates that the existence of other mechanisms within the Bill of Rights, while ameliorating the effect of the absence of a judicial power of invalidation, do not correct it. Moreover, the current situation under the Bill of Rights has received critical comment from the Human Rights Committee and exposes New Zealand to an ongoing and large-scale breach of its obligations under Article 2 of the Covenant.

In 2000, the Associate Minister of Justice commissioned an independent group of experts to re-evaluate human rights protections in New Zealand. Among the terms of reference was the following:[133]

"To develop recommendations for the relationship of one domestic human rights laws to other legislation in a way that best promotes and protects the human rights of New Zealanders in accordance with international conventions. This should include consideration of the primacy or otherwise of human rights law to other legislation."

This paragraph clearly made a link between the need to ensure respect for our international obligations and the interrelationship between domestic human rights laws and other enactments. Yet, other than noting New Zealand's ratification of the Covenant, and the availability of the communication mechanism, the Report made no links between the Covenant and what it referred to as the "primacy" issue. There is no discussion of Article 2.3 of the Covenant; no discussion of the criticisms made of New Zealand on this score by the Human Rights Committee

---

[132] *A Bill of Rights for New Zealand* (1985) AJHR A6, 53–4.
[133] *Re-evaluation of the Human Rights Protections in New Zealand*, above n. 28 at 17.

in 1995; and no acknowledgement that international human rights accountability, in order to be effective, requires extensive accountability and enforcement mechanisms at the *domestic* level as well as the international.

The result is that recommendations were made which will do little to advance New Zealand's compliance with Article 2.3 of the Covenant. While noting the suggestion in *Moonen* that Courts may have the power to make declarations of inconsistency with the Bill of Rights, the review group (with the exception of one member) declined to even recommend the express incorporation of such a device within the Bill of Rights, preferring instead "to leave the judicial practice to evolve".[134] This preference was informed by the history of the White Paper proposal, and by a public perception of the Bill of Rights as a drunk-drivers' charter, which does not "offer something to all New Zealanders".[135] Doubtless it was also informed by the group's earlier conclusion that there are "very few cases . . . genuinely" of conflict between the Bill of Rights and other enactments.[136]

In light of the material traversed above, many of these views can be seen to be infirm. First, the history of the 1985 White Paper only showed reluctance to adopt an entrenched, supreme-law bill of rights, not a bill of rights like the Charter or UK model. Second, perceptions of the Bill of Rights as a criminals' charter are unlikely to change, when it cannot be used elsewhere. In New Zealand that is often the case because in areas outside of the criminal law, statute law regulates so closely that there will often be little room for the Bill of Rights-consistent interpretation, and if in cases of inconsistency there is no mechanism which allows non-criminal New Zealanders to call Parliament to account, then it offers them little. Third, the view that resort to section 4 is infrequent is incorrect.

My point has been to show that there are alternative models available which acknowledge public opposition to a complete (or nearly complete)[137] transfer of power from Parliament to the judges, yet which provide more meaningful mechanisms to redress human rights violations effected through legislation: sections 4 and 10 of the Human Rights Act 1998 (UK) and section 33 of the Canadian Charter 1982. Upon close examination, it is my view that the latter achieves the best balance between parliamentary sovereignty and the need for effective remedies for human rights violations. It is a model worthy of consideration in response to the concerns of the Human Rights Committee expressed at the presentation of New Zealand's last Periodic Report, and which will surely be raised again upon consideration of New Zealand's next Report in 2001.

---

[134] *Re-evaluation of the Human Rights Protections in New Zealand*, above n. 28 at 37.
[135] *Ibid.*
[136] *Ibid*, 36.
[137] The White Paper Bill of Rights allowed amendments to be made by a parliamentary supermajority or by a referendum: ibid, 118, Art. 28 of the Draft Bill of Rights.

5

Human Rights Review and the Public–Private Distinction

MURRAY HUNT*

I INTRODUCTION

Historically, debates about the purpose of bills of rights, and the role of judicial review in protecting those rights, have been conducted on the largely unquestioned liberal premise of a firm distinction between the public and the private spheres. The main preoccupations of constitutional theorists have been how to justify a judicial role in the policing of democratic decision-makers. Reconciling judicial review with democracy has been the constitutional holy grail.

Today, however, any debate about the purpose of judicial enforcement of fundamental human rights norms must take account of the significant shift which is taking place in the locus of power. The worldwide political trend towards "privatisation" in the last two decades of the twentieth century, and the rapid acceleration of processes of globalisation in the last few years, have dramatically altered the landscape, both of politics and law. The power to interfere with what have traditionally been regarded as fundamental human rights has become increasingly concentrated in private hands, at the same time as the ability of democratic decision-makers to control those private actors has correspondingly diminished, as national governments find their freedom to act increasingly constrained by the complex web of overlapping international, supranational, and intergovernmental obligations and agreements in which they are now situated. Contemporary debate about the legitimacy of a judicial role in protecting fundamental values against the exercise of power must address this phenomenon of significant changes in the nature, locus, and configuration of power. One of the implications of this is that any modern account of the justification for constitutional judicial review must consider the justification for a judicial role in reviewing what has traditionally been conceived of as "private law", the law governing "private" relations, for compatibility with human rights norms.

* A much earlier version of this paper was delivered as a lecture in November 1999 in the JUSTICE/University College London seminar series "Fundamental Human Rights Principles: Defining the Limits to Rights", published as J Cooper (ed.), *Understanding Human Rights Principles* (Oxford, Hart Publishing, 2001).

The purpose of this paper is to take stock of where that debate has reached, both in theory and in practice, in New Zealand and the UK, and to argue for the adoption of an approach in both countries which would be an appropriate and legitimate response to the phenomenon described above. The paper is in four parts. First, it considers briefly the New Zealand experience under the New Zealand Bill of Rights Act 1990. Second, it reviews the considerable literature which has been generated on this question in the UK, and the practice of the UK courts in the first six months of the life of the UK's Human Rights Act, and suggests that there has emerged in the UK a very considerable degree of consensus as to the extent to which the law governing "private" relations should now be subjected to human rights norms. Third, it argues that this is a beneficial development which should be taken further, by cutting free altogether from the traditional public–private distinction, and the geometric metaphors which presuppose it, and conceiving instead of human rights review by courts as an exercise to which all law should in principle be subjected, including the law governing "private" relations, whether statute or common law. Fourth and finally, it argues for the adoption by courts of a simple and practical approach to rendering the common law compatible with fundamental rights norms, which acknowledges the importance of subjecting private law to human rights values in modern conditions, and at the same time recognises that there are both normative and institutional limits on judicial law-making in a democratic society.

II THE POSITION IN NEW ZEALAND

Section 3 of the New Zealand Bill of Rights Act 1990 expressly includes the judicial as well as the legislative and executive branches of government in the definition of the bodies to which the Act applies.[1] The significance of this was the subject of some uncertainty in New Zealand courts in the early days of its operation. In *Television New Zealand Ltd* v. *Newsmonitor Services Ltd*,[2] for example, which was a private claim for an infringement of copyright in which the plaintiff sought an injunction to restrain the defendant news monitoring company from publishing news and current affairs material produced by the plaintiff, the significance of the judicial branch being bound by the Bill of Rights was canvassed before Blanchard J in the High Court. Although he did not have to decide the point, because on his view the freedom of expression guarantee relied on did not require any change in the interpretation of the Copyright Act 1994, he recorded his tentative thoughts on the matter as follows:[3]

"I note, that there is no comparable reference to the judicial branch of government in the Canadian Charter of Rights and Freedoms. It may therefore be that our Parliament

---

[1] S. 3(a) New Zealand Bill of Rights Act 1990: "The Bill of Rights applies only to acts done—
(a) By the legislative, executive, or judicial branches of the government of New Zealand".

[2] [1994] 2 NZLR 91.

[3] *Ibid*, 96.

intended to go further in this respect than the Canadian Charter, though, equally, [counsel for the plaintiff] may have been correct in saying that the reference to the judicial branch in s. 3 was included because later in the statute there are sections dealing with exclusively judicial decision-making: minimum standards of criminal procedure, retroactive penalties and double jeopardy and the right to observance of the principles of natural justice. . . . On a wider interpretation it may possibly be that s. 3 requires the Courts to conduct themselves in accordance with the Bill of Rights in terms of their processes and procedures, but that this direction does not extend to the substance of their judgments and the orders which flow out of those judgments. If it was intended that the Bill of Rights is directly to apply in relation to every question of statutory interpretation and every other substantive judicial decision Parliament might have been expected to so enact in plain terms."

It is clear from this passage that Blanchard J was sceptical of the view that the effect of section 3 of the Bill of Rights Act binding the judiciary was to require that the substance of their judgments and orders must be compatible with the Bill of Rights. At the most, in his view, it meant that courts are bound to respect the Bill of Rights when conducting their own processes and procedures. In doubting the defendant's submission that section 3 required the court to interpret statutes consistently with the Bill of Rights even in private litigation, his underlying concern was that the logic of this argument led inexorably to the common law governing private relations being subjected to the Bill of Rights:[4]

"I pointed out to counsel that his argument would indistinguishably embrace non-statutory decision making, eg the granting of an injunction to restrain the dissemination of confidential information which was not protected by a statute. Counsel shrank from my invitation so to extend his argument."

Counsel's timidity in the *Television New Zealand* case proved unwarranted, as in a series of subsequent decisions the New Zealand courts appear to have accepted that the effect of section 3(a) is to require courts to give effect to the Bill of Rights when applying the common law. In *Solicitor-General* v. *Radio New Zealand*,[5] for example, which involved an application to commit the defendant broadcaster for contempt of court for contacting jurors in a murder trial and broadcasting their comments, the Court recorded that it was common ground between the parties that "the New Zealand Bill of Rights Act 1990 applies to these proceedings as applying to acts done by the judicial branch of the Government under s. 3(a)",[6] and that the case involved the right to freedom of expression.

This was taken further in *Duff* v. *Communicado Ltd*,[7] also contempt of court proceedings in respect of comments in the media which had the potential to affect a pending civil trial. Citing the *Radio New Zealand* case, the Court expressly considered whether the common law approach to contempt of court needed any modification because of the New Zealand Bill of Rights Act. The Court considered it

---

[4] *Ibid.*
[5] [1994] 1 NZLR 48.
[6] *Ibid*, 58.
[7] [1996] 2 NZLR 89.

to be bound to carry out this exercise because "[c]ontempt of court, *like any other part of the common law*, is subject to the Bill of Rights by virtue of s. 3(a) thereof".[8]

As in so many other jurisdictions, however, it is in the law of defamation that the clearest statement has been given of the degree to which the common law is affected by the Bill of Rights Act.[9] In *Lange* v. *Atkinson and ACP NZ Ltd*, which was an action for defamation by a former Prime Minister of New Zealand in which the main issue was whether special defences to defamation claims are required to protect political expression, Elias J in the High Court expressly considered the difference between the weak Canadian approach, according to which the Charter values "inform" the development of the common law, and a stronger obligation to ensure that the common law is applied consistently with the Bill of Rights.[10] She expressly preferred the latter because of the presence in New Zealand of section 3:[11]

"It is convenient to deal at the outset . . . with the submission made on behalf of the plaintiff as to the impact of the [New Zealand Bill of Rights] Act upon the common law. [Counsel for the plaintiff] argues that, while the New Zealand Bill of Rights Act may be taken into account in the development of common law, the common law is not subject to the New Zealand Bill of Rights under s. 3. In this he relies upon *Hill* v. *Church of Scientology of Toronto*. . . .

In my view the New Zealand Bill of Rights Act protections are to be given effect by the court in applying the common law. . . . The application of the Act to the common law seems to me to follow from the language of s. 3 which refers to acts of the judicial branch of the Government of New Zealand, a provision not to be found in the Canadian charter. . . . The New Zealand Bill of Rights Act 1990 is important contemporary legislation which is directly relevant to the policies served by the common law of defamation. It is idle to suggest that the common law need not conform to the judgments in such legislation."

It would therefore seem now to be well established that in New Zealand, despite the wrong turn that was almost made by Blanchard J in the early *Television New Zealand* case, the Bill of Rights applies to the common law, including the common law governing disputes between private parties, and that one reason why it does so is that the acts of the judicial branch are expressly made subject to the Bill of Rights by section 3.[12] As will be seen below in the case of the UK, however, commentators continue

---

[8] [1996] 2 NZLR 89, 99 (emphasis added).

[9] See also *Television New Zealand Ltd* v. *Quinn* [1996] 3 NZLR 24, a case, like *Rantzen* v. *Mirror Group Newspapers (1986) Ltd* [1994] QB 670 (CA), concerning the practice of directing juries on damages in defamation actions, in which McGechan J said (at 58): "As a general and opening position, I endorse alignment between jury directions and dictates of the Bill of Rights. It is an inevitability. It is the Court's duty to support freedoms in the Bill of Rights, not to frustrate them."

[10] [1997] 2 NZLR 22, 32.

[11] *Ibid*. Although the point was not expressly considered by the Court of Appeal in its decision on appeal, [1998] 3 NZLR 424, it appears that they approved of Elias J's approach. Her view about the effect of s. 3 is recited in the Court of Appeal's summary of her decision (*ibid*, 431) and the Court of Appeal upheld her decision "broadly for the same reasons" (*ibid*, 428).

[12] As in the UK, however, purely textual arguments can only ever be part of the justification; at least as important is acceptance of the instrumental role of the common law in constituting power relations.

to disagree over the precise nature of the obligation to which courts are subject, and therefore the *extent* to which the common law governing private relations is affected by the Bill of Rights Act. Some, such as Andrew Butler, argue that the Bill of Rights Act applies to the whole of the common law, and that courts are under an obligation to develop the common law so as to achieve compatibility with it.[13] Others take a more cautious approach. Paul Rishworth, for example, argues that the correct interpretation of the position in New Zealand is equivalent to the weaker Canadian approach, that "the common law must be evaluated and developed in line with the values of the Bill of Rights".[14] Rishworth's position flows from his explicit acceptance of the liberal premise that the Bill of Rights is a fetter on state power and not a reason for its exercise, and that it assumes the existence of a sphere of personal autonomy that is not properly regulated by the state. The stronger approach advocated in this paper does not share that premise, but proceeds instead from the premise that all fundamental rights have a positive dimension which imposes on the State a positive obligation to act to secure those rights where threatened by other private actors. Where such rights come into conflict with individual autonomy, prioritising the latter is to be subjected to a process of justification rather than taken as a given fact. This, it is suggested, is also the premise which implicitly underlies the approach taken in the more recent New Zealand cases considered above.

The relevance of the New Zealand experience under section 3 of its Bill of Rights Act is likely to be seen as being of considerable relevance to the position under the UK's Human Rights Act, not least because of the presence of Lord Cooke in the UK House of Lords. In Lord Cooke's view, "the Convention rights . . . will prevail over the common law, in that the courts will have the responsibility of adjusting the common law as far as may be necessary to give effect to such of them as are capable of application".[15]

III THE EMERGING CONSENSUS IN THE UK

When the United Kingdom's Human Rights Act 1998 was passed by Parliament containing a provision expressly making courts "public authorities" for the purposes

---

[13] A S Butler, "The New Zealand Bill of Rights and Private Common Law Litigation" [1991] *NZLJ* 261.

[14] P Rishworth, G Huscroft, S Optican and R Mahoney, *The New Zealand Bill of Rights* (forthcoming 2002).

[15] "The British Embracement of Human Rights" (1999) *EHRLR* 243, 257. See also Lord Cooke's dissent in *Hunter* v. *Canary Wharf* [1997] AC 655 in which, even before the advent of the Human Rights Act, he thought it legitimate for the courts to develop the common law of nuisance so as to make it compatible with various international standards protecting the home against nuisance, regardless of whether the complainant has a proprietary interest; and his speech in the House of Lords in *Reynolds* v. *Times Newspapers* [1999] 3 WLR 1010, explicitly referring to the role of the European Convention in the development of the common law and to the fact that as public authorities it will be unlawful for courts to act incompatibly with Convention rights. Lord Nicholls in the same case also states that when the Human Rights Act takes effect the common law will have to be developed and applied in a manner consistent with the Convention; and Lord Steyn regards the Human Rights Act as reinforcing the constitutional or "higher order" foundation of freedom of expression.

of the Act, and therefore subject to a clear duty to act compatibly with Convention rights,[16] there was every prospect of a highly charged debate erupting between proponents of the limited government school of constitutionalism advocating a narrow, "vertical" interpretation of the Act and the Convention, and advocates of a more social-democratic version of constitutionalism arguing for a more expansive "horizontal" interpretation which can accommodate the positive dimension of fundamental rights.

In fact, far from there being a debate raging between "verticalists" and "horizontalists" in the UK, what has emerged is a remarkable degree of consensus about the fact that the Human Rights Act makes Convention rights relevant to the law governing private relations. The only real area of disagreement, it will be suggested, is over the *extent* to which the common law governing private relations is affected by the Act. The real focus of the disagreement is whether the Act imposes an *obligation* on courts to develop the common law governing private relations in such a way as to give effect to Convention rights, and, if so, the strength of that obligation.

During the period preceding the enactment of the Human Rights Act in 1998 and its coming into force in October 2000, this question of the Act's so-called "horizontal effect" was the subject of a great deal of analysis and speculation. A review of the literature reveals that the positions which have been taken on this question lie along a spectrum between the vertical and the horizontal.

At the extreme "horizontal" end of the spectrum, arguing that the Human Rights Act makes Convention rights directly enforceable against private parties (that is, gives them full horizontal effect) is William Wade. Ever since the publication of the draft Bill, he has consistently argued that the effect of making courts "public authorities" who are obliged to act compatibly with the Convention is that private individuals and bodies are subjected to the Convention rights, which can be enforced directly against them through the courts.[17] Wade's argument is that this conclusion is compelled by both the letter of the Act and its spirit.

This claim that the Act achieves full or direct horizontal effect for Convention rights faces formidable obstacles: it is plainly inconsistent with the scheme of the Act, in which the concept of a "public authority" is central and which goes to the trouble of partially defining what counts as a public authority for the purposes of the Act; it is directly contrary to the explanations of its effect which were given by the Ministers promoting it during its passage; and it does not pay sufficient heed to the nature of Convention rights themselves. Wade's view, however, is a useful reference point in the debate about the reach of the Human Rights Act: it occupies the most extreme position at the "full horizontality" end of the spectrum.

---

[16] Ss. 6(3)(a) and 6(1) respectively of the Human Rights Act 1998.

[17] H W R Wade, "The United Kingdom's Bill of Rights" in The University of Cambridge Centre for Public Law, *Constitutional Reform in the United Kingdom: Practice and Principles* (Oxford, Hart Publishing, 1998) 61; "Human Rights and the Judiciary" (1998) *EHRLR* 522; and "Horizons of Horizontality" (2000) 116 *LQR* 217.

The other end of the spectrum has been occupied by Richard Buxton, a judge on the English Court of Appeal, whose argument comes close to defending the extreme verticalist position, that the Convention rights are entirely irrelevant to the law which governs private relations and the Act therefore has no effect on private law rights and obligations.[18] Buxton argues that there are "substantial limitations" on the effect that the Human Rights Act and the ECHR will have on private law.[19] He recognises, as he must, that even before the HRA indirect use has been made of the ECHR's provisions and values in the interpretation of domestic law, including private law.[20] He also acknowledges that the principle of effectiveness and the fact that courts themselves, as public authorities, have responsibilities imposed on them by the ECHR, "have significance when considering the ability of individuals to resist claims made against them which if upheld would entail a breach of the requirements of the E.C.H.R.".[21] To this extent, therefore, he falls short of being an outright verticalist.

However, in his view there are "substantial limitations" on the effect of the Act on private law because the rights created by the ECHR "are limited to rights against states or against public bodies for which the state is responsible",[22] and human rights values "remain, stubbornly, values whose content lives in public law".[23] On this view, the effects of the Act are safely confined to the realm of public law by asserting the traditional distinction between public and private as if it were uncontroversial that such a clear distinction exists.

A position very close to the "vertical" end of the spectrum has also been taken by Sydney Kentridge. In his comments to a conference on constitutional reform in Cambridge in January 1998, he argued that the inclusion of courts in the definition of "public authority" in the Human Rights Act:[24]

> "means only that the courts in their own sphere must give effect to such fundamental rights as the right to a fair trial, and to more particular rights such as a right to an interpreter. The courts must also in their own sphere observe general prohibitions, such as the prohibition of discrimination."

It did not mean that the Convention applied as between individual litigants, such as the plaintiff and defendant in a defamation case. In such cases the Convention would influence the common law, but only indirectly, on the German *Drittwirkung* model.[25]

---

[18] R Buxton, "The Human Rights Act and Private Law" (2000) 116 *LQR* 48.
[19] *Ibid*, 65.
[20] *Ibid*, 49.
[21] *Ibid*, 52.
[22] *Ibid*, 55.
[23] *Ibid*, 59.
[24] S Kentridge, "The Incorporation of the European Convention on Human Rights" in *Constitutional Reform in the United Kingdom*, above n. 17 at 70.
[25] At a debate between William Wade, Sydney Kentridge, Nicholas Bamforth and the author at a seminar on "The Possible Horizontal Effect of the Human Rights Act 1998" organised by the Cambridge Centre for Public Law on 6 December 2000, Sydney Kentridge appeared to take a position even closer to the vertical end of the spectrum. He argued that the debate about horizontality is an unnecessary distraction, because he has yet to be persuaded that there exists a single situation in which human rights norms would make a difference to the content of private law.

Most writers, however, have adopted a position somewhere between these two extremes. In one sense this is hardly surprising, given that the language of the Act, its legislative history and the case law of the Convention make the more extreme positions difficult to justify.[26] But it is highly significant, because it immediately reveals that the real debate is taking place on a relatively narrow part of the spectrum somewhere in between the two extremes.

A number of writers have advocated an intermediate position, less narrow than the Buxton and Kentridge view, but stopping significantly short of the position that the Convention applies to all law. Ian Leigh, for example, has drawn up a typology of horizontal effect, identifying no fewer than six forms of "horizontal effect" which could be said to arise under the Human Rights Act, five of which he accepts exist.[27] Two of these are the types that Kentridge also acknowledges: "remedial horizontality", whereby judges exercising discretionary powers in private litigation must do so in conformity with Convention rights; and "indirect horizontality", which is the indirect influence the Convention exerts over the general development of the common law as it applies between private parties.

In addition to these, Leigh acknowledges what he labels "direct statutory horizontality", which refers to the fact that even statutes which apply to private relations are still subject to the interpretive obligation in section 3(1) to give effect to Convention rights so far as it is possible to do so. "Public liability horizontality" refers to the fact that under the Act the definition of "public authority" may be wider than the category of bodies or persons for which the state may be liable in Strasbourg. And "intermediate horizontality" refers to the situation where a Convention right may be claimed against a public authority in respect of its failure to take action against a third party whose actions harm the plaintiff.

Leigh therefore acknowledges that the Act has a considerable degree of horizontal effect, but he cannot accept that the Act has what he calls "full or direct horizontal effect" in the sense that courts, as public authorities, are required to create appropriate rights and remedies by developing the common law.[28] He sees this as the most contentious type of horizontal effect and in his view it is unsupported by the drafting of the Act, the scheme of the Convention, or constitutional

---

[26] See M Hunt, "The 'Horizontal Effect' of the Human Rights Act" [1998] PL 423 for the argument that these indicators suggest that the Human Rights Act goes significantly beyond the "indirect effect" of equivalent instruments in Canada and Germany, but stops short of creating entirely new causes of action against private parties.

[27] I Leigh, "Horizontal Rights, the Human Rights Act and Privacy: Lessons from the Commonwealth" (1999) 48 *ICLQ* 57; and see further his contribution to this volume.

[28] *Ibid*, 87. See also G Phillipson, "The Human Rights Act, 'Horizontal Effect' and the Common Law: a Bang or a Whimper?" (1999) 62 *MLR* 824, who argues that no general duty to ensure the compatibility of all private common law with Convention rights can be deduced from the Act. Instead, he argues that the most satisfactory interpretation of the court's duty under s. 6(1) is that "the rights will figure only as principles to which the courts must have regard", *ibid*, 848. Nicholas Bamforth also takes an intermediate position, arguing that the interpretive obligation in s. 3 of the Human Rights Act provides "the true statutory basis for any 'horizontal effect'": "The True 'Horizontal Effect' of the Human Rights Act 1998" (2001) 117 *LQR* 34.

principle elucidated by courts in other jurisdictions which have faced identical problems.[29]

Further along the spectrum from this intermediate group, but falling short of Wade's extreme position of full horizontality, are commentators who argue that private law will be significantly affected by the Human Rights Act, but that the way in which this will happen is more complex than is allowed for by Wade's "simple view". Anthony Lester and David Pannick, for example, explicitly accept that the consequence of courts being public authorities is that they are under a duty to develop the common law in order to achieve compatibility:[30]

> "Because the courts are public authorities, they have a duty to ensure that Convention rights are protected even in litigation between private parties. The obligation of the court under s. 6 will apply where the Convention has effect on the legal relationship between private parties because the state (acting through its courts) is obliged, under the Convention, to protect individuals against breaches of their rights."

Significantly, however, Lester and Pannick are anxious to distinguish this stronger approach from Wade's extreme position that the Human Rights Act has full operation in the sphere of private rights. The correct approach, they argue:[31]

> "involves applying the constitutional guarantee of human rights not only to the relationship between the state and the individual but also to relations between private individuals, but only where the State has a duty under the convention to protect the human rights of one of the parties as against the other, whether by way of claim or defence".

At the time of writing, the UK's Human Rights Act has only been in force for six months,[32] and it is therefore far too early to predict exactly what course the courts will take. From the handful of cases which have so far raised the question, however, the early indications are at the very least that the broad consensus amongst the commentators will be reflected by the courts in practice, and there are also signs that the strong position, that the courts are under a positive obligation to strive to develop the common law to achieve compatibility where possible, may also find favour.[33] So in *Douglas* v. *Hello! Ltd*,[34] for example, a private action for an injunction to

---

[29] Leigh's analysis does not, however, distinguish between an entirely new cause of action and an incremental development in the scope of an existing cause of action, a distinction which is crucial to maintaining a meaningful difference between illegitimate horizontality under the Human Rights Act and permissible development of the common law pursuant to the obligation on courts to act compatibly.

[30] A P Lester and D Pannick (eds.), *Human Rights Law and Practice* (London, Butterworths, 1999) 31–2, n. 3. This also appears to be the view taken by Lord Hope in *R* v. *DPP, ex parte Kebilene* [2000] 2 AC 326, 374–5, who said "It is now plain that the incorporation of the European Convention on Human Rights into our domestic law will subject the entire legal system to a fundamental process of review and, where necessary, reform by the judiciary." See, to similar effect, S Grosz, J Beatson and& P Duffy, *Human Rights: The 1998 Act and the European Convention* (London, Sweet and Maxwell, 2000).

[31] A P Lester and D Pannick, "The Impact of the Human Rights Act on Private Law: The Knight's Move" (2000) 116 *LQR* 380, 384. Beatson and Grosz "substantially agree": "Horizontality: A Footnote" (2000) 116 *LQR* 385, 386.

[32] Although enacted in 1998 the Human Rights Act only came into force in October 2000.

[33] The cases are considered in detail in Ian Leigh's contribution to this volume, and only brief reference is therefore made to them here.

[34] [2001] 2 WLR 992, 1021–2 (CA).

restrain a breach of confidence, Sedley LJ held that the Human Rights Act gave "the final impetus to the recognition of a right of privacy in English law",[35] because by the Act English courts must not only take account of the Strasbourg jurisprudence, which points to a positive institutional obligation to respect privacy, but they must also themselves act compatibly with that Convention right. Significantly, he held that, if the step from confidentiality to privacy was not simply a modern restatement of a known protection but a legal innovation, it was precisely the kind of incremental change for which the Act is designed: one which without undermining the measure of certainty necessary to all law gives substance and effect to the obligation on courts to act compatibly with Convention rights.[36]

In *Venables and Thompson* v. *News Group Newspapers Ltd*[37] the Court went even further in deriving from the Human Rights Act a strong obligation on the courts to render the common law compatible with the Convention in purely private proceedings. The case concerned an entirely novel claim, brought in the tort of breach of confidence, for injunctions against the world to protect the identity and whereabouts and other relevant information concerning two 18 year-olds who had notoriously killed a two year-old boy and who were shortly to be released from detention. In considering whether the court had jurisdiction to grant such injunctions, Dame Elizabeth Butler-Sloss held that the court first had to determine the question of the applicability of the Convention, given that it was being relied upon in private proceedings. After considering the relevant case law of the Convention, she held that the courts were under positive obligations, including, where necessary, the provision of a regulatory framework of adjudicatory and enforcement machinery in order to protect the rights of the individual, and that[38]

> "the duty on the court . . . is to act compatibly with convention rights in adjudicating upon existing common law causes of action, and that includes a positive as well as a negative obligation".

Recognising that it was being asked to extend the domestic law of confidence to grant the injunctions sought, she held that there was a positive duty upon the court to take such steps as may be necessary to achieve the aim of protecting the claimants from serious and possibly irreparable harm in breach of Articles 2 and 3 of the Convention. Since she was satisfied that such a real and serious risk existed, she considered that the court was bound to grant the injunctions sought, in order to act compatibly with the positive obligation on public authorities to protect an individual against breaches of Articles 2 and 3.[39]

---

[35] [2001] 2 WLR 992, 1022 (CA).

[36] *Ibid*, 1026. See also Keene LJ at 1035–6 (the scope of the established cause of action of breach of confidence may now need to be approached in the light of the obligation on the court to act compatibly with Convention rights).

[37] [2001] 2 WLR 1038 (Fam D).

[38] *Ibid*, 1049.

[39] For a further example of judicial acceptance that the Convention applies in private proceedings (this time family law proceedings between parents concerning the removal of a child outside the jurisdiction), see *Payne* v. *Payne* [2001] All ER (D) 142 (13 February 2001) paras. 34 and 81, disapproving

This brief survey of the literature and judicial practice reveals a surprisingly large degree of consensus about the extent to which the law governing "private" disputes is affected by the Act. Most commentators and judges who have so far considered the question appear to be in broad agreement that the Convention is relevant to the development of the common law governing private relations, and the only area of real disagreement is whether, and if so to what extent courts are *obliged* to develop the common law to protect Convention rights. It appears that the debate is not so much about whether the law governing private relations should be compatible with Convention rights (that debate has largely been settled in the UK by the form of the legislation); it seems to be more concerned with the extent to which development of the common law will tread on Parliament's toes. In which case, the issue in the UK has become less a philosophical one about public and private, and more an issue of relative institutional competence between the courts and Parliament.[40]

IV BEYOND THE PUBLIC–PRIVATE DISTINCTION

Much, though not all, of the UK literature proceeds on the assumption that the geometric language of "vertical" or "horizontal" effect is an entirely appropriate metaphor for the meaningful discussion of the extent to which the Human Rights Act applies to "private" relations. The purpose of this part of the paper is to address that question directly, and to argue that the language of horizontality mischaracterises the debate and is likely to lead in the long run to the frustration of one of the central purposes of the Human Rights Act: to make fundamental human rights pervasive in the law in order to give them genuine, practical effectiveness.

The most powerful case for abandoning the language of horizontality has been made by Stephen Sedley in his second Hamlyn Lecture, "Public Power and Private Power".[41] In that lecture, Sedley directly challenges the use of the horizontality metaphor because it is premised on an assumed dichotomy between law's public and its private spheres. The metaphor presupposes that there is a fundamental distinction between the public and the private spheres of law's operation, and by framing the debate in this way it "assume[s] the very thing that needs to be debated".[42] What needs to be debated is not whether or how far rights which are inherently "vertical" in nature should be "extended" into the "private" sphere, but what it means in practical terms for all the institutions of the state, including courts, to be bound to act compatibly with Convention rights.

as "no longer tenable" the view expressed by Buxton LJ in *Re A (Permission to Remove Child From Jurisdiction: Human Rights)* [2000] 2 FLR 225 that the Convention perhaps had no place in this area of litigation.

[40] Though inescapably this remains a normative question, raising difficult issues of legitimacy, and is not merely a value-free, factual question about which decision-maker is "best-placed" to make a decision.

[41] S Sedley, *Freedom, Law and Justice* (London, Sweet & Maxwell, 1999) 19.

[42] *Ibid*, 23.

This is a crucial insight. The vocabulary of "horizontality" commits participants in the discourse to a prior assumption about the separateness of the public and the private spheres which is highly controversial. It concedes the starting point in the debate to those who believe there to be a firm distinction between the public and the private spheres, and who would privilege the private over the public by preserving it immune from the values of public law, including fundamental rights norms. In fact, there is no such firm distinction, because the very presence of law introduces a public element: private relations are in part constituted by both statute and common law, and the state lurks behind both. For those like Stephen Sedley, who reject the notion that there is a firm distinction between public and private, it follows that the horizontality metaphor cannot serve. It skews the debate from the outset by asking the question to be determined in terms which presuppose a certain answer.[43]

The oddness of the assumption that the common law governing private relations is not subject to Convention rights comes into focus when one considers the effect of section 3 of the Human Rights Act. The obligation imposed by that section to interpret primary and subordinate legislation, so far as it is possible to do so, in a manner which is compatible with Convention rights is in its terms an obligation of general application. It applies as much to the interpretation of statutes which regulate private relations, of which there are many, as it applies to statutes of a more "public" nature. This is uncontroversial. Absolutely no one argues that, where there is a Convention right in play, legislation can be interpreted in a way which is incompatible with that right simply because the question of interpretation arises in litigation between private parties.

Not only does the Human Rights Act itself not attempt to distinguish between different types of legislation, it would be unique if it did: it seems to be universally assumed in legal systems with legal protections for fundamental rights that legislation is *always* amenable to scrutiny for compatibility with those rights, even where the question arises in otherwise purely private proceedings. This is presumably because a legislative intervention is always considered to involve some action by the "state" which satisfies the assumed requirement of a "public" dimension. Even in Canada, for example, where the common law governing private relations is immune from direct Charter scrutiny,[44] it was accepted early on in the life of the Charter that even legislation which governs private relations is subject to the Charter.[45] In this country, the recent decision of the House of Lords in *Fitzpatrick*

---

[43] As Stephen Sedley also explains, rejection of the assumed distinction between law's public and private spheres also requires rejection of the language of "Drittwirkung" or "third party effects", since this "again suggests an artificial extension of the natural ambit of rights": *ibid*, 23 n. 11.

[44] *Retail, Wholesale & Department Store Union, Local 580* v. *Dolphin Delivery Ltd* [1986] 2 SCR 573. The position in Canada is that the common law has been held to be affected only *indirectly*, in the sense that its development should be "informed" by the values underlying the Charter: see eg, *Hill* v. *Church of Scientology of Toronto* [1995] 2 SCR 1130.

[45] See eg, *Re Blainey and Ontario Hockey Association* (1986) 26 DLR (4th) 728 (Ont CA), in which a statutory exemption in provincial human rights legislation concerning discrimination was held to be incompatible with the Charter in a case involving private parties. See generally on "direct statutory horizontality" Leigh, above n. 27 at 75–7.

v. *Sterling Housing Association Ltd*,[46] holding that a same-sex partner can qualify as a member of the tenant's family within the meaning of the relevant provision of the Rent Act 1977, entitling him to succeed to an assured tenancy, is a timely reminder of the way in which the judicial interpretation of statutory phrases in legislation governing private relations can have a profound effect on private relations.

The fact that the section 3 interpretive obligation clearly applies in proceedings between purely private parties is an important factor in rejecting the appropriateness of the "horizontality" metaphor. It makes something of a mockery of many of the arguments against the Human Rights Act applying to the common law governing private relations, because many of them are in the nature of objections in principle to human rights having any application in the private sphere at all. Many of Ian Leigh's arguments against the Human Rights Act governing the common law, for example, are based on considerations of certainty and stability:[47]

> "[I]f applied in the private domestic sphere the result would be destabilising, with every personal tort open to reinterpretation in the light of plausible Article 8 arguments on both sides. Such an undesirable exercise in uncertainty risks seriously damaging the balancing of private interests in the common law."

These are arguments of general application in their resistance to the applicability of fundamental rights norms in the "private sphere", and they would apply equally to the applicability of the section 3 interpretive obligation to statutes which regulate private disputes. That too will lead to the reinterpretation of law governing private relations in the light of plausible Convention arguments on both sides, leading inevitably to some uncertainty and instability for old assumptions, but that is precisely what Parliament has sanctioned. Whether private activity is regulated by statute or common law is often entirely fortuitous, and it would be a wholly arbitrary distinction if only part of the legal framework within which private relations are conducted were subjected to scrutiny for compatibility with the Convention.

V HOW CAN THE COMMON LAW BE RENDERED COMPATIBLE?

If the debate about the effect of the Human Rights Act on private law is less about distinguishing public from private than has traditionally been thought, and if the "horizontality" metaphor is therefore to be abandoned, how are UK courts to make sense of their confusing role as public authorities, statutorily obliged to act

---

[46] [1999] 3 WLR 1113. Although the "living instrument" approach to interpretation on which the decision is based was not adopted in order to achieve compatibility with the Convention (the decision in fact goes further than the Strasbourg case law which has yet to recognise the family life of same-sex partners), it is a useful foretaste of the interpretive techniques that will be required by the s. 3(1) obligation.

[47] Leigh, above n. 27 at 73. For similarly cautious arguments, seeking to privilege the common law over statute law in terms of the effect of the HRA, see Phillipson, above n. 28 at 840 ("if the Convention were *always* to override inconsistent common law rules, this could seriously unbalance the common law, which has attempted to reconcile a more comprehensive set of individual interests than has the Convention").

compatibly with the Convention, and therefore to develop the common law where necessary, but at the same time required by the scheme of the Act not to invent entirely new causes of action against private persons, and warned by the Lord Chancellor not to step over the line into forbidden judicial "legislation"?

One of the sure signs of the sheer conceptual difficulty of this question is the prevalence of metaphors. Convention rights have variously been described as the "prism" through which all domestic law must in future be viewed; the "magnetic north" whose gravitational force will rearrange the contours of UK law. The most attractive are undoubtedly those which treat the current law as a sort of background cloth, through the fabric of which the Convention rights will spread like a dye,[48] or into which they will be interwoven.[49] This metaphor has the particular attraction that it captures graphically the reality that the scheme of the model adopted in the UK means that there will be some patches which remain impervious to the dye, or some holes in the fabric which cannot be patched by the most skilled judicial weaver.

Stephen Sedley's rejection of the premise underlying the horizontality metaphor leads him to prefer to talk of the "cascade effect" of the Human Rights Act rather than its "horizontal effect". However, this does not do justice to the effect of the Act, when it is properly understood against the background of the constitutive role of the common law. Cascading implies differentiated levels, with human rights spilling over from one level to another. The implication is that the primary effect of the Act is on statute law, but that the rights it introduces flow over into the common law. Characterising the effect of the Act in this way risks forfeiting the essential insight that statute and the common law are *both* manifestations of the state in private relations, and are *equally* constitutive of them.[50] Rights which "cascade" or "spill over" into the common law might be thought to be of less force by the time they reach that level.[51] In short, "cascade effect" does not really do justice to the force of the Convention's claim under the Human Rights Act to require reshaping of the common law.

This is an important point to keep in mind. The effect of section 6 of the UK's Human Rights Act is that the courts are under an *obligation* to act compatibly with the Convention. They must therefore ensure the common law's compatibility with Convention rights, in so far as it is possible for them to do so. It is not simply a matter of *discretion*: can courts develop the common law in this way if they feel like it? It is a matter of judicial *obligation*. It must be distinguished from the much weaker "indirect effect" doctrine of the Canadian and German approaches. Section 6(3)(a), properly understood against the background of the courts' law-making role in the development of the common law, means that UK courts are not dealing here with

---

[48] Sedley, above n. 41 at 19.

[49] Cooke, above n. 15 at 258.

[50] Moreover, the common law continues to regulate vast areas of private activity which are relatively untouched by statutory intervention.

[51] Cf the now common characterisation of the effect of principles of European public law on our domestic public law as a "spillover effect".

mere common law development in line with the underlying values of the common law. They are dealing with something much more concrete: an obligation to ensure that the common law is not incompatible with an individual's Convention rights, subject only to the constraint implicit in the scheme of the Act that Parliament and not the courts should be responsible for changing the law when that amounts to creating a new cause of action against private persons.

Although metaphors can be illuminating and powerful, they can also become an obstacle to understanding or, worse, a substitute for thought. What is required at this juncture is a more practical, metaphor-free articulation of exactly what is required of courts as a consequence of their being public authorities obliged to act compatibly with Convention rights. In plain language, what is required is that courts must ask themselves, even in private litigation, whether there is a Convention right in play. If there is, they must ask themselves whether the substance of the common law they propose to apply, and the order they propose to make, is compatible with that Convention right. That means subjecting the common law to the same process of scrutiny, including for justification where it interferes with Convention rights, as executive actions and legislation. It also means subjecting values of individual autonomy to the same process of justification when they come into conflict with other fundamental rights, instead of assuming that they are automatically prioritised by the very nature of the exercise of rights-protection.

If application of the common law in the court's order would not be compatible with the Convention right at stake, the court must ask itself whether the common law can be developed so as to avoid the incompatibility. This is only likely to be controversial if it involves filling a gap that exists in the common law scheme of remedies. In trying to decide whether the necessary development in the common law is open to it, the court should remember that it is under an obligation to act compatibly, and should therefore be creative in its incremental development of the common law, but is subject to the ultimate constraint that it must not create entirely new causes of action where nothing analogous previously existed. If (and this is perhaps the most important point) the court decides that the development of the common law that would be required to achieve compatibility would take it beyond its legitimate role of incrementally developing the common law, it should make clear in its judgment that in its view the state of the law is incompatible with the Convention, and requires legislative amendment to remove the incompatibility.

The attraction of this straightforward approach is that it makes the courts' approach to common law compatibility symmetrical with that to statutory compatibility, and therefore fits the scheme of the Human Rights Act, which is to give the courts a central role in ensuring that UK law conforms to the Convention, whilst preserving at the same time a role for Parliament in deciding precisely how such conformity is to be achieved. It achieves a position whereby the Act imposes a judicial obligation to ensure that the law of the UK, including the common law, is compatible with the Convention, except where this would, in the case of statute law, exceed the interpretive obligation in section 3 (in which case a declaration of incompatibility should be given) or, in the case of the common law, exceed the legitimate bounds of common law development, in which case the court should indicate clearly to Parliament its view that the common law is incompatible and requires legislative amendment. On this approach to both types of law, courts cannot avoid the compatibility question: they must carry out the inquiry, and either achieve compatibility themselves, or make clear that there is an incompatibility that they are powerless to redress.

PART II

Liberty and Equality

6

Liberty, Equality and the New Establishment

PAUL RISHWORTH

Equality is one of the most conceptually difficult and challenging issues in modern human rights law. Which characteristics of persons should attract judicial scrutiny when selected by government as reasons for differentiating between citizens? With whom does one compare the complainant group? May courts extend the benefits of government programmes or legislation to excluded groups who share the same characteristics as the included? How much should context—that the government programme is ameliorative in purpose, for example—count in equality cases?

Justice Binnie's account of the Supreme Court of Canada's progress in struggling with equality rights in the Canadian Charter is both fascinating and reassuring. It is reassuring because of the evident compassion and humility in the Court's effort to make a constitutional right meaningful for people, while avoiding its over-extension such that all legislative distinctions are rendered suspect and vulnerable to judicial review. For her part, Hilary Charlesworth chronicles the international dimension of the right to equality. The equality jurisprudence there is in its formative stages, and is being outrun by the aspirations of commentators. In part this is because an equality right is, as she concludes, a vehicle for social justice. When so conceived, the equality jurisprudence of any court or tribunal is likely often to disappoint, if not because of the institutional inability of courts and tribunals to deliver social justice, then because of differing conceptions in the community of what counts as success.

Some of these differing conceptions are exposed when we focus on the interaction of the right to equality with the various "liberty rights"—freedom of expression, religion and association. Here it helps to distinguish two types of case in which equality rights might be invoked. One is where government has acted through the legislature or the administration, and equality rights are invoked by members of a group to contend that they have suffered discrimination. Here the equality right may function as a shield against the imposition of burdens by government, or perhaps as a chisel with which to fine-tune or augment the distribution of benefits so as to include the claimant group. These are the types of cases that Justice Binnie and Hilary Charlesworth are principally concerned with. The second type of case is where government has restricted liberty rights in order to promote the equality rights of particular groups, seeking to protect them from the words and deeds of private actors. Nadine Strossen's contribution takes us into that second field, where she confronts and rejects the claim that restrictions on freedom of expression in the field of pornography and hate speech are justified if they tend to reduce attitudes and acts of discrimination by private actors. This is not, of course, a view born of any lack of concern for those who suffer discrimination. Rather, Strossen's view, and that of the American Civil Liberties Union which she heads, is that these types of restrictions are simply not effective, and worse, that they may often be counterproductive.

In a case of the first type, there will typically be two parties: government, and a claimant group contending that government has discriminated. But in the second type of case, there are typically three parties whose rights and interests are at stake: (1) government, (2) a litigant contending that its *liberty* rights to freedom of expression or association are infringed, and (3) a group in whose *equality* interests government claims to have restricted the litigant's expression or association. It is unlikely that a group in this last category will be a party to the litigation, but it is likely that they will be there as an intervenor.

I want to explore briefly the implications of making a public commitment to equality through bills of rights and anti-discrimination codes, and to ask whether this leaves any room for competing visions about human nature and hence competing visions about what true equality might mean. I then seek to link that inquiry to a second contemporary debate—whether a bill of rights has "indirect horizontal effect" because of the requirement that judges develop a "bill of rights-consistent" common law. Does this mean that a bill of rights indirectly imposes upon private persons and associations a duty to respect the rights (including equality rights) of others, and if this is so is there any room for private dissent from the values and assumptions that the bill of rights affirms?

I   PUBLIC VALUES AND THE NEW ESTABLISHMENT

While the US First Amendment explicitly proscribes the "establishment of religion", modern human rights law tends to conflate the concepts of free exercise and establishment, reducing them to their common denominator of "freedom". A person is not truly free in religious matters if the state takes a religious position and seeks to extract tokens of obeisance to that religion from its citizens. This was the insight of the Supreme Court of Canada in *R* v. *Big M Drug Mart Ltd*, where it held that Sunday observance laws backed by criminal sanctions infringed the freedom of religion of all Canadians, since they were obliged by law to perform a religiously significant act:[1]

> "In proclaiming the standards of the Christian faith, the Act creates a climate hostile to, and
> gives the appearance of discrimination against, non-Christian Canadians. It takes religious

---

[1] [1985] 1 SCR 295, 337.

values rooted in Christian morality and, using the force of the State, translates them into a positive law binding on believers and non-believers alike."

It was no answer that all persons remained free to believe, internally, what they liked. Freedom of religion required freedom from the imposition of a religious position by the state. In short, freedom of religion means freedom *from* religion.

In a secular and pluralistic world the benefits of religious freedom have, of course, been extended more broadly. Article 18 of the International Covenant on Civil and Political Rights (ICCPR) protects freedom of thought, conscience, and belief as well as religion. The right was expanded to protect non-theistic world views. This suggests, logically, a parallel principle of anti-establishment operating in the secular sphere. The right to freedom of "thought, conscience and belief" implies that one must equally be free from the coercion that is wrought when the state proclaims or endorses official "positions" on contestable *non*-religious matters.[2] Indeed, the Human Rights Committee, in General Comment 22 speaks to this very possibility:[3]

> "If a set of beliefs is treated as official ideology in constitutions, statutes, proclamations of ruling parties, etc, or in actual practice, this shall not result in any impairment of the freedoms under article 18 or any other rights under the Covenant nor in any discrimination against persons who do not accept the official ideology or who oppose it."

The reality, of course, is that states must inevitably pursue or affirm ideologies upon which opinions may reasonably differ amongst its citizens. A government's position on matters such as free trade, universal access to public health and pensions, employment law, the way it should treat its citizens, and so on will all reflect some underlying vision and values. For the most part these values will be widely shared in the community, and that will be how they came to be reflected in law in the first place. Criminal law is an obvious example, even though there is debate at its margins (the criminalisation of marijuana, for example). In other areas, law may move ahead of a significant portion of the community, or in a different direction. Even so, everyone is obliged to order their affairs in accordance with the law, even if they withhold their own approval of that law and vigorously seek to change it. That is how democracy works. But the more that laws reach into the private sphere, affecting matters of self-expression and association between citizens, the more onerous may be the imposition on persons and groups who disagree. Their very ability to maintain and propagate competing views and to advance them democratically may be impaired. Indeed, this may be part of the intended effect of some laws, which may explicitly seek to advance some values and discourage others from taking hold.

While bills of rights express the right to equality in general terms, statutory anti-discrimination codes are usually quite specific, and contain a number of provisions that preserve a private and unregulated sphere. Though they regulate employment,

---

[2] For discussion of this in the US context, see M McConnell, "The New Establishmentarianism" (2000) 75 *Chicago Kent L Rev* 453. As will be seen, I adapted part of Professor McConnell's title for my own.

[3] UN Doc HRI/GEN/1/Rev 1 at 35 (1994) para. 10.

for example, anti-discrimination codes usually exclude employment in the home, along with the employment and ordination decisions of religious institutions, and workplaces with small numbers of employees. Though they regulate housing, they usually do not apply to decisions such as the choice of a flatmate, or the rental of a room in one's home. Exemptions from the coverage of anti-discrimination legislation may be quite broad. In New Zealand, for example, the anti-discrimination law does not apply to the membership decisions of private clubs. The values thereby manifested in anti-discrimination laws are respect and tolerance, alongside some conception of a sphere for private and uncompelled virtue (which carries with it, of course, the possibility of divergence from state-espoused virtue). For their part, bills of rights too postulate a private sphere of autonomy; along with protecting life, liberty and security of the person, that is their very purpose. The private sphere has become the battle ground in a series of recent cases, pitting the liberty rights of private associations and persons against the equality rights of groups. These take the pattern of anti-discrimination codes, or similar, being wielded as a sword against private associations which in turn raise constitutional liberty rights as a shield.

In *Boy Scouts of America* v. *Dale* the question was whether the Boy Scouts were bound to admit homosexual leaders to membership.[4] The Scout leadership contended their admission would be contrary to the values of the association. They lost in the New Jersey Supreme Court but a 5–4 majority of the US Supreme Court reversed, holding that the Boy Scouts were entitled to a constitutional exemption from New Jersey's anti-discrimination code in relation to their selection of leaders. The majority rested its decision on the freedom of expressive association enjoyed by Boy Scouts as an institution. Freedom of association is not explicitly protected by the US First Amendment but is held to be a facet of freedom of expression, since groups will often form to express, by their association, a commitment to shared ideas and principles. The key contests in the case became, first, whether the Boy Scouts *had* a message at all about sexual orientation that was capable of First Amendment protection and, second, whether the presence of a gay leader would impair them in expressing it. The flavour of the arguments can be seen from the following extract from the brief of the ACLU which, perhaps surprisingly, intervened on behalf of Dale:[5]

"All that an organization can really be understood to have 'said' by retaining someone protected against discrimination by the civil rights laws is that the organization obeys the law. If anything, that is a message that the Boy Scouts presumably endorses."

But the majority of the Court did not accept this. They held that if the Scouts' leadership asserted a position about homosexuality then it was not for the Court to say the Scouts had no such position. And as to whether compliance with the law by having gay leaders would burden that message, the Court concluded:[6]

---

[4] 530 US 640 (2000).

[5] http://www.aclu.org/court/boyscouts_v_dale.html (visited 23 May 2001).

[6] 530 US 640, 655–6 (2000).

"The presence of an avowed homosexual and gay rights activist in an assistant scout-master's uniform sends a distinctly different message from the presence of a heterosexual assistant scoutmaster who is on record as disagreeing with Boy Scouts policy. The Boy Scouts has a First Amendment right to choose to send one message but not the other."

And, in a passage that one might have thought was straight from an Americal Civil Liberties Union brief, the Court said:[7]

"[T]he fact that an idea may be embraced and advocated by increasing numbers of people is all the more reason to protect the First Amendment rights of those who wish to voice a different view."

The case therefore exemplified the struggle between the freedom of belief for some, and the right of others to be free from discrimination. The 5–4 split reflects the keenness of that struggle.

A broadly similar issue was faced by the Supreme Court of Canada in *British Columbia College of Teachers* v. *Trinity Western University*.[8] The College of Teachers had refused to certify the teacher training programme of a private Christian university on the grounds that its trainees were each required to promise to abstain from homosexual acts. It was said by the College, which had a statutory certification power, that these students were therefore likely to harbour discriminatory attitudes against gay people which may in their subsequent teaching careers manifest as discriminatory acts. But no evidence was adduced about any particular acts of discrimination.[9] This case, too, pitted the liberty right of religious freedom for the university and its students against the equality rights of gay and lesbian school pupils. The Christian University had prevailed in the Court of Appeal, but in a 2–1 split decision. The Supreme Court of Canada affirmed that result by an 8–1 majority, noting that Canada's Constitution and the provincial human rights code each reflected a sphere of protected autonomy for religious institutions which would be impaired if "their graduates are de facto considered unworthy of fully participating in public activities".[10] The threshold at which restrictions were justified, said the Court, is when belief manifests itself in discriminatory *conduct*.[11] It was a legal error for the College to elevate the right to equality over the right simply to hold religious beliefs.

What are we to make of these cases where emanations of the state sought to extract from private organisations the same values that the state has affirmed in its anti-discrimination law?

The UN Human Rights Committee was not oblivious to the inevitability of official positions being taken and the need for protecting dissenters. Its point, made

---

[7] 530 US 640, 660 (2000).

[8] 2001 SCC 31.

[9] This proved the telling gap in the case. As TWU had been training teachers for some years, with only the last year of training taking place outside the institution, one might have expected the danger to have manifested itself, if danger it were. (The case arose because of the College's refusal to allow that final year of instruction and oversight to be operated by TWU.)

[10] *Ibid*, para. 35.

[11] *Ibid*, para. 36.

in relation to religion but equally applicable to non-religious belief, is that when the state takes a position persons must not be penalised for differing from it. State ideologies must, it says, permit full recognition of other freedoms in the Covenant. Two safeguards were mentioned: first, the requirement that laws and practices leave room for the protected freedoms of thought, association and expression (and indeed other Covenant rights); second, that there be no discrimination on the ground of not sharing the ideology.

The question then becomes: what counts as an impairment by the state of freedom of thought or expression, or as discrimination? It cannot be the mere taking of an official position or ideology, because government could not work if that were so. Mere disagreement with a law and its assumptions cannot be a ground for constitutional challenge. There is no guarantee that citizens and groups will be able to maintain their beliefs without some cost, and there are limits to the extent that a state can immunise persons from the inevitable consequence of their being in a minority. The question is really one of degree. At what point does the impairment of thought, conscience and belief become too much? This is ultimately a question of balancing constitutional rights against the legitimate reasons for their limitation, a familiar scenario in modern comparative constitutional law. It is important, however, that the exercise not be distorted by incorrect conceptions about the way in which rights operate. I take that up next.

II INDIRECT HORIZONTALITY

A current controversy, especially in the UK and to a lesser extent in NZ, is the extent to which a bill of rights might be invoked by litigants in private litigation, where no legislation is in issue and hence there is no state action apart from the presence of the judge who will decide the case. The argument for indirect horizontal effect is that the judge must make the common law conform to the dictates of the bill of rights. That ensures its indirect horizontal effect, for it is said that private persons would then need to order their affairs in a manner that conforms to the rights protected by the bill of rights.

The exact nature of the required adjustment to common law is seldom made clear by contributors to this debate, for it is often conducted at a high level of generality. But it assists to begin with two propositions that most would accept. First, it is surely difficult to argue that the totality of a bill of rights is to be replicated as a set of private common law obligations. If that were intended, why would the bills of rights of NZ and the UK not say so directly? In any event, much of the content of bills of rights is simply not apt to this type of replication (consider the right to vote, and the various criminal procedure rights).

The second proposition is that it is quite appropriate for judges to develop the common law with regard to the values affirmed in a bill of rights. After all, what the citizenry has chosen to affirm as beyond the power of *government* is undoubtedly relevant to developing the law between *citizens*, even if not necessarily dispositive. That said, there are some who regard this focus on the "values" of a bill of rights as somehow not capturing the full scope of what a bill of rights ought to mean for the common law and private conduct, and who contend for a stronger judicial obligation—that judges are positively "bound" to apply the Bill of Rights when developing common law applicable between private persons.

I have some difficulty, however, envisaging a real case that might ever turn on whether a judge regarded herself as "bound" in this way, as opposed to being required to consider the values affirmed by the bill of rights.[12] Indeed, the notion of a judge being bound by a bill of rights in their adjudication role is deeply problematic at a conceptual level, for it suggests that judicial decisions at all levels might be conceived (by the disappointed litigant) as fresh *judicial* breaches of a bill of rights justifying fresh proceedings against the judge.[13]

But behind the esoteric debate about judicial obligation lies, I suspect, a much more substantial issue. It concerns competing visions of society and how a bill of rights might transform it. The orthodoxy, of course, is that bills of rights are designed to limit the power of government for the benefit of private persons and institutions. This necessarily presupposes a private sphere, something that will *result* from the enforcement of those limits on government and that explains the reason for a bill of rights in the first place. On that view, the values underlying a bill of rights include that conception of autonomy and liberty alongside all the other rights (including equality of treatment by government).

On the other hand, the rival conception is that bills of rights are or ought to be equally concerned with protecting and promoting the rights of minorities against both public *and* private power, the latter said (not without justification) to be growing in significance in the modern era. It is argued that this conception is justified because the state is ultimately responsible for rights infringements in the private sphere. Its refusal or omission to regulate is tantamount to tacit approval or empowerment of private actors. In that sense government is present everywhere, whether by action or inaction. A bill of rights ought to control it when it is absent as well. The answer, on this alternative view, lies with indirect horizontality, whereby judges are made responsible by a bill of rights for developing the law applicable between private persons in a rights-respecting fashion. This will be relevant not only in deciding what the common law is, but also in other bill of rights applications such as statutory interpretation. It might make a difference even there if one regards private persons as bound to respect rights in the bill of rights.

---

[12] It is notable that even in the flagship case for suggested indirect horizontality of the New Zealand Bill of Rights, the first instance decision in *Lange* v. *Atkinson* [1997] 2 NZLR 22, no election was required between these two conceptions since it was common ground that the bill of rights appropriately informed the development of the common law. Nor did the matter arise in the Court of Appeal ([1998] 3 NZLR 424; [2000] 3 NZLR 385) where in any event the actual significance of the Bill of Rights (however its application might be conceived) to the result reached is not made clear.

[13] It might be said, of course, that judicial immunity precludes actions against a judge based on the content of his or her judgment, but if that is so it merely serves to demonstrate how little really turns on the suggestion that judges are "bound" to make the common law conform to the Bill of Rights. See also L'Heureux-Dubé J in *Dagenais* v. *The Queen* [1994] 3 SCR 835 at 910–11.

Many of the premises of that alternative view can be granted. However, in my view it still does not follow that a bill of rights, as opposed to ordinary legislation, is the means for imposing obligations upon persons to respect the rights of others. Any argument premised on the values of the bill of rights (or, if one prefers, its actual text and not its "values") must reckon with the fact that both text and values affirm a fundamental *difference* between the state and a private citizen. In short: yes, the bill of rights can potentially affect the common law between citizens. But when discerning its impact one must not lose sight of the crucial fact that it is a bill of rights *whose concern is with limiting the power of government*. It is emphatically not intended to require that citizens demonstrate a commitment to the same values as the state. Indeed, in large part, it is designed to preserve the freedom to differ.

The two cases discussed above each raised the horizontal application issue in one of its manifestations. These were, it is true, cases where *government* had acted, either through legislation (as in the *Boy Scouts* Case) or through the exercise of a discretion under legislation (as in the *Trinity Western* Case). They took the form, noted at the outset, of government purporting to act to protect the interests of Group A by restricting the freedom of Group B. But the horizontality issue was latent in these cases since, if a bill of rights is seen as empowering citizens against each other by requiring their relations *inter se* to be informed by bill of rights values, then it is all the easier to say that Group A is owed rights by Group B. The refutation, by those arguing for indirect horizontality, of any truly private sphere therefore diminishes the claim of groups for a right to dissent from the values affirmed in the public sphere. This results in bill of rights litigation taking a new and different hue: instead of government having to justify the restrictions it has placed on the liberty rights of B, we find that B is instead required to defend its own treatment of the equality rights of A. These cases take on the character of a contest between competing rights in the bill of rights, when the true position is that they are in fact a contest between the rights of B and the power of government, albeit a power that may have been exercised in the *interests* of A.

The significance of the point is illustrated by *Living Word Distributors Ltd* v. *Board of Film and Literature Review*,[14] a decision of the Court of Appeal of New Zealand. The context was censorship. New Zealand law allows bans and restrictions on publications that are "objectionable". The test for "objectionable" is whether the publication:[15]

> "describes, depicts, expresses, or otherwise deals with matters such as sex, horror, crime, cruelty, or violence in such a manner that the availability of the publication is likely to be injurious to the public good".

The case concerned two US-made videos dealing with homosexuality from a fundamentalist Christian perspective. One critiqued the move to add sexual orientation to the US Civil Rights Act as a prohibited ground of discrimination. The second was a video made in 1989 about the then growing AIDS problem in the

---

[14] [2000] 3 NZLR 570.
[15] S. 3(1) of the Films, Videos and Publications Classification Act 1993.

United States, contending that the public health response had been hi-jacked by gay activists seeking to legitimise homosexual practices. Though the second video concluded with an exhortation to the religious community to help AIDS sufferers and to donate money for the running of hospices, much of the content of each video was devoted to portraying the homosexual life as promiscuous and given to an array of sexual practices that the videos' makers saw as immoral.

The New Zealand legislation gave further direction to the censorship body in applying the criterion of "objectionable". One provision was especially apposite. This was whether the video:[16]

"Represents (whether directly or by implication) that members of any particular class of the public are inherently inferior to other members of the public by reason of any characteristic of members of that class, being a characteristic that is a prohibited ground of discrimination specified in section 21(1) of the Human Rights Act 1993."

Amongst the prohibited grounds of discrimination in the Human Rights Act is sexual orientation. The videos were said to depict gay and lesbian persons as inherently inferior on that basis, by depicting their lifestyle as immoral and wrong. And so the case shaped as a contest between, on one hand, freedom of expression for the videos' importers and potential viewers in New Zealand and, on the other, freedom from discrimination for gay and lesbian persons. Each group had, it seemed, a right affirmed in the New Zealand Bill of Rights.

The Board of Film and Literature Review saw the case as requiring that it decide which right prevailed. It did not consider the ACLU's argument that they are mutually reinforcing. Indeed, the Board cited instead from an article by a principal exponent of the contrary view, Mari Matsuda.[17] It concluded that the censorship legislation required it to prefer the right against discrimination in priority to the right to freedom of expression. The High Court on appeal agreed, and it was left for the Court of Appeal to correct the error, which it did in these terms:[18]

"[I]n terms of the statutory scheme there is no direct clash of rights. . . . *The Bill of Rights is a limitation on governmental, not private conduct.* The ultimate inquiry under s. 3 involves balancing the rights of a speaker and of the members of the public to receive information under s. 14 of the Bill of Rights as against the state interest under the 1993 Act in protecting individuals from harm caused by the speech. And the fundamental error on the part of the High Court was in treating s. 19 as prevailing over s. 14."

This, of course, is a strong statement of the orthodoxy. It accepts that the *state* was not discriminating against gays and lesbians through its censorship legislation. Indeed, the legislation to be interpreted and applied was seeking to advance the interests of gay and lesbian persons, as well as other protected groups (including religious groups). And it could not be said that *private* persons—such as the videos' makers, importers and potential viewers—owed rights under the Bill of Rights to

---

[16] *Ibid*, s. 3(3)(e).
[17] "Public Response to Racist Speech: Considering the Victim's Story" (1989) 87 *Mich L Rev* 2320.
[18] [2000] 3 NZLR 570, 584 per Richardson P, Gault, Keith and Tipping JJ, emphasis added. I disclose that I was one of the counsel for the appellant in this case.

refrain from that discrimination. This meant that no *Bill of Rights* right was in direct play other than freedom of expression for the videos' importers and potential audience. In affirming that orthodoxy the Court of Appeal returned the Bill of Rights to its appropriate position, and quashed the orders banning the videos.

Of course, nothing in the above analysis precludes the promotion by Government, through law, of equality between groups of citizens. This is a legitimate governmental objective. But the contest must then be conceived as one between the *right* to freedom of expression on the one hand, and the governmental *interest* in affirming egalitarian values amongst its citizens on the other. When this key conception is kept in mind, it becomes apparent that the Bill of Rights does not directly require the imposition of its public values upon private citizens and associations such that private bodies must themselves espouse them. In other words, *Dale* and *Trinity Western* are rightly decided from a New Zealand perspective.

It is important to be clear what the above argument does and does not entail. Murray Hunt describes my position on the horizontal application of a bill of rights as explicitly premised on the liberal ideal that a bill of rights protects a sphere of private autonomy against intrusion by the state. It will be apparent that I accept that characterisation of my position. A private sphere of autonomy and immunity from coercion is the intended result of the proper operation of a bill of rights. But it is necessary to add that the proper scope of the private sphere is always contestable, if only because there is always the possibility of legislation that seeks to regulate the private sphere. The point is that a bill of rights supplies the rules for that contest by assigning considerable weight to the rights that it protects from intrusion by the state. By transmuting the contest into one between competing rights that "clash", we risk losing our commitment to the values that a bill of rights establishes. To repeat, this does not mean that the liberty rights are not capable of limitation in pursuit of other substantial interests. But rights in the bill of rights ought to be given the a priori value that a bill of rights assumes they should have, and not reduced in impact by the elevation to "clashing rights" of what are really "competing interests" advanced to justify their limitation.

7

Equality Rights in Canada: Judicial Usurpation or Missed Opportunities?

JUSTICE IAN BINNIE*

The role and function of Canadian judges in the protection of human equality is controversial. Whatever I say on the topic is likely to aggravate critics of judicial activism and their opponents, the critics of judicial inertia, in about equal measure. At the moment, in Canada, the indignation of the critics of judicial activism is in the ascendant. Our Court recently, by an 8–1 majority,[1] held that the Ontario Family Law Act violated the Canadian Charter of Rights and Freedoms insofar as it excluded same sex couples, whose relationship had soured, from the dispute resolution provisions provided to opposite sex couples. The decision was denounced in Parliament by the Leader of the Opposition.[2] He complained that the decision was pure social policy and as such should be made by elected politicians not appointed judges.

On the other hand, critics of judicial inertia have got in some good licks too. They like to criticise the Supreme Court as a "court of lost opportunities". In a 1995 case involving relationship breakdown between spouses of the *opposite* sex, the Court ruled that it was not discriminatory to impose the tax liability for child support payments wholly on the custodial parent (usually the woman), with a tax deduction wholly to the non-custodial parent (usually the man).[3] In a more recent case, a young widow was outraged that she was refused Charter relief against the denial of a widow's pension.[4] She was told that as a 30 year-old healthy member of the workforce, she could not be considered a member of a disadvantaged group. While there was age differentiation between young widows

---

* Much of the basic research for this paper was done by my law clerk, Cathy Hawara, to whom I am greatly indebted. In discussing the jurisprudence of the Court it is, I hope, self-evident that the views expressed here are entirely my own.

[1] *M & H* v. *Attorney-General of Ontario* [1999] 2 SCR 3.

[2] Preston Manning, Leader of the Reform Party, lamented the fact that the Supreme Court was, as he saw it, becoming the favoured venue for deciding major social policies, rather than the legislatures and Parliament. He criticised "activist" Supreme Court decisions on social policy, pointing to the striking down of abortion laws; deciding how British Columbia must spend scarce health-care dollars; reading "sexual orientation" into the human rights legislation of the province of Alberta when the legislature had explicitly refused to include it; and stripping the legislatures of their authority to set the salaries of judges they appoint.

[3] *Thibaudeau* v. *Canada* [1995] 2 SCR 627.

[4] *Law* v. *Canada (Minister of Employment and Immigration)* [1999] 1 SCR 497.

and older widows, the Court held that this differentiation was unrelated to the mischief for which the framers had crafted equality rights, namely the promotion of human dignity.

I do not intend to wade into the merits of this debate between activism and inertia. The Court has explained its reasons in these cases (at what still another set of critics says is inordinate length). My more modest objective is to put the current debate on judicial activism in a more historical perspective. I want to talk a little about the creation of the Charter in the constitutional debates of 1980 and 1981, the fears of those who saw in it an erosion of parliamentary sovereignty as well as the expectations of those who sought a level of protection for vulnerable minorities which they believed the political system, for all its advantages, had failed to deliver.

I then want to trace in brief outline the evolution of the Court's interpretation of equality rights in section 15 of the Charter, from its initial formulation in *Andrews* v. *Law Society of British Columbia*[5] to its present embodiment in *Law* v. *Canada (Minister of Employment and Immigration)*,[6] *M & H* v. *Attorney-General of Ontario*,[7] and *Corbière* v. *Canada (Minister of Indian and Northern Affairs)*.[8]

I THE VISION

The Canadian Charter of Rights and Freedoms was part of the great constitutional turmoil of 1980–1982.[9] The Trudeau government proposed to patriate the Constitution from the United Kingdom, by which was meant bringing home the power to amend it without resort to Westminster. At the same time, the Charter was entrenched as a human rights limitation on the legislative and executive powers of Canadian governments at both the federal and provincial level.[10] Many people who supported patriation were opposed to the Charter, and resented the Charter and patriation being bundled together in a single legislative package.

The Charter was opposed by several of the ten provincial governments, in some cases on grounds of principle and in some cases for reasons of political strategy.[11] One product of this political negotiation was the addition to the Charter of section

---

[5] [1989] 1 SCR 143.

[6] [1999] 1 SCR 497.

[7] [1999] 2 SCR 3.

[8] [1999] 2 SCR 203.

[9] Political arguments over patriation of the Constitution also caused constitutional turmoil in 1927, 1932, 1967 and 1976.

[10] To the extent that Canadians may also suffer discrimination at the hands of private persons (as opposed to the State), all Canadian jurisdictions have enacted human rights legislation prohibiting discrimination on various grounds.

[11] Newfoundland, for example, sought the transfer of some fisheries jurisdiction from the federal to the provincial government as part of the "patriation package". Trudeau said he couldn't see the logic of bargaining human rights against barrels of fish.

33,[12] which allows legislative bodies to "override" specified provisions of the Charter, including equality rights, for five years, renewable indefinitely.

Trudeau's vision of equality had a certain nobility:[13]

> "The very adoption of a constitutional charter is in keeping with the purest liberalism, according to which all members of a civil society enjoy certain fundamental, inalienable rights and cannot be deprived of them by any collectivity (state or government) or on behalf of any collectivity (nation, ethnic group, religious group, or other). To use Maritain's phrase, they are 'human personalities', they are beings of moral order—that is, free and equal among themselves, *each having absolute dignity and infinite value*. As such, they transcend the accidents of place and time, and partake in the essence of universal Humanity. They are therefore not coercible by any ancestral tradition, being vassals neither of their race, nor to their religion, nor to their condition of birth, nor to their collective history."

I emphasise the words "absolute dignity and infinite value". While the Supreme Court has made it clear that it does not accept an "original intent" approach to constitutional interpretation,[14] it is nevertheless of interest that with the recent decisions in *Law* and *M & H*, concluding almost 15 years of judicial interpretation, this concept of human dignity may have achieved the centrality in section 15 that the framers apparently intended it to have.

II THE CONSTITUTIONAL DEBATES

As part of the patriation exercise, both Houses of the federal Parliament appointed a Special Joint Committee to consider and report on the various issues pertaining

---

[12] "33. (1) Parliament or the legislature of a province may expressly declare in an Act of Parliament or of the legislature, as the case may be, that the Act or a provision thereof shall operate notwithstanding a provision included in section 2 or sections 7 to 15 of this Charter.

(2) An Act or a provision of an Act in respect of which a declaration made under this section is in effect shall have such operation as it would have but for the provision of this Charter referred to in the declaration.

(3) A declaration made under subsection (1) shall cease to have effect five years after it comes into force or on such earlier date as may be specified in the declaration.

(4) Parliament or the legislature of a province may re-enact a declaration made under subsection (1).

(5) Subsection (3) applies in respect of a re-enactment made under subsection (4)."

[13] R Graham (ed.), *The Essential Trudeau* (Toronto, M & S, 1998) 80 (emphasis added).

[14] See *Re British Columbia Motor Vehicle Act* [1985] 2 SCR 486, 509:

"Another danger with casting the interpretation of s. 7 in terms of the comments made by those heard at the Special Joint Committee Proceedings is that, in so doing, the rights, freedoms and values embodied in the *Charter* in effect become frozen in time to the moment of adoption with little or no possibility of growth, development and adjustment to changing societal needs."

Re British Columbia Motor Vehicle Act is an awkward precedent for the critics of judicial activism because the Court refused to read down the words "fundamental justice" to mean no more than procedural justice. The Court explained that in doing so it was merely following the plain meaning of the text of s. 7, as the critics contend the Court should do. Chief Justice Lamer (as he became) reasoned that if the framers had intended no more than procedural justice, they presumably would have used those well-understood words. Use of the word "fundamental", he thought, must betoken something more than procedure. Yet, the decision that s. 7 included "substantive justice" was one of the most controversial in Charter history.

to the Constitution, including the entrenchment of a charter of rights. The Joint Committee sat for over eight weeks and heard representations from 104 individuals and groups, many of them focused on equality rights. The more vociferous their demands, and the more sympathetic the federally constituted Joint Committee appeared to become,[15] the more apprehensive became some of the provincial premiers. Although the Charter was being constructed in Ottawa, its structures would be felt equally in the provincial capitals. Amongst others, Alberta Premier Peter Lougheed and Manitoba Premier Sterling Lyon were strong opponents of the Charter as antithetical to parliamentary supremacy. The flavour of Premier Lougheed's criticism was prophetic, having regard to the Supreme Court's decision in *Vriend*[16] 20 years later to declare unconstitutional the refusal of Alberta's provincial legislature to recognise sexual orientation as a prohibited ground of discrimination:[17]

> "The principle of legislative supremacy would be undermined. The courts would become the chief forum for determining what is permissible under an entrenched bill of rights. To a great extent, this has been the case in the United States. One of the consequences has been to involve the courts in the adjudication of a wide range of social questions, which in the interests of society are best debated and resolved in legislatures."

Premier Sterling Lyon of Manitoba sounded similar warnings during the Federal-Provincial Conference of First Ministers on the Constitution:[18]

---

[15] The present Prime Minister, Mr Jean Chrétien, was the Minister of Justice and Attorney-General of Canada at the time.

[16] *Vriend* v. *Alberta* [1998] 1 SCR 493.

[17] Premier Lougheed's position was put forward in a paper entitled "Harmony in Diversity: A New Federalism for Canada" (Government of Alberta, 1978) 22:

> "The Government of Alberta believes that the rights of Alberta citizens are well protected by the [ordinary statutes] *Alberta Bill of Rights* and the *Alberta Individual's Rights Protection Act*. The primacy clauses of these acts and the upholding of their provisions by the courts has provided the best protection of rights for Albertans.
>
> While there are many proposals for and against entrenchment of human rights in the Constitution, it can be argued that the best guarantee of rights is a vigilant legislature which can take the necessary steps to ensure that the rights of citizens are safeguarded and meet the demands and needs of a changing society. This argument is based upon the concept that the role of legislatures in protecting rights would be significantly diminished if a bill of rights were to be entrenched in the Constitution. . . . Legally enacted bills of rights do not preclude the courts from upholding these rights. The commitment of legislatures to guarantee rights is best secured by incorporating primacy provisions, such as are found in Alberta's legislation.
>
> Further, to entrench rights in the Constitution is to risk the limitation of rights not enumerated therein, to make it very difficult to amend these rights, and to limit the scope of their application."

[18] Premier Lyon elaborated the point in his September 9, 1980 speech in the Manitoba Legislature.

> "The system of Parliamentary responsible democracy which exists in Canada recognizes and protects the rights of our citizens on an evolving basis, without making judgments as to which rights are fundamental and which are of only secondary importance.
>
> A decision to entrench a Charter of Rights, Prime Minister, would, in effect, move our familiar and traditional and successful Parliamentary form of government towards that of a republican system—replacing a system of protection of rights that has worked in Canada for 113 years with a system that, with respect, has not worked as well in the United States.
>
> There is no historical justification for the entrenchment of a Charter of Rights in the Canadian Constitution. The need for such a fundamental change in our system cannot be demonstrated."

"Prime Minister, you have described the entrenchment of a Charter of Rights as a mechanism that would give more power to the people. In fact, Sir, it takes power from the people and places it in the hands of men, albeit men learned in law, but not necessarily aware of every day concerns of Canadians."

The controversial aspect of the Charter was thus not so much the vision of human rights it embodied as fear of the intrusive policy role it seemed to confer on the judges. One wag suggested that the Charter would represent the greatest transfer of power in history from elected Liberals to the unelected Liberals whom the elected Liberals had put on the bench.

One of the groups most apprehensive of this qualitative jump in judicial power was the judiciary.[19] The report of a former distinguished Chief Justice of Ontario, Chief Justice James McRuer, was wheeled out to combat the Charter-ites. In his report, he contrasted the purity of the Canadian model with what he saw as an American "constitutional straight jacket" south of the border:[20]

---

[19] Justice Jean Beetz of the Supreme Court of Canada was heard to complain that the politicians had changed job descriptions on him without consultation. Justice Lamer, now our Chief Justice, made a similar point in a speech to the Empire Club of Canada:

"Some people speak as if these new responsibilities under the *Charter* are simply judges seeking more power. Nothing could be further from the truth. The judiciary did not seek these responsibilities and we certainly did not assign them to ourselves. They were given to, indeed imposed upon, the judiciary by politicians. It was a job given to us, either deliberately or by default, by the democratic process. As for the suggestion that judges intrude into the legislative sphere, the truth is that many of the toughest issues we have had to deal with have been left to us by the democratic process. The legislature can duck them. We can't. Think of abortion, euthanasia, same sex benefits to name a few. Our job is to decide the cases properly before us to the best of our abilities. We can't say we are too busy with other things or that the issue is too politically sensitive to set up a royal commission. We do our duty and decide."

Quoted in Epstein J's reasons in *M* v. *H* (1996) 132 DLR (4th) 538, 564 (Ont Gen Div).

[20] The following passage from his report, *Royal Commission: Inquiry into Civil Rights* (Toronto: Queen's Printer, 1969) 1591, was read to the Special Joint Committee:

"In considering the entrenchment method versus the definition of human rights by ordinary statute we must keep clearly in mind the age of rapid social change that we live in—change that is hard to foresee. Behind the accelerating rate of change lie the new technologies that have come from a great explosion of new knowledge in the natural sciences. A similar and related explosion is going on in the social sciences of which the advance of learning and knowledge in politics and law are a part."

[After deploring the US "constitutional straight jacket", he continued (pp. 1592–3)]

"The modern democratic Parliament on the British model, which we have in Canada at the Federal level and in the Provinces, not only has the superior constitutional title for privacy in major decisions of social policy, but it has the matching institutional design and procedure. It does not focus on special individual conflicts as the courts are bound to do but on social problems in a general way. Royal commissions and parliamentary committees can conduct hearings and investigations where a great variety of interested parties and experts may make their reasoned submissions. The whole expertise of the civil service is directly available. Then, after due deliberation, the government can stand behind a statutory solution that deals with law reform and control of social problems with as much generality and particularity as the social need for regulation and the use of public resources seems to call for. The fact is that the well drafted statute passed in a democratic parliament under the cabinet system with full debate and under scrutiny of freely expressed public opinion is the most flexible and sophisticated form of law making available under a constitutional system that puts human individual rights first."

"There is both need and pressure for government to know more and do more about more things. In these circumstances governments dare not lock themselves into a constitutional straitjacket where repeated deadlock is likely in the solution of grave social problems. This is precisely what has happened in the past in the United States and what we would do if we followed the American example of sweeping judicial supremacy for life-appointed judges over the democratic legislative body that contains the elected representatives of the people."

Others feared the judiciary for the opposite reason. They saw judges less as legal revolutionaries than as defenders of the establishment. They wanted the Charter to speak with such aggressive clarity that even the most inert bench would be unable to interpret it into virtual extinction, as they believed had been done in the 1960s and 1970s to the Canadian Bill of Rights.

The chosen field of battle for these contending forces was the Parliamentary Joint Committee. More than any other provision of the Charter, the language of section 15 ("equality rights") reflects the contributions of public interest groups. They criticised the draft wording of section 15(1) because it offered limited non-discrimination guarantees rather than a broad equality right. During the Special Joint Committee's clause-by-clause consideration of the Charter, a number of amendments were proposed and accepted. Section 15(1), as amended, was re-styled "Equality Rights". There is no need here to belabour the details. It is, however, of interest to set out the two versions side by side.

The original draft:

"Non-discrimination rights
Everyone has the right to equality before the law and to the equal protection of the law without discrimination because of race, national or ethnic origin, colour, religion, age or sex."

The final version:

"Equality rights
Every individual is equal before and under the law and has the right to the equal protection and equal benefit of the law without discrimination and, in particular, without discrimination based on race, national or ethnic origin, colour, religion, sex, age or mental or physical disability."

You will note that addition of the words "and, in particular" was seemingly designed to bifurcate the section, thereby liberating the first branch (the broad equality right) from the confines of the second branch (the traditional grounds of prohibited discrimination). In so far as the Court was later criticised for engaging in social engineering under the guise of "interpreting" section 15 without a political mandate, it is worth emphasizing the very specific political mandate reflected in these sweeping amendments in section 15(1).

III MIXED EXPECTATIONS IN THE EARLY YEARS

The framers of the Charter delayed the implementation of section 15 for three years in order to allow legislatures the time needed to undertake what was expected to be a massive overhaul of legislation to reflect the newly entrenched equality guarantee. The delay, combined with the broad language of the section itself, caused many minorities to hold out high hopes for the effective pursuit of equality rights before the courts.

Others were more sanguine. I had a good vantage point from which to see events unfold. In September 1982, I was appointed Associate Deputy Minister of Justice for the federal government, and, until returning to private practice four years later, had overall responsibility for the conduct of the government's early Charter cases. The bureaucracy took a more modest view of the Charter than did the Prime Minister. There was a sense that, subject to a few bells and whistles, things in the courts would go on pretty much as before. We soldiered on in support of writs of assistance,[21] if exercised reasonably, Her Majesty's prerogative to test cruise missiles if she wanted to,[22] and even went into battle to defend the religiously-problematic Lord's Day Act on the basis that, although religious in origin, Sunday had become for most people simply a "pause day" without much religious significance.[23]

The limited view of the Charter advocated by the federal Department of Justice reassured some Charter critics. Premier Sterling Lyon of Manitoba even accepted an appointment to the Manitoba Court of Appeal.

On the other side of the ideological divide, so to speak, the critics of judicial inertia more or less dared the judges to live up to the Charter's potential. In 1983, the late Professor Walter Tarnopolsky, subsequently a judge of the Ontario Court of Appeal, warned that the "timid judiciary" would need "courage enough to take up the challenge". He wrote:[24]

> "[I]ncluding a bill of rights in the basic constitutional document and providing for its entrenchment in that document could be, and probably is, important . . . to convince a reluctant judiciary that the legislators were serious when they attempted to adopt a bill of rights that would have overriding effect. Thus, since the newly agreed-on charter would constitute Part I of the Constitution Act, 1982, its status as a constitutional and entrenched bill of rights can no longer be denigrated by a timid judiciary."

Equality rights, in particular, became a focus of expectation. Professor Peter Hogg, one of New Zealand's least sheep-like exports to Canada, described section 15 as potentially the "most intrusive provision of the Charter".[25] David Harris, in an article entitled "Equality, Equality Rights and Discrimination under the Charter of Rights and Freedoms",[26] argued that judges

---

[21] *R v. Sieben* [1987] 1 SCR 295; *R v. Hamill* [1987] 1 SCR 301.

[22] *Operation Dismantle Inc v. R* [1985] 1 SCR 441.

[23] *R v. Big M Drug Mart* [1985] 1 SCR 295.

[24] W Tarnopolsky, "Human Rights and Constitutional Options for Canada" in S M Beck and I Bernier (eds.), *Canada and the New Constitution: The Unfinished Agenda*, vol. 1 (Montreal, The Institute for Research on Public Policy, 1983) 281, 291.

[25] P Hogg, *Constitutional Law of Canada*, 2nd edn. (Toronto, Carswell, 1985) 797.

[26] (1987) 21 *UBC L Rev* 389.

"are being asked to turn their backs on the traditional understandings of "equality before the law", associated in the Anglo-Canadian tradition with Dicey, and to embrace with enthusiasm the equal protection jurisprudence of the United States".

Professor Lynn Smith, in an article entitled "A New Paradigm for Equality Rights,"[27] continued the drumbeat:

"The significance of the paradigm shift embodied in the Charter will be felt, if it occurs, in the next decades. If it does not occur, it will be because it has been thwarted through inertia, resistance to change, or opposition to the kinds of equality principles it entails, since the potential for it in the *Charter* is clear."

Of course, court watchers who didn't share this enthusiasm for judicial activism had their champions as well. Professor Marc Gold advocated a more modest view of the courts' role as guardians of the Constitution:[28]

"[T]he courts ought to respect the pluralism in the allocation of values that is inherent in the conception of justice implicit in the Charter. Only where it is clear that the legislation was enacted in disregard of the inherent worth and dignity of the class burdened by the law should the courts intervene. In approaching this question, a court should be modest in its assumption that it alone understands what does or does not abrogate human dignity. Assuming that the political process is functioning tolerably well, such cases will be rare."

With conflicting expectations on both fronts, the Supreme Court was left to give meaning and content to a constitutional equality guarantee which seemingly was given few outside boundaries by the framers.

IV THE GRAMMATICAL STRUCTURE OF SECTION 15

Four specific equality rights are guaranteed to every Canadian under section 15(1), namely equality "*before* and *under* the law and . . . the right to the equal *protection* and equal *benefit* of the law *without discrimination*" (emphasis added). As mentioned earlier, section 15 as amended in the Joint Committee is double-barreled. The broad concept of equality is accompanied by an anti-discrimination provision listing nine enumerated personal characteristics (ie, race, national or ethnic origin, colour, religion, sex, age, or mental or physical disability). Grammatically, these personal characteristics are presented as a subset of equality ("and, in particular"). In practice, some observers of the Court's section 15 jurisprudence claim that the sub-clause came to swallow up the broader right to equality. Discrimination on the basis of personal characteristics certainly emerged as the controlling concept in the elaboration of equality rights in Canada.

---

[27] L Smith et al (eds.), *Righting the Balance: Canada's New Equality Rights* (Saskatoon, The Canadian Human Rights Reporter Inc, 1986) 355, 383.

[28] M Gold, "A Principled Approach to Equality Rights: A Preliminary Inquiry" (1982) 4 *Supreme Court L R* 131, 158.

As I will point out in a moment, the critics of judicial activism who advocate a "plain meaning" of the Charter have a difficult time making their case on section 15. A plain meaning approach would probably extend, not reduce the scope given by the judiciary to equality rights. Judicial activism, in that sense, has resulted in a contraction, not an expansion, of judicial policy making.

Another key issue that emerged was the relationship between section 15 and section 1, which subordinates freedom from discrimination (however broadly or narrowly defined) to "such reasonable limits as are demonstrably justified in a free and democratic society".[29] The issue was whether the balancing of individual rights against the collective values of society should take place within section 15 (in the US style) or only in section 1 (an idea that Canada borrowed in part from the European Convention on Human Rights). Professor Peter Hogg opted for the latter, advocating that:[30]

"[w]hen a law draws a distinction between individuals, *on any ground*, that distinction is sufficient to constitute a breach of s. 15, and to move the constitutional issue to s. 1".

A second school of thought considered that some of the balancing should be done in section 15 itself, before resort to section 1. They argued that the word "discrimination" imported into the section 15 analysis the concepts of "reasonableness", "rationality" and "fairness".[31] While the Supreme Court largely agreed with Professor Hogg on the need to confine social justification to section 1 of the Charter, the Court rejected his more generous approach to the grounds of inequality. The Court concluded that a legislative distinction did not necessarily amount to discrimination.

V THE FALSE SUNRISE

Some of the judges in these early Charter cases, perhaps ignited by the Trudeau vision, perhaps emboldened by the respected Professor Hogg's generous approach to section 15, opened the courts to all kinds of inequality complaints that had nothing to do with personal attributes or characteristics. A glance at these cases shows

[29] S. 1, a unique feature of the Canadian Charter of Rights and Freedoms, is a limiting provision pursuant to which the state can attempt to justify its infringement of a guaranteed right or freedom, thus safeguarding an impugned state action. The Supreme Court had already stated that the right guaranteeing sections must be kept "analytically separate from s. 1" (*Andrews* v. *Law Society of British Columbia* [1989] 1 SCR 143, 178). The main reason for this separation is the different attribution of the burden of proof. As McIntyre J states in *Andrews*, "[i]t is for the citizen to establish that his or her *Charter* right has been infringed and for the state to justify the infringement" (*ibid*). S. 1 provides as follows:

The *Canadian Charter of Rights and Freedoms* guarantees the rights and freedoms set out in it subject only to such reasonable limits prescribed by law as can be demonstrably justified in a free and democratic society.

[30] P Hogg, above n. 26 at 800 (emphasis added).
[31] The decision of McLachlin JA (as she then was) of the Court of Appeal for British Columbia in *Andrews* v. *Law Society of British Columbia* (1986) 27 DLR (4th) 600 was a leading proponent of this school of thought.

what section 15 might have become had the courts pushed ahead with the "plain meaning" interpretation, as opposed to a "purposive" interpretation, of section 15(1).

In *Streng* v. *Township of Winchester* [32] the plaintiff was involved in a motor vehicle accident as a result of which he sustained severe injuries. He alleged a breach by the Township of its duty to keep the roadway in good repair. Pleading the distraction of his prolonged hospitalisation, he failed to commence his action until after the expiry of the abbreviated three-month limitation period applicable to claims against municipalities. He mounted a constitutional attack on the limitation period, alleging a violation of his equality rights as guaranteed by section 15(1) of the Charter. He argued that he should not be defeated by a special limitation not confronted by plaintiffs who had the good fortune to be injured by someone other than a municipal employee. Smith J, of the Ontario High Court of Justice, agreed that there was a *prima facie* breach of section 15(1):[33]

> "[M]ust there be 'discrimination' based upon human attributes and characteristics before s. 15 is triggered? As already indicated, I think not.
>
> It seems to me that s. 15 should be so interpreted as to allow the courts to strike down all irrelevant or unreasonable classifications that result in certain individuals having the benefit of a law or the protection of a right, in this instance the right to claim damages, and yet in the case of other individuals similarly situated having the same right taken away. The class created here is that of persons suffering personal injuries as a result of the negligence of others. The class may be further narrowed by including only those suffering injuries in car accidents. All members of such a class are entitled to expect, in the normal course, to be treated alike."

Smith J ultimately found the shortened limitation period to be an infringement of the plaintiff's equality rights guaranteed by section 15(1) which could not be saved under section 1 of the Charter. Smith J ordered the action against the township be allowed to go forward. This decision was never appealed.

Jones v. *Ontario (Attorney General)* [34] involved another broad equality challenge. In that case the applicant, a full-time fire-fighter, intended to run as a candidate in an upcoming civic election. Section 38(1) of the Municipal Act [35] required him to resign from his position with the fire department in the event of his election to the council. Other candidates did not face this loss of livelihood. The applicant sought a declaration that this "discriminatory" provision was of no force or effect as against him pursuant to s. 52(1) of the Constitution Act 1982. According to Reid J, "[s]ection 38 clearly draws a line between those who may run in a municipal election without having to sacrifice their employment and those who may not."[36]

While he agreed with the applicant that this constituted an infringement of his equality rights, he found this infringement to be justified in a free and democratic

---

[32] (1986) 31 DLR (4th) 734 (Ont HC).
[33] *Ibid*, 741.
[34] (1988) 65 OR (2d) 737 (Ont HC).
[35] RSO 1980, c 302.
[36] (1988) 65 OR (2d) 737, 741.

society pursuant to section 1 of the Charter. The application was consequently dismissed, but the broad equality principle was affirmed.

One final example. In *Piercey Estate* v. *General Bakeries Ltd*[37] the plaintiff was the widow of one of the defendant's employees, who died while performing his employment duties. As the deceased's dependent, she filed a claim with the Workers' Compensation Commission for benefits as the surviving dependent spouse and was duly paid compensation. She considered the quantum of the benefits to be unsatisfactory. She therefore commenced a legal action against the defendant for the damages suffered as a result of its negligence. In its defence, the employer invoked the protection of sections 32 and 34 of the Workers' Compensation Act 1983, which stated that the right to compensation under the Act was in lieu of all other rights of action. In turn, the plaintiff challenged the constitutionality of these statutory provisions denying her the same access to the courts as other tort victims possessed. Chief Justice Hickman decided that the bar in the impugned Workman's Compensation Act was unconstitutional. The right to litigate in the courts is a fundamental right, he ruled, and went on to say:[38]

> "No substitute has been devised, to date, to replace the courts as the guardian of the liberty and freedom of all Canadians and to deprive a class of citizens of access to the courts is at variance with the intent of the *Charter* and in particular, s. 15 thereof."

Hickman CJ concluded that this violation of section 15(1) was not justified under section 1 of the Charter. However, as the Charter did not apply retrospectively to save her action, the particular claim was dismissed.[39]

This broad interpretation of equality rights under section 15(1) of the Charter, based on what the judges considered the "plain meaning" of the text, obviously engaged the courts in assessing the policy merits of a wide variety of classifications and distinctions. This raised new concerns about the respective roles of the courts and the legislatures. The concerns were apparently shared by the judges of the Supreme Court of Canada.

In 1989, the Supreme Court finally pronounced itself on the framework to be applied to equality claims under section 15(1) of the Charter. In *Andrews* v. *Law Society of British Columbia*[40] McIntyre J, for the Court, rejected Professor Hogg's emphasis on the broad equality rights and instead found the words "without discrimination" to be a "form of qualifier built into s. 15 itself" which serves to "*limit* those distinctions which are forbidden by the section".[41] The *Andrews* decision

---

[37] (1986) 31 DLR (4th) 373 (Nfld SC).

[38] *Ibid*, 384.

[39] As Hickman CJ's view on the breach of s. 15 was expressed in *obiter*, this issue was referred by the Lieutenant-Governor in Council to the Newfoundland Court of Appeal, which subsequently found that no violation of s. 15 had occurred; while the regime did create an inequality, it was not sufficient to condemn the impugned legislation under the Charter. The Supreme Court, in reasons delivered orally by La Forest J, dismissed the appeal. I intend to return shortly to this decision of the Supreme Court.

[40] [1989] 1 SCR 143.

[41] *Ibid*, 181 (emphasis added).

effectively closed the door to a large number of section 15 claims which had previously been moving confidently through the courts.

VI THE SUPREME COURT'S FIRST PRONOUNCEMENTS ON SECTION 15(1):
ANDREWS v. LAW SOCIETY OF BRITISH COLUMBIA

Mark Andrews, a British citizen and graduate of Oxford University, challenged the constitutional validity of section 42 of the Barristers and Solicitors Act,[42] which allowed only Canadian citizens to be called to the bar of British Columbia. Permanently resident in Canada, he satisfied all requirements other than Canadian citizenship for admission to the Law Society. He commenced legal proceedings for a declaration that the impugned provision of the Barristers and Solicitors Act violated section 15(1) of the Charter. Unsuccessful before the Supreme Court of British Columbia,[43] he appealed to the Court of Appeal of that province, where his appeal was allowed.[44] In the Supreme Court of Canada,[45] three judges wrote opinions: the reasons of McIntyre J had the support of the majority of the Court with respect to the section 15(1) issue, while Wilson J commanded the support of a differently composed majority on the section 1 determination. The appeal was accordingly dismissed.

McIntyre J began his analysis with his concept of equality. He stated that section 15(1) was not to be considered a general guarantee of equality and that not every difference in treatment would necessarily result in constitutionally prohibited inequality. Furthermore, in what was seen as a great step forward for the protection of equality rights, McIntyre J rejected as seriously deficient the "similarly situated" test which required that individuals similarly situated should be treated similarly, whereas individuals who were differently situated should be treated differently. In other words, as long as the similarly situated individuals were equally discriminated against, there could be no violation of equality rights.[46] McIntyre J

---

[42] RSBC 1979, c 26.

[43] (1985) 22 DLR (4th) 9, per Taylor J.

[44] (1986) 27 DLR (4th) 600, per McLachlin JA for Hinkson and Craig JJA.

[45] The following constitutional questions were formulated by the Chief Justice ([1989] 1 SCR 143, 159):

"(1) Does the Canadian citizenship requirement to be a lawyer in the province of British Columbia as set out in s. 42 of the *Barristers and Solicitors Act*, RS.B.C. 1979, c. 26 infringe or deny the rights guaranteed by s. 15(1) of the *Canadian Charter of Rights and Freedoms*?

(2) If the Canadian citizenship requirement to be a lawyer in the province of British Columbia as set out in s. 42 of the *Barristers and Solicitors Act*, R.S.B.C. 1979, c. 26 infringes or denies the rights guaranteed by s. 15(1) of the *Canadian Charter of Rights and Freedoms*, is it justified by s. 1 of the *Canadian Charter of Rights and Freedoms*?"

[46] This test reached a zenith of sorts in the Supreme Court's decision in *Bliss* v. *Attorney General of Canada* [1979] 1 SCR 183. In that case, a pregnant woman who was denied unemployment benefits because of her pregnancy, challenged the relevant sections of the Unemployment Insurance Act 1971 as being inconsistent with the provisions of s. 1(b) of the Canadian Bill of Rights. The Court found that there could be no discrimination on the basis of sex since all pregnant women were equally being denied the benefits the claimant had sought to obtain.

rejected this concept of equality as formalistic, noting that it could have been used to justify Nazi treatment of the Jewish population in Europe.[47] Nevertheless, his view was that not *all* distinctions should be considered even *prima facie* violations of section 15 of the Charter.

To determine which distinctions would be acceptable under section 15(1), McIntyre J first looked to the language of the provision. He acknowledged that the specific inclusion of the four equality rights was "an attempt to remedy some of the shortcomings of the right to equality in the *Canadian Bill of Rights*", as well as a reflection of "the expanded concept of discrimination being developed under the various Human Rights Codes since the enactment of the *Canadian Bill of Rights*".[48] McIntyre J considered section 15 to have a large remedial component, but was quick to add that equality rights had been granted with the express direction that they be *without discrimination*. As he considered that the concept of "discrimination" was the central feature of section 15, it became essential to offer a definition of that concept. McIntyre J wrote:[49]

> "I would say then that discrimination may be described as a distinction, whether intentional or not but based on grounds relating to *personal characteristics* of the individual or group, which has the effect of imposing burdens, obligations, or disadvantages on such individual or group not imposed upon others, or which withholds or limits access to opportunities, benefits, and advantages available to other members of society. Distinctions based on *personal characteristics* attributed to an individual solely on the basis of association with a group will rarely escape the charge of discrimination, while those based on an individual's merits and capacities will rarely be so classed."

Having considered both the concepts of equality and discrimination and their relative importance in section 15 challenges, the final issue to be considered before an analytical framework could be set out was the issue of justification. The extent of the protection offered by section 15(1) would be determined by the respective roles assigned to sections 1 and 15 of the Charter in the analytical framework.

Having rejected the "open grounds" approach advocated by Professor Hogg, McIntyre J went on to reject the still more restrictive approach advanced by McLachlin JA (as she then was) in the Court of Appeal's decision in *Andrews*. This approach, which imported the limiting concepts of "reasonableness" and "fairness" into the section 15 analysis, permitted important balancing of values to take place in the definition of the equality right itself, and downplayed the importance of section 1. Its principal impact was to increase the onus on the claimant to prove the violation of the right and to reduce the number of cases where the government would be called upon to justify an infringement. In the end, McIntyre J opted for a third approach, described as the "enumerated or analogous grounds" approach. Under this approach, section 15(1) is considered to include a built-in qualifier ("without discrimination") and is limited to the prohibition of discrimination based

---

[47] [1989] 1 SCR 143, 166.
[48] *Ibid*, 170.
[49] *Ibid*, 174–5 (emphasis added).

on "enumerated or analogous grounds" relating to the personal attributes of the claimant. In McIntyre J's words:[50]

> "The third or "enumerated and analogous grounds" approach most closely accords with the purposes of s. 15 and the definition of discrimination outlined above and leaves questions of justification to s. 1."

In summary, McIntyre J adopted a purposive rather than a "plain words" approach to section 15(1). He held that when courts are faced with a section 15 challenge, the claimant must show (a) "that he or she is not receiving equal treatment before and under the law or that the law has a differential impact on him or her in the protection or benefit accorded by law"; (b) that the distinction be based on an enumerated or analogous ground [personal characteristics]; and (c) that the distinction involves prejudice or disadvantage to the claimant. If the court is satisfied that the claimant has discharged his or her burden of proof,[51]

> "any justification, any consideration of the reasonableness of the enactment; indeed, any consideration of factors which could justify the discrimination and support the constitutionality of the impugned enactment would take place under section 1."

As mentioned earlier, at the section 1 stage, the burden of proof lies on the person relying on the impugned provision, usually the government.

In *Andrews* itself, McIntyre J found that a legislative distinction between citizens and non-citizens was discriminatory. The discrimination in this case was not based on an enumerated ground. However, McIntyre J held that citizenship was an *analogous* ground as non-citizens are a good example of a "'discrete and insular minority' who come within the protection of s. 15".[52] The words "in particular" showed that the *enumerated* personal characteristics in section 15 were not intended to be exhaustive.

McIntyre J wrote for the majority of the Supreme Court with respect to section 15. However, as noted above, he was outvoted with regard to the outcome of the section 1 analysis.[53] Whereas in *Oakes* the Court had said the justification for any Charter breach had to be related to "concerns which are pressing and substantial", both McIntyre and La Forest JJ (in dissent) were of the view that the *pressing and substantial*[54] standard was too onerous for the legislatures. They considered it suffi-

---

[50] [1989] 1 SCR 182.

[51] *Ibid.*

[52] *Ibid*, 183.

[53] *Ibid*, 158.

[54] The analysis to be conducted when considering the possible justification of the infringement under s. 1 was set out by Chief Justice Dickson in R v. *Oakes* [1986] 1 SCR 103, 138–9. It is necessary that the objective underlying the impugned statute or governmental action relates "to concerns which are pressing and substantial in a free and democratic society before it can be characterized as sufficiently important". Then, it must be shown "that the means chosen are reasonable and demonstrably justified. This involves 'a form of proportionality test'". The Chief Justice went on to state:

> "There are, in my view, three important components of a proportionality test. First, the measures adopted must be carefully designed to achieve the objective in question. They must not be arbitrary, unfair or based on irrational considerations. In short, they must be rationally connected to the objective. Second, the means, even if rationally connected to the objective in this first sense, should impair

cient to say the "*legitimate* exercise of the legislative power for the attainment of a *desirable* social objective"[55] satisfied the first step of the section 1 inquiry. Under this more deferential approach, McIntyre and La Forest JJ found the violation of section 15 to be saved under section 1. They would have allowed the appeal and dismissed the complaint.

However, Wilson J, speaking for the majority on the section 1 issue, maintained the traditional *Oakes* burden on the state and wrote that while this burden might have been excessive had *every* distinction been found to be a violation of section 15, this was not the test espoused by the Court. The "pressing and substantial" standard was most appropriate in light of the more tightly circumscribed grounds of discrimination. She held that the infringement of Andrews' equality rights could not be justified in a free and democratic society. Consequently, the appeal was dismissed and Mr Andrews got his admission to the bar of British Columbia, where he continues in active practice, already a historic figure before the age of 40.

Andrews is a tough sell for those who profess to be alarmed about judicial activism. Earlier decisions such as *Streng, Jones*, and *Piercy Estate* had proven to be false harbingers of a new judicial order. The Court had, it is true, given a reasonably generous interpretation to the way in which personal attributes or characteristics could be used in the section 15 analysis, but this was already familiar ground in the interpretation of provincial human rights legislation. Critics of judicial activism complain that judges sometimes have insufficient sensitivity to the limits of the institutional competence of the courts to receive, sift and analyse social science evidence and to pronounce upon policy options. In *Andrews*, I think, the Court recognised, as much as anything else, the limitations to its constitutional role and institutional competence. The judges shrank from the mandate arguably conferred by the "plain text" of section 15(1) as amended by the Joint Committee. They preferred "purpose" to "plain text" for the many very good reasons that are littered through the jurisprudence. The result, however, was to contract rather than expand their job description.

VII THE DOWNDRAFT CREATED BY *ANDREWS*

Two other decisions of the Supreme Court must also be considered at this juncture in order to draw an accurate picture of the Court's early pronouncements on section 15(1) of the Charter. The first was *Re Workers' Compensation Act, 1983* (Nfld).[56] At the heart of this reference, as mentioned earlier, was a continuation of the issues raised in *Piercy Estate*. The provincial government sought a determination of the constitutionality of the provisions of the Workers' Compensation Act,

---

'as little as possible' the right or freedom in question: *R v. Big M Drug Mart Ltd* . . . Third, there must be a proportionality between the *effects* of the measures which are responsible for limiting the *Charter* right or freedom, and the objective which has been identified as of 'sufficient importance' ".

[55] [1989] 1 SCR 143, 184, per McIntyre J (emphasis added).
[56] [1989] 1 SCR 922.

which provided that the right to compensation under that Act was in lieu of all other rights of action. The Court of Appeal for Newfoundland disagreed with the trial judge and declared that the impugned sections passed muster under section 15(1) of the Charter. There was thus no need to call for a section 1 justification. The Supreme Court agreed. The personal attributes or characteristics of the claimant were not the basis of the denial of access to the courts and the complaint thus fell outside the "purposive interpretation" of section 15(1) developed in *Andrews*.[57]

The second decision, released shortly after *Andrews*, was *R v. Turpin*.[58] In that appeal, the Court considered the constitutional validity of certain provisions of the Criminal Code which granted residents of the province of Alberta charged with murder the right to elect trial by judge alone, while residents of all other provinces and territories were required to be tried by judge and jury.[59] The accused in this case were charged in Ontario but, nevertheless, wanted to be tried by a judge sitting without a jury. They challenged the constitutional validity of the relevant sections of the Criminal Code, claiming that these infringed upon their rights to equality without discrimination on the basis of residence.[60]

Wilson J, writing for a unanimous Court, applied the *Andrews* framework and first considered whether the effect of the impugned provisions was to deny the appellants any of their four basic equality rights under section 15. Defining the right to equality before the law "purposively" as a right "designed to advance the value that all persons be subject to the equal demands and burdens of the law and not suffer any greater disability in the substance and application of the law than others",[61] Wilson J nevertheless concluded that only differential treatment which is "discriminatory" for purposes of section 15(1) is a distinction based on the "*personal characteristics*" of the individual or group. According to Wilson J, section 15(1) was designed to remedy or prevent discrimination against those "groups suffering social, political and legal disadvantage in our society".[62] She found that it could not be said of the appellants that they were members of such a "discrete and insular minority".[63] The interest advanced by the appellants was not the kind of interest section 15 was intended to protect. As the appellants did not "constitute a disadvantaged group in

---

[57] La Forest J stated briefly (*ibid* at 924):

"We are all of the view that *The Workers' Compensation Act, 1983*, S.N. 1983, c. 48 . . . does not, in these circumstances, constitute discrimination within the meaning of s. 15(1) of the *Canadian Charter of Rights and Freedoms* as elaborated by this Court in *Andrews* v. *Law Society of British Columbia* [1989] 1 S.C.R. 143, subsequent to the filing of a notice of appeal as of right. The situation of the workers and dependents here is in no way analogous to those listed in s. 15(1) as a majority in *Andrews* stated was required to permit recourse to s. 15(1). The appeal is accordingly dismissed".

[58] [1989] 1 SCR 1296.

[59] It should be noted that the relevant provisions of the *Criminal Code* were amended during the course of the proceedings.

[60] This case makes an interesting comparison with *Corbière* v. *Canada (Minister of Indian and Northern Affairs)* [1999] 2 SCR 203.

[61] [1989] 1 SCR 1296, 1329.

[62] *Ibid*, 1333.

[63] *Ibid*.

Canadian society within the contemplation of s. 15", they were not victims of discrimination within the meaning of section 15(1) and the impugned provisions were therefore found to be constitutionally valid.

If the Supreme Court's position in *Andrews* left any doubt, these two decisions unequivocally closed the door to all equality challenges which were not based, directly or indirectly, on personal characteristics. The Court limited the scope of section 15 to what it perceived was the intended purpose of the framers of the Charter, that is, the protection of historically disadvantaged groups in Canadian society and other victims of false stigma or prejudicial myths and stereotypes.

VIII ATTEMPTED DEPARTURES FROM THE *ANDREWS* FRAMEWORK

While the Supreme Court maintained more or less the course first charted in *Andrews*, this was at times only by the slimmest of majorities. Differences came to the forefront in 1995 as the Court released its judgments in three key decisions on equality rights: *Miron v. Trudel*,[64] *Egan v. Canada*[65] and *Thibaudeau v. Canada*.[66] In all three appeals, while the majority applied the analytical framework established in *Andrews*, other approaches were proposed, some to further narrow it, others to broaden the reach of section 15(1) significantly.

In *Miron v. Trudel*, the appellant was involved in a motor vehicle accident and subsequently made a claim for accident benefits for loss of income and damages against his common law spouse's insurance policy. The insurer denied his claim on the basis that he did not fall within the statutory definition of "spouse", which was restricted to married persons only. Mr Miron, who considered himself a "common law" spouse, challenged the constitutional validity of this definition, alleging that it discriminated against him on the grounds of marital status. McLachlin J, writing for the four judges[67] who most closely followed the previous analysis of the Supreme Court in *Andrews*, confined the analysis to the following steps:[68]

> "First, the claimant must show a denial of 'equal protection' or 'equal benefit' of the law, as compared with some other person. Second, the claimant must show that the denial constitutes discrimination. At this second stage, in order for discrimination to be made out, the claimant must show that the denial rests on one of the grounds enumerated in s. 15(1) or an analogous ground and that the unequal treatment is based on the stereotypical application of presumed group or personal characteristics."

Applying this test to the facts of the case, McLachlin J found the definition of "spouse" to be discriminatory and in violation of section 15(1) of the Charter. This put the onus on the provincial government to justify under section 1 the exclusion of "common law" spouses.

---

[64] [1995] 2 SCR 418.
[65] [1995] 2 SCR 513.
[66] [1995] 2 SCR 627.
[67] She wrote for herself, Sopinka, Cory and Iacobucci JJ.
[68] [1995] 2 SCR 418, 485.

The notion that the state could not constitutionally differentiate between married and unmarried couples, even for the purpose of insurance benefits, disturbed Gonthier J. In his view, the provincial law was designed to reinforce the institution of marriage. Writing for four of the nine judges,[69] dissenting, he proposed a modified version of the section 15 analytical framework. He proposed an additional step which further restricted the scope of section 15(1). In considering whether a distinction was based on a prohibited personal characteristic, he said, the Court must determine precisely "the personal characteristic shared by a group and then [assess] its *relevancy* having regard to the functional values underlying the legislation".[70]

Adopting the orthodox "contextual approach" to section 15, Gonthier J's inquiry looked into whether the distinction complained of "rests upon or is the expression of some *objective* physical or biological *reality*, or *fundamental value*"[71] (ie, such as the institution of marriage). Where these conditions are present, the distinctions *relevant* to the functional values underlying the legislation cannot be said to be discriminatory.[72] Applying the test to the facts, Gonthier J concluded that while the first two steps were satisfied, the third could not be, thus rejecting the contention that the definition of "spouse" infringed upon the claimant's equality rights. Gonthier J was of the view that, given the importance of marriage as a fundamental social institution in Canadian society, distinctions based on marital status created by laws seeking to define marriage and attribute rights and obligations to married individuals were relevant to the functional values underlying the legislation, and therefore could

---

[69] Gonthier J wrote for himself, Lamer CJ, La Forest and Major JJ.

[70] Emphasis added. In context, his words were ([1995] 2 SCR 418, 435–6):

"The analysis to be undertaken under s. 15(1) of the *Charter* involves three steps. The first step looks to whether the law has drawn a distinction between the claimant and others. The second step then questions whether the distinction results in disadvantage, and examines whether the impugned law imposes a burden, obligation or disadvantage on a group of persons to which the claimant belongs which is not imposed on others, or does not provide them with a benefit which it grants others. . . . It is at this second step that the direct or indirect effect of the legislation is examined.

The third step assesses whether the distinction is based on an irrelevant personal characteristic which is either enumerated in s. 15(1) or one analogous thereto.

. . .

This third step thus comprises two aspects: determining the personal characteristic shared by a group and then assessing its relevancy having regard to the functional values underlying the legislation."

[71] *Ibid*, 438 (emphasis added)

[72] McLachlin J explained her reasons for rejecting the "relevance" approach as follows (*ibid*, 491):

"Relevance as the ultimate indicator of non-discrimination suffers from the disadvantage that it may validate distinctions which violate the purpose of s. 15(1). A second problem is that it may lead to enquiries better pursued under s. 1. As pointed out by this Court in *Andrews* v. *Law Society of British Columbia* . . . an analysis within s. 15 of whether the distinction was reasonable leaves little to s. 1, because in determining reasonableness, one must look at the conflicting state interest and determine if its importance outweighs the denial of equality. The same difficulties arise with asking whether the unequal treatment is justified because the distinction is relevant to the legislative goal. If any professed relevance suffices, unevaluated and unweighed, then few claims would pass s. 15(1). On the other hand, an evaluation of the degree of relevance of the ground of distinction to the legislative goal necessarily involves weighing the legislative purpose against the seriousness of the unequal treatment. Under the scheme of the *Charter*, such questions are better posed under s. 1."

not be considered discriminatory. Gonthier J also examined whether the appellants were members of a disadvantaged group, as an additional *indicium* of discrimination, but again, found that unmarried couples could not be identified as such. In the end, Gonthier J, for Lamer CJ, La Forest and Major JJ, would have dismissed the appeal.

Gonthier J's "relevancy" test would clearly have reduced the number of successful claimants under section 15(1), and reduced the demand on governments to justify their adverse "distinctions" under section 1. The point here, I think, is that the underlying inspiration for Gonthier J's approach was his sense that elected governments speak for the people in matters of social policy, and their social policy decisions should, within reasonable limits, be respected.

The decisive vote in *Miron* was cast by L'Heureux-Dubé J. In her concurring reasons she agreed with McLachlin J that there had been a violation of the claimant's equality rights, and that this violation was not justified in a free and democratic society. She differed from McLachlin J's reasons as to the proper approach to be taken to section 15(1) and reiterated her approach in the *Egan* case, to which I will now turn. In the end, the *Miron* appeal was allowed and "common law" spouses were admitted to insurance benefits.

The appellants in *Egan* v. *Canada*, James Egan and John Norris Nesbit, were homosexuals involved in a long term, intimate and committed relationship. When Egan reached the age of 65, he became eligible to receive old age security and a guaranteed income supplement pursuant to the provisions of the Old Age Security Act. The Act also provided an allowance for the spouse of a pensioner. Nesbit claimed to satisfy every condition of "spouse" except gender. Egan said the definition of "spouse" was of no force or effect as it discriminated on the basis of sexual orientation and was consequently in violation of section 15(1) of the Charter. Their claim was dismissed both before the Federal Court and the Federal Court of Appeal.

Once again, the judges of the Supreme Court were split as to the proper test to be applied to section 15(1) challenges. A cornucopia of four separate judgments was delivered. La Forest J, writing for Lamer CJ, Gonthier and Major JJ, applied the "relevancy" test developed by Gonthier J in *Miron* v. *Trudel*. The distinction drawn by the legislation between married or common law couples and same sex couples was deeply rooted in society's fundamental values and traditions, that is, the fundamental importance of marriage as a social institution firmly anchored "in the biological and social reality" that heterosexual couples have the capacity to procreate. That potential for procreation also exists in the context of common law relationships but not, in the ordinary way, with same sex couples. La Forest J concluded that[73]

"[b]ecause of its importance, legal marriage may properly be viewed as fundamental to the stability and well-being of the family and, as such, . . . Parliament may quite properly give special support to the institution of marriage".

---

[73] [1995] 2 SCR 513, 536.

La Forest J was of the view that the distinction drawn by Parliament in this case was relevant to these functional values underlying the Old Age Security Act. A *relevant* distinction, he concluded, cannot be discriminatory. Accordingly, it was not necessary for La Forest J to consider section 1 and he voted to dismiss Egan's appeal.

The final outcome was determined by a single vote, that of Sopinka J. While he disagreed with La Forest J on the section 15 analysis, he reached the same conclusion as La Forest J because he considered that the infringement was saved under section 1 of the Charter. Sopinka J developed a more flexible approach to section 1 than had been laid down in *Oakes* by giving deference to the choices made by Parliament in coming to terms with this "novel concept".[74] Egan's appeal was consequently dismissed.

For present purposes, however, the important point about *Egan* was the attempt by L'Heureux-Dubé J, dissenting, to enlarge the section 15 methodology beyond the limits placed by *Andrews*, which she described with faint praise as "an extremely good start". Equality challenges were becoming more complicated. She said that the emergence of divergent approaches taken to section 15 cases before the Supreme Court indicated that the members of the Court were not necessarily operating "with the same underlying purpose in mind".[75]

Examining the language of the equality provision of the Charter, L'Heureux-Dubé J suggested it was obvious that section 15 was not meant as a guarantee of *formal* equality, but rather, was intended to guarantee *substantial* equality: "equality without discrimination" generally. As in *Andrews*, it was important to define the concept of "discrimination". However, while McIntyre J had defined discrimination by reference to the enumerated grounds, L'Heureux-Dubé J proposed to tie "equality" to another similarly elusive concept, that of "human dignity" (shades of Pierre Elliot Trudeau!). She described the purpose of section 15 in these words:[76]

> "[A]t the heart of s. 15 is the promotion of a society in which all are secure in the knowledge that they are recognized at law as equal human beings, equally capable, and equally deserving. A person or group of persons has been discriminated against within the meaning of s. 15 of the *Charter* when members of that group have been made to feel, by virtue of the impugned legislative distinction, that they are less capable, or less worthy of recognition or value as human beings or as members of Canadian society, equally deserving of concern, respect, and consideration. These are the core elements of a definition of 'discrimination'—a definition that focuses on *impact* (i.e. discriminatory effect) rather than on constituent *elements* (i.e. the grounds of distinction)."

As McLachlin J had done in *Miron*, L'Heureux-Dubé J made clear that she did not agree with the "relevancy" approach taken by La Forest J.[77] Nor did she accept as

---

[74] [1995] 2 SCR, 576.

[75] *Ibid*, 541.

[76] *Ibid*, 545 (emphasis in original).

[77] More specifically, she states at [1995] 2 SCR 513, 547:

> "Consequently, it fails to take into account the possibility that a distinction that is relevant to the purpose of the legislation may nonetheless still have a discriminatory *effect*. If s. 15 is about recognizing the equal worth and dignity of each human being, it seems counter-productive to say that this sense

exhaustive the "grounds" approach set out in *Andrews*, which was an "imperfect vehicle" for giving equality rights their full effect.[78] Instead, L'Heureux-Dubé J proposed her own approach to section 15 in an attempt to "put discrimination first".[79]

Two factors, she said, must be considered at the final stage: the nature of the group affected (i.e, has this group suffered historical disadvantage; is it currently vulnerable to stereotyping or marginalisation; is the claimant a member of a "discrete and insular minority"?) and the nature of the affected interest (ie, does the distinction restrict the claimant's access to a fundamental social institution or does the distinction constitute a complete non-recognition of a particular group?). The "nature of the affected interest", in her view, may or may not involve personal attributes or characteristics.

In the third case, *Thibaudeau* v. *Canada*, the three divergent approaches again surfaced and while the majority and minority were differently constituted, allegiances did not change with respect to the judges' approaches. As noted above, *Thibaudeau* involved the tax deductibility of child support payments. The Court unfortunately split along gender lines 7–2 and held the allocation of the tax burden to be quite consistent with equality rights, L'Heureux-Dubé and McLachlin JJ dissenting.

After the release of the trilogy, members of the Court openly acknowledged the existence of an internal divide with respect to the proper analytical framework to be applied to section 15 claims (see for example *Benner* v. *Canada (Secretary of State)*[80] and *Eldridge* v. *British Columbia (Attorney General)*[81]), but were able to

of equal worth has not been impugned merely because the legislative distinction is relevant to some legitimate legislative purpose."

[78] According to L'Heureux-Dubé J, "[t]his approach inquires into whether the characteristics *of the ground* are sufficient to constitute a basis for discrimination, rather than into the absence or presence of discriminatory *effects* themselves" (*ibid*, 549).

[79] *Ibid*, 552–3:

"In my view, for an individual to make out a violation of their rights under s. 15(1) of the *Charter*, he or she must demonstrate the following three things:

(1) that there is a legislative distinction;

(2) that this distinction results in a denial of one of the four equality rights on the basis of the rights claimant's membership in an identifiable group;

(3) that this distinction is "discriminatory" within the meaning of s. 15.

. . .

A distinction is discriminatory within the meaning of s. 15 where it is capable of either promoting or perpetuating the view that the individual adversely affected by this distinction is less capable, or less worthy of recognition or value as a human being or as a member of Canadian society, equally deserving of concern, respect, and consideration. This examination should be undertaken from a subjective-objective perspective: i.e. from the point of view of the reasonable person, dispassionate and fully apprised of the circumstances, possessed of similar attributes to, and under similar circumstances as, the group of which the rights claimant is a member."

[80] [1997] 1 SCR 358. In this case the Court held unanimously that a provision in the *Citizenship Act* unconstitutionally discriminated by age between groups of children born abroad to Canadian mothers. Iacobucci J stated "[a]s I have previously concurred with the test of Cory and McLachlin JJ, my own preference is for their approach, and I apply it in these reasons. However, the result in this appeal is in my opinion the same no matter which test is applied" (at 393).

[81] [1997] 3 SCR 624. In this case the Court held unconstitutional British Columbia's refusal to supply special assistance to the blind who sought health services under the provincial medicare plan. At 669, La Forest J wrote again for a unanimous court, "[w]hile this Court has not adopted a uniform approach to s. 15(1), there is broad agreement on the general analytic framework."

resolve appeals on the basis that whichever approach was adopted, the result would be the same.

Let me pause here to suggest that there was nothing in these cases to rock the foundations of parliamentary democracy. Within the limited sphere of operations carved out by *Andrews*, the Court was doing useful work relieving discriminatory provisions that operated harshly against individuals because of personal characteristics over which they had no—or very limited—control, and which the government in question had failed to justify. The Workmen's Compensation scheme had not been overthrown. The Crown's priority in collecting taxes and other debts had not been put to the judicial sword. The courts were involved in social policy from time to time, but it was a role that was inescapable given the Charter mandate conferred by the democratically elected framers. While the critics of judicial inertia grumbled from time to time, the critics of judicial activism were hard pressed to demonstrate any realisation of their constitutional anxieties, apart from the basic principle that was inevitable from the outset, namely that the country had been moved by the democratically-elected framers from a state of parliamentary supremacy to one of constitutional supremacy.[82]

IX THE CORONATION OF "HUMAN DIGNITY" AS THE KEY TO SECTION 15 IN THE COURT'S UNANIMOUS DECISION IN *LAW*

In *Law* v. *Canada (Minister of Employment and Immigration)*[83] the Court undertook a heroic synthesis of its section 15 jurisprudence. The previously divided Court was unanimous. In *Law* the appellant challenged the constitutionality of certain provisions of the Canada Pension Plan, which provided for a survivor's pension paid to the surviving spouse whose deceased partner had made sufficient contributions to the CPP and met certain other eligibility criteria. However, the appellant widow was only 30 years old when her husband died, she was not disabled and she was not responsible for dependent children. Her application for survivor's pension was rejected, as were her subsequent appeals to the Minister of National Health and Welfare, the Pension Plan Review Tribunal, the Pension Appeals Board and the Federal Court of Appeal. The appellant argued that by imposing an age threshold for the receipt of the survivor's pension, the CPP discriminated against her on the basis of her age and that this infringement upon her equality rights could not be justified in a free and democratic society.

The Supreme Court found it difficult to see Mrs Law as a classic victim of discrimination, although clearly she had suffered a detriment (denial of a pension) for no reason other than her relative youth, good health and absence of dependent children. The Court was forced to reexamine its equality jurisprudence in terms of the *purpose* of section 15. The result was to move the idea of human dignity to the

[82] Dickson CJ, "Keynote Address" in F E McArdle (ed.), *The Cambridge Lectures 1985* (Montreal, Yvon Blais, 1985) 3–4.
[83] [1999] 1 SCR 497.

more central position that Trudeau had asserted for it 15 years earlier. Iacobucci J, speaking for the Court, related the "purpose" of section 15 firmly to the concept of human dignity. He did this by conducting an extensive review of the Supreme Court's equality jurisprudence and extrapolating these propositions:[84]

"It may be said that the purpose of s. 15(1) is to prevent the violation of essential human dignity and freedom through the imposition of disadvantage, stereotyping, or political or social prejudice, and to promote a society in which all persons enjoy equal recognition at law as human beings or as members of Canadian society, equally capable and equally deserving of concern, respect and consideration.

. . .

What is human dignity? . . . Human dignity means that an individual or group feels self-respect and self-worth. It is concerned with physical and psychological integrity and empowerment. Human dignity is harmed by unfair treatment premised upon personal traits or circumstances which do not relate to individual needs, capacities, or merits. It is enhanced by laws which are sensitive to the needs, capacities, and merits of different individuals, taking into account the context underlying their differences. Human dignity is harmed when individuals and groups are marginalized, ignored, or devalued, and is enhanced when laws recognize the full place of all individuals and groups within Canadian society."

While the emphasis on human dignity does not liberate section 15 from "personal characteristics", it provides additional elbow room in defining what personal characteristics are. It opens up the search for "analogous grounds". At the same time, it qualifies and disciplines the whole exercise to conform to the *purpose* of the constitutional protection. Charter claimants must show that a differential treatment denies them their human dignity. The analysis is nevertheless to be conducted within the general framework of the *Andrews* analysis. Iacobucci J suggested that a court called upon to determine a discrimination claim under section 15(1) should make three broad inquiries:[85]

"First, does the impugned law (a) draw a formal distinction between the claimant and others on the basis of one or more personal characteristics, or (b) fail to take into account the claimant's already disadvantaged position within Canadian society resulting in substantively differential treatment between the claimant and others on the basis of one or more personal characteristics? If so, there is differential treatment for the purpose of s. 15(1). Second, was the claimant subject to differential treatment on the basis of one or more of the enumerated and analogous grounds? And third, does the differential treatment discriminate in a substantive sense, bringing into play the *purpose* of s. 15(1) of the *Charter* in remedying such ills as prejudice, stereotyping, and historical disadvantage? The second and third inquiries are concerned with whether the differential treatment constitutes discrimination in the substantive sense intended by s. 15(1)."

Having restated the section 15 analysis in more purposive terms, Iacobucci J then undertook the synthesis of the Court's existing section 15 jurisprudence to outline

---

[84] *Ibid*, 529–30.
[85] *Ibid*, 524 (emphasis added).

more detailed guidance. He identified what he called contextual "factors" which may be invoked by claimants to show that the legislation has a demeaning effect on their dignity. The first contextual factor is pre-existing disadvantage. If the claimant can show he or she is a member of a group which has already suffered disadvantage and stereotyping, it must be determined whether further differential treatment will contribute to "the promotion of their unfair social characterization". A second contextual factor is stereotyping. Where the impugned legislation does not take into account the actual situation and circumstances of the claimant, it will rarely escape a charge of discrimination. Another contextual factor is the ameliorative purpose or effects of the legislation. An ameliorative purpose or effect which does not include more advantaged individuals or groups may not violate their human dignity. Iacobucci J then referred to a fourth contextual factor, the nature of the affected interest, picking up a theme in L'Heureux-Dubé J's dissenting reasons in *Egan*. The economic, constitutional and societal importance of the interest being denied provides an indication as to whether the claimant's dignity has been demeaned.

Applying this framework to the facts of the appeal, the Court could not find that adults under the pension cut-off age of 45 constituted an historically disadvantaged group or that their differential treatment promoted the view that they were less worthy of concern, respect or consideration. In addition, the impugned legislation had a clearly ameliorative purpose for older surviving spouses whose need for financial aid by the government was likely to be greater. The differential treatment was not discriminatory and section 15(1) was not violated. It was therefore not necessary for the Court to consider section 1 of the Charter.

The Supreme Court's decision in *Law* essentially constitutes a reassertion of the principles it established in *Andrews* in 1989, with the exception of the new emphasis on the protean concept of "dignity". While on the one hand the Court appeared unwilling to narrow the application of section 15(1) by importing the concept of "relevance" as developed by the reasons of La Forest and Gonthier JJ in *Egan* and *Miron*,[86] the Court also did not jettison the enumerated and analogous grounds approach despite the urging of L'Heureux-Dubé J. The concept of "dignity", while facilitating claims which the Court believes conform to the purpose of the Charter, at the same time means that not all distinctions which have an adverse effect will result in a violation of the claimant's equality rights.

X SUBSEQUENT DDECISIONS

The Court, possibly stressed by the effort required to achieve unanimity in *Law*, somewhat fractured when confronted shortly thereafter with the controversial

---

[86] Gonthier J concurred with the reasons in *Law*. As will be seen, he viewed the notion of "correspondence" as keeping alive the nub of his concept of relevance; La Forest J had retired on 30 September 1997, before the case was heard.

issues of the rights of same sex couples in *M & H* v. *Attorney-General of Ontario*[87] and Indian band government in *Corbière* v. *Canada (Minister of Indian and Northern Affairs)*.[88] The first case, *M & H*, in particular, has galvanised the critics of judicial activism[89] although, in reality, the decision was largely compelled by the words "in particular" in section 15(1).[90]

M & H involved two women whose same-sex relationship had lasted a number of years. During that time, they undertook several business ventures together. It appeared on the whole that H was more entrepreneurial, and M was more domestically oriented. Upon the breakdown of their relationship, in addition to seeking the settlement of their financial affairs in court, M made a claim for spousal support pursuant to the provisions of the Family Law Act.[91]

She was confronted, as *Egan* had been four years earlier, with a definition of spouse that limited the benefit to members of the opposite sex. Unlike *Egan* however, M was not seeking a government financial benefit. She wanted to be treated as a "spouse" for purposes of access to Ontario's Family Law Act, which set up a procedure to address the financial ramifications of people emerging from relations of intimacy and financial interdependence. She argued that people in that position should be able to rely on spousal assistance rather than state assistance, irrespective of the gender of the partners. The Family Law Act procedure, she pointed out, had nothing to do with marriage. It expressly covered "common law" relationships. The exclusion, by omission, related to same sex relationships.

The leading judgment on the section 15(1) issue was written by Cory J, who concluded that the claimant's exclusion from the support system resulted in a violation of her human dignity. In the case of homosexuals, the pre-existing disadvantage was clear. Cory J considered that the differential treatment could only exacerbate their disadvantage and their vulnerability. The challenged legislation completely failed to take into account the claimant's actual situation as a partner in a same-sex couple. As to the obviously ameliorative purpose of the legislation, Cory J found it did nothing to "lessen the charge of discrimination".[92] The exclusion undermined rather than advanced the objective of providing an effective means to resolve issues of financial dependency arising out of the collapse of an intimate relationship. Moreover, not only is the "interest" protected by the Family Law Act financially significant, but denial of this interest serves to further the misconception that same-sex couples do not form intimate and lasting relationships of economic interdependence.

Having applied the contextual and purposive analysis to section 15(1) expounded in *Law*, Cory J came to the conclusion that the differential treatment

---

[87] [1999] 2 SCR 3.

[88] [1999] 2 SCR 203.

[89] Building as it did on the Court's previous decision on sexual orientation in *Vriend* v. *Alberta* [1998] 1 SCR 493.

[90] An appeal to the Court's previous jurisprudence does not impress critics of judicial activism, who dismiss it as "self citation".

[91] RSO 1990, c F 3.

[92] [1999] 2 SCR 3, 57.

imposed upon the claimant was discriminatory as it constituted a clear denial of her basic human dignity. Iacobucci J then stepped in to address the issue of justification under section 1 of the Charter. The objective of the impugned provision was to provide "for the equitable resolution of economic disputes when intimate relationships between financially interdependent individuals break down", and to alleviate "the burden on the public purse to provide for dependent spouses".[93] These were pressing and substantial objectives. However, a rational connection could not be said to exist since, if anything, the inclusion of same-sex couples in the support system would have directly furthered its stated objectives of domestic equity. It could not be said that the claimant's equality rights were "minimally" impaired as she was denied totally any participation in the support regime. Alternate equitable or contractual remedies were inadequate substitutes. Finally, there could simply be no proportionality between the effect of the measure and the objective when, in practice, the measure chosen by the legislature impedes the realization of its objective. The infringement of the claimant's equality rights could not be saved under section 1.[94]

The outcome clearly turned (as Gonthier J's dissent demonstrated) on how one characterised the purpose of these particular provisions in the Family Law Act. For the majority, the legislation had little to do with marriage and everything to do with working out the finances of a broken down, economically interdependent sexual relationship. Given that view of the purpose, the gender of the participants was irrelevant. Applying the analysis in *Law*, which had not itself attracted much controversy, there was little "judicial activism" in pronouncing the Family Law Act unconstitutionally under-inclusive.

Similarly, the still more recent decision in *Corbière* involved the complaint of a group of Indian band members who were disenfranchised from voting for band government because they chose (or were obliged) to live off reserve. The issue is of considerable importance in Canada. Many aboriginal people have recently been restored to band membership. Most of those are women (or their children) who lost band membership when they married non-Indians, although their brothers kept band membership if they married non-Indians, and their non-Indian wives

---

[93] [1999] 2 SCR 3, 72.

[94] The lone dissent was written by Gonthier J, who differently characterised the purpose of the impugned provisions. In his view (*ibid*, 91):

"this legislation seeks to recognize the specific social function of opposite-sex couples in society, and to address a *dynamic* of dependence unique to both men and women in opposite-sex couples that flows from three basic realities. First, this dynamic of dependence relates to the biological reality of the opposite-sex relationship and its unique potential for giving birth to children and its being the primary forum for raising them. Second, this dynamic relates to a unique form of dependence that is unrelated to children but is specific to heterosexual relationships. And third, this dynamic of dependence is particularly acute for women in opposite-sex relationships, who suffer from pre-existing economic disadvantage as compared with men."

Given his view of the specific purpose of the legislation, the claimant's dignity could not, he said, be violated. In essence, his position, a philosophical one, continues to advocate a greater degree of deference towards the policy choices made by Parliament and the legislatures with respect to the traditional institutions of Canadian society of which marriage is a perfect example.

became Indians. In *Attorney General of Canada* v. *Lavell*,[95] the claimant failed in her attempt under the *Canadian Bill of Rights* to challenge the validity of these provisions. Subsequent restoration of these women and their offspring by statutory amendment to band membership did not, under the existing law, carry with it restoration of a vote in band elections.

In *Corbière* the Court found the "analogous ground" to be a combination of Indian status (which is not legally immutable, although of great importance to an individual's culture and identity) and residence off-reserve. Exclusion of non-resident band members from the right to vote was held to violate their basic human dignity by compounding their pre-existing disadvantage and vulnerability. Denial of the fundamental right to participate in the governance of their band denied them a say with respect to important financial, territorial and cultural interests which went beyond the local concerns of reserve residents.

The Court ruled that this violation of section 15(1) could not be saved under section 1 of the Charter. A more sophisticated legislative scheme could more minimally infringe the section 15(1) rights of off-reserve members by retaining purely local matters for a locally elected government, while allocating matters that affect the band as a whole to a governing structure that includes non-residents as well as residents.

Corbière is an interesting case. It shows the flexibility of the section 15 analysis when appropriately triggered by some strong factual findings of a trial judge.

XI THE POTENTIAL FOR CONFLICT WITH THE LEGISLATURES

Prima facie infringement of the section 15 right does not necessarily result in a violation of the Charter because under section 1, as stated, the section 15 right itself is "subject to such reasonable limits as can be demonstrably justified in a free and democratic society".

I think I have said enough to show that the content of the rights themselves is a source of continuing controversy, and it doesn't seem to matter to some critics whether the courts adopt a plain meaning interpretation (as in the scope of "fundamental justice" in section 7) or a more purposive construction (as in section 15 equality rights).

Life doesn't get any easier when the battle shifts to the "reasonable limits" saving provision of section 1 of the Charter. Issues of particular difficulty arise when the Court feels compelled by the Constitution to strike a different balance between the individual right (s. 15) and collective rights (s. 1) than the legislative majority thought appropriate. In *Vriend* for example, the Alberta legislature specifically considered a measure to make sexual orientation a prohibited ground of discrimination in its Individual Rights Protection Act and voted it down.

The potential for conflict is further aggravated when the Court addresses the remedy for a Charter violation. Does the Court simply declare the violation to exist

---

[95] [1974] SCR 1349.

and send it back to the legislature for reconsideration or a section 33 override?[96] Or does the Court try to fix the problem itself, using its limited arsenal of interpretive powers to read out, read in, read up or read down the words used by the legislature in the impugned provision to eliminate the feature that rendered it unconstitutional?

A Section 1: Justifying the Community Interest

In *Egan*, it will be recalled, the Court held that a gay civil servant's equality rights were denied when his same sex partner's income supplement was denied, but that the denial was justified. The basis was that[97]

> "government must be accorded some flexibility in extending social benefits, and does not have to be pro-active in recognizing new social relationships, it is not realistic for the Court to assume that there are unlimited funds to address the needs of all".

In *McKinney* v. *University of Guelph*[98] mandatory retirement at age 65 was held *prima facie* to discriminate on the basis of age, but was saved under section 1 because of "[r]amifications relating to the integrity of pension systems and the prospects for younger members of the labour force".[99]

Some critics complain that in these cases the judges were too quick to read down the "plain meaning" of section 1 which requires the Court, it is said, to reach an independent decision about the justification for the *prima facie* infringement, as opposed to showing "deference" to the legislature. On the other hand, in *Andrews*, *Miron* v. *Trudel* and *Oakes* itself, the government's section 1 justification was rejected.

It was confirmed in *Andrews*, as we have seen, that the "balancing" of social and individual interests should be done in section 1 rather than in section 15. The fundamental issue under section 1 is whether the Court is satisfied that the impugned legislation is directed to concerns that are pressing and substantial, and if so that the infringement of the individual right is no more than rationally and demonstrably necessary (or proportional) to meet such pressing and substantial concerns.[100] As we have also seen, the justificatory onus is on the party (usually the government) seeking to uphold the infringing measure, not on the claimant.

This analytical framework raises at least three areas of difficulty, namely the standard of review, the existence of an evidentiary record, and the sometimes mixed motives of governments called upon to offer a section 1 justification.

---

[96] See s. 33(1), above n. 12.
[97] [1995] 2 SCR 513, 572 per Sopinka J.
[98] [1990] 3 SCR 229.
[99] *Ibid*, 302 per La Forest J, quoting from (1986) 57 OR (2d) 1, 32, per Gray J.
[100] See eg, *R v. Oakes* [1986] 1 SCR 103; *RJR Macdonald v. The Queen* [1995] 3 SCR 199; and *Dagenais v. Canadian Broadcasting Corp* [1994] 3 SCR 835.

(a) The Standard of Review

The issue here is the degree of deference that ought to be paid to the policy choices of elected legislatures. The most striking insight into this issue, I think, was provided in *RJR MacDonald v. The Queen*,[101] which dealt not with equality rights but with free speech. The issue was the constitutional validity of federal legislation that required cigarette companies to put explicit and dire health warnings on their own packages ("SMOKING CAN KILL YOU"). The legislation was struck down. La Forest J, dissenting, relied on the huge body of scientific research linking cigarette smoking to cancer and held that the government's "compelled speech" measure was a "reasonable" response to a pressing and substantial public concern. However McLachlin J, for the majority, held that the government had to do more than just prove smoking is bad. The issue was, more narrowly, to weigh the justification for warnings on cigarette packages against free speech concerns. In justifying *compelled* speech (ie, the compulsory warning), the government had to do more than just show it was acting "reasonably"; it had to rationally demonstrate that the interference with free speech went no further than was necessary.[102] Critics of judicial activism say the *RJR Macdonald* test was insufficiently deferential to members of Parliament who, after all, carry the high responsibility for the health of the population, and should be given policy scope to deal with recognised health hazards. Critics of judicial inertia say that anything less than the McLachlin J approach would have abdicated the Court's responsibilities under the Constitution to uphold free speech, however unfashionable the cause, and would have reduced the Court to a rubber stamp of the will of the parliamentary majority.

(b) The Evidentiary Record

The Court has said on numerous occasions that section 1 justifications require an evidentiary base ("*Charter* decisions should not and must not be made in a factual

---

[101] *Ibid.*

[102] *Ibid*, 328–9, per McLachlin J:

"First, to be saved under s. 1 the party defending the law (here the Attorney General of Canada) must show that the law which violates the right or freedom guaranteed by the *Charter* is "reasonable". In other words, the infringing measure must be justifiable by the processes of reason and rationality. The question is not whether the measure is popular or accords with the current public opinion polls. The question is rather whether it can be justified by application of the processes of reason. In the legal context, reason imports the notion of inference from evidence or established truths. This is not to deny intuition its role, or to require proof to the standards required by science in every case, but it is to insist on a rational, reasoned defensibility.

Second, to meet its burden under s. 1 of the *Charter*, the state must show that the violative law is 'demonstrably justified'. The choice of the word 'demonstrably' is critical. The process is not one of mere intuition, nor is it one of deference to Parliament's choice. It is a process of *demonstration*. This reinforces the notion inherent in the word 'reasonable' of rational inference from evidence or established truths."

vacuum"[103]). The difficulty, as noted in *RJR Macdonald*, is that often facts do not exist, or are unprovable, or, as in *Operation Dismantle*,[104] are considered undisclosable by the state for reasons of national defence. More often, the section 1 justification consists of competing policies, neither of which is "right" or "wrong". In such cases, particularly where the policy controversy amounts to a competition for scarce resources, the Court is more willing to adopt a position of deference to the legislature.

(c) Governments Who Would Rather Switch Than Fight

Governments may lack not only the means but the desire to defend legislation. This is particularly the case where an election has brought about a change of the party in power. In *Miron* v. *Trudel*, for example, a Conservative government in Ontario had restricted compulsory motor vehicle insurance benefits to married "spouses". This was challenged as discrimination as the basis of marital status.[105] The New Democratic Party government that replaced the Conservatives by the time the legislation reached the Supreme Court had no sympathy for the previous government's philosophic position and declined to offer a section 1 justification for its legislation. This put the Court in an awkward position. The adversarial system doesn't work when one of the adversaries throws in the towel, and leaves the Court to pronounce on the constitutionality of legislation without full argument on both sides. As it happened, I benefited from Ontario's intransigence in that case because I was retained by the Supreme Court to act as *amicus curiae* to address the section 1 issue. We put together an evidentiary record that showed the definition of "spouse" was not in fact based on any philosophic position (the Conservative government had itself extended spousal benefits to "common law" spouses in a variety of other statutes) but on the vagaries of its legislative priorities and timetable. We showed the impact a judicial enlargement of the word "spouse" would have in dozens of federal and provincial statutes. We also filed actual evidence that demonstrated the cost to the state of extending spousal insurance benefits to unmarried common law spouses. At the end of the day, I could not find much of a rational basis for restricting spousal benefits to married couples in light of the broader statutory purpose, and said so.[106] As in *M & H* four years later, the "pith and substance" of the impugned law seemed to address the financial needs of financially interdependent conjugal couples who

---

[103] *MacKay* v. *Manitoba* [1989] 2 SCR 357, 361 per Cory J. I should add that the Court is frequently provided with massive "Brandeis briefs" addressing the "legislative facts" on which the state's action was premised (or is afterwards rationalised), as opposed to the "adjudicative facts" of the particular case being litigated. However, the reality is that many of these issues do not lend themselves to evidentiary proof one way or the other.

[104] *Operation Dismantle* v. *R* [1985] 1 SCR 441.

[105] An analogous ground: [1995] 2 SCR 418, 497 per McLachlin J.

[106] I may have been too much of an advocate in my analysis. The majority adopted a similar position (*ibid*, 506) but one of the dissenting judges felt I had not been imaginative enough in putting forward a pro-marriage option (*ibid*, 478).

had been devastated by a tragic accident, and was not about the philosophy of protecting marriage as a socially desirable institution.

On occasion, of course, the government may not wish to tackle controversial human rights issues, and would prefer the courts to be seen to be challenging the majoritarian view. This issue was touched on by Chief Justice Lamer in an interview:[107]

> "Q. People talk about an activist court, but do you think it's because there are inactive legislators?
> A. I've heard that being said. It's not for me to criticize legislators, but if they choose not to legislate, that's their doing. If they prefer to leave it up to the court, that's their choice. But a problem is not going to go away because legislators aren't dealing with it. People say we're activist, but we're doing our job."

A number of critics disparage what they call the "Charter made me do it defence" and say the judges should stick to the "plain text" of its provisions. My purpose is not to argue with these critics, but simply to outline some of the issues underlying Charter interpretation that give rise to the controversy in the first place. Judges do not initiate the controversies they are required to decide, and are obliged to interpret the Charter as best they can using the traditional tools of constitutional interpretation. For the reasons already mentioned, I think the plain meaning of several key provisions of the Charter, if taken literally, would have conferred far more power on the courts than the courts have been willing to accept.

XII REMEDIES AVAILABLE FOR EQUALITY BREACHES

Where a court has found a violation of a Charter right or freedom that cannot be justified under section 1 of the Charter, it must then turn its attention to the remedial clauses of the Constitution. Section 52(1) of the Constitution Act 1982 gives to the Charter overriding effect over federal or provincial statutes "to the extent" they are found to be inconsistent with Charter guarantees of rights and freedoms.[108] However, where the statute itself withstands constitutional scrutiny, but the actions taken under it infringe an individual's rights or freedoms, an individual remedy can be granted by a court pursuant to section 24(1) of the Charter:

> "Anyone whose rights or freedoms, as guaranteed by this *Charter*, have been infringed or denied may apply to a court of competent jurisdiction to obtain such remedy as the court considers appropriate and just in the circumstances."

The language of section 24(1) is very broad indeed, and the extent to which the Court fashions an "intrusive" remedy under sections 52 and 24 is often seen as a function of judicial activism or judicial restraint, as the case may be. The leading

---

[107] *The Ottawa Citizen*, 12 July 1999.

[108] S. 52 reads: "The Constitution of Canada is the supreme law of Canada, and any law that is inconsistent with the provisions of the Constitution is, to the extent of the inconsistency, of no force or effect."

decision on constitutional remedies is the Supreme Court's decision in *Schachter* v. *Canada*.[109] The majority opinion of Lamer CJ developed an approach which the Court considered consistent with the respective roles of the legislatures and the courts. He outlined a number of techniques that would avoid the drastic measure of striking down an entire law or an impugned provision in an otherwise valid statute. These included severing (or "reading out") particular words (eg, eliminating the words "of opposite sexes" in the definition of spouse in *M & H*), reading down (ie adopting a narrow interpretation to save constitutionality), reading up (the opposite) and "reading in" certain words to fill a legislative gap (eg, the words "sexual orientation" into the prohibited grounds of discrimination in *Vriend*).

Severance and "reading in" are described by Lamer CJ as being techniques which allow courts to "interfere with the laws adopted by the legislature as little as possible".[110] Nevertheless, conscious of the limitation of the Court's constitutional role, the technique will only be applied where it can be safely assumed that "the legislature would have passed the constitutionally sound part of the scheme without the unsound part"[111] or with the additional element unconstitutionally omitted in the first place. The Chief Justice indicated that when this assumption cannot fairly be made, the courts should not embark on a course of action that is properly reserved for the elected representatives, especially where there are financial or budgetary implications.

The Supreme Court's decision in *Vriend* v. *Alberta* is a contentious example of the application of the remedial options spelled out in *Schachter*. Having held that the omission of sexual orientation as a prohibited ground of discrimination in Alberta's Individual's Rights Protection Act constituted an unjustified violation of the appellant's equality rights, the issue was whether to send the problem back to Alberta or "read in" the words "sexual orientation" into the Act, and leave it to Alberta, if it wished, to override the Court's opinion under section 33. In the end

---

[109] [1992] 2 SCR 679. *Schachter* involved a challenge to a provision of the *Unemployment Insurance Act* that conferred parental leave benefits upon adoptive parents. The exclusion of natural parents from this scheme was held to be an unjustified infringement upon natural parents' equality rights. The appellant sought the extension of these benefits to natural parents by way of reading in, but the Court concluded that the remedy sought encroached on the role of Parliament with a suspended declaration of invalidity. Lamer CJ commented (at 723–4):

"Without a mandate based on a clear legislative objective, it would be imprudent for me to take the course of reading the excluded group into the legislation. A consideration of the budgetary implications of such a course of action further underlines this conclusion. . . . the excluded group sought to be included likely vastly outnumbers the group to whom the benefits were already extended.

Given the nature of the benefit and the size of the group to whom it is sought to be extended, to read in natural parents would in these circumstances constitute a substantial intrusion into the legislative domain. This intrusion would be substantial enough to change potentially the nature of the scheme as a whole. . . . Parliament and the provincial legislatures are much better equipped to assess the whole picture in formulating solutions in cases such as these. Clearly, the appropriate action for the Court to take is to declare the provision invalid but to suspend that declaration to allow the legislative body in question to weigh all the relevant factors in amending the legislation to meet constitutional requirements."

[110] *Ibid*, 696.
[111] *Ibid*, 697.

a majority did read the words "sexual orientation" into the impugned provision, citing with approval an observation from the Ontario Court of Appeal's decision in *Haig* v. *Canada*:[112]

> "[It is] inconceivable . . . that Parliament would have preferred no human rights Act over one that included sexual orientation as a prohibited ground of discrimination. To believe otherwise would be a gratuitous insult to Parliament".

Iacobucci J, for the majority, considered that this extension would not involve serious budgetary repercussions and would have no deleterious impact on the overall thrust of the legislation. In answer to the call for judicial restraint where a legislature has clearly made its will known, Iacobucci J replied that[113]

> "the closest a court can come to respecting the legislative intention is to determine what the legislature would likely have done if it had known that its chosen measures would be found unconstitutional".

Major J dissented on the issue of remedy. In his view, "reading in" was not an appropriate remedy to an unjustified Charter violation where the "Legislature's opposition to including sexual orientation as a prohibited ground of discrimination is abundantly clear on the record".[114] Under those circumstances, Major J was of the view that it was not open to the majority to assume that Alberta's Legislature would nevertheless have passed the Individual's Rights Protection Act had sexual orientation been included as a prohibited ground of discrimination. Furthermore, armed with the knowledge that the omission would prove to be unconstitutional, Major J observed that the legislature could choose from several ways to address the under-inclusiveness of the legislation.[115] It could, for example, override the Court's finding of invalidity by resort to the provisions of section 33 of the Charter.[116]

Section 33 of the Charter may be of particular interest to those who offer principled resistance to any erosion of parliamentary sovereignty in the area of human

---

[112] [1998] 1 SCR 493, 569, citing (1992) 9 OR (3d) 495, 508 per Krever JA.

[113] *Ibid*, 574.

[114] *Ibid*, 586.

[115] His suggestions included (*ibid*, 586–7)

"[s]exual orientation may be added as a prohibited ground of discrimination to each of the impugned provisions. In doing so, the Legislature may choose to define the term "sexual orientation", or may devise constitutional limitations on the scope of protection provided by the [*Individual's Rights Protection Act*]."

[116] In the end, Major J concluded (*ibid*, 587):

"The responsibility of enacting legislation that accords with the rights guaranteed by the *Charter* rests with the legislature. Except in the clearest of cases, courts should not dictate how underinclusive legislation must be amended. Obviously, the courts have a role to play in protecting *Charter* rights by deciding on the constitutionality of legislation. Deference and respect for the role of the legislature come into play in determining how unconstitutional legislation will be amended where various means are available.

Given the apparent legislative opposition to including sexual orientation in the [*Individual's Rights Protection Act*], I conclude that this is not an appropriate case for reading in. It is preferable to declare the offending sections invalid and provide the Legislature with an opportunity to rectify them."

rights. Section 33 permits Parliament or one of the provincial legislatures to "over-ride" a judicial declaration of invalidity in respect of some (but not all) Charter rights, including equality rights. It reads as follows:

> "Parliament or the legislature of a province may expressly declare in an Act of Parliament or of the legislature, as the case may be, that the Act or a provision thereof shall operate notwithstanding a provision included in s. 2 or sections 7 to 15 of this *Charter.*"

Prime Minister Trudeau accepted section 33 in an effort to accommodate the fears for parliamentary democracy of Alberta, Manitoba and others, and there are many who criticised the concession, including his successor, Brian Mulroney. For present purposes however, the point is that if the elected representatives conclude that the courts have gone too far in promulgating social policy under the guise of constitutional law, they can override the courts' decisions. This may attract a certain amount of political heat,[117] but the override power is there to be exercised. The ongoing interchange between the courts and the legislatures has been described as a "dialogue".[118] It is not an easy dialogue, but then neither judges nor legislators were promised a rose garden in Charter-land.

XIII   CONCLUSION

I suggest that the Supreme Court cannot fairly be convicted of either judicial usurpation *or* missed opportunities. On one of the central criticisms, namely that the Court's "judge-made law" too often ignores the "plain text" of the Charter, I hope I have said enough to show that in the case of section 15 equality rights, the plain text approach would arguably have *increased* the Court's role in shaping the country's social and cultural policy.

---

[117] When the Charter came into force, the province of Quebec passed an act which added a standard-form "notwithstanding" clause pursuant to s. 33 to each statute in force in the province at the time. This clause was routinely added to each new statute. This practice was an act of protest by the separatist government in Quebec against the Charter, but was abandoned in 1985 with the election of the Liberal Party to power. Later, in 1988, Quebec again resorted to the use of s. 33 after the Supreme Court's decision in *Ford* v. *Quebec* [1988] 2 SCR 712, in which the Court ruled that a law banning the use of languages other than French on commercial signs infringed upon freedom of expression as guaranteed by the Charter. The only other province which has invoked the override power of s. 33 is Saskatchewan, in an effort to protect from Charter scrutiny back-to-work legislation which that province's court of appeal had declared unconstitutional. The use of s. 33 in that case ultimately proved to be unnecessary as the Supreme Court later found the statute in question constitutionally valid: *RWDSU* v. *Saskatchewan* [1987] 1 SCR 460.

[118] Peter Hogg writes in "The *Charter* Dialogue Between Courts and Legislatures (Or Perhaps *The Charter of Rights* Isn't Such A Bad Thing After All)" (1997) 35 *Osgoode Hall L J* 75, 79–80:

> "Where a judicial decision is open to legislative reversal, modification, or avoidance, then it is meaningful to regard the relationship between the Court and the competent legislative body as a dialogue. In that case, the judicial decision causes a public debate in which *Charter* values play a more prominent role than they would if there had been no judicial decision. The legislative body is in a position to devise a response that is properly respectful of the *Charter* values that have been identified by the Court, but which accomplishes the social or economic objectives that the judicial decision has impeded."

Whether or not you believe the Court has got it right will largely depend on the expectations against which you measure the results. To those who felt comfortable with the Canadian Bill of Rights, the Court's equality decisions may be seen as activism, albeit activism dictated by the framers, whose mandate is most vividly demonstrated in the amendments to section 15(1) made by the Joint Committee of elected politicians. To the public interest groups that persuaded the Joint Committee to adopt the amendments, the Court's equality decisions may from time to time have come as a disappointment, but a disappointment tempered, surely, by an understanding that "reasonable limits" had to be accepted by the judiciary in defining their proper role in a constitutional democracy.

In any event, it can be said, I think, that the section 15 jurisprudence does not disclose any judicial appetite for a general overhaul of the legal landscape. The Court recognised its constitutional and institutional limitations from the beginning, as evidenced by the comments of La Forest J in *Andrews*.[119]

> "[I]t was never intended in enacting s. 15 that it become a tool for the wholesale subjection to judicial scrutiny of variegated legislative choices in no way infringing on values fundamental to a free and democratic society. . . . I am not prepared to accept that all legislative classifications must be rationally supportable before the courts. Much economic and social policy-making is simply beyond the institutional competence of the courts; their role is to protect against incursions on fundamental values, not to second guess policy decisions."

Prime Minister Trudeau expressed on behalf of the framers a sweeping vision of human dignity, but it fell to the courts to translate the vision into practice. If the result of the Court's judgments has been to produce tight but manageable anxiety in the minds of both critics of judicial activism and critics of judicial inertia in about equal measure, the judiciary may have performed one of the great navigational feats of modern jurisprudence.

---

[119] [1989] 1 SCR 143, 194 (emphasis in original).

8

Concepts of Equality in International Law

HILARY CHARLESWORTH

I INTRODUCTION

International law has influenced the design and interpretation of many modern constitutional systems of rights. It has also played a significant role in the interpretation of constitutional systems that have little explicit connection with international law, particularly in the area of human rights. How can international law contribute to debates about the meaning and forms of equality in national contexts? This paper surveys the way that such notions have been used in international treaties and how they have been developed in international jurisprudence. It then considers how international law might be developed to respond to manifestations of inequality.

II INTERNATIONAL LAW

The concept of equality is traditionally considered in international law in the context of the principle of the equality of states, a concomitant of traditional notions of sovereignty.[1] The assumption is that all states are equal players in the creation and application of international law, whatever their size, population, geography or wealth. Woodrow Wilson proposed including provisions relating to religious and racial equality in the Covenant of the League of Nations in 1919, but these were strongly resisted by British government at the behest of Australia and New Zealand. The latter two countries were concerned that treatment of their indigenous populations would be made subject to international scrutiny, as well as their restrictive immigration policies.[2] Ideas of equality and non-discrimination with respect to people were not given prominence until the Charter of the United Nations and these concepts remained linked with the notion of state equality. Thus the preamble to the Charter appears to consider sovereign and human equality as comparable in its reference to the determination "to reaffirm faith . . . in the equal rights of men and women and of nations large and small". Article 1.3 of the Charter goes

---

[1] I Brownlie, *Principles of Public International Law* (Oxford: Oxford University Press, 5th ed, 1998) 289–90.
[2] W McKean, *Equality and Discrimination Under International Law*, 5th edn. (Oxford, Clarendon Press 1983) 14–20.

on to declare as one of the purposes of the United Nations the promotion and encouragement of respect "for human rights and fundamental freedoms for all without distinction as to race, sex, language, or religion".[3]

In 1966, the UN General Assembly adopted two general human rights treaties: the International Covenants on Economic, Social and Cultural Rights ("ICE-SCR")[4] and on Civil and Political Rights ("ICCPR").[5] Both invoke the idea of non-discrimination with respect to enjoyment of the rights they contain.[6] The ICCPR also contains a specific guarantee of equality and non-discrimination. Article 26 states:

> "All persons are equal before the law and are entitled without any discrimination to the equal protection of the law. In this respect, the law shall prohibit any discrimination and guarantee to all persons equal and effective protection against discrimination on any ground such as race, colour, sex, language, religion, political or other opinion, national or social origin, property, birth or other status."

The general commitment to equality in the UN Charter and the ICCPR has been given greater detail in two specific treaty contexts. The first UN treaty devoted entirely to equality and non-discrimination was the International Convention on the Elimination of Racial Discrimination (ICERD, adopted by the General Assembly in 1965.[7] The Convention builds on the Charter references to dignity and equality and translates them into the context of race discrimination, which is defined as:[8]

> "any distinction, exclusion, restriction or preference based on race, colour, descent, or national or ethnic origin which has the purpose or effect of nullifying or impairing the recognition, enjoyment or exercise, on an equal footing, of human rights and fundamental freedoms in the political, economic, social, cultural or any other field of public life".

The second specific international legal context in which notions of equality and non-discrimination have been developed is that of sex. In 1979, the UN General Assembly adopted the Convention on the Elimination of All Forms of Discrimination Against Women (CEDAW).[9] In many respects, its provisions parallel those of the Race Discrimination Convention. For example, the definition of discrimination in the CEDAW is very similar to that in the ICERD:[10]

> "any distinction, exclusion or restriction made on the basis of sex which has the effect or purpose of impairing or nullifying the recognition, enjoyment or exercise by women, irrespective of their marital status, on a basis of equality of men and women, of human

---

[3] See also UN Charter, Art. 55.
[4] 999 UNTS 3.
[5] 999 UNTS 171.
[6] ICCPR, Arts. 2.1 and 3; ICESCR, Arts. 2.2 and 3.
[7] 660 UNTS 195.
[8] Art. 1.1.
[9] 1249 UNTS 13.
[10] Art. 1.

rights and fundamental freedoms in the political, economic, social, cultural, civil or any other field".

Some other forms of discrimination have been dealt with in international instruments that do not have the status of treaties. Thus a Declaration on the Elimination of All Forms of Intolerance and of Discrimination Based on Religion or Belief was adopted by the General Assembly in 1981.[11]

While principles of equality and non-discrimination are well established in international legal instruments, their development in international jurisprudence has been more halting. In the inter-war period, the Permanent Court of International Justice considered a number of cases dealing with the treatment of minorities in Europe. In *Minority Schools in Albania*[12] the Court gave a broad reading to the idea of equality of national minorities, accepting that it involved the preservation of a minority's own institutions. It noted that:[13]

> "[e]quality in law precludes discrimination of any kind; whereas equality in fact may involve the necessity of different treatment in order to attain a result which establishes an equilibrium between different situations".

The Permanent Court's successor, the International Court of Justice, has also developed a principle of non-discrimination on the basis of race. In the *South West Africa Cases*[14] Judge Tanaka (dissenting on the majority's decision that the applicant states, Liberia and Ethiopia, did not have standing to bring the action) rejected a claim by South Africa that differential treatment on the basis of race was consistent with international law. He accepted that some forms of differential treatment may be consistent with the overall goal of equality, but that such distinctions must be established to be reasonable or in "conformity with justice". Judge Tanaka insisted that any distinctions on the basis of race could not meet this test and were automatically illegal.[15]

The Human Rights Committee, which monitors the ICCPR, adopted a General Comment on the equality and non-discrimination provision, Article 26, in 1989.[16] The General Comment proposes a definition of the term "discrimination", unelaborated in the text of Article 26 itself. It refers to the definitions of discrimination in both the Race Discrimination Convention and the Women's Convention and states that:[17]

> "the Committee believes that the term 'discrimination' as used in the Covenant should be understood to imply any distinction, exclusion, restriction or preference which is based

---

[11] GA Res 36/55, reprinted in (1982) 21 ILM 205.

[12] 1935 PCIJ series A/B, no 64.

[13] *Ibid*, 19.

[14] 1962 ICJ Rep 319; 1966 ICJ Rep 4.

[15] *Ibid*, 314.

[16] *Human Rights Committee: General Comment No 23 (Art 26) (1989)* UN Doc HRI/Gen/1/Rev 1 at 26 (1994). General Comments are adopted under Art. 40(4) of the ICCPR, and are intended to guide states parties in applying the provisions of the Treaty and in preparing their periodic reports under Art. 40.

[17] *Ibid*, para. 7.

on any ground such as race, colour, sex, language, religion, political or other opinion, national or social origin, property, birth or other status, and which has the purpose or effect of nullifying or impairing the recognition, enjoyment or exercise by all persons, on an equal footing, of all rights and freedoms".

This account of discrimination is a relatively broad one: it does not require proof of a discriminatory intention and it covers both direct and indirect discrimination.

Another feature of the General Comment is its statement that equality does not always mean identical treatment. It acknowledges the possibility of different treatment in particular circumstances (for example, the prohibition in the ICCPR on the imposition of the death sentence on those under eighteen or on pregnant women).[18] The General Comment also points out that:[19]

"the principle of equality sometimes requires States parties to take affirmative action in order to diminish or eliminate conditions which cause or help to perpetuate discrimination prohibited by the Covenant".

The Comment observes that:[20]

"not every differentiation of treatment will constitute discrimination, if the criteria for such differentiation are reasonable and objective and if the aim is to achieve a purpose which is legitimate under the Covenant".

This statement appears to draw on the jurisprudence of the European Court of Human Rights, which has accepted that ostensibly discriminatory laws may nevertheless not violate human rights if they have been adopted in pursuit of a legitimate aim and there is a reasonable relationship of proportionality between the means employed and the aims sought to be realised.[21] As we shall see, these criteria allow wide latitude to states.

The Human Rights Committee has considered many individual communications or complaints of violations of Article 26 brought under the Optional Protocol to the ICCPR. Overall, however, the views of the Committee on the scope of Article 26 have been limited. Generally, the Human Rights Committee has found laws that discriminate on their face between women and men to breach Article 26. Thus Mauritian legislation that required foreign husbands of Mauritian nationals to apply for residence permits, but did not make the same requirement of foreign wives of Mauritian nationals, was declared to have violated several provisions of the ICCPR, including Article 26.[22] So too a Peruvian law that prevented a married woman from taking legal action with respect to matrimonial property was held to breach Article 26.[23]

---

[18] Art. 6.5.
[19] Above n. 16 at para. 10.
[20] Para. 13.
[21] Eg, *Belgian Linguistics Case* 1 EHRR 252 (1968).
[22] Communication no 35/1978, *Ameeruddy-Cziffra* v. *Mauritius*.
[23] Communication no 172/1984, *Avellanal* v. *Peru*. See also Communication no 716/1996, *Pauger* v. *Austria*, in which a widower successfully invoked Art. 26 to challenge Austrian laws that gave widowers lower pension benefits than widows in the same position.

The Human Rights Committee has, however, quite readily tolerated some forms of direct (or "facial") discrimination. For example, *Vos* v. *The Netherlands*[24] raised the issue of discrimination with respect to access to a disability allowance on the death of a spouse. Dutch law allowed men with a disability to retain the right to a disability allowance when their wives died; but on the death of their husbands disabled women were only eligible for a widow's pension, which in Ms Vos' case was less than the disability pension. Ms Vos had been divorced for 22 years at the time of her former husband's death and had been supporting herself when she became disabled. The Human Rights Committee found no violation of article 26 in this case, although two members of the Committee dissented. It accepted the Dutch government's justification of the distinction as reasonable and objective for a number of reasons. First, it accepted that at the time of the legislation's enactment "it was customary for husbands to act as bread-winners for their families".[25] Second, it stated that the law was necessary "to avoid the necessity of entering the person concerned in the records of two different bodies".[26] Third, it noted that generally the widow's pension was more than the disability allowance because most married women worked part-time and therefore qualified for only partial disability benefits.[27]

The views of the Human Rights Committee in *Vos* are unsatisfactory.[28] They depend on outmoded historical assumptions about the working habits of women and privilege administrative convenience over the guarantees in Article 26. Moreover, the decision assumes that there must be some type of discriminatory intent for the legislation to violate Article 26 and does not address the actual effect of the legislation in Ms Vos' case. This approach is also at odds with that of the Committee's General Comment, adopted in the same year.

Later cases involving Article 26 in which the Committee has adopted views continue a limited analysis of equality and non-discrimination. Generally the Committee appears to avoid basing a decision on Article 26 if there is another plausible ground. For example, in *Ballantyne, Davidson and McIntyre* v. *Canada*[29] the Human Rights Committee considered a Quebec law prohibiting the use of English in commercial signs and in the name of businesses. The authors of the communications were English speaking small business people and they invoked Article 26 as one of the grounds of their complaint on the basis that their French-speaking commercial competitors had no restrictions on the use of their mother tongue. This ground was rejected by the Committee (although it did accept that a violation of freedom of expression under article 19 of the ICCPR had occurred) on the basis that:[30]

---

[24] Communication no 218/1986.

[25] *Ibid*, para. 8.6 (citing the Netherlands' elucidation of the legislation).

[26] *Ibid*, para. 8.8.

[27] *Ibid*, para. 8.9.

[28] See the discussion of *Vos* in A Bayefsky, "The Principle of Equality or Non-Discrimination in International Law" (1990) 11 *HRLJ* 1, 15.

[29] Communications nos 359/1989 and 385/1989.

[30] *Ibid*, para. 11.5.

"[the] prohibition [of use of English] applies to French speakers as well as English speakers, so that a French speaking person wishing to advertise in English, in order to reach those of his or her clientele who are English speaking, may not do so".

This argument does not address the issue that the relevant inequality was the inability of the authors to use their mother tongue in their business signage and name.

Article 26 was one ground of another case against Canada, *Gauthier*,[31] in which a journalist had been denied full membership of the Parliamentary Press Gallery. The Committee did not consider the Article 26 aspect of the case, and found a violation of Article 19.2. An individual opinion signed by four members of the Committee,[32] however, discussed Article 26 in the following terms:[33]

"Article 26 stipulates that all persons are equal before the law. Equality implies that the application of laws and regulations as well as administrative decisions by Government officials should not be arbitrary but should be based on clear coherent grounds, ensuring equality of treatment. To deny the author, who is a journalist and seeks to report on parliamentary proceedings, access to the Parliamentary press facilities without specifically identifying the reasons, was arbitrary. Furthermore, there was no procedure for review. In the circumstances, we are of the opinion that the principle of equality before the law protected by article 26 of the Covenant was violated in the author's case."

The individual opinion signals a possible shift in jurisprudence on Article 26, suggesting that the provision carries with it at least some of the safeguards of the notion of natural justice as developed in administrative law.

In 1999, the Human Rights Committee adopted its views in *Waldman* v. *Canada*,[34] which raised the issue of discrimination on the basis of religious belief. The Province of Ontario fully funded Catholic schools but not the schools of other religious denominations. The author, who sent his children to Jewish schools, argued that this constituted, among other things, a violation of Article 26. The Canadian Supreme Court had rejected a parallel argument made under section 15 of the Canadian Charter of Rights and Freedoms on the grounds that the Canadian Constitution guaranteed Catholics' rights to a religious education. The Human Rights Committee by contrast did not accept that a constitutional provision could of itself override the norm of equality in Article 26. Unequal treatment must be based on "reasonable and objective criteria"[35] and the special support given to Catholic schools did not meet this standard.

In 2000, the Human Rights Committee adopted a significant General Comment on Article 3 of the ICCPR, which provides that all persons should enjoy the rights set out in the Covenant equally.[36] The Comment focuses on the human rights of women and goes beyond the idea of formal equality that informs the Committee's

---

[31] Communication no 633/1995.

[32] Lord Colville, Elizabeth Evatt, Ms Cecilia Medina Quiroga and Mr Hipolito Solari Yrigoyen.

[33] See also the individual opinions of Prafullachandra N Bhagwati and Rajsoomer Lallah. Compare that of David Kretzmer, rejecting this view of Art. 26.

[34] Communication no 694/1996.

[35] Para. 10.6.

[36] UN Doc CCPR/C/21/Rev.1/Add.10, 29 March 2000.

views in *Vos*. It refers to the way women's inequality is often deeply bound up in tradition and culture and emphasises the need for states to identify the practical obstacles to women's enjoyment of human rights. The General Comment also calls on states to prohibit discrimination against women by both public and private agencies. However, the Comment assumes that in most cases equality is achieved when women and men are treated the same way with respect to human rights and does not specifically address the issue of biases inherent in the definition of some human rights.

III   INADEQUACIES OF THE INTERNATIONAL LEGAL ACCOUNT OF EQUALITY AND NON-DISCRIMINATION

Compared with many national legal systems, then, the international legal system has been very slow to develop the concept of equality. There are a number of significant fault lines in the international legal understanding of equality and I will address three of them.

First, international law has developed a hierarchy of forms of discrimination. Discrimination based on race is typically regarded as considerably more serious than other forms of discrimination. This hierarchy can be seen most clearly in judicial and academic discussion of norms that have attained the status of *ius cogens* (peremptory norms of international law from which no derogation is permitted) or are obligations *erga omnes* (binding all states). Thus in the *Barcelona Traction* case, the International Court of Justice referred to the category of *erga omnes* obligations as including specifically "the basic human rights of the human person, including protection from slavery and racial discrimination".[37] So too, the only form of discrimination regularly mentioned in lists of *ius cogens* norms is racial discrimination.[38] Other forms of discrimination are seen as more easily justified, and in some cases as integral to community values, particularly in the case of discrimination against women.

Although discrimination on the grounds of sex is proscribed by treaty, and the Women's Convention has over 160 parties, its lesser status in the hierarchy is indicated by the extraordinary pattern of reservations made by states. More than fifty states have entered reservations to the Convention,[39] many of which undermine the basic obligations set out in the treaty. The most sweeping reservations have been made in the name of religious and cultural rights.[40] For example, New Zealand has made a reservation to provisions of the Convention with respect to the Cook Islands "to the extent that the customs governing the inheritance of certain Cook Islands chief titles may be inconsistent with [Articles 2(f) and 5(a)]".

---

[37] Second Phase, 1970 ICJ Rep 3, 32.

[38] Eg American Law Institute, *Restatement (Third) of the Foreign Relations Law of the United States* (St Paul, American Law Institute, 1987) para. 702.

[39] See <http://untreaty.un.org/>.

[40] See H Charlesworth and C Chinkin, *The Boundaries of International Law: A Feminist Analysis* (Manchester, Manchester University Press, 2000) 102–9.

As we have seen, treaty prohibition of discrimination has been fully developed only in the limited contexts of race and sex. In its interpretation of Article 26 of the ICCPR, which contains a broader list of prohibited grounds of discrimination, the Human Rights Committee has occasionally found discrimination on the basis of nationality or political opinion to violate the provision.[41] Despite the reference in Article 26 to "other status", implying that the list of prohibited grounds is not closed, there has been little development outside the specified grounds. Thus international law has not seemed able yet to respond to issues of inequality on the basis of disability or sexuality. In *Toonen* v. *Australia*[42] a gay activist, Nicholas Toonen, argued that Tasmania's criminalisation of male homosexual acts violated both his right to privacy under Article 17 of the ICCPR and his right to non-discrimination under Article 26. The Human Rights Committee found the Tasmanian law violated Article 17, but was much more circumspect with respect to the discrimination argument, despite the Australian government's explicit support for a discrimination analysis. In a cryptic paragraph, the Committee stated simply:[43]

> "The State party has sought the Committee's guidance as to whether sexual orientation may be considered an 'other status' for the purposes of article 26. . . . The Committee confines itself to noting, however, that in its view, the reference to 'sex' in article . . . 26 is to be taken as including sexual orientation."

One of the problems in analysing sexuality as an issue of privacy rather than one of discrimination is that it challenges neither the idea that homosexuality is immoral nor the elements of anti-homosexual bias. In other words, an Article 17 privacy approach simply limits the actions a state may take in protecting community morality.[44] An individual opinion by Mr Bertil Wennergren in the *Toonen* case takes up the Australian invitation to consider Article 26, arguing that the distinctions drawn between heterosexual and homosexual activity in the Tasmanian legislation violate the principle of equality before the law, although he also makes the curious connection between the reference to "sex" in Article 26 and sexual orientation.

A second problem with the international legal system's treatment of discrimination is that it has been difficult to deal with more than one form of discrimination at one time. For example, when the Committee on the Elimination of Racial Discrimination ("CERD") was faced with a communication raising issues of both race and sex discrimination, it adopted a very narrow approach. In *Yilmaz-Dogan* v. *Netherlands*[45] an employer had sought to terminate the employment of a Turkish woman who was pregnant on the basis that:

---

[41] Eg Communication no 586/1994, *Adam* v. *Czech Republic*; Communication no 309/1988, *Valenzuela* v. *Peru*.

[42] Communication no 488/1992.

[43] Para. 8.7.

[44] See D Kane, "Homosexuality and the European Convention on Human Rights: What Rights?" (1988) 11 *Hastings Int'l & Comp L Rev* 447, 467.

[45] Communication no 1/1994.

"[w]hen a Netherlands girl marries and has a baby, she stops working. Our foreign women workers, on the other hand, take the child to neighbours or family and at the slightest setback disappear on sick leave under the terms of the Sickness Act. They repeat that endlessly. . . . [W]e cannot afford such goings-on."

After a Dutch court had ratified the dismissal, and an appeal court had rejected a claim of racial discrimination, Ms Yilmaz-Dogan made a complaint to CERD. The Committee agreed that the termination of employment was based on racial discrimination, but did not address discrimination on the basis of gender stereotypes. Indeed the Chair of CERD, Michael Banton, has termed attempts to consider the intersection of race and gender "fundamentally misconceived".[46]

A third problem in international law with respect to equality and non-discrimination is its elision of the two concepts. It is widely accepted that equality and non-discrimination are positive and negative statements of the same principle.[47] In other words, equality means absence of discrimination and non-discrimination between groups will produce equality. This approach however limits the transformative possibilities of the idea of equality and non-discrimination: it confines the meaning of equality to a guarantee of equal opportunity.

There has been much debate over the limitations of the concept of equal opportunity in the context of race and sex. In the context of sex, it has been pointed out that the approach of insisting that women and men be treated similarly falters when women and men are not in the same position either because of physical difference or because of structural disadvantage. Feminists have debated, for example, whether the ability to become pregnant should be legally acknowledged as a difference between women and men or regarded as a merely temporary "disability".[48] More fundamentally, the "similar treatment" theme of equal opportunity requires women to conform to a male-defined world. For example, to enjoy a right to paid work, women generally may need considerably more support (maternity leave, childcare) than men.[49] In dealing with individual cases of discrimination rather than structural inequality, the principle of equal opportunity can solve a limited number of discrete problems and fails to address the underlying causes of sex discrimination. The principle of equal opportunity, Nicola Lacey has said, is "inadequate to criticise and transform a world in which the distribution of goods is structured along gender lines".[50] It assumes "a world of autonomous individuals starting a race or making free choices [that] has no cutting edge against the argument that men and women are simply running different races".[51]

---

[46] Quoted in A Gallagher, "Ending the Marginalization: Strategies for Incorporating Women into the United Nations Human Rights System" (1997) 19 *HRQ* 283, 304.

[47] McKean, above n. 2 at 287–8; Bayefsky, above n. 28 at n. 1.

[48] Eg W Williams, "Equality's Riddle: Pregnancy and the Equal Treatment-Special Treatment Debate" (1985) 13 *N Y U Rev L & Social Change* 325; L Finley, "Transcending Equality Theory: A Way Out of the Maternity and Workplace Debate" (1986) 86 *Col L Rev* 1118.

[49] A Phillips, "Introduction" in A Phillips (ed.), *Feminism and Equality* (Oxford, Blackwell, 1987) 1, 8.

[50] N Lacey, "Legislation Against Sex Discrimination: Questions From a Feminist Perspective" (1987) 14 *J L & Soc* 411, 415.

[51] *Ibid*, 420.

The promise of equality as "sameness" to men only gives women access to a world already constituted by men.[52] In other words, equality is understood as aiming at a single, assimilationist endpoint.[53]

The problematic notions of equality and non-discrimination in international law are underlined in the way that the term "special measures" is used in the both the Race Convention and the Women's Convention. Thus the Race Discrimination Convention states:[54]

> "Special measures taken for the sole purpose of securing adequate advancement of certain racial or ethnic groups or individuals requiring such protection as may be necessary in order to ensure such groups or individuals equal enjoyment or exercise of human rights and fundamental freedoms shall not be deemed racial discrimination, provided, however, that such measures do not, as a consequence, lead to the maintenance of separate rights for different racial groups and that they shall not be continued after the objectives for which they have been taken have been achieved."

The approval of "special measures" in the international context indicates that the prohibition of discrimination goes beyond the narrow notion of formal equality and recognises the significance of equality of outcome. However, the treaty description of affirmative action assumes that special measures will be simply temporary methods to counteract inaccurate views that, given the same opportunities, blacks cannot achieve the same things as whites or that women cannot perform exactly like men.[55] In other words, "special" treatment is seen as allowing the disadvantaged group to become just like their advantaged competitors. The basis of equality and non-discrimination, then, is sameness.

This approach raises a number of questions. One is that it contemplates a single utopian standard of equality: non-discrimination means allowing progression to an already established standard. It is not clear how differences between groups might fit in with this analysis. Another question is that if "special measures" are seen simply as compensation for past discrimination, their scope will be quite narrow and will not necessarily respond to the structures of discrimination that allow the continuation of equality.[56] A third issue is the emphasis on the temporary nature of special measures: it assumes that special measures are a form of discrimination in themselves and should be done away with at the earliest opportunity. Critics of special measures of course make a similar assumption, but give the principle of non-discrimination priority in all circumstances. For both the proponents and critics of special measures as they are understood in international law, non-discrimination is assumed to be a basic principle of justice.

---

[52] C Dalton, "Where We Stand: Observations on the Situation of Feminist Legal Thought" (1987) 3 *Berkeley Women's LJ* 1, 5.

[53] B Gaze, "Some Aspects of Equality Rights: Theory and Practice" in B Galligan and C Sampford (eds.), *Rethinking Human Rights* (Sydney, The Federation Press, 1997) 190.

[54] Art. 1.4.

[55] F Olsen, "Feminism and Critical Legal Theory: An American Perspective" (1990) 18 *International Journal of the Sociology of Law* 199, 203.

[56] See I M Young, *Justice and the Politics of Difference* (Princeton, Princeton University Press, 1990) 194.

Another problem with the linkage of equality and non-discrimination is that it emphasises fault by particular actors in particular cases and distracts attention from the broader situation of "victims" of discrimination and indeed the acceptance of many forms of discrimination as normal or based on acceptable principles of "merit".[57] Moreover, as Stephen Sedley has pointed out, the legal process is itself "based on assumptions which can turn procedures designed to achieve evenhandedness into engines of oppression".[58] For example, rules of criminal procedure can lead to disadvantage and injustice in the context of rape trials.

IV CONCLUSION

I have suggested that the international legal understanding of equality is a narrow one and that it has little impact in dealing with many forms of injustice. It has been overtaken by more progressive accounts of equality developed in national legal systems. The international law linkage of equality with the idea of non-discrimination has constrained its potential. An alternative approach is to reduce the focus on non-discrimination and to develop a broader idea of equality. Iris Marion Young has proposed an analysis of inequality in terms of oppression and domination, rather than in terms of discrimination in the distribution of social goods. She notes that:[59]

> "[w]hile discriminatory policies sometimes cause or reinforce oppression, oppression involves many actions, practices, and structures that have little to do with preferring or excluding members of groups in the awarding of benefits".

Young's arguments are useful in international law. They suggest a much richer understanding of equality and inequality that would promote the "participation and inclusion of all groups in institutions and positions."[60] In this light, for example, special measures would not be seen as an exception to the overriding principle of non-discrimination, but one strategy to deal with structures of oppression and domination. Linking the idea of equality with non-domination also allows consideration of the history and context of inequality and relative distributions of power. While this reorientation would be a profound one in international law, it would make the notion of equality a proper vehicle for social justice.

---

[57] *Ibid*, 195–6.
[58] S Sedley, "How Laws Discriminate" 21: 9 *London Review of Books* (29 April 1999) 25, 26.
[59] Above n. 56 at 195.
[60] *Ibid*.

9

Liberty and Equality: Complementary, Not Competing, Constitutional Commitments

NADINE STROSSEN*

I INTRODUCTION

The American Civil Liberties Union ("ACLU") sparks a lot of disagreement and controversy—not surprisingly, since the rights we defend also spark a lot of disagreement and controversy. Still, among both our supporters and our critics, there is a consensus that we are very influential. For example, a comprehensive history of the ACLU by Samuel Walker, published by Oxford University Press, opens with these words:[1]

> "The history of the American Civil Liberties Union is the story of America in this century. . . . When the ACLU was founded . . . the promises of the Bill of Rights had little practical meaning for ordinary people. Today, there is a substantial body of law in all the major areas of civil liberties: freedom of speech and press, separation of church and state, free exercise of religion, due process of law, equal protection, and privacy. The growth of civil liberties since World War I represents one of the most important long-term developments in modern American history, a revolution in the law and public attitudes . . . The ACLU can legitimately claim much of the credit—or be assigned the blame, if you prefer—for the growth of modern constitutional law."

Now, of course I champion dissenting views, so let me quickly turn to one of the most prominent critics of the ACLU, and the rights we defend, the arch-conservative Judge Robert Bork, the nominee to the Supreme Court who was rejected by the Senate in 1987 following an extremely bitter battle. Since then, Judge Bork has remained an influential commentator. In 1996, he wrote a best-selling book with the apocalyptic title, *Slouching Towards Gomorrah*.[2] His thesis was

* For assistance with research and drafting footnotes, Professor Strossen gratefully acknowledges her Chief Aide, Amy L Tenney, her Academic Assistant, Kathy Davis, and her Research Assistants, Jaci Flug, Anna Genet, Mara Levy, Kara Miller, Michael Nordskog, Maria Pedraza, Janice Purvis, Hanna Slan and Elena Vournas.

[1] S Walker, *In Defense Of American Liberties: A History Of The ACLU* (New York: Oxford,University Press, 1990) 3–4.

[2] R H Bork, *Slouching Towards Gomorrah: Modern Liberalism and American Decline* (New York, Regan Books, 1996).

that the US has degenerated into radical libertarianism and radical egalitarianism. And the chief culprits, in his view, are the ACLU and what he sees as our hand-maidens—namely, the US Supreme Court Justices![3] I am not sure that all members of the Court would share that view! In any event, Bork's criticism of the ACLU is something I take as a backhanded compliment. Here is a sample:[4]

> "[T]he American Civil Liberties Union . . . has had, through litigation and lobbying, a very considerable effect upon American law and culture. . . . The ACLU is the premier litigating and lobbying arm of modern liberalism, and it has been extremely successful."

As both Walker and Bork concur, despite their differing views about civil liberties issues, the ACLU has been very influential. Therefore, for better or worse, many of the positions we have advocated are now reflected in US constitutional law.[5] Moreover, while those positions are often controversial even within the US, the divisions are not along partisan or ideological lines. That is certainly true, for instance, of the defence of controversial, offensive expression, including racist expression.

Consider, for example, the Court's most recent decision in this area, in 1992.[6] It endorsed the ACLU's argument that a so-called "hate speech law" was unconstitutional, even when applied to the odious racist message conveyed by burning a cross inside the fenced yard of an African-American family. The Court's ringing opinion, with its bracing vision of a robust free speech guarantee, was authored by no less distinguished a conservative than Justice Antonin Scalia.[7]

Let me cite another prominent illustration of the US Supreme Court's broad-ranging support for a civil libertarian approach to free speech, its twin decisions upholding the First Amendment right to burn the US flag in political protest, in 1989 and 1990.[8] These rulings are still extremely controversial among the general public,[9] and the target of serious, ongoing campaigns to amend the Constitution.[10] In contrast, in the Court itself, these rulings did not provoke the sort of divisions one might have expected. They were joined not only by the two most liberal Justices at the time, Justices Brennan and Marshall, but also by two at the opposite

---

[3] R H Bork, *Slouching Towards Gomorrah: Modern Liberalism and American Decline* (New York, Regan Books, 1996), 96–7.

[4] *Ibid*, 97–8.

[5] See eg, Walker, above n. 1 at 4.

[6] *RAV* v. *City of St. Paul* 505 US 377 (1992).

[7] The Court recognised that this symbolic expression could be constitutionally prohibited under many laws, such as those prohibiting arson, vandalism, and trespass. See *ibid*, 379–80. It stressed, though, that this expression could not be prohibited under a law that focused on the ideas it conveyed—in this case, a city ordinance prohibiting expression that "arouses anger, alarm or resentment . . . on the basis of race, color, creed, religion or gender". *Ibid*, 391.

[8] *United States* v. *Eichman* 496 US 310 (1990); *Texas* v. *Johnson* 491 US 397 (1989).

[9] See L Saad, "Most Americans Would Give Old Glory Legal Protection" (visited 20 March 2001) <http://www.gallup.com/poll/releases/pr990706.asp>.

[10] See L Alvarez, "Measure to Ban Flag Burning Falls 4 Votes Short in Senate", *New York Times*, 30 March 2000, A24, see also, D E Rosenbaum, "In Recurring Debate, House Votes to Ban Flag-Burning", *New York Times*, 25 June 1999, A18.

end of the spectrum—again, our favourite conservative civil libertarian ally, Justice Scalia, along with his conservative colleague, Anthony Kennedy.

Let me cite one final, more recent, and even more striking example here, of the US Supreme Court's consensus—along with the ACLU—on an important civil liberties issue where the public and politicians are deeply divided. I am referring to the ACLU's 1997 Supreme Court victory in a landmark First Amendment case, the first to address the constitutional status of that brave new medium, cyberspace. I am so proud that this case will go down in history under the name of *Reno* v. *ACLU*.[11] And I am thrilled that this ruling, declaring cyberspace a free speech zone, was essentially unanimous.[12]

I must stress that neither I nor the ACLU are American chauvinists. To the contrary! We work closely with our counterparts around the world, human rights activists and organisations.[13] Significantly, the ACLU's position—the so-called "American" position—on controversial free speech issues, such as "hate speech," has been endorsed by some human rights organisations in other countries, including Canada, and by some international human rights organisations, including Human Rights Watch and Article 19, the International Centre Against Censorship. Article 19, which is based in London, of course takes its name from the free speech guarantees in the Universal Declaration of Human Rights[14] and the International Covenant on Civil and Political Rights.[15] That is significant, since the robust free speech positions that this organisation espouses reflect its interpretation not of the US Constitution, but rather of international human rights treaties that have been ratified by countries all over the world.

The ACLU has always advocated an increased role for international law within the US legal system.[16] Unfortunately, on this point, we have not prevailed. The US lags far behind most other countries in ratifying international human rights treaties, and even when it does ratify, it does so only in the most qualified and limited way, to avoid any additional human rights protections, above and beyond

---

[11] 521 US 844 (1997).

[12] Justice O'Connor wrote a partial dissent, joined by Chief Justice Rehnquist, which concluded that the challenged cybercensorship law, the Communications Decency Act, should be constitutional only concerning a tiny percentage of online communications: those involving one adult and one or more minors (but not more than one adult). See *ibid*, 896–7. As the majority noted, however, many communications of this type would likely be between family members—eg, emails between parents and their own children—thus raising constitutional problems even concerning this relatively narrow portion of the Act's scope. See *ibid*, n. 32.

[13] See generally *ACLU International Human Rights Task Force, ACLU International Civil Liberties Report* (Los Angeles, The Task Force, May 1999).

[14] Universal Declaration of Human Rights, GA Res 217A III, UN GAOR, 3d Sess, UN Doc A/810 at 71 (1948).

[15] International Covenant on Civil and Political Rights, GA Res 2200A (XXI), 21 UN GAOR Supp (No 16) at 52, UN Doc A/6316 (1966), 999 UNTS 171, opened for signature, 19 December 1966 (entered into force 23 March 1976) (hereinafter "ICCPR").

[16] See eg, P L Hoffman and N Strossen, "Enforcing International Human Rights Law in the United States" in L Henkin and John L Hargrove (eds.), *Human Rights: An Agenda for the Next Century* (Washington DC, American Society of International Law, 1994) 477; N Strossen, "Recent US and International Judicial Protection of Individual Rights: A Comparative Legal Process Analysis and Proposed Synthesis" (1990) 41 *Hastings LJ* 805, 806.

those already recognised under established US law.[17] Moreover, the US Supreme Court maintains an isolationist stance, refusing to consider customary international law even in the most limited way—namely, as a non-binding guide to interpreting ambiguous terms in US legal authorities.[18]

The ACLU has joined with our colleagues in the international human rights movement to criticise these stances, and we are in good company. One important ally, for example, is Supreme Court Justice Ruth Bader Ginsburg. Significantly, before she became a judge, Ruth Bader Ginsburg was both an ACLU lawyer and a comparative law scholar. In a major lecture she delivered in New York City in 1999, she chastised her Supreme Court colleagues for being insufficiently attentive to legal developments beyond US borders.[19]

Now, let me say a word about the substantive inter-relationship between US and international law in terms of liberty and individual rights. In some important respects, US law gives more protection to individual rights than international law does. The paradigmatic case in point is one I have already mentioned—US law's free speech protection for even the most controversial, "politically incorrect", ideas. This stance is one facet of US law's strong protection of controversial expression conveying politically unpopular views, including criticism of political leaders and their policies in harsh, even defamatory, terms.[20]

On the other hand, in other important respects, US law gives less protection to individual rights than international law does. Here the paradigmatic case in point is our Supreme Court's consistent rejection of constitutional challenges to the death penalty.[21] Under international human rights law, in stark contrast to US Supreme Court rulings, the death penalty may not be administered against individuals who were minors or mentally impaired at the time they committed the crime.[22] Moreover, there is a developing body of international customary law treating the death penalty as inherently "cruel" and "inhumane", thus contravening general

---

[17] See eg, L Henkin et al (eds.), *Human Rights* (New York, Foundation Press, 1999) 783; L Henkin, "US Ratification of Human Rights Conventions: The Ghost of Senator Bricker" (1995) 89 *AJIL* 341, 341.

[18] See eg, Strossen, above n. 16 at 808–9.

[19] R Bader Ginsburg and D Jones Merritt, *Affirmative Action: An International Human Rights Dialogue* (Fifty-First Cardozo Memorial Lecture, 1999).

[20] See eg, *New York Times* v. *Sullivan* 376 US 254 (1964). See also N Strossen, "A Defence of the Aspirations—But Not the Achievements—of the U.S. Rules Limiting Defamation Actions by Public Officials or Public Figures" (1985–1986) 15 *Melb U L Rev* 419.

[21] See eg, *Stanford* v. *Kentucky* 492 US 361 (1989) (rejecting challenges to death sentences of individuals who were minors, aged 16 and 17, when they committed the capital crimes); *Penry* v. *Lynaugh* 492 US 302 (1989) (rejecting challenge to death penalty for mentally retarded defendant); *McCleskey* v. *Kemp* 481 US 279 (1987) (rejecting constitutional challenge to death penalty on African-American man for murdering white man, despite statistics indicating racially-biased patterns in capital sentencing); and *Gregg* v. *Georgia* 428 US 153 (1976) (holding that death penalty does not violate constitutional prohibition on cruel and unusual punishment).

[22] See eg, ICCPR, above n. 15 at Pt III, Art 6, paras. 1 & 5; J H Wyman, Comment, "Vengeance is Whose?: The Death Penalty and Cultural Relativism in International Law" (1997) 6 *J Transnat'l L & Pol'y* 543, n. 94.

prohibitions on any such punishments that are contained in both international and domestic human rights laws.[23]

In the ACLU's ideal world, all individual rights would receive the maximum protection consistent with civil libertarian principles, and, in support of our claims for each right, we would cite whatever source of legal authority offered the most protection—not only the US Constitution, but also, alternatively, state constitutions, federal or state statutes, or international human rights principles. This is an upward-ratcheting approach. In other words, the US Constitution—as interpreted by the Supreme Court—sets a floor under our individual rights, but it should not set a ceiling over them.

Under this civil libertarian approach, to the extent that increased protection for individual rights is offered by other binding legal authorities, domestic or international, they should prevail over US constitutional law. In contrast, though, whenever these other authorities purport to undermine rights protected by the US Constitution, the Constitution trumps them.[24] In the same vein, we believe that government officials should respect fundamental rights even if they are not expressly articulated in any constitution, treaty, or any other explicit source of law.[25]

What is a right that deserves the type of legal protection I have outlined? Believe me, I understand that one person's cherished "individual right" is another person's abhorred anti-social crime. For example, in the US, these diametrically opposed labels are currently being applied to everything from abortion, to physician-assisted suicide, to homosexual relationships.

Moreover, even if we could agree on what qualifies as a right *prima facie*, we still face another essential question: What are the legitimate limits on that right? Even though we civil libertarians are often described as "absolutists", I am not aware of anyone who does not acknowledge some legitimate limits on individual freedom. To be sure, civil libertarians do insist that, to justify any such limit, government must bear a heavy burden of proof. And, in general, the US Supreme Court has agreed with that approach.[26]

A third important question about the scope of individual rights is, what do we do when one right is in conflict, or at least in tension, with another? In the US, we have had many, ongoing debates about purported conflicts between liberty and equality—or, as sometimes phrased, between "civil *liberties*" and "civil *rights*".

The ACLU has played a prominent role in these debates, since we always have been committed to defending all fundamental rights for all individuals.[27] In our

---

[23] See eg, K T Prinzo, Note: "The United States—'Capital' of the World: An Analysis of Why the United States Practices Capital Punishment While the International Trend is Towards its Abolition" (1999) 24 *Brooklyn J Int'l L* 855.

[24] See Strossen, above n. 16 at 810.

[25] See eg, N Strossen, "What Constitutes Full Protection of Fundamental Freedoms?" (1992) 15 *Harv J L & Pub Pol'y* 43; N Strossen, "Religion and Politics: A Reply to Justice Antonin Scalia" (1997) 24 *Fordham Urb L J* 427, 436.

[26] See eg, N Strossen, "Civil Liberties" (1993) 4 *Geo Mason U Civ Rts L J* 253.

[27] See eg, N Strossen, "In the Defense of Freedom and Equality: The American Civil Liberties Union Past, Present, and Future" (1994) 29 *Harv CR-CL L Rev* 143.

view, these basic rights are not only libertarian in nature, but also egalitarian. Accordingly, we take criticism from partisans on both sides of this purported divide. We are regularly attacked by libertarians on the right side of the political spectrum for supporting egalitarian measures such as affirmative action pro-grammes[28] and enhanced penalties for discriminatory crimes.[29]

Correspondingly, we are also regularly attacked by egalitarians on the left side of the political spectrum for our libertarian opposition to restrictions on expression that, in their view, undermines equality. The major example here is what Americans generally call "hate speech", that is, expression that reflects dislike or discrimination on the basis of race, gender and so forth.[30] Another prime example is actually a specific type of "hate speech"—namely, sexist speech that is sexually explicit.[31] In the US and elsewhere, some outspoken feminists have sought to ban such expression, which they label as "pornography".[32]

I referred above to the "purported" conflict between liberty and equality. Of course, these rights can conflict with each other, but that is true for all rights. And it is certainly not true, as some maintain, that liberty and equality are inherently, or even usually, at odds with each other. To the contrary, these rights tend to be mutually reinforcing, including in the controverted contexts I have just mentioned, hate speech and pornography.[33]

II THE INDIVISIBILITY OF ALL RIGHTS IN GENERAL

Let me start with the general notion of the indivisibility of all rights, for all indi-viduals. This is not just an ACLU credo, but it is essentially the law of the land in the US. For example, in the First Amendment context, this concept is reflected in the rule of "content" or "viewpoint-neutrality", which the Supreme Court has called the "bedrock principle"[34] of our free speech jurisprudence: that government may never limit speech just because any listener, or even the majority of the com-munity, disagrees with or is offended by its content or viewpoint.

Despite the fact that this approach is firmly entrenched in US law, it still meets with a lot of public resistance, at least on first impression. Everyone wants to make

[28] See eg, N Strossen, "Quota Czars" (1997) *J Am Citizenship Pol'y Rev* 3 (responding to J Gavora, "The Quota Czars" (1997) *J Am Citizenship Pol'y Rev* 22); see also N Strossen, "Blaming the Victim: A Critique of Attacks on Affirmative Action" (1992) 77 *Cornell L Rev* 974.

[29] See eg, N Strossen, "Hate Crimes: Should They Carry Enhanced Penalties?—Yes: Discriminatory Crimes" (1993) 79 *ABAJ* 44 (debate with Nat Hentoff).

[30] See eg, R Delgado and J Stefancic, "Hateful Speech, Loving Communities: Why Our Notion of 'A Just Balance' Changes So Slowly" (1994) 82 *Calif L Rev* 851; see also, eg, R Delgado and D H Yun, "Pressure Valves and Bloodied Chickens: An Analysis of Paternalistic Objections to Hate Speech Regulation" (1994) 82 *Calif L Rev* 871.

[31] See eg, M E Gale and N Strossen, "The Real ACLU" (1989) 2 *Yale J L & Feminism* 161.

[32] See eg, A Dworkin, *Pornography: Men Possessing Women* (London, Women's Press, 1981); see also, eg, C A MacKinnon, "Pornography as Defamation and Discrimination" (1991) 71 *BU L Rev* 793.

[33] See eg, N Strossen, "Hate Speech and Pornography: Do We Have to Choose Between Freedom of Speech and Equality?" (1996) 46 *Case W Res L Rev* 449.

[34] *Texas* v. *Johnson* 491 US 397, 414 (1989).

"just one exception" to the First Amendment for the particular idea or expression that s/he considers the most dangerous or odious. For that reason, former Supreme Court Justice Hugo Black, a great First Amendment champion, declared:[35]

> "I do not believe that it can be too often repeated that the freedoms of speech, press, petition and assembly guaranteed by the First Amendment must be accorded to the ideas we hate or sooner or later they will be denied to the ideas we cherish."

I can illustrate the counter-intuitive nature of the viewpoint-neutrality principle by recounting a story involving my own beloved father. Sadly, he died recently, but that means I take special joy in reminiscing about him, including through this anecdote. Dad had retired in San Diego, California. About a dozen years ago, I was invited to give a lecture there, following some well-publicised, ugly incidents of anti-Semitic and racist expression. I was asked to explain why the ACLU defends free speech even for racist and religious bigots, and why we win those cases. My father came to hear my talk. Now, mind you, he was not a card-carrying ACLU member! But he still came because he had not heard me give a speech since my high school commencement address—which, incidentally, he also disagreed with! Anyway, Dad listened very attentively and politely to this more recent talk of mine. Afterwards, he came up to me and said: "I appreciate that excellent explanation about the ACLU's positions and constitutional law. I now understand that the ACLU is correctly interpreting the First Amendment. Thank you for making it clear to me that the problem is the First Amendment."

I do not mean to pick on my dear Dad unfairly. To the contrary, his reaction was quite typical. Often, people do not realise the importance of defending free speech for ideas that they find offensive or abhorrent until or unless their own ideas are subject to censorship, because other people find them offensive or abhorrent.

Let me cite another story that makes this point. Its protagonist is an African-American schoolteacher in Florida named Bill Maxwell. He told his own story in a newspaper column whose title I find most apt: "The ACLU is Quintessential American Group." He refers to the ACLU case that epitomises not only our organisation's commitment, but also our Constitution's commitment, to an indivisible defence even of the most hateful and hated expression. I am referring to the famous—or infamous—"Skokie case", in which we defended the free speech rights of neo-Nazis to march in Skokie, Illinois, a city with not only a large Jewish population, but, even more poignantly, a large population of Holocaust survivors.[36]

While the Skokie case was, and still is, very controversial among the general public, it was very straightforward as a legal matter, involving a classic application of the "viewpoint-neutrality" aspect of the "indivisibility" principle. Still, Bill Maxwell's experience confirms that these principles are hard to accept as such— namely, as abstract principles—and that they make far more sense to most people

---

[35] *Communist Party of the United States* v. *Subversive Activities Control Board* 367 US 1, 137 (1961) (Black J, dissenting).
[36] *Collin* v. *Smith* 578 F 2d 1197 (7th Cir), cert denied, 479 US 916 (1978); *Village of Skokie* v. *National Socialist Party* 69 Ill 2d 605 (1978).

when they bring about some concrete, practical, personal benefit for them, or for people with whom they agree. Here is what he wrote:[37]

> "Like millions of other Americans, I have a love/hate relationship with the ACLU. I donate money to it because I support its absolutist positions on civil liberties. Often, though, I curse this high-minded group and swear I'll never give it another dime.
>
> The last time I fell out of love and canceled my membership was in 1977, when the ACLU defended the right of the American Nazi Party to demonstrate in Skokie, Illinois.
>
> Ironically, I needed the ACLU a year later when three [other] black teachers and I tried to distribute a handbill critical of our university's hiring policies. No other teachers or administrators supported us. In fact, placards produced by our colleagues labeled us as 'racists,' 'niggers' and 'educated monkeys.' But the ACLU took our case and won. Our attorney explained that although the university community saw us as 'obnoxious subversives,' we had a constitutional right to speak.
>
> Suddenly, I recalled the Skokie Nazis. The next day I mailed a check to the ACLU."

Bill Maxwell's experience and insight about the concept of indivisibility extends beyond free speech to all other rights. Across the board, people understandably tend to be more supportive of rights that they can imagine being exercised by themselves, by people like them, or by people they like. Therefore, the ACLU's least popular causes—and our Constitution's least popular clauses—protect the rights of people who are seen as society's most different, most despised, and most, well, *anti-social* members—namely, those accused of crime.[38] It is very difficult for most people to look beyond the facts of a particular case—for example, a heinous murder—and to see the overarching constitutional or civil liberties principles at stake. Justice William Brennan noted this fact in a dissent from a Supreme Court opinion rejecting a constitutional challenge to the death penalty, despite powerful evidence that it is applied in a racially discriminatory fashion:[39]

> "It is tempting to pretend that minorities on death row share a fate in no way connected to our own, that our treatment of them sounds no echoes beyond the chambers in which they die. Such an illusion is ultimately corrosive, for the reverberations of injustice are not so easily confined. . . . [T]he way in which we choose those who will die reveals the depth of moral commitment among the living."

Hard as it is for most people to appreciate the importance of the constitutional and civil liberties principles at stake in the criminal justice system, it is even harder for most people to empathise with those who invoke these principles, since most people do not contemplate that they themselves might be in situations where they would want to be protected by those same principles. There are, though, amusing, ironic incidents where even the most hardened, conservative champions of "law and order" suddenly become born-again advocates of constitutional rights—and

---

[37] Letter from Bill Maxwell to Nadine Strossen (on file with the author).

[38] Strikingly, out of the 27 separate rights that are guaranteed in the Bill of Rights, a full 16—almost 60%—secure the rights of individuals who have been accused or convicted of crime. The Constitution's framers clearly recognised that these rights would be the most embattled, and most in need of constitutional, judicial protection against communities and popularly elected officials.

[39] *McCleskey* v. *Kemp* 481 US 279, 344 (1987).

even of the ACLU—after they have had the unexpected, and unpleasant, experience of finding themselves on the wrong side of the criminal law.

Perhaps the best example is former US Attorney General Ed Meese, who served under President Ronald Reagan. Both Reagan and Meese got a lot of political mileage from their "tough-on-crime" stances. Meese actually denounced the ACLU as "a criminal's lobby";[40] after all, as he told the press, you would not be accused of a crime unless you were guilty.[41] He said that right before he himself became the target of a criminal investigation, facing charges of alleged financial improprieties under income tax and conflict of interest laws.[42] At that point, Meese quickly underwent what I like to call a "conviction conversion"—in both senses of the word "conviction"! It should be stressed that Meese, along with the vast majority of people who are investigated for suspected criminal activity, was not convicted; indeed, he was not even indicted.[43]

Another great example of the "conviction conversion" phenomenon is another top aide of President Reagan, Lyn Nofziger, who wrote the following letter to an ACLU official:[44]

"This letter is to thank you . . . and . . . all those other members of the ACLU who agreed that your organization should intervene on my behalf. I am most appreciative. . . .

Although, as you can imagine, there are many times when I have not agreed with the ACLU, I have never doubted your willingness to stand up and be counted on issues and cases where you believe the Constitution is being violated. I am greatly pleased that you believe mine is one of those cases.

Over the last two years and $1.5 million, I have learned more about our legal system than I ever wanted to know. I have also learned that the courts and the Congress only sometimes believe that the Constitution, including the [F]irst [A]mendment, means what it says. That is why it is important to have organizations such as the ACLU watchdogging those who believe that their ideas of what constitutes the common good override the words of the Constitution.

I'm sure many of my conservative friends will look askance at your involvement in my case and my appreciation of your involvement. They have not been caught in the toils of the American legal system; I have.

Thank you once again."

III THE INDIVISIBILITY OF LIBERTY AND EQUALITY—"CIVIL LIBERTIES" AND "CIVIL RIGHTS"

With that general understanding of indivisibility in mind, let me turn to the more specific, to answer the increasingly common claim that there is an inherent,

---

[40] See E Walsh, "Meese's Viewpoint On ACLU Efforts Called His Own", *Washington Post*, 15 May 1981, A13.

[41] See "Meese's Miranda Reply Shocking to Law Experts", *Chicago Tribune*, 10 October 1985, C8.

[42] See G Lardner Jr and R Marcus, "Ethics Office to Assess Meese's Conduct", *Washington Post*, 28 July 1988, A6.

[43] See "Edwin Meese; The Last Word?", *The Economist*, 23 July 1988, 21 (UK ed p. 37).

[44] Letter from Lyn Nofziger, former aide to President Reagan, to Kate Martin, Legislative Counsel, American Civil Liberties Union (29 September 1988).

irreconcilable conflict between so-called "classic civil liberties" and so-called "civil rights". Most pointedly, this argument contends that the classic civil libertarian protection of free speech undermines the equality rights of groups that traditionally have suffered discrimination.[45]

This claim assumes that there is something special about the relationship between free speech and equality rights that sets it apart from relationships among other rights. This assumption, in turn, reflects two basic misconceptions. First, it presumes that equality rights are different from other rights because they, unlike others, can conflict with free speech. Second, it presumes that equality rights are necessarily and consistently in tension with free speech. Both of these presumptions are wrong.

First, all rights can come into conflict with all other rights, and often do. Even within the realm of classic civil liberties, there are conflicts. For example, we must often wrestle with tensions between free speech and privacy,[46] between free speech and due process,[47] and between free speech and non-establishment of religion.[48] Yes, equality rights are sometimes in tension with free speech. But that does not distinguish them from any other rights.

Moreover, the fact that equality rights sometimes are in tension with free speech—just as other rights sometimes are—does not mean that equality rights are inevitably or even usually in conflict with free speech. To the contrary, free speech and equality rights often go hand in hand.

One prime illustration of the often mutually-reinforcing nature of free speech and equality rights comes from one of the newest civil rights movements, the movement for lesbian and gay rights. For this important cause, defending freedom of speech and promoting equality are essentially inseparable and indistinguishable.[49] For a gay person, the first, necessary step in seeking equal rights is "coming out of the closet", or publicly acknowledging one's sexual orientation. This act is at once both an exercise of free speech rights and an *assertion* of equality rights.

Conversely, those who discriminate against lesbians and gay men often simultaneously attack their free speech and equality rights. A prominent example is the US military's discriminatory "Don't Ask, Don't Tell" policy. Under this policy, even the most outstanding, brave, and patriotic members of our military will be drummed out not only for engaging in homosexual conduct, but also for just

---

[45] See eg, M J Matsuda, C R Lawrence III et al, *Words That Wound: Critical Race Theory, Assaultive Speech, and the First Amendment* (Boulder, Westview Press, 1993).

[46] See eg, E Volokh, "Freedom of Speech and Information Privacy: The Troubling Implications of a Right to Stop People From Speaking About You" (2000) 52 *Stan L Rev* 52.

[47] See eg, N Strossen, "Free Press and Fair Trial: Implications of the O.J. Simpson Case" (1995) 26 *U Tol L Rev* 647.

[48] See eg, N Strossen, "A Framework for Evaluating Equal Access Claims by Student Religious Groups: Is There a Window for Free Speech in the Wall Separating Church and State?" (1985) 71 *Cornell L Rev* 143.

[49] See eg, W B Rubenstein, "Since When is the Fourteenth Amendment Our Route to Equality? Some Reflections on the Construction of the 'Hate-Speech' Debate from a Lesbian/Gay Perspective" in H L Gates et al (eds.), *Speaking of Race, Speaking of Sex: Hate Speech, Civil Rights, and Civil Liberties* (New York, New York University Press, 1994) 280.

saying something that indicates their sexual orientation, even if they had never engaged in any sexual conduct. That is the "Don't Tell" prong of the policy.[50] Accordingly, in the ACLU's constitutional challenge to this policy, which we brought jointly with the Lambda Legal Defense Fund, we argued that it is doubly unconstitutional, violating both equality and free speech rights, and the lower court agreed with us on both scores.[51]

It should not be surprising that there is often a positive relationship between free speech and equality, and between censorship and inequality. After all, at bottom, free speech and equality are simply different facets of the same broader underlying values: respect for individual autonomy and dignity and for societal diversity and pluralism. In a society that respected the autonomy and dignity of all individuals, all people would be free to express their views, no matter what their views or who they were. Likewise, in a society that respected diversity and pluralism, all individuals would be free to express any ideas, regardless of whether the speaker or the idea diverged in any way from societal norms.

In short, contrary to the "rights vs liberties" critique, we can vigorously defend liberty at the same time we defend equality. Indeed, we cannot vigorously defend either unless we vigorously defend both. Moreover, I believe it is conceptually impossible for a dedicated human rights advocate even to draw a meaningful distinction between liberty and equality, let alone to see them as somehow inalterably in opposition to each other. How could we possibly claim to have secured individual liberty, if certain individuals are denied liberty because they belong to certain societal groups? Conversely, how could we possibly claim to have secured meaningful equality for all groups of people, if that equality does not encompass the exercise of individual freedom?

These interrelationships are clearly illustrated by one of the major battles the ACLU is now actively fighting all over the US: against the purported crime of "DWB," or "driving while black or brown".[52] Of course, it violates classic civil liberties for police officers to interfere with individuals' freedom of movement and privacy, and to subject them to unjustified, abusive, harassing searches and seizures. But it also violates core civil rights principles for police officers to inflict these abuses systematically upon members of racial minorities.

In fact, no matter what the issue, the ACLU's clients, sadly, are disproportionately members of racial and other relatively disempowered minority groups.[53] That

---

[50] Section 571 of the National Defense Authorization Act for Fiscal Year 1994, (Subtitle G—Other Matters), Pub L 103–60, 107 Stat 1547 (codified at 10 USC sec 654 (1993)).

[51] *Able* v. *United States*, 968 F Supp 850 (EDNY 1997), rev'd, 155 F3d 628 (2d Cir 1998). The ACLU and Lambda decided not to appeal from the Second Circuit's decision overturning our lower court victory.

[52] See N Strossen, "The Road to Freedom" *Intellectual Capital*, 24 September 1998. <http://www.intellectualcapital.com/issues/98/0924/icopinions2.asp>; see also American Civil Liberties Union, "Is Jim Crow Justice Alive and Well in America Today?" (visited 20 March 2001) <http://www.aclu.org/profiling/index.html>.

[53] See Report to the ACLU's National Board from the Executive Committee's Subcommittee on the Race Commission Report entitled *Integrating the ACLU: A Report to the National Board from the Executive Committee* (29 September 1999) (on file with the New Zealand Law Review).

is certainly true throughout the entire criminal justice system—everything from police brutality, to violations of prisoners' rights, to the administration of the death penalty. In all these contexts, our clients are mainly people of colour. And the same is true of many other human rights issues, ranging from children's rights to women's rights. Even censorship efforts disproportionately target expression by or on behalf of sexual, racial, and other minority groups.[54]

These patterns reflect the political reality that members of minority groups are, by definition, not well-represented by the majoritarian, elected branches of government. It also reflects the economic reality that, alas, members of minority groups are disproportionately poor[55] and hence, for this reason too, especially vulnerable to government abuses.

The noted constitutional law scholar Kenneth Karst well explained the symbiotic relationship between liberty and equality, and between civil liberties and civil rights, in a classic article with this apt title: "Equality as a Central Principle in the First Amendment". He wrote:[56]

"[T]he constitutional values of equality and liberty are fundamentally linked by the notion that equal access to certain institutions and services is a prime component of any meaningful liberty. This link is reflected in the language of egalitarian movements. The civil rights movement of the 1960s, for example, marched under the banner of 'Freedom' even though its chief objective was equal access—to the vote, to education, to housing, even to lunch counters. 'Liberation' is today a theme of more than rhetorical significance in egalitarian causes such as the women's movement."

IV SUPPRESSING HATE SPEECH AND PORNOGRAPHY WOULD UNDERMINE, RATHER THAN ADVANCE, EQUALITY

I will now illustrate the indivisible, mutually reinforcing relationship between free speech and equality in the especially controverted contexts of "hate speech" and pornography. On these points, again, I am speaking not only for American civil libertarians, but also for American constitutional law. It also bears repeating that these views are endorsed by human rights advocates and organisations in some other countries, as well as some international human rights groups.

I will start by briefly explaining the traditional US constitutional approach to "hate speech" and pornography, which coincides with the civil libertarian approach. I will then address the equality-based arguments that have been advanced for changing it.

The arguments for relaxing the traditional speech-protective standards concerning "hate speech" have been vigorously asserted in the US in the recent past, just

---

[54] See N Strossen, *Defending Pornography: Free Speech, Sex, and the Fight For Women's Rights* (New York, Doubleday, 1995) 56–7, 104–5, 217–46; see also *Paris Adult Theater* v. *Slaton* 413 US 49, 73 (1973) (Brennan J, dissenting).

[55] See "Race Divisions May Be Greater Than in 1960s", *Chicago Tribune*, 1 March 1998, C8.

[56] K Karst, "Equality as a Central Principle in the First Amendment" (1975) 43 *U Chi L Rev* 20, 43–4.

as they have been in many European and other countries. Specifically, it has been argued that "hate speech" has fostered increased discrimination and violence against members of minority groups or other groups that are relatively powerless in the political system, such as women. Conversely, it is argued that censoring hate speech would reduce intergroup discrimination and violence.

Although I reject these arguments, I think they are important and worthy of being taken seriously. Indeed, I take these arguments so seriously that I have written one book,[57] and co-authored another,[58] in response. The book that I wrote focuses on pornography, and the book that I co-authored focuses on "hate speech". I am proud that my co-authors include such prominent advocates of equality rights as Henry Louis Gates, Chair of the Afro-American Studies Department at Harvard University, and William Rubenstein, a prominent gay rights scholar and activist. They all join me in arguing that censorship damages both egalitarian and libertarian principles.

A Traditional US Constitutional/Civil Libertarian Approach

American law's traditional protection of all types of hate speech, including sexist speech, reflects two cardinal principles. The first specifies what is *not* a sufficient justification for restricting speech, and the second prescribes what *is* a sufficient justification.

(a) Speech May Not Be Suppressed Because of Disapproval of its Viewpoint

The first of these basic principles requires "viewpoint neutrality". As I explained earlier, this principle holds that government may never limit speech just because any listener—or even, indeed, the majority of the community—disagrees with or is offended by its content or the viewpoint it conveys. The Supreme Court has called this the "bedrock principle" of our proud free speech tradition under American law.[59] In recent years, the Court has steadfastly enforced this fundamental principle to protect speech that conveys ideas that are deeply unpopular with or offensive to many, if not most, Americans—for example, burning an American flag in a political demonstration against national policies,[60] and burning a cross inside the fenced yard of an African-American family that had recently moved into a previously all-white neighborhood.[61]

The "viewpoint-neutrality" principle was also essential to protect expression by pro-civil rights demonstrators during the Civil Rights Movement in the 1960s. In

---

[57] See Strossen, above n. 54.
[58] See N Strossen, "Regulating Racist Speech on Campus: A Modest Proposal?" in H L Gates et al (eds.), *Speaking of Race, Speaking of Sex: Hate Speech, Civil Rights, and Civil Liberties* (New York, New York University Press, 1994) 181.
[59] *Texas* v. *Johnson* 491 US 397, 414 (1989).
[60] *Ibid*; *United States* v. *Eichman* 496 US 310 (1990).
[61] *RAV* v. *City of St. Paul* 505 US 377 (1992).

many of the Southern communities where Martin Luther King and other civil rights activists demonstrated and aired their ideas, their views were seen as deeply offensive, abhorrent, and dangerous to traditional community mores and values concerning race relations. Efforts to censor and punish these expressions, though, were thwarted by court rulings enforcing the "viewpoint-neutrality" principle.

The same fate has befallen antipornography laws touted by some feminists, which would have proscribed sexually explicit expression that is "subordinating" or "degrading" to women, as a violation of women's civil rights. In striking down one such law, the US Court of Appeals for the Seventh Circuit—the highest court to issue a ruling in this area—explained the fatal flaw of viewpoint discrimination as follows:[62]

> "Speech treating women in the approved way—in sexual encounters 'premised on equality' . . . —is lawful no matter how sexually explicit. Speech treating women in the disapproved way—as submissive in matters sexual or as enjoying humiliation—is unlawful no matter how significant the literary, artistic, or political qualities of the work taken as a whole. The state may not ordain preferred viewpoints in this way."

(b) Speech with a Disfavoured Viewpoint is Better Countered by More Speech, Not Suppression

The viewpoint neutrality principle reflects the philosophy, first stated in pathbreaking opinions by former US Supreme Court Justices Oliver Wendell Holmes and Louis Brandeis, that the appropriate response to any speech with which one disagrees in a free society is not censorship but counterspeech—*more* speech, not *less*. Persuasion, not coercion, is the solution.[63] Accordingly, the appropriate response to hate speech is also not to censor it, but to answer it.

Rejecting this philosophy, the movements to censor "hate speech" and pornography target that expression precisely because of its viewpoint—specifically, a biased viewpoint. For this reason, the US courts have unanimously struck down laws punishing "hate speech" or pornography.

The constitutionally-commanded counterspeech strategy is better than censorship not only in principle, but also from a practical perspective. This has been demonstrated in the context of the movement to censor "hate speech" on college and university campuses, which began to gain substantial support in the US in the late 1980s. The ACLU successfully challenged "hate speech codes", prohibiting certain racist and other discriminatory expression on campuses, invoking traditional First Amendment principles. We have also argued, and I continue to believe, that these codes do not effectively advance equality or reduce discrimination. One reason for this conclusion has to do with the potentially empowering experience of responding to hate speech with counterspeech.

I say "potentially", since I realise that the pain and anger and other emotions provoked by being the target of "hate speech" could well have an incapacitating

---

[62] *American Booksellers Ass'n v. Hudnut* 771 F 2d 323, 325 (1985) (7th Cir), aff'd 475 US 1001 (1986).
[63] See eg, *Whitney v. California* 274 US 357, 377 (1927) (Brandeis J, concurring).

effect, preventing any counterspeech on the part of the target himself or herself. Even in such a situation, though, other members of the community who are outraged by the hate speech could engage in counterspeech, and that is likely to have a more positive impact than any censorial response they might undertake. Moreover, once other community members raise their voices to denounce the hate speech, it should be easier for the target to join with them in doing so.

Counterspeech transforms students who would otherwise be seen, and see themselves, largely as victims into activists and reformers. It underscores their dignity, rather than undermines it. One excellent example of the effective use of counterspeech comes from Arizona State University in Tempe, Arizona. Under the leadership of a law professor on that campus, Charles Calleros, the faculty and administration rejected any code that outlawed "hate speech" or punished students who expressed it. Instead, they endorsed an educational or counterspeech response to any "hate speech". Interestingly enough, as a Latino, Charles Calleros is himself a member of a minority group. As such, though, he believes that censoring hate speech is no better for advancing non-discrimination and equality than it is for free speech. And, based on his university's actual experience with the non-censorial, more-speech response to hate speech, Professor Calleros' original speech-protective views have been reinforced.

Professor Calleros has written about the positive impact of the non-censorial approach to "hate speech" at Arizona State University, explaining how it has been empowering and supportive for the targets of the "hate speech", and also educational and promotive of tolerance and anti-discrimination values for the university community as a whole.[64] I would like to quote his description of the first "hate speech" incident under the pro-educational, non-censorial campus policy:[65]

"[F]our black women students . . . were understandably outraged when they noticed a racially degrading poster near the residence of a friend they were visiting in Cholla, a campus dormitory. Rather than simply complain to their friends . . . , they took positive action. First, they spoke with a Resident Assistant who told them that they could express their feelings to the owners of the poster and encourage them to remove it. . . . The students knocked on the door that displayed the racist poster and expressed their outrage in the strongest terms to the occupant who answered the door. . . . He agreed that the poster was inappropriate, removed it, and allowed the women to make a photocopy of it.

[T]he four students then met with the staff director of Cholla. That director set up a meet for all members of Cholla. . . . [A] capacity crowd showed up. . . . All seemed to accept the challenging conclusion that the poster was protected by the First Amendment, and I regard what followed as a model example of constructive response.

First, the black women who discovered the poster explained as perhaps only they could why the poster hurt them deeply. . . . The Anglo-American students assured the black

---

[64] C R Calleros, "Paternalism, Counterspeech, and Campus Hate-Speech Codes: A Reply to Delgado and Yun" (1995) 27 *Ariz St LJ* 1249; and "Reconciliation of Civil Rights and Civil Liberties After *RAV* v. *City of St. Paul*: Free Speech, Antiharassment Policies, Multicultural Education, and Political Correctness at Arizona State University" (1992) *Utah L Rev* 1205.

[65] Letter to the Editor, "African-American Women Respond to Poster with Courage, Intelligence", *State Press*, 15 February 1991, 5.

women that they did not share the stereotypes reflected in the poster, yet all agreed that they would benefit from learning more about other cultures. The group reached a consensus that they would support ASU's Black History events and would work toward developing multicultural programming at Cholla. The four women who led the discussion expressed their desire to meet with the residents of the offending dormitory room to exchange views and to educate them about their feelings and about the danger of stereotyping. I understand that the owner of the poster is planning to publish an apology in [the campus] newspaper today and a personal communication with the four women would be an excellent follow-up. . . .

The entire University community then poured its energy into the kind of constructive action and dialogue that took place in the Cholla meeting. Students organized an open forum. The message was this: at most, a few individuals on a campus think that the racist poster is humorous; in contrast, a great number of demonstrators represent the more prevalent campus view that degrading racial stereotypes are destructive. Such a message is infinitely more effective than disciplining the students who displayed the racist poster."

In addition to empowering the students who encountered the racist poster, and educating the students who had displayed it, the non-censorial response to this "hate speech" incident generated constructive steps to counter bias campus-wide. One of the student leaders of this constructive college-wide response was Rossie Turman, who was then Chairman of the African-American Coalition at Arizona State University. Turman's leadership in supporting both free speech and non-discrimination earned him much recognition, including an award from a major civil rights organisation, the Anti-Defamation League. As one press account stated:

"Turman and other campus minority group leaders handled their anger by calling a press conference and rally to voice their concerns and allow students and administrators to speak. . . . Within days, the ASU Faculty Senate passed a previously-proposed domestic diversity course requirement. Turman said: "When you get a chance to swing at racism, and you do, you feel more confident about doing it the next time. It was a personal feeling of empowerment, that I don't have to take that kind of stupidity. . . . The sickest thing would have been if the racists had been kicked out, the university sued, and people were forced to defend these folks. It would have been a momentary victory, but we would have lost the war."

After this incident, Rossie Turman went on to be elected student body President at ASU, the first African-American to hold that position on a campus with an African-American student population of only 2.3 per cent. Upon his graduation from college, he went to Columbia Law School. Therefore, for him, what could have been a disempowering, victimising experience with "hate speech" became an empowering, leadership-development experience—not despite the absence of censorship, but because of it.

In contrast with the "more-speech" response to "hate speech" adopted by Arizona State University, a censorial response does not empower the maligned students. To the contrary, it may well perpetuate their victimisation. Worse yet, ironically, censoring "hate speech" may well empower verbal abusers, by making them into free speech martyrs. This point was captured by an editorial in the *Progressive* magazine:[66]

> "[T]he attempt to ban or punish hateful speech does nothing at all to empower the presumed victims of bigotry. Instead, it compels them to seek the protection of authorities whose own commitment to justice is often, to put it mildly, less than vigorous. Restraining speech increases the dependency of minorities and other victims of hate and oppression. Instead of empowering them, it enfeebles them."

(c) The "Clear and Present Danger" Requirement

Laws suppressing "hate speech" or pornography also violate the second core principle of US free speech law: that a restriction on speech can be justified only when necessary to prevent actual or imminent harm to an interest of "compelling" importance, such as violence toward others. As former Supreme Court Justice Oliver Wendell Holmes observed in a much-quoted opinion, the First Amendment would not protect someone who falsely shouted "Fire!" in a theatre and caused a panic.[67] This is often summarised as the "clear and present danger" requirement.

This second core free speech principle entails two essential prerequisites for justifying any speech restrictions: 1) that the expression will cause direct, imminent harm to a very important interest; and 2) that only by suppressing the expression can we avert such harm. Each of these requirements is crucial for preserving free expression, and neither is satisfied by advocates of suppressing "hate speech" or pornography.

To be restricted consistent with the "clear-and-present-danger" principle, speech must *clearly* pose an *imminent* danger, not just a more speculative, attenuated connection to potential future harm. Allowing speech to be curtailed on the ground that it might indirectly lead to possible harm sometime in the future would inevitably unravel free speech protection. After all, *any* speech might lead to potential danger at some future point. Therefore, if we banned the expression of all ideas that might induce individuals to take actions that could endanger important interests, such as public safety, scarcely any idea would be safe, and surely no idea that challenged the status quo would be.

Earlier in this century, the US Supreme Court did apply this relaxed, so-called "bad tendency" approach to free speech; the Court allowed speech to be suppressed if it might tend to cause some future harm. Precisely this approach stifled all progressive voices and causes until shockingly recently, from the labour movement to the Civil Rights movement. For example, during the World War I era and the ensuing "Red Scare," thousands of Americans were imprisoned just for expressing pacifist or socialist views. Likewise, at the height—or depth—of the Cold War, members of left-wing political groups were punished just for criticising

---

[66] "The Speech We Hate" 56(8) *The Progressive*, 8 August 1992, 8, 8–9.
[67] *Schenck* v. *United States* 249 US 47, 52 (1919).

capitalism or advocating Marxism. Given this history, I find it ironic that self-described "leftists" or "progressives" now seek to resurrect the very same censorial standards that were so long used to suppress their ideas.

In the modern era, though, the Supreme Court has resoundingly repudiated this bad tendency rationale for suppressing controversial speech. Moreover, in the modern era, the Court also has recognised the crucial distinction between advocacy of violent or unlawful conduct, which is protected, and intentional, imminent incitement of such conduct, which is not. The Court enshrined this distinction in a landmark 1969 decision, *Brandenburg* v. *Ohio*.[68] In *Brandenburg*, the Court unanimously upheld the First Amendment rights of a Ku Klux Klan leader who addressed a rally of supporters, some of whom brandished firearms, and advocated violence and discrimination against Jews and blacks. The Court held that this generalised advocacy was neither intended nor likely to cause immediate violent or unlawful conduct, and therefore could not be punished.

The Supreme Court has consistently applied *Brandenburg's* critical distinction between protected advocacy and unprotected incitement to shelter inflammatory expression of every stripe, including fiery rhetoric in support of civil rights causes and protests.[69]

As I have explained, before the government may restrict expression, it must show not only that the expression threatens imminent serious harm, but also that the restriction is necessary to avert the harm. Undeniably, the interests that advocates of censoring hate speech and pornography seek to promote—the equality and safety of minority groups and women—are supremely important. But advocates of suppressive laws cannot even show that these laws would effectively promote the safety and equality of minority groups and women, let alone that they are necessary to do so. Indeed, these laws may well do more harm than good in terms of safety and equality.

Space does not permit elaboration of the many reasons for these conclusions, which I have discussed in detail in my books about "hate speech" and pornography. Here, I will list the reasons for these conclusions, and then elaborate on three of them.

B Summary of Reasons Why Suppressing Hate Speech and Pornography Does Not Promote Equality

First, let me sum up the reasons why suppressing "hate speech" in general does not promote, and may well undermine, racial and other types of equality. As I explained earlier, the concept of illegal pornography advocated by some feminists is a type of "hate speech"—specifically, sexist speech that is sexually explicit. Accordingly, the following conclusions about hate speech apply to this concept of pornography, too.[70]

---

[68] 395 US 444 (1969).

[69] See eg, *NAACP* v. *Claiborne Hardware Co.* 458 US 886 (1982).

[70] See Strossen, above n. 58, 224–9 (1994) (elaborating on the following conclusions).

- Censoring hate speech increases attention to, and sympathy for, bigots.
- It drives bigoted expression and ideas underground, thus making response more difficult.
- It is inevitably enforced disproportionately against speech by and on behalf of minority group members themselves.
- It reinforces paternalistic stereotypes about minority group members, suggesting that they need special protection from offensive speech.
- It increases resentment against minority group members, the presumed beneficiaries of the censorship.
- Censoring "hate speech" undermines a mainstay of equal rights movements, which have always been especially dependent on a robust concept of free speech.
- An "anti-hate-speech" policy curbs the candid intergroup dialogue concerning racism and other forms of bias, which is an essential precondition for reducing discrimination.
- Positive intergroup relations will more likely result from education, free discussion, and the airing of misunderstandings and insensitivity, rather than from legal battles; in contrast, "anti-hate-speech" rules will continue to generate litigation and other forms of controversy that increase intergroup tensions.
- Last but far from least, censorship is diversionary, making it easier to avoid coming to grips with less convenient and more expensive, but ultimately more meaningful, strategies for combating discrimination. Censoring discriminatory expression diverts us from the essential goals of eradicating discriminatory attitudes and conduct.

Now I will list the specific reasons why suppressing pornography does not promote, and may well undermine, the critically important goals of reducing discrimination and violence against women. Many of these parallel my analysis of "anti-hate-speech" laws:

- Censoring pornography would suppress many works that are especially valuable to women and feminists.[71]
- Any pornography censorship scheme would be enforced in a way that discriminates against the least popular, least powerful groups in our society, including feminists and lesbians.[72]
- It would perpetuate demeaning stereotypes about women, including that sex is bad for us.[73]
- It would perpetuate the disempowering notion that women are essentially victims.[74]
- It would distract us from constructive approaches to countering discrimination and violence against women.[75]

---

[71] See Strossen, above n. 54 at 203–6.
[72] *Ibid*, 224–44.
[73] *Ibid*, 107–12.
[74] *Ibid*, 114–18.
[75] *Ibid*, 268–79.

- It would harm women who voluntarily work in the sex industry.[76]
- It would harm women's efforts to develop their own sexuality.[77]
- It would strengthen the power of the right wing, whose patriarchal agenda would curtail women's rights.[78]
- By undermining free speech, censorship would deprive feminists of a powerful tool for advancing women's equality.[79]
- Finally, since sexual freedom, and freedom for sexually explicit expression, are essential aspects of human freedom, censoring such expression would undermine human rights more broadly.[80]

Now let me expand on three of the reasons why censoring either hate speech or pornography would be as dangerous for equality rights as free speech rights.

C A Robust Freedom of Speech is Especially Important for Advancing Egalitarian Causes

First and foremost, all those who seek equal rights and freedom have an especially important stake in securing free speech. Throughout history, free speech consistently has been the greatest ally of those seeking equal rights for groups that have been subject to discrimination. For example, the 1960s Civil Rights movement in the United States was particularly dependent on a robust concept of free speech, one that was capacious enough to encompass "hate speech". Absolutely critical to the success of that movement were the landmark rulings of the US Supreme Court under the leadership of Chief Justice Earl Warren—not only the Warren Court's rulings dealing directly with the Constitution's equal rights guarantee, but also its rulings upholding a capacious concept of free speech, extending even to the most provocative and controversial speech.[81]

Important as the Court's equal protection rulings were for advancing the civil rights cause, those rulings could not even have been achieved, let alone effectively implemented, without the organising and litigating efforts of the NAACP (National Association for the Advancement of Colored People), without the speeches and demonstrations of Martin Luther King and other civil rights leaders and activists, and without the press coverage that mobilised the support of the American public and the national government.

All of these essential foundations for advances in civil rights depended upon the Warren Court's broad, vigorous conception of free speech—a conception sufficiently broad and vigorous that it necessarily also encompassed "hate speech" and

---

[76] See Strossen, above n. 54 at 179–98.

[77] *Ibid*, 171–8.

[78] *Ibid*, 81–2, 90–1.

[79] *Ibid*, 217–44.

[80] *Ibid*, 56–8, 218–20.

[81] See N Strossen, "Freedom of Speech in the Warren Court" in B Schwartz (ed.), *The Warren Court: A Retrospective* (New York, Oxford University Press, 1996) 68.

other forms of speech that now are said to undermine equality. The Warren Court record conclusively shows that, in the words of historian Samuel Walker, "The . . . civil rights movement depended on the First Amendment."[82]

Civil rights leaders concur in this judgment. In the words of Benjamin L Hooks, former Executive Director of the NAACP, "The civil rights movement would have been vastly different without the shield and spear of the First Amendment."[83] Likewise, Eleanor Holmes Norton, an African-American woman who served as Director of the Equal Employment Opportunity Commission, and who now represents the District of Columbia in Congress, succinctly summarised the positive, symbiotic relationship between free speech and equality during the Civil Rights Movement when she said: "There was always the First."[84]

In his 1994 book, *Hate Speech: The History of an American Controversy*, Samuel Walker shows that, throughout the twentieth century, the equality rights of African Americans and other minority groups were dependent on an expansive concept of protected free speech. He further documents that the major American civil rights organisations consistently opposed efforts to restrict any speech viewed as hateful or dangerous, because they realised that their own speech certainly was so viewed in many Southern and other communities. As Walker concluded, "[t]he lessons of the civil rights movement were that the interests of racial minorities and powerless groups were best protected through the broadest, most content-neutral protection of speech."[85] These speech-protective principles allowed protestors to carry their messages to audiences who found them highly offensive and threatening to their most deeply cherished views of themselves and their way of life. Equating civil rights activists with Communists, subversives, and criminals, government officials mounted inquisitions against the NAACP, seeking compulsory disclosure of its membership lists and endangering the members' jobs and lives. As Professor Harry Kalven concluded, "[o]nly strong principles of free speech and association could—and did—protect the drive for desegregation".[86]

These principles allowed protestors to carry their messages to audiences who found them highly offensive and threatening to their most deeply cherished views of themselves and their way of life. Martin Luther King Jr wrote his historic letter from a Birmingham jail,[87] but the Warren Court later struck down the Birmingham parade ordinance that King and other demonstrators had violated, holding that it had breached their First Amendment rights.[88]

The more disruptive forms of civil rights protest, such as marches, sit-ins, and kneel-ins (which some observers credit as being the most effective) were especially

---

[82] S Walker, above n. 1 at 241.

[83] Statement quoted in Phillip Morris Companies, Inc, Press Release (7 May 1990).

[84] See Walker, above n. 1 at 241.

[85] S Walker, *Hate Speech: The History of an American Controversy* (Lincoln, University & Nebraska Press, 1994) 126.

[86] H Kalven Jr, *The Negro and The First Amendment* (Chicago, University of Chicago Press, 1965) 6.

[87] M L King, "Letter From the Birmingham Jail" in M L King, *Why We Can't Wait* (New York, Harper & Row, 1964) 77.

[88] *Shuttlesworth* v. *Birmingham* 394 US 147 (1969).

dependent on generous judicial constructions of the free speech guarantee.[89] Notably, many of these protective interpretations initially had been formulated in cases brought on behalf of anti-civil rights demonstrators. Similarly, the insulting and often racist language that militant black activists hurled at police officers and other government officials was also protected under the same principles and precedents.[90]

The mutually reinforcing relationship between a strong free speech guarantee and equality rights obtains for other equality movements, in addition to the Civil Rights Movement on behalf of African Americans. As I have argued in *Defending Pornography: Free Speech, Sex, and the Fight for Women's Rights*,[91] the movement for equal rights for women, including reproductive freedom, has always depended upon strong protection of free speech for ideas that many communities have seen as offensive, wrong, and dangerous. The same pattern holds for the lesbian and gay rights movement, as I explained above.

D Censorship Has Consistently Been Used to Suppress Civil Rights Causes

Just as free speech has always been the strongest weapon to *advance* equal rights causes, correspondingly, censorship has always been the strongest weapon to *thwart* them. Ironically, the explanation for this pattern lies in the very analysis of those who want to curb hate speech and pornography. They contend that racial minorities and women are relatively disempowered and marginalised. I agree with that analysis of the problem, and am deeply committed to working toward solving it. Indeed, I am proud that the ACLU is, and long has been, on the forefront of the struggles for racial justice, women's rights, and other equality movements.

But I strongly disagree that censorship is a solution for our society's persistent discrimination. To the contrary, precisely because women and minorities are relatively powerless, it makes no sense to hand the power structure yet another tool that it can use—and does and will use—to further suppress them, in both senses of the word "suppress". Consistent with the analysis of the censorship advocates themselves, the government will inevitably wield this tool, along with all others, to the particular disadvantage of already disempowered groups.

(a) *"Anti-Hate Speech" Laws Have Stifled Human Rights Causes*

Laws censoring hate speech are inevitably enforced disproportionately against speech by and on behalf of those who lack political power, including government

---

[89] See eg, *NAACP* v. *Claiborne Hardware Co* 458 US 886 (1982); *Gregory* v. *Chicago* 394 US 111 (1969); *Cox* v. *Louisiana*, 379 US 536, 550 (1965) and *Edwards* v. *South Carolina* 371 US 229 (1963).

[90] See *Brown* v. *Oklahoma* 408 US 914 (1972); *Gooding* v. *Wilson* 405 US 518, 523 (1972); *Lewis* v. *New Orleans* 415 US 130 (1974).

[91] See Strossen, above n. 54 at 224–9.

critics, and even members of the very minority groups who are the laws' intended beneficiaries. This conclusion is confirmed by the enforcement record of all censorship measures, around the world, and throughout history. The pattern of discriminated-against, disempowered groups being disproportionately targeted under censorship measures extends even to measures that are allegedly for their benefit, including laws against "hate speech" and pornography.

This was the conclusion reached by the respected international human rights organisation, Human Rights Watch, based on actual experience and observations in countries around the world. In 1992, Human Rights Watch issued a report and policy statement opposing any restrictions on "hate speech" that go beyond the narrow confines permitted by traditional US First Amendment principles. In a comprehensive report, Human Rights Watch explained its position as follows:[92]

> "[This] policy [applies] free speech principles in the anti-discrimination context in a manner that is respectful of both concerns, believing that they are complementary, not contradictory. While we recognize that the policy is closer to the American legal approach than to that of any other nation, it was arrived at after a careful review of the experience of many other countries.
>
> This review has made clear that there is little connection in practice between draconian 'hate speech' laws and the lessening of ethnic and racial violence or tension. Furthermore, most of the nations which invoke 'hate speech' laws have a long way to go in implementing the provisions of the Convention for the Elimination of Racial Discrimination calling for the elimination of racial discrimination. Laws that penalize speech or membership are also subject to abuse by the dominant racial or ethnic group. Some of the most stringent 'hate speech' laws, for example, were in force in South Africa during the apartheid era, when they were used almost exclusively against the black majority."

Similar conclusions were generated by an international conference organised by the international free speech organisation, Article 19, in 1991. It brought together human rights activists, lawyers, and scholars, from fifteen different countries, to compare notes on the actual impact that" anti-hate-speech" laws had in their respective countries, in promoting equality, and countering bias and discrimination.[93] The conclusion from these proceedings was clear: there was not even any correlation, let alone any causal relationship, between the enforcement of anti-hate-speech laws in particular countries and an improvement in equality or intergroup relations in those countries. These findings were summarised by Article 19's Legal Director, Sandra Coliver:[94]

> "[L]aws which restrict hate speech have been flagrantly abused by the authorities. Thus, the laws in Sri Lanka and South Africa have been used almost exclusively against the

---

[92] Human Rights Watch, "Hate Speech" and Freedom of Expression: A Human Rights Watch Policy Paper 4 (1992).

[93] I was honoured to participate in that memorable gathering. The conference papers were subsequently published in an excellent book, S Coliver (ed.), *Striking A Balance: Hate Speech, Freedom of Expression and Non-Discrimination* (London, Article 19 and Human Rights Centre, University of Essex, 1992).

[94] S Coliver, "Hate Speech Laws: Do They Work?", *ibid*, 363, 373–4.

oppressed and politically weakest communities. . . . In Eastern Europe and the former Soviet Union these laws were vehicles for the persecution of critics who were often also victims of state-tolerated or sponsored anti-Semitism. Selective or lax enforcement by the authorities, including in the United Kingdom, Israel and the former Soviet Union, allows governments to compromise the right of dissent and inevitably leads to feelings of alienation among minority groups.

Such laws may also distract from the need for effective legislation to promote non-discrimination. The rise of racism and xenophobia throughout Europe despite laws restricting racist speech, calls into question the effectiveness of such laws in the promotion of tolerance and non-discrimination. One worrying phenomenon is the sanitized language now adopted to avoid prosecution by prominent racists in Britain, France, Israel and other countries, which may have the effect of making their hateful messages more acceptable to a broader audience."

Other illustrations abound. For example, the Turkish government has invoked its law against inciting racial hatred to bring thousands of prosecutions against Turkish writers, journalists, academicians, and scientists who have criticised the government's war against Kurdish separatists. In 1995, the Turkish government prosecuted a US journalist accused of "inciting hatred" by writing an article on that same topic.[95] Likewise, Singapore's authoritarian, long-time governing party has threatened to sue the main opposition party, the Workers' Party, for inciting racial hatred.[96]

These examples are consistent with a worldwide pattern throughout history. Thus, former US Supreme Court Justice Hugo Black made the following trenchant observation, in dissenting from a 1952 decision upholding a "hate speech" law (which has been overturned implicitly by subsequent decisions[97]):[98]

"If there be minority groups who hail this holding as their victory, they might consider the possible relevancy of this ancient remark: 'Another such victory and I am undone'."

The first individuals prosecuted under the British Race Relations Act of 1965, which criminalised the incitement of racial hatred, were black power leaders. Their overtly racist messages undoubtedly expressed legitimate anger at real discrimination, yet the statute drew no such fine lines, nor could any similar law possibly do so. Rather than curbing speech offensive to minorities, this British law instead has been used regularly to curb the speech of blacks, trade unionists, and anti-nuclear activists. Perhaps the ultimate irony of this law, intended to restrain the National Front, a neo-Nazi group, is that it instead has barred expression by the Anti-Nazi League.

The British experience is typical. None of the anti-Semites who were responsible for arousing France against Captain Alfred Dreyfus was ever prosecuted for group libel. But Emile Zola was prosecuted for libelling the French clergy and

[95] K Couturier, "U.S. Reporter Caught Up in Turkey's Crackdown on Press", *The San Francisco Chronicle*, 11 October 1995, A8.
[96] "Singapore Campaign Ends in Threats of Lawsuits", *New York Times*, 2 January 1997, A4.
[97] See L H Tribe, *American Constitutional Law*, 2nd edn. (Mineola, Foundation Press, 1988) 927.
[98] *Beauharnais* v. *Illinois* 343 US 250, 275 (1952) (Black J, dissenting).

military in his classic letter "J'Accuse", and he had to flee to England to escape punishment.

Similarly, Professor Eric Stein has documented that although the German Criminal Code of 1871 punished offenses against personal honour,[99]

"The German Supreme Court . . . consistently refused to apply this article to insults against Jews as a group—although it gave the benefit of its protection to such groups as 'Germans living in Prussian provinces, large landowners, all Christian clerics, German officers, and Prussian troops who fought in Belgium and Northern France'."

Canada's "anti-hate-speech" law has also led to the suppression of expression by members of minority groups. For example, enforcing this law, Canadian Customs officials seized 1500 copies of the book *Black Looks: Race and Representation* by the African-American feminist scholar, bell hooks, which had been en route to Canadian universities. Other such perverse applications of the law were cited by the dissenting opinion in the Supreme Court of Canada's decision upholding this law—by a narrow 5–4 vote—under Canada's Charter of Rights and Freedoms. The dissent noted:[100]

"Although [the law] is of relatively recent origin, it has provoked many questionable actions on the part of the authorities. . . . [I]ntemperate statements about identifiable groups, particularly if they represent an unpopular viewpoint, may attract state involvement or calls for police action. Novels such as Leon Uris' pro-Zionist novel, *The Haj*, face calls for banning. . . . Other works, such as Salman Rushdie's *Satanic Verses*, are stopped at the border on the ground that they violate [the law]. Films may be temporarily kept out, as happened to a film entitled *Nelson Mandela*, ordered as an educational film by Ryerson Polytechnical Institute. . . . Arrests are even made for distributing pamphlets containing the words 'Yankee Go Home'."

The international pattern also holds true in specific, localised contexts—namely, on university and college campuses. Again, the British experience is instructive. In 1974, in a move aimed at the National Front, the British National Union of Students (NUS) adopted a resolution that representatives of "openly racist and fascist organizations" were to be prevented from speaking on college campuses "by whatever means necessary (including disruption of the meeting)".[101] The rule had been designed in large part to stem an increase in campus anti-Semitism. But following the United Nations' cue, some British students deemed Zionism a form of racism beyond the bounds of permitted discussion, and in 1975 British students invoked the NUS resolution to disrupt speeches by Israelis and Zionists, including the Israeli ambassador to Great Britain. The intended target of the NUS resolution, the National Front, applauded this result. The NUS itself, in contrast, became disenchanted by this and other unintended consequences of its resolution and repealed it in 1977.

---

[99] E Stein, "History Against Free Speech: The New German Law Against the 'Auschwitz'—and Other—'Lies' " (1986) 85 *Mich L Rev* 277, 286.

[100] *R v. Keegstra* [1990] 3 SCR 697, 895 per McLachlin J.

[101] A Neier, *Defending My Enemy: American Nazis, the Skokie Case, and the Risks of Freedom* (New York, Dutton, 1979) 155–7.

The British experience parallels what has happened in the United States, as evidenced by the campus "hate speech" codes for which enforcement information is available.[102] One such code was in effect at the University of Michigan from April 1988 until October 1989. Because the ACLU brought a lawsuit to challenge the code (which resulted in a ruling that the code was unconstitutional),[103] the university was forced to disclose information that otherwise would have been unavailable to the public about how it had been enforced. This enforcement record, while not surprising to anyone familiar with the consistent history of censorship measures, should come as a rude awakening to any who believes that "anti-hate-speech" laws will protect or benefit racial minorities, women, or any other group that has traditionally suffered discrimination.

During the year and a half that the University of Michigan rule was in effect, there were more than twenty cases of whites charging blacks with racist speech. More importantly, the only two instances in which the rule was invoked to sanction racist speech (as opposed to other forms of "hate speech") involved the punishment of speech by or on behalf of black students. The only student who was subjected to a full-fledged disciplinary hearing under the Michigan rule was an African-American student accused of homophobic and sexist expression. In seeking clemency from the punishment that was imposed on him after this hearing, the student asserted that he had been singled out because of his race and his political views.[104]

Others who were punished at the University of Michigan included several Jewish students accused of engaging in anti-Semitic expression (they wrote graffiti, including a swastika, on a classroom blackboard, saying they intended it as a practical joke), and an Asian-American student accused of making an anti-black comment (his allegedly "hateful" remark was to ask why black people feel discriminated against; he said he raised this question because the black students in his dormitory tended to socialise together, making him feel isolated).

Likewise, the student who in 1989 challenged the University of Connecticut's "hate speech" policy, under which she had been penalized for an allegedly homophobic remark, was Asian-American. She claimed that other students had engaged in similar expression, but that she had been singled out for punishment because of her ethnic background.[105]

---

[102] See N Strossen, "Frontiers of Legal Thought (II) The New First Amendment: Regulating Racist Speech on Campus: A Modest Proposal?" (1990) *Duke LJ* 484, 554–5.

[103] *Doe* v. *University of Michigan* 721 F Supp 852 (ED Mich 1989). The ACLU also successfully challenged a "hate speech" code at the University of Wisconsin. See *UWM Post, Inc* v. *Board of Regents of University of Wisconsin System* 774 F Supp 1163 (ED Wis 1991).

[104] See Plaintiff's Exhibit Submitted in Support of Motion for Preliminary Injunction at 1, *Doe* v. *University of Mich* 721 F. Supp. 852 (ED Mich 1989) (No. 89-CV-71683-DT) (black student used term "white trash" in conversation with white student); *ibid*, 5 (at beginning of preclinical dentistry course, recognised as difficult, faculty member led small group discussion, designed to "identify concerns of students"; dental student said that he had heard, from his minority roommate, that minorities have a difficult time in the course and were not treated fairly; the faculty member, who was black, complained that the student was accusing her of racism).

[105] Representing this student, the ACLU persuaded the university to drop the challenged policy. See *Wu* v. *University of Conn* No. Civ H89-649 PCD (D Conn 1989).

And the first complaint filed under Trinity College's then-new policy prohibiting racial harassment, in 1989, was against an African-American speaker who had been sponsored by a black student organisaton, Black-Power Serves itself.

(b) Anti-pornography Laws Have Stifled Feminists, Reproductive Freedom Advocates and Lesbian/Gay Expression

Just as "anti-hate-speech" laws consistently have been used to suppress speech on behalf of disempowered individuals, the same is true of all forms of censorship. That generalisation certainly pertains to censorship of sexual expression. Whatever particular epithet is used for the targeted expression—be it "obscenity," or "pornography," or "indecency"—the end-result is always the same: at risk is any expression with any sexual connotation, and at particular risk is any expression on behalf of women, women's rights, reproductive freedom, and lesbian and gay sexuality. My book on pornography provides many examples, but for now I will confine myself to two, one historic, and one current.

The historic example goes back to the ACLU's first decade and one of our first clients, the pioneering birth-control advocate, Margaret Sanger. She was repeatedly harassed, persecuted, prosecuted—and even convicted and imprisoned—for daring to give women information about their bodies, their health, their sexuality, and their child-bearing options. The instrument of her repression was the 1873 Comstock Law, the first national anti-obscenity law in the US. The information she wanted to give women, to assist them to take charge of their own bodies and lives, was deemed criminally obscene.[106]

Sadly, not much has changed. Let me cite one current incarnation of this same pattern: cybercensorship laws. While the advocates of these laws say that they are protecting us against "cyberporn"—again that demonised epithet—in fact, the laws criminalise any expression with any sexual content, no matter how valuable the expression may be either in general or to women in particular.

Alas, it is still true, at the dawn of the new millennium, that women and sexual orientation minorities are relatively disempowered, and that their rights are relatively unpopular causes. Moreover, there is reason to fear that these groups and causes are going to continue to be embattled. Consider, for example, the most comprehensive assessment of American students' attitudes, the annual survey of incoming college students that is conducted by UCLA's Higher Education Research Institute and the American Council on Education. Since the early 1990s, that survey has shown decreasing support for reproductive freedom and gay rights. Among students who entered college in 1999, only 52.7 per cent believe that abortion should be legal, and 30.3 per cent said that "it is important to have laws prohibiting homosexual relationships".[107]

---

[106] Strossen, above n. 54 at 226–7.
[107] See generally, L J Sax et al, *American Freshman: National Norms for Fall 1999* (Higher Education Research Institute, 1999).

These anti-choice and anti-gay-rights attitudes are manifest in the many anti-choice and anti-gay actions by government officials and citizens all over the country, ranging from legislative assaults on the rights to literal assaults on the individuals who seek to exercise them. Therefore, it is not surprising that courts have concurred with the ACLU that prime targets of all the cybercensorship laws would include any expression concerning women's sexual and reproductive health and options, as well as any concerning lesbian and gay sexuality. This sad-but-true fact is illustrated by the clients that the ACLU has represented in our challenges to cybercensorship laws.

I find it particularly striking, for instance, that one of our clients in *Reno* v. *ACLU*[108] was the Planned Parenthood Federation of America, the organisation that Sanger founded, against the Internet era's first federal cybercensorship law, which criminalised the very same information. Consider, also, just a few of the ACLU's other clients in challenges to cybercensorship measures that endangered their expression:

—American Association of University Women–Maryland, which promotes equity, education, self-development over the life span, and positive societal change, for all women and girls, working to remove barriers and to develop opportunities to enable women and girls to reach their full potential;
—Books for Gay and Lesbian Teens/Youth Page, which has a website operated by a teenaged high school student, listing books that may be of interest to gay and lesbian youth;
—Critical Path AIDS Project, an AIDS treatment and prevention information project that offers AIDS treatment and safer sex information that is specifically geared toward young people;
—Full Circle Books, one of the oldest and largest feminist bookstores in North America;
—Human Rights Watch, the largest US-based international human rights organisation, which documents and challenges human rights abuses around the world, many of which involve sexual abuse against women;
—Obgyn.net, a comprehensive international online resource centre for professionals in obstetrics and gynaecology and the women they serve, offering up-to-the-minute information, clinical reference collections, and discussion forums;
—*Philadelphia Gay News*, the award-winning weekly;
—PlanetOut, a website that serves as an online community for gay, lesbian, bisexual and transgendered people, a valuable resource for "closeted" people who do not voluntarily disclose their sexual orientation due to fear of others' reactions;
—Queer Resources Directory, one of the largest online distributors of gay, lesbian and bisexual resources;
—*Riotgrrl*, a magazine aimed at young feminists;
—*Salon Magazine*, a leading general interest online magazine, whose feature articles address sexuality, among other topics, and which also includes a regular

---

[108] 521 US 844 (1997).

column entitled "Sexpert Opinion" by feminist author and sex therapist Susie Bright;

—Sexual Health Network, which provides information about sexuality geared toward individuals with disabilities, including articles on erectile dysfunction, the use of sex toys, and sexual surrogacy as a form of sexual therapy;

—Stop Prisoner Rape, which is dedicated to combating sexual abuse in our nation's prisons, including among the fastest growing segment of our nation's prison population—women;

—The Safer Sex Page, which maintains a large archive of information about minimising the risks of sexually transmitted diseases;

—Jeff Walsh, editor of Oasis Magazine, a monthly online magazine for lesbian, gay, bisexual, and questioning youth, which includes news, reviews, and safer sex advice columns written by and for gay and lesbian youth.

The courts have agreed with us that the online expression of the foregoing individuals and organisations is subject to prosecution under the various cybercensorship laws that have been touted as "protecting children" from "cyberporn"—no matter how much serious value that expression has in general, and no matter how much serious value it has for the causes of women's rights, reproductive freedom, and lesbian/gay rights in particular. I consider it tragic that so-called "radical feminists" have joined with the so-called "religious right" to call for criminalising this type of material. Far from harming women, exactly the opposite is true.

The same pattern obtains even when the law supposedly targets sexual expression that is demeaning to women. That is clearly shown by the experience in Canada. In 1992, in a case called *R v. Butler*,[109] the Supreme Court of Canada held that, henceforth, Canada's obscenity law would bar sexual materials that are "degrading" or "dehumanising" to women. Alas for women, however, the enforcement record under this law has followed the familiar pattern; it has harmed the very groups that it was supposed to help. As my book documents in detail, the particular victims of Canada's new censorship regime have been women, feminists, and lesbians and gay men, their writings and their bookstores.[110] This point was acknowledged even by the Women's Legal Education and Action Fund (LEAF), the Canadian feminist pro-censorship organisation, that Catharine MacKinnon co-founded, and which had initially supported the *Butler* decision. Yet, in a 1993 press release, LEAF was forced to recognise that *Butler* had backfired:[111]

> "Since the *Butler* decision, Canada Customs [and] police forces . . . have exploited [the] law to harass bookstores, artists, AIDS organizations, sex trade workers, and safe sex educators. Lesbian and gay materials have been particularly singled out."

The extent to which Canada's supposedly pro-feminist anti-pornography law actually has had a devastating impact on lesbian and gay writings was dramatically

---

[109] [1992] 1 SCR 452.
[110] Strossen, above n. 54 at 229–39.
[111] "Historic Gathering Condemns Targeting of Lesbian and Gay Materials and Sex Trade Workers" *LEAF News Release* (Women's Legal Education and Action Fund, Toronto, 21 June 1993).

brought home by a collection of works that have been banned in Canada under this law. Published by Cleis Press, a lesbian-oriented publisher in Pittsburgh, the title of this collection is a clever wordplay, *Forbidden Passages*.[112] It was published in an effort to raise funds for Little Sisters Bookstore in Vancouver, a gay and lesbian-themed bookstore that was driven to the brink of bankruptcy as a result of Canada's anti-pornography regime.[113] The authors whose banned-in-Canada works are represented in the collection include Kathy Acker, Dorothy Allison, Susie Bright, Dennis Cooper, Diane DiMassa, Marguerite Duras, bell hooks, Richard Mohr, John Preston and Jane Rule. Pat Califia, the transgendered feminist writer and activist who wrote the book's introduction, summed up the feminist (and gay/lesbian) anti-censorship message as follows:[114]

> "You may not agree with many of the things I've said, or some of the positions I take in my work. Perhaps you won't like some of the pieces that appear in *Forbidden Passages*. But don't you think you ought to have the right to read them in the first place? . . . If you buy only one gay or feminist book this year, it should be *Forbidden Passages*. . . . Buy this book, hold a benefit, make a donation. Gag the state, before it chokes you!"

E Censorship is Diversionary; It Makes it Easier to Avoid Coming to Grips With Less Convenient and More Expensive, But Ultimately More Meaningful, Strategies for Combating Discrimination

Like all censorship schemes, proposals to restrict "hate speech" and pornography divert attention and resources from constructive, meaningful steps to address the societal problems at which the censorship is aimed, including discrimination and discriminatory violence. Focusing on sexist images or other forms of biased expression diverts us from both the root causes of such discrimination and violence—of which the expression is merely one symptom—and from actual acts of discrimination and violence. Canadian feminist Varda Burstyn made this point in opposing censorship of pornography:[115]

---

[112] K Acker et al, *Forbidden Passages: Writings Banned in Canada* (Pittsburgh, Cleis Press, 1995).

[113] See *Little Sisters Book and Art Emporium* v. *Canada* (2000) 193 DLR (4th) 193 (sustaining, in part, the challenge by Little Sisters Bookstore, its directors and shareholders, and a civil liberties organisation, to the portion of the Canadian Customs Act that incorporated the *Butler* concept of illegal obscenity). The majority acknowledged that Canadian Customs officials administered the law in a way that was "oppressive and dismissive" (p. 216) of free expression and the equality rights of the Bookstore's personnel and patrons, since the effect of this discriminatory administration "was to isolate and disparage [them] on the basis of their sexual orientation" (pp. 216–17). However, the majority ascribed these violations to the way the law was applied, not the way it was written. Therefore, the majority struck down only the portion of the law that imposed the onus (burden of proof) on an importer to show that the challenged material was not obscene. Three Justices dissented in part, concluding that the law should be declared of no force and effect, since it caused "systematic and consistent violations of their constitutional rights" (p. 291), including the denial of important pieces of literature to ordinary Canadians, an "effect [that] particularly significant for homosexuals" (p. 287).

[114] *Ibid*, 23.

[115] V Burstyn, "Beyond Despair: Positive Strategies" in V Burstyn (ed.), *Women Against Censorship* (Vancouver, Douglas & McIntyre, 1985) 152, 179.

"Feminists who oppose censorship . . . do not have another slogan, another quick solution, another panacea to offer in its place. We do have a comprehensive list of tasks we must carry out to bring sexism and violence to an end. Working on any one of these is more helpful – immediately, not in the distant future – than supporting censorship of any kind today, for these tasks get at the structural basis of sexism and violence, and thus insure that we will have a future."

My book on pornography concludes with a chapter, "Toward Constructive Approaches to Reducing Discrimination and Violence Against Women", which explores specific alternatives to censoring pornography that are at least as effective—if not more so—in promoting women's dignity, equality, and safety.[116] In the remainder of this paper, I will make the same point specifically focusing on "hate speech" more broadly—not only sexually explicit, sexist speech.

The counter-productive, diversionary impact of censorship has been demonstrated by recent experience in the US, in the context of the movement to implement campus "hate speech" codes. Too many universities have adopted such codes at the expense of other policies that would constructively combat bias and promote tolerance. After realising this trade-off, some former advocates of campus "hate speech" codes have become disillusioned with them. One example is the minority student who was initially a leading advocate of one of the earliest campus "hate speech" codes, at the University of Wisconsin, Victor DeJesus. After the ACLU successfully challenged that code under the First Amendment, he opposed the University's efforts to rewrite the code in the hope of coming up with something that would pass constitutional muster. As the *New York Times* reported:[117]

"Victor DeJesus, co-president of the Wisconsin Student Association, said that he initially supported the hate speech rule, but that he had changed his mind because he felt the regents were using it as an excuse to avoid the real problems of minority students. 'Now they can finally start putting their efforts into some of our major concerns like financial aid, student awareness and recruitment retention,' Mr. DeJesus said."

Recognising the diversionary nature of campus hate speech codes, the ACLU policy on this subject expressly urges colleges and universities to respond to bias through a range of constructive alternatives. These alternative approaches, all of which could be implemented in the non-campus context as well, are not only consistent with free speech rights, but would also make a more meaningful contribution toward reducing inter-group prejudice, discrimination, and violence:[118]

"All students have the right to participate fully in the educational process on a nondiscriminatory basis. Colleges and universities have an affirmative obligation to combat racism, sexism, homophobia, and other forms of bias, and a responsibility to provide equal opportunities through education. To address these responsibilities and obligations, the ACLU advocates the following actions by colleges and universities:

116 Strossen, above n. 54 at 265–79.
117 "U of Wisconsin Repeals Ban on 'Hate Speech'", *New York Times*, 14 September 1992, A10.
118 ACLU, Policy Guide of the American Civil Liberties Union, Policy #72a, Free Speech and Bias on College Campuses 159.

(1) to utilize every opportunity to communicate through its administrators, faculty and students its commitment to the elimination of all forms of bigotry on campus;

(2) to develop comprehensive plans aimed at reducing prejudice, responding promptly to incidents of bigotry and discriminatory harassment, and protecting students from any such further incidents;

(3) to pursue vigorously efforts to attract enough minorities, women and members of other historically disadvantaged groups as students, faculty and administrators to alleviate isolation and to ensure real integration and diversity in academic life;

(4) to offer and consider whether to require all students to take courses in the history and meaning of prejudice, including racism, sexism and other forms of invidious discrimination;

(5) to establish new-student orientation programs and continuing counseling programs that enable students of different races, sexes, religions and sexual orientations to learn to live with each other outside the classroom;

(6) to review and revise course offerings as well as extracurricular programs in order to recognize the contributions of those whose art, music, literature and learning have been insufficiently reflected in the curriculum of many American colleges and universities;

(7) to address the question of *de facto* segregation in dormitories and other university facilities; and

(8) to take such other steps as are consistent with the goal of ensuring that all students have an equal opportunity to do their best work and to participate fully in campus life."

I would like to comment on a few of these non-censorial strategies for addressing bias and discrimination, to underscore their efficacy. First, it is important for people in leadership positions in any community in which "hate speech" occurs to denounce and dissociate their institutions from the discriminatory attitudes that such expression reflects. One good example of this kind of statement was provided in 1985 by the then-President of Harvard University, Derek Bok, who circulated a letter to the entire Harvard community in response to a sexist flyer that an undergraduate fraternity had distributed. He wrote:[119]

"The wording of the letter was so extreme and derogatory to women that I wanted to communicate my disapproval publicly, if only to make sure that no one could gain the false impression that the Harvard administration harbored any sympathy or complacency toward the tone and substance of the letter. Such action does not infringe on free speech. Indeed, statements of disagreement are part and parcel of the open debate that freedom of speech is meant to encourage; the right to condemn a point of view is as protected as the right to express it. Of course, I recognize that even verbal disapproval by persons in positions of authority may have inhibiting effects on students. Nevertheless, this possibility is not sufficient to outweigh the need for officials to speak out on matters of significance to the community—provided, of course, that they take no action to penalize the speech of others."

---

[119] D Bok, "Reflections on Free Speech: An Open Letter to the Harvard Community", Winter 1985, *Educ Rec* 4, 6.

Likewise, six years later, when some Harvard students displayed Confederate flags—usually viewed as a racist symbol, particularly offensive to African-Americans—and another displayed a swastika in response to the flags, Harvard President Bok issued another thoughtful statement strongly criticising the displays but equally strongly defending free speech principles. He wrote, in part:[120]

"To begin with, it is important to distinguish clearly between the appropriateness of such communications and their status under the First Amendment. The fact that speech is protected by the First Amendment does not necessarily mean that it is right, proper, or civil. In this case, I believe that the vast majority in this community believes that hanging a Confederate flag in public view—or displaying a swastika in response—is insensitive and unwise . . . because any satisfaction it gives to the students who display these symbols is far outweighed by the discomfort it causes to many others. I agree with this view and regret that the Harvard students involved saw fit to behave in this fashion.

One reason why the power of censorship is so dangerous is that it is extremely difficult to decide when a particular communication is offensive enough to warrant prohibition or to weigh the degree of offensiveness against the potential value of the communication. If we begin to forbid flags, it is only a short step to prohibiting offensive speakers. Do we really want Harvard officials (or anyone else) to begin deciding whether Louis Farrakhan or Yasser Arafat or David Duke or anyone else should be allowed to speak on this campus? Those who are still unconvinced should remember the long, sorry history of preventing Dick Gregory and other civil rights activists from speaking at Southern universities on grounds that they might prove 'disruptive' or 'offensive' to the campus community, not to mention the earlier exclusion of suspected communists for fear that they would corrupt students' minds.

In addition, I suspect that no community can expect to become humane and caring by restricting what its members can say. The worst offenders will simply find other ways to irritate and insult. Those who are not malicious but merely insensitive are not likely to learn by having their flags or their posters torn down. Once we start to declare certain things 'offensive,' with all the excitement and attention that will follow, I fear that . . . the resulting publicity will eventually attract more attention to the offensive material than would ever have occurred otherwise. . . .

In conclusion, then, our concern for free speech may keep the University from forcibly removing the offensive flags, but it should not prevent us from urging the students involved to take more account of the feelings and sensibilities of others. Most of the time, I suspect, we will succeed in this endeavor. By so doing, I believe that we will have acted in the manner most consistent with our ideals as an educational institution and most likely to help us create a truly understanding, supportive community."

Moving from the university campus to the larger community, the same strategy was followed by US President Bill Clinton in response to what is frequently termed "hate radio"—call-in talk shows in which the hosts and listeners harshly criticise the government, government officials, and racial and other groups in our society—immediately after the tragic bombing of the federal building in Oklahoma City in April 1995. Clinton, along with many others, believed that the anti-government rantings on such radio programmes had fanned the type of sentiments that could

---

[120] "Bok Issues Free Speech Statement", *Harvard University Gazette*, 15 March 1991, 1, 4.

well have motivated or encouraged those responsible for the bombing. Accordingly, Clinton condemned the ideas conveyed by "hate radio", while stressing that he was not calling for any kind of censorial reaction to it. Instead, he exercised his own free speech rights, from his "bully pulpit", to send a very powerful message against bias and violence, explaining:[121]

> "Yes, stand up for freedom of speech. Yes, stand up for all our freedoms, including the freedom of assembly and the freedom to bear arms. . . . But remember this: with freedom . . . comes responsibility. And that means that even as others discharge their freedom of speech, if we think they are being irresponsible, then we have the duty to stand up and say so to protect our own freedom of speech."

A study by a professor at Smith College in Massachusetts demonstrated the effectiveness of this kind of counter-speech in combating bias and prejudice. It showed that when a student who hears a statement conveying discriminatory attitudes also promptly hears a rebuttal to that statement—especially from someone in a leadership position—then the student will probably not be persuaded by the initial statement. Dr Fletcher Blanchard, a psychologist at the college who conducted the experiment, concluded that "[a] few outspoken people who are vigorously anti-racist can establish the kind of social climate that discourages racist acts."[122] Thus, this study provides empirical social scientific support for the free speech maxim, discussed above, that the appropriate response to any speech with which one disagrees is not suppression but rather counter-speech.

Social scientific studies also underscore the efficacy of another non-censorial alternative to suppressing "hate speech": affirmative action measures to increase the participation of members of minority groups in the relevant communities. The most pertinent studies have been done on countering homophobia, but they also have implications for redressing other forms of bias. These studies show that the most constructive way to decrease people's negative attitudes toward lesbians and gay men is to give them an opportunity to get to know and interact with lesbians and gay men in settings such as school and work, where they are collaborating on common endeavours. Accordingly, by helping to ensure that members of various minority or disempowered groups are represented on campus and in the workplace, affirmative action measures can play a positive role in reducing present and future prejudice and discrimination.

In 1992, Human Rights Watch issued a report on discriminatory violence in Germany. It opposed the suppression of "hate speech" against the ethnic minorities and immigrants who have been the targets of such violence. Instead, it called for a number of the alternative non-censorial measures endorsed in the ACLU policy.[123] For example, Human Rights Watch urged the German government, at

---

[121] Remarks to Students at Iowa State University in Ames, 31 *Weekly Comp Pres Doc* 710 (25 Apr 1995).

[122] D Goleman, "New Way to Battle Bias: Fight Acts, Not Feelings", *New York Times*, 16 July 1991, C1; Fletcher A Blanchard et al, "Reducing the Expression of Racial Prejudice" (1991) 2 *Psychol Sci* 101, 105.

[123] Human Rights Watch/Helsinki, *"Germany for Germans": Xenophobia and Racist Violence in Germany* (New York, Human Rights Watch, 1995).

national and local levels, to undertake affirmative action efforts. It urged the government to hire members of the embattled minority groups to police forces and other agencies that deal both with these groups themselves and with the public at large.[124]

The Human Rights Watch report on Germany also endorsed another of the alternative measures urged by the ACLU: outlawing and punishing actual violent or discriminatory conduct. In Germany, as in many other countries, free speech and associational rights of bigots are suppressed at the same time that their actual violent or discriminatory conduct are not effectively curbed; the appropriate and effective response should be precisely the opposite. Accordingly, the Human Rights Watch report recommended that German officials pass laws against discrimination, enforce those laws, and take stepped-up action against discriminatory violence, but it opposed banning speech and meetings as counterproductive:[125]

> "This report focuses on acts of violence by right-wing extremists and the response of the German state. While viewing extremist violence with great concern, Human Rights Watch/Helsinki at the same time opposes laws that prohibit the expression of anti-foreigner or anti-Semitic sentiments, as well as laws that prohibit groups that hold such views from forming associations and holding public gatherings, so long as that speech, association or assembly does not rise to the level of incitement to or participation in violence. . . .
>
> While such measures may be popular politically and may even appear to be effective in the short-run, Human Rights Watch/Helsinki is concerned that over the long run such measures are not only not effective to counter bigotry, but they may even be counterproductive. Draconian bans turn bigots into victims, driving them underground and creating a more attractive home for the unstable and insecure people who are drawn to such groups. . . .
>
> The exercise of these rights in a hateful fashion short of incitement to violence can best be countered by other forms of speech, association and assembly, such as anti-racist demonstrations and anti-racism educational efforts, without infringing the rights themselves. Furthermore, while prohibitions on these rights may be adopted to protect minorities, they are often used by majoritarian governments against minority groups."

The theme that censoring "hate speech" is not effective—and may well be counter-productive—in responding to discrimination in Germany goes back to pre-Hitler Germany, during the Weimar Republic. The problem was not that the Nazis enjoyed too much free speech, as I have often heard claimed. Rather, the problem was that the Nazis got away with murder—literally. They therefore deprived everyone else, including anti-Nazis, Jews, and other minorities, of free speech.

This point was forcefully made by Aryeh Neier, a German Jew who fled to the US with his immediate family, but whose extended family was exterminated in the Holocaust. As Executive Director of the ACLU in the late 1970s, Neier led the

---

[124] *Ibid*, 11.
[125] *Ibid*, 5, 70–1.

ACLU during the controversial *Skokie* case.[126] In his eloquent book about that controversy, Aryeh Neier refuted common misperceptions about free speech and the rise of Nazism in Weimar Germany as follows:[127]

"The impression that Weimar was a free society is fostered by the great flowering of arts, music, and theater that took place in Berlin in the 1920s. But lacking a government with the will and the strength to enforce the provisions of the constitution and the laws against politically motivated violence, Weimar did not safeguard the liberties of Germans. The constitution itself was so lightly regarded that the Nazis didn't bother to repeal it when they took over. They left it in place but ignored it.

The Nazis did not defeat their political opponents of the 1920s through the free and open encounter of ideas. They won by terrorizing and murdering those who opposed them. . . .

The history of the Weimar Republic . . . does not support the views of those who say that the Nazis must be forbidden to express their views. The lesson of Germany in the 1920s is that a free society cannot be established and maintained if it will not act vigorously and forcefully to punish political violence. It is as if no effort had been made in the United States to punish the murderers of Medgar Evers, Martin Luther King, . . . and the other victims of the effort in the 1960s to desegregate the Deep South. There would have been hundreds of additional murders if the federal government of the United States had not stepped in to bring prosecutions where local law-enforcement agencies evaded their duty.

Prosecutions of those who commit political violence are an essential part of the duty the government owes its citizens to protect their freedom to speak. Violence is the antithesis of speech. Through speech, we try to persuade others with the force of our ideas. Violence, on the other hand, terrorizes with the force of arms. It shuts off opposing points of view."

IV CONCLUSION

I would like to close by quoting a powerful, timeless statement by former Supreme Court Justice Hugo Black. Significantly, Black is as honoured for his championship of equality rights as for his free speech absolutism. In this 1951 statement, Justice Black was specifically referring to the ideology of Communism, which was then seen as especially harmful, and hence especially worthy of suppression. But Justice Black's wise words apply equally to the ideologies of racism and sexism, which are now seen as especially harmful, and hence especially worthy of suppression.

With twenty-twenty hindsight, today we see how exaggerated were our earlier fears that Communist authoritarianism would defeat libertarian rights. I fervently hope that, within another generation, we will have a similar view about current concerns that racism and sexism could triumph over egalitarian rights. In both cases, free speech plays a vital role in defeating doctrines at odds with human rights. Thus, as Justice Black repeatedly reminded us, in the very situations when it seems

---

[126] Above n. 36.
[127] Neier, above n. 101, 167.

we have the most to fear in defending free speech—then, above all, do we actually have even more to fear in not defending free speech:[128]

"Fears of [certain] ideologies have frequently agitated the nation and inspired legislation aimed at suppressing . . . those ideologies. At such times the fog of public excitement obscures the ancient landmarks set up in our Bill of Rights. Yet then, of all times, should [we] adhere most closely to the course they mark."

---

[128] *American Communications Ass'n v. Douds* 339 US 382, 453 (1950) (Black J, dissenting).

PART III
Group and Indigenous Rights

10

Group Rights and Constitutional Rights

TIM DARE

I INTRODUCTION

Until quite recently, liberal political theorists found the notion of group rights hard to swallow. The diverse strands of political liberalism were united by the idea that individuals, rather than groups or collectives, were the primary social and political entities: thus one often saw the terms "liberalism" and "liberal individualism" used interchangeably. Groups or collectives certainly featured in liberal theory so understood, as states or societies, but were cast as potential threats to the liberty of individuals. Hence, liberalism was primarily concerned with limiting state or social intrusions upon the liberty of citizens. Its central question was how one could have both recognition of individual liberty as a primary value, and civil society with its necessary limitations upon that liberty.[1]

A couple of developments placed pressure on this view of the central task of liberalism. One was the communitarian complaint that liberalism failed to appreciate the social nature of persons. Put shortly, communitarians argued that liberalism could not give priority to the choices of individuals over the claims of the communities in which those individuals were embedded, since their choices were meaningful only when understood within the relevant community or cultural context.[2] Another development was the perception that liberal individualism could not adequately respond to the increasing claims of minority cultures living within multicultural liberal states. Such claims seemed not properly understood as claims by individuals against collectives. Rather, they seemed to be claims to a right to preserve certain collectives, or aspects of certain collectives, even against the wishes of a majority of the individuals living within the state in which that collective was located and even—perhaps—where an implication of the preservation of the collective was the apparent loss of autonomy rights by members of the collective.

Some liberals, moved by these communitarian and multicultural arguments, have been concerned to defend liberalism's ability to recognise the importance of groups and group-rights without abandoning its core principles: to defend the

---

[1] Typical liberal answers included limiting legitimate interventions to those necessary to prevent harm, or to those to which individuals had consented, or to which they would or should have consented under some idealised conditions.

[2] See for instance A MacIntyre, *After Virtue: A Study in Moral Theory* (Notre Dame, Notre Dame University Press, 1981); M Sandel, *Liberalism and the Limits of Justice* (Cambridge, Cambridge University Press, 1982); and C Taylor, *Hegel and Modern Society* (Cambridge, Cambridge University Press, 1979).

possibility of "liberal culturalism" as opposed to "liberal individualism". Hence Will Kymlicka, the author of perhaps the most influential liberal response to these challenges, describes his project as being "to show that the relationship between liberalism and minority rights is more complex, and less antagonistic, than is normally supposed".[3] The papers in this section can be read as contributions to this debate. The authors seek to place the claims of minority cultures—with particular concern for New Zealand Maori—within a broadly liberal framework. I think this background debate is usefully kept in mind when reading the contributions. It allows us to see what is at stake, why some routes are preferred over others, and why some moves are more controversial than others.

Even if they accept the idea of group rights, constitutional democracies face a further question: should those rights be given constitutional protection? Hence, there are two broad clusters of questions under consideration—roughly those about the nature and coherence of group rights and those about "constitutionalisation".

II GROUP RIGHTS

Kymlicka has recently suggested that there is an emerging consensus on liberal culturalism: "the view that liberal democratic states . . . must . . . adopt various group-specific rights or policies which are intended to recognise and accommodate the distinctive identities and needs of ethnocultural groups."[4] At least at first glance, the papers in this section seem to support Kymlicka's suggestion. All three contributors state early in their pieces that "there is no logical difficulty with the idea of group rights",[5] that "the idea . . . of groups bearing rights is neither obviously incoherent nor obviously wrong",[6] that "individual and group rights . . . reflect different limbs of a single body that can be made to work in unison. . .".[7] However, this apparent consensus may not be as deep as first glance suggests. We can see some of the more interesting differences in the contributions to this collection by Andrew Sharp and Jeremy Waldron.

Sharp begins with a distinction between two ways of understanding groups and group rights. One way of accommodating these phenomena within a broadly liberal framework—the way that requires the least modification of liberal individualism—is to hold on to the idea that individuals are the primary moral entity, while acknowledging that some individual interests require recognition of the importance of group membership. Here group rights—derivative group rights—are justified by appeal to the interests or choices of the members of the group (p. 225):

---

[3] W Kymlicka, *Liberalism Community and Culture* (Oxford, Clarendon Press, 1989) 5.

[4] W Kymlicka "Introduction: An emerging consensus?" (1998) 1 *Ethical Theory and Moral Practice* 143, 148.

[5] J Waldron, "Taking Group Rights Carefully" p. 203.

[6] A Sharp, "Should Maori Group Rights be Part of a New Zealand Constitution?" p. 222.

[7] E Durie "Constitutionalising Maori" p. 241.

"Whatever the complicated facts about individual judgment of and choices about membership of groups, it is the individual who is, so to say, the fundamental moral particle: the basic element of ethical and thus legal life."

We recognise group rights and group interests only because we see that some of the rights and interests of individuals are, perhaps necessarily, fostered by group membership. Alternatively, and more radically from a liberal perspective, we may understand groups as having moral standing in their own right, not as derivative but as primary—Sharp calls them "fundamental"—moral entities. The defender of fundamental groups and fundamental group rights "insists that the group is the fundamental moral particle of social life, and that *its* good, *its* interests and *its* rights are foundational" (p. 226).

The significance of this distinction to Sharp's final view on group rights lies in two further features of his position. First, his initial endorsement of group rights—his insistence that "the idea . . . of groups bearing rights is neither obviously incoherent nor obviously wrong"—applies only to derivative groups and derivative group rights. Fundamental group rights, he goes on to argue, and we will look at his argument in a moment, "are intellectually and therefore prescriptively incoherent, and should be resisted not only as incoherent but also as in practice foolish and damaging" (p. 223).

Second, he maintains that the notion of derivative group rights cannot do justice to the claims that are actually made on behalf of Maori. Claims to special rights for Maori tend to be claims for fundamental group rights: "The notion is that Maori as a whole, and/or various traditional Maori groupings, have *fundamental group rights* to rule by virtue of being . . . *fundamental* groups" (p. 223). The conclusion, of course, is that many claims to special rights for Maori must be rejected, since they are claims to fundamental rights (though it must be noted immediately that Sharp thinks there may be other, more promising—and more individualist—grounds for such claims).

Sharp's argument that fundamental group rights "should be resisted not only as incoherent but also as in practice foolish and damaging" is long and complex. Its crucial claim, however, seems to be that, as a logical matter, fundamental groups are unable to deal with conflict and disagreement. Fundamental groups, he claims, cannot generate adequate decision-making procedures. This is not merely a claim that such groups will be unable in practice to manage disagreement. Sharp's contention is that the inability to generate decision-making procedures is a logical consequence of the nature of such groups. The theory of fundamental groups, he writes (p. 233),

"yields the conclusion that where there is disagreement among or within fundamental groups then there is no judge or decision-maker, and so the conflicts in question are . . . an inescapable *logical outcome* of disagreement in conditions of the theory of the fundamental group".

Call this the "agency-condition". It is the idea that "the entity to which rights are attributed be capable of agency—that is, that it [must] be capable of making claims and exercising choices" (Waldron, p. 203).

I wish to raise two issues for Sharp's use of the agency condition. One asks whether it is true that groups—even fundamental groups—cannot satisfy the condition. The other will lead us into some broader issues in rights theory and question whether it matters whether they can do so.

First, I am not convinced that fundamental groups cannot forge ways of making decisions in the face of disagreement. As Sharp points out, it will not always be easy to specify just what it is that marks the boundary of a group. Commonly, however, the identification criteria are likely to include some set of beliefs, traditions, and cultural practices. Suppose one of the distinctive, "group-constituting" cultural practices of a group was one that identified a particular individual or class or lineage as having authority to speak for the group. Perhaps in this group, the answer to questions about what should be done is universally accepted to lie in the traditions of the group, and the members of some class—the elders perhaps—are equally universally agreed to be the people who can say determinatively what the traditions require. Whenever there is a decision to be made, the relevant individual or class is consulted and a decision is issued. And it is not that the members of the group think that there was *ever* an individualist decision to adopt these decision procedures: as far as they are concerned, this is just the way their group does things. The cultural practice of making decisions as the group does—whatever it is—is likely to be supported by other cultural practices, equally constitutive of the group: perhaps group members just cannot imagine that a decision produced by the appropriate practice could be wrong; or perhaps they cannot imagine that the decision could be questioned as inimical to the interests of the group, let alone as unacceptable because it failed to give adequate weight to the interests of individual members; or perhaps the tradition of respect for elders is such that it is universally regarded as improper—maybe even literally unthinkable—to question their decisions. Would not this fundamental group have a way of resolving disputes?

Let me make a bolder claim. I hope the hypothetical decision-making practices I have sketched are not too far-fetched. Note, however, that the distinctive, group-constituting cultural practices that comprise a group's decision-making procedures could have *any* content. Far-fetched examples are easy to imagine: groups that appeal to planets, volcanoes, chicken entrails, and so on.[8] Possibilities that are more plausible may be even more challenging. Might not there be a fundamental group whose decision-making practices look *just like* those we normally associate with individualist or derivative-group societies? Imagine a group that decides between alternative actions by staging the following ritual. All members over a certain age are gathered together. The occupant of an office set just this task explains the alternatives to them. Each member is asked to signal "yes" or "no" in some suitably ritualistic manner. According to the cultural practice, "the view of the group" is "yes" if most of its members signal "yes", and "no" if most members signal "no". The ritual looks individualist, but no one in the group thinks of it that way. None

---

[8] Though Joseph Raz thinks some such procedures could not be authoritative: "Authority, Law and Morality" (1985) 68 *Monist* 295, 301.

think its point is to find "a majority view", or that the view of the group is reducible to the view of a majority of its members. The aim is to find "the view of the group", which is as surely revealed here by counting what would elsewhere be called votes as it is in other communities by consulting planets, volcanoes, chicken entrails, or elders. Members of the group shake their heads when outsiders suggest that a particular ritual produced a "close result", they cannot understand those who commiserate with them for being on the "losing side", and so on. If we are puzzled as to why anyone would have such a view of what we think of as voting, we might imagine that one of the constitutive views of the group is that their decision-rituals are guided by a spiritual force who sees to it that the right view is revealed. The spirit cares not whether the view is revealed by a bare or clear majority, and certainly is not interested in the views of individual members. And, since the members believe their conduct to be guided by this spirit, neither are they. Although the content of the decision procedure—what it calls upon the group to do to make decisions—appears to be a function that aggregates individual views, its outcome is not, and is not believed to be, reducible to such views. What this suggests is that *formal features* of the decision procedures of a group will not settle whether the decision procedure, or the group who deploys it, is more or less individualist. That will be settled by the way in which the members of the group regard the decision procedures, whatever they may be.

I think Waldron agrees with most of this. He too rejects the agency-condition. We will see in a moment that he does so in part because he endorses a theory of rights that does not require agency of rights holders. However, even if we do apply the condition, he continues, there is no logical reason to think that it cannot be satisfied by groups. Although this goes by quickly, his arguments sound not unlike those advanced above. He argues that we cannot assume that the ostensibly collective decisions we see all around us—elections for instance—are not genuinely collective or group decisions just because they are most readily understood as functions over individual preferences: "True", Waldron writes (p. 203),

> "our best understanding of collective decision is in terms of a function over individual decisions (such as majority-rule in a simple case). But such a function operates as *the content of a rule* which specifies how collective decisions are made; and that is not at all the same as saying that the collective decision may be reduced to the individual decisions to which the function applies."

Waldron does not address the distinction between fundamental and derivative groups, and so it is unclear whether he would think that a group could employ decision-making procedures with ostensibly individualist content and still count as a fundamental group (though, of course, I think the preceeding arguments suggest that he should be happy to do so!).

I want to return to the initial—and perhaps less ambitious—claim that fundamental groups might have distinctive, group-constituting, cultural practices that give them perfectly adequate, non-derivative, ways of resolving disputes. Notice that there are some responses to this suggestion that are not available to Sharp. He cannot object, for instance, that such decision-making procedures are inadequate, or unfair, or improper—whether from a moral or practical point of view—because they do not give sufficient weight to the interests of individuals. Liberal individualists, and liberal collectivists prepared to go no further than derivative group rights, may well hold such reservations, but—even if well founded from an individualist or derivative perspective—the reservations have limited force against the fundamental group theorist. First, they do not show fundamental group rights to be *logically* incoherent: we may not like them as decision-making procedures but they could work tolerably well. Second, we need to be careful in raising such arguments not to beg the question against our opponents.[9] It will not do to say, for instance, that a fundamental group decision-making procedure is unfair or ineffective *because it is insufficiently individualist.* Not only is that not a logical matter, it also begs the question against less individualist opponents, who may well accept that their way of doing things is not very individualist but ask "so what?". Objecting to the content of fundamental group decision procedures on the grounds that they are not sufficiently individualist is to assume at the outset that adequate procedures must be individualist, and that is just what is at issue.

I move to a second issue for Sharp's views about fundamental groups. We have seen that Waldron does not think that the agency-condition excludes groups from the class of potential rights-holders. Waldron has another, more general ground for rejecting the agency-condition that has its roots in a broader division within rights-theory.[10] It is commonly thought that the various rights-theories can be gathered into two broad types: choice theories (sometimes called will theories) and interest theories (sometimes called benefit theories). Choice theory is motivated by the idea that what matters about moral entities is their capacity to make choices—to value, to plan, to order, to exercise will. Rights protect this special capacity. From here, choice theory defines rights as "an option or power of waiver over the enforcement of a duty". Rights-holders are those who can demand or waive performance, who can choose to sue or not sue. Interest theory starts from the idea that what matters most is not capacity to choose, to value and so on, but the possession of morally important interests: interests that warrant especially powerful protection. According to interest theory, a person has a right within a normative system whenever the protection or advancement of some interest of that person is recognised by the normative system as a sufficient reason for imposing duties on others. If we can mount an argument within a normative system—a moral theory or a legal system perhaps—to show that some interest is or should be afforded special protection, we will have made out a case for the allocation of a right and the imposition of duties necessary for the protection of that right.

Various reasons are advanced for preferring one or other of these theories. I will not dwell upon them here, except to say that among them is the obvious one that

---

[9] Sadly, one cannot use the expression "begs the question" without clarification, for it has been appropriated by sports commentators to mean "raise a question that must be answered". In fact, of course, an argument that begs the question is one that assumes the truth of its own conclusion.

[10] Waldron mentions the point, but it goes by quickly and I think warrants emphasis.

the choice theory will not readily allocate rights to entities that are incapable of exercising choice or agency. Of course, if one starts from the idea that such agency is *precisely what matters*, this may seem no bad thing; *aliter* if one rejects that starting point. Hence, those who believe that things such as animals, small children, the environment and groups (perhaps including fundamental groups) have interests of sufficient importance to warrant the special protection of rights, are likely to find themselves drawn to interest, rather than choice, theories of rights.[11] If one is an interest theorist all of these entities are potential rights-holders, provided only that one can attribute interests (presumably derivatively or fundamentally) to them— though that, of course, may not be a straightforward matter.

Having the distinction between these two types of theory on the table allows us to make a few quick points. First, as remarked, the position Waldron takes on the distinction gives him a second reason to reject the agency-argument against group rights. Waldron describes the interest theory as "the most persuasive analytical treatment" of when an entity may be said to have a right, and reports that he can see no reason to think groups might not satisfy the conditions specified by the interest theory for status as rights-holder. It is hardly surprising, then, that he is unmoved by the "agency-argument" against group-rights: under the interest theory, the capacity to make decisions does not settle status as a rights-holder. Second, by the same token, having the distinction on the table makes clear that Sharp's central argument against fundamental group rights rests upon an unstated theory of rights that makes agency a condition for status as a rights-holder. It allows us to see that a full defence of Sharp's position must show not just that groups cannot satisfy the agency-condition, but also that it matters whether they can do so or not. Third, the discussion, and in particular Sharp's use of the agency condition, suggests the debate between choice and interest theories may have a good deal of significance for our views on group rights. It allows us to see some issues that might otherwise be passed over; to see, for instance, that the apparent consensus between Sharp and Waldron may not be as deep as it at first seemed. Perhaps it also identifies questions that need further work in the group rights area.

I have suggested that Sharp's rejection of fundamental group rights flows from his sympathy for a choice theory of rights. There is an intriguing thread toward the end of his paper that is not easily understood in this light. Having argued that fundamental group rights are incoherent, Sharp writes that "[h]owever this may be . . . the practice of fundamental group rights is a fact. . . . How might one think about this?" (p. 236). Sharp uses the question as a segue into some more practical matters. From a theoretical perspective, however, the distinction between interest and choice theories might allow us to resolve the apparent tension between the ideas that fundamental group rights are both "intellectually and therefore prescriptively incoherent" and "a fact". Fundamental group rights could be incoherent

---

[11] Such theorists may concede that at least some of the entities they wish to treat as rights-holders are unlikely to satisfy the agency condition (the environment is a clear example), or, like Waldron in his contribution to this volume, may think agency is not the key, even if one can argue that the agency condition could be satisfied.

from the perspective of choice theory but not so from that of interest theory: those who in fact claim them—use them even—might be appealing, perhaps implicitly, to some version of the latter theory. I wonder, indeed, whether Sharp himself might feel more at home within interest theory. "[I]t is as certain as anything can be", he writes at the end of his paper, "that so long as Maori continue to be victims of marked relative deprivation they will continue not only to suffer in groups but to act in groups" (p. 240). An interest theorist may well think that the common interest in the alleviation of suffering and deprivation, which Sharp takes to be sufficient to generate and maintain groups, is also sufficient to generate interest based group rights (without supposing, of course, that this settles whether those rights should be given constitutional protection).

III CONSTITUTIONAL RIGHTS

As noted at the outset, even if they accept the idea of group rights, constitutional democracies face a further question: should those rights be constitutionally protected? Should Maori rights be part of a New Zealand constitution? The contributors divide on these questions: Eddie Durie favours development of constitutional protection of Maori rights. Waldron and Sharp are at least more reticent.

Durie favours constitutional protection, even though he believes that the interaction of international instruments and domestic law currently provides greater protection for Maori interests than is generally appreciated, since "the protection of Maori rights remains limited by the fact that the New Zealand Bill of Rights is not 'higher law'" (p. 252). He begins with a very quick tour of constitutions that make special provision for minority cultures, from which he draws a positive lesson. The constitutions remind us, he suggests, "of the issues of equality, protection from discrimination, recognition of indigenous status, and the compatibility of unity and diversity" (p. 249). Perhaps they do, though without further analysis it is hard to be sure they do so by themselves honouring these concerns. Certainly one cannot read section 10 of the Fijian Constitution, affirming "the right to equality before law without discrimination *other than on grounds of race or ethnic origin*" (emphasis added), without being reminded of some of the difficult issues surrounding multicultural, if not minority, rights.

Durie does not believe that recognition of minority group rights is inconsistent with imposing limits upon what the holders of those rights may do: it is possible to combine unity and diversity, to retain "the ideal of a single set of human rights standards while valuing the rights of groups to self-determination and to live according to their own values and practices" (p. 257). I am sure there is a defensible position here. Rights can vary as to their content, so there is no in-principle reason why a rights-holder might not have a right to do x, where x is specified in ways that exclude "denying freedom of speech to women". The "right to x" is no less a right because its content is prescribed: the limitation goes to the content and identity of the right, not to its status as a right. Having said that, however, I wonder whether someone who claims a right "to self-determination and to live according to their own values and practices" would be satisfied with limited versions of these rights. This pragmatic reservation has a "conceptual" counterpart: we can express the conceptual reservation by noting that the descriptions "right to self-determination" and "right to live according to one's own values and practices" cannot be applied to rights with just any content.

I have another "semantic" quibble with the presentation of Durie's position. Durie describes his position as flowing from the "judicious application of the doctrine of cultural relativism" (p. 242). The term "cultural relativism" has a long, and not entirely happy, history in western analytic philosophy. Crudely, in that tradition, it names the combination of the meta-ethical view that no moral viewpoint has universal validity—that moral truth and justifiability, if they exist, are always relative to a set of cultural beliefs—and the normative ethical view that it is wrong to judge those who have different moral values, let alone to oblige them to adopt a different set of values, since their values are as valid as any alternative. I shall not spend any time chronicling the very familiar arguments against at least the simple forms of the view.[12] I do not think we need to do so, because I do not think Durie's position *is* relativist. Durie does not believe that there are no a-cultural standpoints from which to judge the practices of cultures, or that it is always wrong to judge those who have different values. He is quite prepared to impose the standards set by international instruments of law, to call upon universal standards to set moral and legal minimums, to retain the ideal of a single set of human rights. These strategies are not obviously available to the relativist.

I think Durie appeals to relativism to underpin a principled tolerance. But he does not need to do so and, I think, should not do so. He need not do so, because one does not need to be a relativist to be tolerant. A "universalist" need only think that whatever universal principles there are, there is more than one way of organising a society that is consistent with those principles. Such a person might think that universal principles establish a threshold. All of the many and varied ways of living that fall above it are to be tolerated; *ceteris paribus*, those that fall below it should be pressed to change. Durie should not appeal to relativism to support a principled tolerance, because relativists face a peculiar difficulty when it comes to tolerance. For a relativist, tolerance will be a moral value only in those societies where tolerance is in fact valued. If a society does not value tolerance, then, in that society, tolerance is not morally valuable. And since relativists think there are no a-cultural standpoints from which to criticise a society's moral view, relativists cannot criticise societies for which tolerance is not a value, even where those intolerant societies act intolerantly, whether toward their own members or toward others.

---

[12] However, I cannot resist reporting Bernard Williams' marvellously acerbic estimation of its "vulgar and unregenerate form" as "possibly the most absurd view to have been advanced even in moral philosophy". *Morality: An Introduction to Ethics* (New York, Harper & Row, 1972) 21. Williams' assessment is motivated by the tension between relativism's meta-ethical and normative claims: how can it be (normatively) universally wrong to criticise and compel if (meta-ethically) nothing is universally wrong? For a recent, accessible, and more sympathetic treatment, see D Wong, "Relativism" in P Singer (ed.), *A Companion to Ethics* (Oxford, Blackwell, 1993) 442–50.

But, as I have said, since I do not think Durie is a relativist, these remarks are probably of merely academic interest. My principal, semantic, point is that given that his position is not relativist, it should not be so described. At the very least, if this is more than a matter of nomenclature—if Durie really does want to defend a combination of cultural relativism and moral and legal universalism—much more needs to be said about how those apparently inconsistent notions are to be reconciled.

Waldron takes it as settled that group rights are a logical possibility. Most of his paper is given over to consideration of the "further question": assuming there can be such rights—assuming even that there are such rights—should they be constitutionally protected? Waldron presents a number of arguments to think that we should at least proceed with care. He stresses that none of these arguments, alone or in concert, settles the further question. But each counsels caution. I focus on one of the arguments that seems to be an implication of, or to underpin, many of the others. Waldron emphasises this argument in his conclusion, where he writes (p. 220):

> "Claims of rights are always asserted in peremptory tones: that's part of the politics of rights. They do not invite discussion: they close it down. . . . Precisely because rights *are* peremptory, and tend to close down compromise and reconsideration, we ought to be very careful which rights we recognize, and be sure that we understand the nature and complexity of the issues that such rights-talk claims to settle."

I begin consideration of Waldron's argument by looking at a very brief remark he makes about the effect the United States Constitution has had on constitutional discussion in that country. Waldron grants that the Constitution has not shut down all discussion. "[P]eople in the United States", he writes, ". . . remain divisively garrulous on topics like freedom of speech and abortion, both of which are supposed to have been settled at the constitutional level (p. 206 n. 10)" But Waldron does not think *public* discussion is the issue—or at least not directly. Even though public debate continues, "the constitutional 'gag' is successful in ensuring that the topic does not come up in any forum where popular discussion might make a difference" (n. 10). The forum Waldron has in mind is the legislature, where politicians are able and intended—barring entrenched constitutional provision—to do something about the views that have been aired in public debate.[13] Waldron mentions the ongoing public debate in the United States to make a point about the necessary location of effective constitutional discourse.

I will come back to that point in moment. Before doing so, I want to draw attention to another distinction that seems to lie hidden in Waldron's remark about public constitutional debate in the United States. His examples of constitutionally settled matters that remain the focus of "divisively garrulous" public debate are freedom of speech and abortion. I am not sure whether these two constitutional issues are properly treated as of a kind in the context of the current discussion. I

---

[13] That Waldron stresses the importance of the legislature will not surprise those who know his other work, especially *Law and Disagreement* (Oxford, Clarendon Press, 1999).

wonder whether they draw attention to two rather different ways in which we might understand the constitutionalisation issue. Here is the idea: public discourse about abortion is very often about whether or not there should *be* a right to abortion. Public discourse about freedom of speech, by contrast, typically accepts that there should be such a right, and focuses upon its scope.[14] Of course, a strand of the abortion debate is about when in the course of a pregnancy abortion should available, so the abortion debate might also seem to be about the scope, rather than the existence, of the right. Still, many contributors to the abortion debate think there simply should not be a right to abortion, while hardly any contributors to the freedom of speech debate think that there simply should not be a right to freedom of speech. Waldron's concern is that constitutionalisation gags effective political discourse. How does this concern bear upon the two sorts of constitutional issue— those like freedom of speech and those like abortion? If it were true that nobody, or almost nobody, denied that there should be a right to freedom of speech, might not we properly take *that* question off the political agenda? Of course, as Waldron points out, discussion about freedom of speech continues. But, if I am right, that discussion is for the most part about the scope of the right not its existence.[15] Provided the gagging effect of constitutionalisation goes to the latter, and there is no genuine dissent over that, then no genuine dissent is silenced. Now it may be an implication of this view—if my assumption about the nature of the abortion debate is correct—that we should take a different view of abortion. If it is true that divisions over that issue focus on the very existence of the right, rather than its scope, and if that is indeed a relevant distinction, then perhaps the question of the existence of the right to abortion was removed from the ordinary discourse of politics prematurely. Now I do not intend to address the appropriateness of constitutional protection of the right to abortion. I am interested in the possibility that there are different types of constitutional issues that need to be taken into account in developing a position on constitutionalisation.[16] If the distinction I have sketched is plausible then constitutionalisation may not always be inappropriate, even if we accept Waldron's arguments about its aim and effects. And we might note that Kymlicka has recently proposed that the view that certain group-specific rights are legitimate[17]

"has arguably become the dominant position in the literature today, and most debates are about how to develop and refine the position rather than whether to accept it in the first place".

There may seem to be a ready response to this talk of different kinds of constitutional issues. Perhaps we need to distinguish between the sort of disagreement that lies behind the abortion debate—disagreement that, far from making constitutionalisation

---

[14] I owe this distinction to my colleague Vanya Kovach.

[15] Sometimes, of course, questions of scope will not be easy to distinguish from questions of existence.

[16] We can accept the distinction and the claim for its significance even if we do not accept that it is properly illustrated by abortion and freedom of speech.

[17] W Kymlicka, above n. 4 at 148.

inappropriate, is the very thing that makes it necessary—and the sort of uncertainty and lack of settled understanding that Waldron thinks makes constitutionalisation inappropriate in the group-rights case, and which result in part from the fact that we are "just beginning to think about [group rights]". The dramatic disagreement over abortion is surely not due to the fact that we are just beginning to think about the issue. Is the idea that people know what is at stake in the abortion debate, even though deep moral disagreement remains, and hence that constitutionalisation is not inappropriate? I am not sure how all of this would play out in a fuller treatment. I am not sure we do know what is at stake in the abortion debate, and I am a little sceptical that the difference between disagreement and lack of understanding, if indeed that is what Waldron has in mind, will explain why we are happy to grant constitutional protection to some issues, but not to others.

I am going to return, however, to the question of the necessary location of effective constitutional discourse. Waldron writes as though it is analytically true that "rights are peremptory", that "the aim of constitutionalising an issue is to remove it from the ordinary discourse of politics". But I think these claims are empirical and contingent. They turn upon particular constitutional forms and practices, some of which seem to lessen the force of Waldron's arguments against constitutionalisation. Consider some of Eddie Durie's examples. Under Article 215 of the Brazilian Constitution, the State "ensures a person full exercise of their cultural rights and access to sources of national culture and supports and encourages the appreciation and diffusion of cultural manifestations". It is hard to believe that such a provision would act as a gag, that it would close it down discussion. Surely we would expect long and difficult discussion about the meaning of the terms and the scope of the provision: What does "full exercise of cultural rights" mean? What obligations does the right to "access to sources of national culture" generate? What is a "source of national culture"? And so on. Or consider section 15(1) of the Canadian Charter of Rights and Freedoms, which provides in part that "[e]very individual is equal before and under the law . . .". This provision has been a central plank in an argument by Wilfrid Waluchow that the Canadian Charter *requires* courts to "display a significant measure of moral reasoning", to "engage in substantive arguments of political morality", to "strike a balance between competing moral and political interests".[18] Again, the constitutionalisation of equality rights in Canada does not seem to have shut down discussion, or to have "made a form of words canonical in saying what the right amounts to".

We have already seen that these points will not satisfy Waldron. Even allowing that constitutionalisation has not operated as a gag in these cases—even allowing as he does that "divisively garrulous" public debate continues, constitutionalisation has shifted the focus of discussion to the courts, removing discussion from the "ordinary discourse of politics" and "cut off politically effective discussion" (p. 206). But, again, I am not sure that this is an analytic matter. I think it will depend upon the factors I mentioned earlier, upon particular constitutional forms

---

[18] W Waluchow, *Inclusive Legal Positivism* (Oxford, Clarendon Press, 1994) 154.

and practices. Nor am I sure how serious it is even where it is true. As for the particular constitutional forms, the effect of constitutionalisation on legislatures will depend in part on factors such as the scope of constitutional protection: given constitutional protection of limited scope, legislatures may be able to do a good deal "around" the constitution. And as to the seriousness of removing issues from the ordinary discourse of politics, note that there is at least one sense in which constitutionalisation does not have that effect: decisions about *what is to be constitutionalised* will continue to be made by legislatures after full and open public debate. Furthermore, if constitutional courts can function as Waluchow claims they do— engaging in substantive moral reasoning—might not discussion in the courts meet some of the concerns that drive our desire for political debate? Such courts may reflect public opinion in their moral reasoning, for instance. Arguably, the Canadian courts simply could not have produced certain interpretations of the Charter had they not been sensitive to slow shifts in public opinion about what equality required in particular cases. If this is right, constitutionalisation may have preserved public input, even if it has reduced the direct input of and to legislatures. In Waldron's terms, the *courts* could be a "forum where popular discussion might make a difference".

One of the issues here is what we think we are doing when we grant constitutional protection. Waldron writes that "the aim of constitutionalising an issue is to remove it from the ordinary discourse of politics" (p. 206). But why should that be our aim? I have suggested, not originally of course, that it is not realistic: no matter how carefully we try to provide a canonical form of words, issues of interpretation and opportunity for debate will remain. And we may not even be *trying* to settle debate or to say in a precise way what the right in question amounts to. Instead, we may be attempting to "flag" a value or interest as one we think warrants special protection. We may think this about a value, while conceding that there remain divisions about its proper application. I suggested that freedom of speech might be such a right, where there was consensus on the existence of the right but ongoing debate about its proper application. In such circumstances we might be prepared to allow the courts to settle the scope of the right we agree exists. We would expect courts, operating with appropriate sensitivity to ongoing public and political debate, to spell out the details of the right, to judge in particular cases whether the community consensus would be properly extended in this way or that. And we might welcome ongoing political and public debate, anticipating that it will be fed into the interpretation and application of the constitution.

One, perhaps interesting, implication of this view is that the use of general terms, though a vice in legislation for which we have authoritative or determinative ambitions, may be a virtue in constitutions. In determinative legislation, general terms undercut the authority of the legislation. Terms like "fair" and "unconscionable" not only invite but require courts to specify their application conditions. But if we have a quite different aim when we constitutionalise, these may not be failures: they may be ways of encouraging just the sort of debate and interpretation that, concurring with Waldron, we think is desirable. Constitutional form may be a way of resisting the gagging we agree is a bad thing. The Treaty of Waitangi may be a particularly striking example. One sometimes hears that it is regrettable that there are different versions of the Treaty, in different languages: it certainly makes interpretation more difficult. But these difficulties may be embraced rather than regretted. The Maori and English versions of the Treaty force precisely the desired reflection and debate. Given the place of the Treaty, and its bilingual forms, there is no avoiding engagement over the meaning of its terms, and not just engagement within one culture, but necessarily within and between both.

Broader issues remain. Many will think that courts should *not* be engaged in moral reasoning or discussion; that law which requires such excursus is a bad thing; and that courts should not take account of public opinion on the proper interpretation of constitutional terms, no matter how slowly and carefully they move: I have argued as much against Waluchow's interpretation of constitutional cases.[19] We will not settle this issue here. For current purposes, it will be enough to suggest that, if the sort of view I have sketched is even plausible, then Waldron's claims are not analytic: they do not flow from the nature of constitutionalisation, but instead from contingent facts about particular constitutional forms and practices. The proper response to different forms and practices, and so the force of Waldron's arguments, will depend upon deeper, prescriptive views: views about the proper role of courts, legislatures, and the public in constitutional discourse; about the proper forum of constitutional debate; about whether constitutions *should* gag or should take issues off the political agenda; about what we should place within their ambit if they do gag; and so on. Again, nothing I have said will settle these issues. Here, as throughout these introductory remarks, I hope merely to have unearthed some issues and questions that will add to the interest of the papers that follow.

---

[19] T Dare, "Wilfrid Waluchow and the Argument from Authority" (1997) 17 *OJLS* 347. Waluchow has recently responded in "Authority and the Practical Difference Thesis" (2000) 6 *Legal Theory* 45.

11

Taking Group Rights Carefully

JEREMY WALDRON

I

There is no logical difficulty with the idea of group rights. According to the most persuasive analytical treatment of the subject, an individual is said to have a right when an aspect of its well-being (its interest) is a sufficient reason for holding some other individual or individuals to be under a duty.[1] As far as I can tell, none of these conditions is inapplicable in principle to groups: a human community may be treated as an individual for certain purposes (*vis-à-vis* other groups or *vis-à-vis* the wider society); we should not foreclose on analytical grounds the possibility that a community might have interests of its own which require recognition in moral and political discourse; nor should we rule out the possibility that those interests rise to a level of moral importance that commands recognition by other entities or individuals in the form of duties. I am not saying these conditions are satisfied in fact. I am certainly not saying they are satisfied wherever group rights are claimed. But if there are reasons for opposing talk of group rights in general (or specific claims about group rights), or for insisting that they be reduced to the rights of individual men and women, they are not analytical reasons.

Some may want to add to these conditions a further requirement that the entity to which rights are attributed be capable of agency—that is, that it be capable of making claims and exercising choices.[2] But this cannot be ruled out on logical grounds either. We are perfectly familiar with the idea of collective decision, and indeed one of the most commonly invoked group rights—the right to national self-determination—is a right to have decisions by the group made politically effective. True, our best understanding of collective decision is in terms of a function over individual decisions (such as majority-rule in a simple case). But such a function operates as *the content of a rule* which specifies how collective decisions are made; and that is not at all the same as saying that the collective decision may be reduced to the individual decisions to which the function applies. To say that a group decides by majority-rule is not at all the same as saying that a group decision is nothing but the decisions of a majority of its individual members.

---

[1] J Raz, "Right-Based Moralities" in J Waldron (ed.), *Theories of Rights* (Oxford, Oxford University Press, 1984) 182. This is generally known as the "interest theory" of rights.

[2] For influential versions of the "choice theory" of rights, see H L A Hart, "Are There Any Natural Rights?" in Waldron (ed.), *Theories of Rights*, above n. 1 at 77, 81–3 and J Feinberg, "The Nature and Value of Rights" (1970) 4 *Journal of Value Inquiry* 243.

Nothing that has been said so far suggests that there *are* group rights: all I have said is that the possibility cannot be dismissed out of hand. To show that there are group rights, we will have to identify a class of distinct and identifiable communities that it makes sense to treat as individuals for certain purposes; and we will have to show that those communities have interests that are in fact important enough to justify holding other individuals (other groups, or maybe other people) to be under duties, or that certain recognisable duties are appropriately controlled by the decisions of these groups. Only if we show all that—for an actual case—will we have shown that the logically impeccable notion of group rights actually applies to something real.

Apart from what I have already said, the remarks about group rights that I present in this paper are not analytic, but practical or pragmatic. I want to consider not the logical question of whether there *might be* group rights—that, as we have seen, is settled—nor the existential question of whether there *are* group rights, but the practical consequences of recognising such rights and giving them a place in political discourse and in legal and constitutional arrangements.

II

How can one distinguish between the existence and the practical recognition of a right? I have already conceded that there may well be such things as group rights. If they exist, how can they not be recognised?[3] This is not just an ontological point, it is a moral one. If a right exists, then it generates certain correlative duties; and surely it is not up to us—especially not as a pragmatic matter—to decide whether we are going to accept and fulfill these duties or not. Indeed, if there is any sense to the claim that rights are "trumps" over social utility,[4] then we must not let considerations of social utility stand in the way of recognising rights. And that's what my pragmatic consideration appears to do.

The objection may be answered as follows. The language of rights gets deployed in several different ways in moral and political philosophy. (Mostly it is an advantage that the language of rights can face several ways, so to speak, but here it contributes some confusion.) The normative claim that *X has a right (against Y) that Y do P* can be parsed as follows. As we have already seen, it can be parsed as a claim about the basis of a duty:

(1) An aspect of X's well-being is, in itself, a reason for holding some others (for example Y) to be under a duty to do P.

Or it can be parsed as a claim about the importance of a duty:

(2) The reasons—for example, those referred to in (1)—for holding that Y should do P are tremendously important, more important perhaps than any requirement associated with the ordinary pursuit of the general good.

---

[3] I owe this point to Joseph Raz.
[4] R Dworkin, *Taking Rights Seriously*, rev. edn. (London, Duckworth, 1977) xi.

Or it can be parsed as a claim about law:

(3) Y's duty to do P should be a legal duty, recognised by the courts and enforceable by them, at the suit of X.

Clearly these are not the same thing, and (1) by itself entails neither (2) nor (3). Most arguments for the *existence* of group rights fall into category (1). Along the lines that I set out on the first page of this paper, they try to show that a group as well as a natural person can occupy the role of 'X' in (1). A group may have a genuine good or interest (which cannot be reduced analytically to the good or the interests of the individual members of the group). And, defenders of group rights argue, unless other entities or other people like Y treat them with some respect and promote them, these goods—these genuine goods of groups—will be lost.

But showing this does not show that (2) is true. (2) is a very strong claim. It asserts that when a right is invoked, we are in the presence of a reason that pushes aside reasons that are normally taken to be sufficient for grounding or overriding claims of social duty. A common form of argument for giving rights this "trumping" force refers us to the well-nigh absolute importance of respect for human persons: the principle of respect for persons, it is said, sometimes requires us to bear the costs that are involved in forgoing the pursuit of social utility for the sake of protecting the basic interests of certain individuals.[5] Other arguments for treating rights as trumps refer us to particular difficulties with utilitarian aggregation.[6] It is quite unclear how these arguments would play out with regard to groups. For even if groups are thought to be important or valuable, that does not mean they command moral respect in the way natural persons are supposed to command moral respect. Certainly from the mere fact that a group exists and has a good of its own, it does not follow that the aggregated interests of individuals (inside or outside the group) may or must be subordinated to the good of the group, in the way that making group rights "trumps" would suggest.

Still less does the recognition of a right in sense (1) commit us to any proposition about the legalisation of group rights. Some have argued that rights as such commit us to some sort of talk about law or something like law: H L A Hart, for example, once argued that when talk of rights is in the air, there is an implicit suggestion that the use of force (and thus the mechanism of law) is not inappropriate to secure what is required.[7] If so, then a further condition must be made out beyond (1) to establish that groups have rights in this sense: we must establish that the duties which are based on the group's interests are duties which it is not inappropriate to *enforce*. It is easy to see how this might be a pragmatic matter, even if the truth of (1) and (2) is not.

---

[5] See, for example, A Margalit, *The Decent Society* (Cambridge, Mass., Harvard University Press, 1996) chs. 2 and 4.

[6] I mean, for example, the argument about "external preferences" in Dworkin, above n. 4 at 234*ff.*

[7] H L A Hart, "Are There Any Natural Rights?" in Waldron (ed.), *Theories of Rights*, above n. 1 at 77, 79–80.

Something similar is true of the constitutionalisation of group rights. Even if we were to accept some connection between (1) and (3), we might hesitate—again for pragmatic reasons—before moving to

(4) The constitution should be such that X has a legally enforceable right that Y should do P.

Formulations like (4) are designed to make the legal rights they refer to permanent and irremovable features of the legal system. (Or if they are not made literally irremovable, the idea is to make it as difficult as possible to remove them, compatible with lip-service to the idea that the constitution represents the will of the people whose law and politics it structures.) Even if we accept (1) and (2) and (3), as applied to group rights, we may have serious pragmatic doubts about proceeding to (4). I will mention two connected considerations (though I have argued extensively elsewhere against any knee-jerk inference from the moral importance of human rights to the desirability of constitutional rights).[8]

First, the aim of constitutionalising an issue is to remove it from the ordinary discourse of politics. As Stephen Holmes has pointed out, constitutional provisions are often supposed to operate as "gag rules" in circumstances where we fear that continued discussion of some issue, in a political forum, may do more harm than good.[9] (We fear that if the issue is debated and voted on, the discussion may be divisive and an appallingly unjust result may emerge.) In a way, constitutional provisions are supposed to be argument-stoppers; it is their job to peremptorily close down political discussion of a topic or make it less likely that the topic will ever be raised.[10] Now obviously, in imposing a gag rule, a delicate balance has to be struck, as between the dangers that one anticipates from continued discussion, and the felt need to persevere with discussion on the topic in question in order to determine the basis on which it will be settled. I guess the case for a gag rule is strongest where we fear grave dangers from continued deliberation and we either do not care about the exact basis on which the issue is settled or we are confident we have already reached an appropriate basis. If, however, the basis on which the issue should be settled is unclear and the dangers from continued discussion are not so grave, then the constitutionalisation of the matter would be inadvisable.

I suspect that the latter point sums up our current position with regard to group rights. We are just beginning to think about them, and it would seem quite unnecessary and inappropriate to cut off politically effective discussion at this point. Some may worry that such discussion will lead to a denial of recognition for group rights. But at the moment, we are unsure whether there even *are* any group rights, and if

---

[8] See J Waldron, "A Right-Based Critique of Constitutional Rights" (1993) 13 *OJLS* 18 and *Law and Disagreement* (Oxford, Oxford University Press, 1999) 10–17 and 211–312.

[9] S Holmes, *Passions and Constraint: On the Theory of Liberal Democracy* (Chicago, University of Chicago Press, 1995) 10ff and 202ff.

[10] It seldom works of course: people in the United States, for example, remain divisively garrulous on topics like freedom of religion and abortion, both of which are supposed to have been settled at the constitutional level; but the constitutional "gag" is successful in ensuring that the topic does not come up in any forum where popular discussion might make a difference.

so, what recognition of them commits us to. So long as this remains unclear or controversial, it would seem wrong to close the discussion down, simply for fear that one side rather than the other might prevail.

We should remember, secondly, that constitutionalising a legal right is usually a process that makes some form of words canonical in saying what the right amounts to. I think one lesson of American constitutional experience is that the words of each provision in the Bill of Rights tend to take on a life of their own, becoming the obsessive catch-phrase for expressing everything one might want to say about the right in question.[11] Of course, every law has its text; and any sensible political deliberation that's intended to be effective is organised around a formulated motion that is supposed to be the centre of debate and eventually the subject of a vote.[12] The difference between the texts which are the focus of ordinary politics (for example legislative politics) and those which are embodied in a constitution, is that the former (for example the text of a statute) can be readily amended to meet our evolving sense of how best to get at the real issues at stake.[13] Constitutional texts cannot be readily amended: indeed it is thought part of the advantage of constitutionalisation that they cannot be. Now, of course, our understanding of constitutional provisions does evolve over time (and it is appropriate that it should). But this tends to happen through the haphazard and unaccountable politics of the judiciary, without any guarantee that it will correspond to changes in the sentiments and opinions among the people.

For these reasons, then, the proponent of a given right may be hesitant about embodying it in a constitutionally entrenched bill of rights. He may worry about the loss in our ability to evolve a free and flexible discourse of politics, particularly in regard to relatively new topics—like group rights—on which many of us don't yet know what to think, let alone what to say.

III

Martha Minow has pointed out that "when [a] system assigns rights to individuals, it actually sets in place patterns of relationships".[14] A theory of rights is not simply a list of demands: since Kant, it has been taken to imply that the demands can be organised into a vision of society, a *Rechtstaat*, a whole array of reciprocal rights and

[11] For example, First Amendment doctrine in America is obsessed to the point of scholasticism with the question of whether some problematic form of behavior that the state has an interest in regulating is to be regarded as "speech" or not. ("Is pornography *speech*?" "Is burning the Stars and Stripes *speech*?" "Is topless dancing *speech*?", and so on.) The same is true for other formulae of American constitutional doctrine: "cruel and unusual punishment", "free exercise" of religion", "due process of law", etc.

[12] See Waldron, *Law and Disagreement*, above n. 8, ch. 4.

[13] And of course this process of evolving phraseology is even easier if we are talking about legal recognition in the form of common law principles and precedents, and easier still if rights take the form of "conventional" understandings subscribed to in the political community at large, as they have in New Zealand for many years.

[14] M Minow, *Making All the Difference: Inclusion, Exclusion and American Law* (Ithaca, Cornell University Press, 1990) 277.

duties integrated around a concept of the person as the dominant single status of equality in moral and political life.[15] Rights should be thought of as a well-ordered network of duties and responsibilities, not just line-item claims on some enumerated charter or bill.[16]

Some of the worries that people have about group rights relate to this question of order, organisation, systematicity. What happens to the systematics of rights, when we begin attributing rights, not just to natural individuals, but to groups and communities of natural individuals? The traditional systematicity of rights involves relations like correlativity, universalisability and reciprocity: X's right is correlative to Y's duty; but if X's right is universalisable (attributable to anyone who is relevantly like X) then Y's duty may be reciprocated by a similar duty that is owed to Y by X, in virtue of Y's similar right. These relations, explicated by Hohfeld and others, are well understood,[17] at least where X and Y are entities of the same type—both natural individuals or both sovereign states, for example. But it is quite unclear how a system of rights is supposed to work when some of the right-bearing entities are natural individuals and others are groups or communities. Once again, I do not mean that therefore group rights must be ruled out *a priori*, on grounds of theoretical untidiness. I mean that this issue of systematicity should give us pause in our enthusiasm for group rights.

In response to this someone may complain that we have little difficulty recognising the rights of firms and corporations in a legal environment that also consists of individual right-holders. We attribute rights to corporations, associating the capacity to bear rights with the attribution of *legal* personality rather than natural individuality. So what is the problem with attributing rights to communities or groups? If IBM and Hoffmann-La Roche are allowed to be right-bearers, it seems a bit harsh to deny that status to the community of French-speaking Canadians or the people of Malawi. Sure, the attribution of rights to groups as well as individuals faces certain difficulties, particularly with regard to the rights of a group against its members or the rights of the members against the group. But the example of corporations shows that the difficulty can be overcome with enough will (and enough money).

We should be cautious, though, about this analogy with corporate personality. Talk of the rights of corporations makes sense in the context of a complicated and articulated theory of what corporate personality amounts to. If Jeremy Bentham and H L A Hart are right in their suggestion that the meaning of terms like "corporation" can be elucidated only by *paraphrasis*[18]—that is, by a consideration of the

---

[15] See I Kant, *The Metaphysics of Morals*, translated by Mary Gregor (Cambridge, Cambridge University Press, 1991) 55–8 (on the doctrine of right).

[16] I have developed this argument in J Waldron, *Liberal Rights: Collected Papers 1981–1991* (Cambridge, Cambridge University Press, 1993) 26–34, and also in "The Role of Rights in Practical Reasoning: Rights versus Needs" (2000) 4 *Journal of Ethics* 115.

[17] See W N Hohfeld, *Fundamental Legal Conceptions* (New Haven, Yale University Press, 1923) and C Wellman, *A Theory of Rights: Persons under Laws, Institutions, and Morals* (Totowa, Rowman & Allanheld, 1985).

[18] See H L A Hart, "Definition and Theory in Jurisprudence" (1954) in his collection *Essays in Jurisprudence and Philosophy* (Oxford, Clarendon Press, 1983) 26ff.

whole context in which they appear—then we cannot talk glibly about an analogy with the human rights of groups unless we are prepared to transplant something like the whole apparatus and context of company law into the area of ethnic and national communities.[19]

In the area of corporations, positive law provides strict and clear criteria for determining (for example, for purposes of liability) the identity of a corporation and for tracing the impact of corporate rights and responsibilities on the rights and responsibilities of natural individuals. For example, legal rules provide a basis for determining whether a given company is the same as a company that existed in the past, and for determining whether a given individual is a shareholder or officer of that company and what his share of its assets and liabilities amounts to. There is law governing the rights of shareholders *vis-à-vis* the corporation and its officers, and the rights and duties which the corporation, its officer and shareholders owe to employees, creditors and other stakeholders in the corporation's activities. If a shareholder wants to renounce his equity in the company, there are rules about the basis on which he may do so, and rules for the settling of any outstanding claims against the company so far as he is concerned. There are rules about conflict-of-interest, insider trading, mergers, competition and limited liability. These rules are complex and intricate and they have been tested (and are still being tested) against all the challenges that the ingenuity of monetary interest can mount against them.

In this regard, it is important to understand that the situation we face in existing law is *not* that we have already recognised group rights as such but unfairly confined the benefit of that recognition to corporations. Instead we have developed a very specific body of corporate law, which enables us to attribute legal rights specifically to *groups of this kind*. But we have not developed any comparable body of law—we have not made any comparable doctrinal preparation—for the according of rights to other sorts of groups, such as the ethnic communities for which group rights are currently claimed.

We found it necessary to develop this intricate body of law for corporations because of the potential for an immense and confusing maze of conflicts of interest, as between shareholders, officers, employees, creditors etc. The prospect for such conflicts and confusion in the cases of other kinds of community is also formidable. Consider these cases, for example.

(i) The Irish people are said to have a right to self-determination; but does that mean that a majority in the Irish Republic can determine the fate of those in the North? Or does it mean a majority of all of those resident on the island of Ireland? Or must the people of the six northern counties be regarded as a separate community with self-determination rights, even though that is part of the very point at issue? Indeed, why not also look to the United Kingdom, as presently constituted, or the whole community consisting of the various peoples of the British Isles, to see whose decisions should be determinative in this regard?

---

[19] The argument in this paragraph and the next is adapted from my essay, "Can Communal Goods Be Human Rights?" in Waldron, *Liberal Rights*, above n. 16 at 339, 361–2.

(ii) The Welsh and the Quebecois are said to have a right to their language; but what if a large number of people living in Wales or Quebec want to opt out of their Welshness or Frenchness and assert their identity as anglophone? Do the groups in question (the Welsh community, the francophone Quebecois community) have rights against their members (the persons who make up the respective groups)? If so, are these rights limited, and by what principle? And how are these group rights related to the opinions, decisions and aspirations of individual members?

(iii) In the 1989 American case of *Mississippi Band of Choctaw Indians* v. *Holyfield*,[20] the US Supreme Court recognised the jurisdiction of tribal authorities over Indian children born off the reservation, in a case where an Indian mother had gone off the reservation specifically for the purpose of relinquishing her child to non-Indian adoptive parents. Is this a fair result, in relation to the rights of the group and the rights of the individual mother?

(iv) In a recent New Zealand case about Maori fishing rights,[21] the Court of Appeal had to consider whether schemes to settle Maori grievances about the expropriation of fishing rights in the nineteenth century should be focused solely on traditional tribes or *iwi* or whether beneficiaries might also include more recently constituted Urban Maori Authorities (UMA). The process whereby redress for historic injustice is sought under the auspices of the Treaty of Waitangi (1840) has been dominated, on the Maori side, by representatives of the traditional *iwi*, for they through their chiefs were of course the original signatories to the Treaty. The settlement reached in regard to fisheries provided, in effect, that the assets held by the Treaty of Waitangi Fisheries Commission be distributed to *iwi*. A number of UMA challenged this settlement, on the grounds that it would not benefit a very large number of urban Maori no longer affiliated with *iwi*. The response for the Commission was that since *iwi* had had the fishing rights wrongfully taken away from them, it is to *iwi* that they should be returned: UMA had not suffered comparable injustice, for they did not exist at the time the expropriations took place, and so they were not entitled to any redress. But the *iwi* no longer have anything like the comprehensive responsibility for their members' welfare that they had at the time of the violations. For a great many Maori people living in cities, perhaps the majority, the functions formerly performed by *iwi* are performed either by the Government, or by UMAs. In what sense then—beyond a merely formalistic sense—can we say that the *iwi* of 2001 are the same as the *iwi* of (say) 1860, and that the former are the exclusive heirs of the latter's grievances?

Problems like these can quickly become viciously circular, because the identity of the group is often exactly the issue at stake—or at least implicated in the issue at stake—in the asserted content of the alleged group right (or the challenge to it). Talk of individual rights has at least this advantage over talk of group rights: the identity of natural individuals is seldom disputed in the controversies in which their rights are thought to be involved.

---

[20] 490 US 30 (1989).

[21] For example, *Te Waka Hi Ika o Te Arawa* v. *Treaty of Waitangi Fisheries Commission* [2000] 1 NZLR 285.

Yet again, I would stress that in principle there is no logical reason why these difficulties might not be overcome—in these particular cases or in general. But a lot of thought—and no doubt a great deal of experience—will be necessary before they are overcome. I think we are closer to the beginning of this process of thinking things through than proponents of group rights sometimes admit.[22] For that reason, the analogy with the well-established existence and recognition of the rights of corporate entities might be a little premature.

IV

I want to turn now to a difficulty that promises to make talk of group rights much more problematic, politically, than talk of either corporate or individual rights. (Again the argument I shall make is not supposed to display an insuperable logical difficulty, but a set of reasons for hesitation before we accord group rights the prominent place that their proponents seek in the legal and political landscape.)

The most familiar group rights claim—as well as one of the most powerful (and, to its opponents, the most troubling)—is the right of national self-determination. This is a right that is implicit in the sovereign independence of many existing states, and it is also a right voiced explicitly by various minorities in existing states in their effort to change national borders or bring a new state (for example a secessionist state) into existence. The claim is that a particular community has a right to order its own affairs, on a basis that is responsive to the culture and traditions of the group and the desires and ideology of its members. Now I am not going to attempt anything like a full account of the grounds and limitations of the right to self-determination in this paper.[23] But it is pretty clear that the right to self-determination is most plausible when two conditions come together. The first condition is that the community in question has (or under favourable conditions is likely to have) a basis for organising itself as a full political community and civil society: I mean it has (or under favourable conditions is likely to have) a basis in its culture, traditions, and internal politics for arranging and orchestrating all the things which it is appropriate for an independent state and legal system to arrange and orchestrate.[24] I will abbreviate this condition as:

---

[22] For some excellent cutting-edge work, see: I M Young, *Justice and the Politics of Difference* (Princeton, Princeton University Press, 1990); W Kymlicka, *Multicultural Citizenship: A Liberal Theory of Minority Rights* (Oxford, Clarendon Press, 1995); M S Williams, *Voice, Trust, and Memory: Marginalized Groups and the Failings of Liberal Representation* (Princeton, Princeton University Press, 1998); and J Levy, *The Multiculturalism of Fear* (Oxford, Oxford University Press, 2000).

[23] There is a useful account in A Margalit and J Raz, "National Self-Determination", reprinted in J Raz, *Ethics in the Public Domain: Essays in the Morality of Law and Politics* (Oxford, Clarendon Press, 1994) 110.

[24] Of course people disagree about what things it is appropriate for an independent state and legal system to arrange and orchestrate; so they will disagree about (a). That is not a problem: a good theory of X explains disagreement about X, rather than making disagreement evaporate.

(a)   the group or community, G, has a *basis*, B_g, for self-determination.

The second condition is that the community is viable as a political entity, which means it must be territorially distinct. Given the way the states-system is currently organised,[25] only a community whose members (or most of whose members) live together in a distinct territory can be recognised as a state. A community is not viable as a self-governing entity if large numbers of its members are permanently dispersed amongst others who do not regard themselves as members of that community (and are not regarded as members of that community), or if large numbers of non-members (in the same sense) are dispersed among members in the community that the latter regard as their territory. I will abbreviate this condition as

(b)   G must be politically *viable*.

Of course viability is a matter of degree, and also a contestable matter. What counts as *the community* in the relevant sense may be debatable: there may be different views about who is a member of G and why. And of course "large numbers" is a relative term too. I assume, however, that the limiting cases of viability are those where the political entity that is envisaged will itself have a minority problem; or where the fulfillment of its aspirations requires ethnic cleansing or large-scale immigration or both.

The demand for group rights is often heard from or on behalf of groups who have sought self-determination but failed, often because they do not satisfy condition (b). A group, G, may have what I have called a *basis* for self-determination, B_g, but not be viable as a political unit, for one reason or another. Or even if G is viable, some other much more powerful political unit (which I shall refer to as "H") may hold G permanently in thrall. Sometimes G will look for a form of political "autonomy" within H that falls short of self-determination. Often, however, G remains fully within H, and its members remain full members of H, undistinguished in most regards from other members of H who are not members of G; but G nevertheless advances claims to group rights in the hope that such rights will become part of the normal functioning of H, the larger entity.

But the aspiration to some form of *rule* by G over its members is seldom wholly eliminated. It is often there in the background, in the form of B_g, informing the claims of right that G puts forward. True, in the situation I have described, G puts forward its rights-claims as a *ruled* entity rather than a potential ruler: it claims its group rights against H, the larger group that rules G and G's members and everyone else in the society. But the *content* of the claims put forward by this ruled group often consist of something like claims to rule.[26] They are claims to some sort of

---

[25] For "states-system", see H Bull, *The Anarchical Society: A Study of Order in World Politics* (New York, Columbia University Press, 1977) 13ff. See also M Wight, *Systems of States* (Leicester, Leicester University Press, 1977) chs. 4 and 5.

[26] An analogy would be Carol Pateman's view of the claims of Lockean individuals against Lockean political society: they present themselves as claims by ruled individuals; but they are really the claims of fathers for vindication of their rule over their households. See C Pateman, *The Sexual Contract* (Cambridge, Polity Press, 1988).

limited hegemony over the members of G—over what language they speak, or who they marry, or how they bring up their children. They are claims that have implications for members' participation in G, their contribution to G, and their possible exit from G. These claims draw upon the basis, B_g, that would exist for a self-determination claim if the other condition of viability were satisfied. For the non-satisfaction of (b) need not affect condition (a). B_g may remain fully (albeit for-lornly) in place: the group may have a cultural basis for self-rule—which means, of course, the rule of the group over its members and their affairs—but just no hope of ever securing self-rule in the fullest sense. We must remember, too, that "self-rule" in the case of a group means something different from self-rule in the case of a natural individual. In the latter case, self-rule means something like personal autonomy. But in the case of a group, self-rule means that individuals in the group *will be ruled* by those who can claim to speak in the name of the group. And lim-ited self-rule, short of full self-determination, does not detract from this difference.

I think this point makes claims of group rights particularly problematic from the point of view of modern political discourse. Our modern talk of rights as trumps is in its element when claims are made against the state by individuals: enormous problems arise when we try to make sense of the claim that these individual rights may have to be balanced against the rights that the state has (or society has) against the individuals. True, people often talk that way. They say, "What about the rights of society? Or what about the rights of the majority?" when some individual or minority claim is being advanced.[27] But this way of speaking tends to introduce confusion into the whole idea of rights. It was one of the contributions of Ronald Dworkin's seminal essay "Taking Rights Seriously", to warn us against this confu-sion. Acknowledging the possibility that rights may conflict with one another, and that therefore one trumping right may sometimes have to give way to another, Dworkin insisted that this point cannot be applied to "the rights of society":[28]

> "It is true that we speak of the 'right' of society to do what it wants, but this cannot be a 'competing right' of the sort that may justify the invasion of a right against the Government. The existence of rights against the Government would be jeopardized if the Government were able to defeat such a right by appealing to the right of a demo-cratic majority to work its will. A right against the Government must be a right to do something even when the majority thinks it would be wrong to do it, and even when the majority would be worse off for having it done. If we now say that society has a right to do whatever is in the general benefit, or the right to preserve whatever sort of environment the majority wishes to live in, and we mean that these are the sort of rights that provide justification for overruling any rights against the Government that may conflict, then we have annihilated the latter rights.

---

[27] "Rights of the majority" may be a loose way of referring to the voting rights of individuals (who may make up a majority on some issue). If so, it is a misleading way. The voters have rights as individ-uals, to be equal one among another in the ordering of their affairs. But the majority does not have rights as a group; and the collective decision-rule which looks for a majority does not accord rights to any such group.

[28] Dworkin, above n. 4 at 194.

> In order to save them, we must recognize as competing rights only the rights of other members of the society as individuals."

Now the situation with group rights is sufficiently complicated that the argument Dworkin makes (assuming it is valid) cannot be a reason for ruling them out *tout court*. The rights of G are not on an exactly similar footing as the rights of H or its majority. But, once again, there is ample reason here for caution—lest the "subaltern" character of rights in general be diminished by admitting into ordinary political discourse rights which are really rights to rule rather than rights against one's rulers.

A defender of group rights may protest the point I have developed in this section. The discourse of group rights, he may say, *is* subaltern discourse: it is the discourse of the subordinated, the marginalised, the under-privileged. As we have seen, there is a sense in which this is undeniable: G claims its rights as a group from a subordinate position *vis-à-vis* H. But this should not let us lose sight of the rather different character of the relation as between G itself and its members that G aspires to, when it makes its claim for group rights from this subordinate position. After all, we should bear in mind that the rights-claim is not being made on or in behalf of the individual members of G. Defenders of group rights are strongly opposed to any individualist reduction that would boil the group's claims down to claims that could be made on behalf of its individual members. The group is claiming rights *as a group*, rights which may rebound to the benefit of its members, to be sure, but which must not be confused with those individual benefits. Logically, I guess it is possible that the reason for claiming rights as a group is solely in order to enable G to act as a distinct legal person in its dealings with other groups and with the state: for example, the group claims the right to be consulted, or the right to funding from the outside. But it would be quite disingenuous for those who claim group rights for ethnic and national minorities in modern politics to say that all the rights they claim for groups fall into this category. The group rights they claim are in fact rights oriented as much to the exercise of authority inside the group as they are to its relations with outsiders. Or, often, even when they *are* oriented to outsiders, the idea is that the outsiders have limited rights to interference in the group's internal affairs. (Authority claims often have this aspect: one says to an outsider, "It is *for me* to discipline my child or employee, not you."[29]) So group rights do pose paradoxes of authority and domination akin to those that Dworkin was exploring when he considered the phrase "the rights of society". I don't think this is enough to disqualify the very idea of group rights. But, as I have said, it is yet another reason for taking group rights cautiously.

---

[29] See G E M Anscombe, "On the Source of the Authority of the State" in J Raz (ed.), *Authority* (Oxford, Blackwell, 1990) 142.

V

When an individual person invokes a right of privacy or a right of free speech or religious freedom, the right that she invokes refers to and seeks to privilege something about that individual's lifestyle, beliefs, or opinions. She has an opinion, O, about what is good or valuable or worth doing or ultimately true, and she demands that this belief be respected. Respecting O does not require the rest of us to subscribe to it or act on it ourselves; it requires us to let it be believed by her, and to let her express and (if she likes) try to convince as many people as she can of its truth or desirability. Sometimes O may be a belief about how our whole society should be organised: it may be a political belief. But again, the same point applies. The right-based demand that the belief be respected is not a demand that society actually be organised in the way that O indicates; it is at most a demand that the expression of O should be tolerated, that agitation for O should be permitted, and that the political system should be organised so that votes cast on the basis of O should be counted. Thus, a society can be fully respectful of the rights of believers in O even though the society's own laws and policies are not affected by O in anyway: this is what we should expect when the expression of O is permitted in a society but other citizens happen to find O unconvincing. For example, I believe very strongly that estate duties should be set high enough so that inheritance does not make a mockery of the idea of equal opportunity. But this belief is not widely shared and the society I live in is moving in the opposite direction. So, fine: I have lost out in the debate. That does not mean that my rights have been violated in respect of this opinion.

The communities that clamour for group rights also have their own beliefs about how a good society would be organised. (These beliefs are part and parcel of what I referred to earlier as the *basis* of a claim that might be made for self-determination, the basis referred to in condition (a) for a self-determination claim.) But the conditions for respect seem to be different. For group rights, it is not enough to respect the expression of a belief: respect for the group requires respect for its way of life, not just for its holding the belief (or its members' holding the belief) that such-and-such is the way that life should be led.

This becomes particularly apparent in the case of rights that refer to culture. A group, G, whose members live interspersed say with non-members of G in a wider society, H, may claim a right to its culture. Now this certainly entails something like a free expression right, and that is often very important: G may demand that its members be protected when they give voice to various beliefs associated with their culture. But usually it goes beyond that, to an issue of practice, not just expression. The culture—which in other circumstances would form the basis, B_g, of a self-determination claim by G—comprises certain practices relating to things like the education of children, or marriage and the regulation of sexuality, or criminal justice, or issues of life and death from health care to burial rites. And G demands, as a matter of right, that its members be free to engage in those practices, and that they be free too of any requirements imposed by the laws of H that might cut across these practices or interfere with them. Now, to the extent that the practices in question seem like private religious practices, then, some form of accommodation may be possible under the auspices of general liberal toleration. (For example, the wider society, H, might tolerate practices of animal sacrifice by a particular community, even though those practices are repugnant to most members of H.[30]) But to the extent that they implicate the interests of others, beyond the members of G, or members of G for whom the wider community has some special concern or responsibility (like children), then claims of group rights of this kind will pose special problems. How common are these cases likely to be? I think they are likely to be very common, for two reasons. First, the self-determination claim lying at back of the claim for group rights is likely to have been defeated precisely because the members of G are *not* tidily separated from others: in other words, the reason why group rights, short of full self-determination, are being claimed is that the affairs of the members of the group are entangled with the affairs of non-members. Secondly, since the rights-claims in question are not supposed to be reducible to *individual* claims to privacy or religious freedom, there are likely to be dimensions of communal entanglement involved that cannot be parsed on the basis of the voluntary consent of adult individuals.

Let me illustrate these concerns with a real-world problem that displays some of the confusion and entanglement that cultural identity claims are likely to involve. The case comes from Nebraska, of all places, and it concerns the regulation of marriage and sexuality among families of Iraqi refugees settled in Lincoln.[31] The case came to national attention with the arrest and criminal indictment of two Iraqi men who had married the 13 and 14-year-old daughters of Iraqi refugees; the marriages were arranged by the girls' parents, allegedly in accordance with Islamic tradition. When the marriages came to light, the girls were taken into protective custody and the four adults involved were arrested. Because the marriages had been consummated, the bridegrooms were charged with statutory rape under Nebraska law making it illegal for anyone 18 or older to have sex with someone under 18, even with that person's consent. The girls' father was charged with child abuse and their mother with contributing to the delinquency of minors.

The case raised intriguing issues about cultural defences to criminal charges. According to the defence attorney, such child marriage is approved among conservative rural Islamic communities, since it alleviates concern that the girls might otherwise be "dishonoured". Being products of a non-Western culture, the defendants said they saw nothing wrong in what they did. In Iraq, they said, arranged marriages and child marriages are commonplace. "What we have here", averred the lawyer for the bridegrooms, "is an example of a cultural gulf, no doubt

---

[30] See eg, *Church of the Lukumi Babalu Aye Inc* v. *City of Hialeah* 508 US 520 (1993).

[31] See M Talbot, "Baghdad on the Plains", *New Republic*, 11 August 1997, 18; D Terry, "Cultural Tradition and Law Collide in Middle America", *New York Times*, 2 December 1996, A10; P Annin and K Hamilton, "Marriage or Rape?", *Newsweek*, 16 December 1996, 78; and L Volpp, "Blaming Culture for Bad Behavior" (2000) 12 *Yale J L & Human* 89, 103–4.

about it".[32] But the prosecutor dismissed any argument for a cultural defence. "You live in our state", she was quoted as saying, "you live by our laws". And she added: "I have yet to find in the law: 'Oh, and by the way, if you immigrate here from another country none of this applies'."[33]

A lawyer for the young brides gave a slightly different spin on the case. She believed that the girls' father and mother arranged their daughters' marriages because the girls were adapting too readily to American ways. Arranging their weddings to Iraqi men was a way of keeping the girls from going astray culturally.[34] (And indeed, Lincoln police said they learned of the marriages when the 15-year-old girl was reported missing by her father. She had run away, police said, to the home of her 20-year-old boyfriend, Mario Rojas, 20, of Lincoln. Rojas was also charged with statutory rape.)[35]

The bridegrooms were convicted of statutory rape and sentenced to four to six years in prison.[36] The father and the mother pleaded no contest to allegations of being neglectful parents. The two daughters were ordered to remain in a foster home under the legal control of the Nebraska Department of Health and Human Services pending completion of a permanent care plan. As part of a plea agreement, the County Attorney's Office agreed not to file additional abuse charges against the parents related to the care of their four other children, who remain at home. Criminal charges of misdemeanour child abuse against the parents would not be prosecuted if they successfully completed parenting and cultural counselling programmes, their attorneys said.

In case readers are left in any doubt about the messiness of cases like this, let me add one last detail. A lawyer for one of the bridegrooms suggested that the older girl might in fact be seventeen rather than fifteen. (There is an exception to the Nebraska statutory rape law in the case of someone *married* at age 17.) His suspicions were aroused by the fact that the girls' parents and one of the girls all list their birth dates as 1 July. The three Iraqi men (father and bridegrooms) were political refugees, who came to Lincoln, Nebraska after long stays in Saudi Arabian refugee camps, joining about 500 other Iraqis. "It is the habit of refugee camps to routinely

---

[32] S Francis, "An Open-Borders Process Spawns Cultural Conflicts", *The San Diego Union-Tribune*, 12 December 1996, B13.

[33] P Hammel, "Iraqis' Lawyer: Rape Case to Have Global Effect", *Omaha World-Herald*, 20 November 1996.

[34] L Fruhling, "They say Marriage; Law says Rape", *Des Moines Register*, 5 January 1997, 1, quoted in C Weisbrod, "Susanna and the Elders: a Note on the Regulation of Families" [1998] *Utah L Rev* 271. Another report said, however, that the father had threatened to kill his two underage daughters or ship them back to Iraq if they didn't agree to the arranged marriages. The father held a knife to the throat of one of the daughters, the girls' attorney said. The lawyer, Michelle Smith Chaffee of Lincoln, said those threats contradict the idea that the nationally publicised case was one of cultural misunderstanding. "I think it had a lot more to do with this individual man and how he related to his daughters than any cultural differences", Ms Chaffee said. (See "Arranged Marriage Case Heard Iraqi Parents Plead No Contest to Neglect", *Omaha World-Herald*, 5 April 1997.)

[35] See Hammel, above n. 33.

[36] See "Prison Terms for 2 Men In Marrying Young Girls", *New York Times*, 24 September 1997, A14.

assign birth dates." The lawyer said he was trying to get the girls' birth records, but that the Iraqi government was often "not helpful" about this sort of thing.[37]

The case is a challenging one not just because of the tangled fact-situation (though it is very important to remember that such factual thickets are the normal habitat of group rights), but also because the issue of the regulation of child sexuality is not normally something that modern societies are content to leave to families or private individuals. At least till late-teenagerhood, many societies claim the right to impose prohibitions on allowable sexual activity and heavy punishments on those who engage in or procure sexual activity with children under the age of consent. It is not seen as a matter of conscience or religious practice or internal family regulation. It is seen as a matter for the society as a whole, as part of its obligation to the children for whom it has an ultimate responsibility. At the same time, the case reminds us that different societies approach this issue on quite different bases. In response to the enduring question of how the sexuality of teenagers is to be governed, society H_1 may answer "Arranged marriages at age 13 or 14." A second society, H_2 may answer "Postponement of marriage to at least age 18, and prohibition on all unsupervised extra-marital contact between the sexes." And H_3 may answer, as most US states have answered, "Unsupervised dating strongly encouraged from age 15, but an absolute prohibition on all sexual activity until age 18." Each society may criticise the answer given by each of the others. The Nebraska case reveals H_3's opposition to the answer given in H_1. And no doubt members of H_1 and H_2 will return the compliment, criticising H_3's approach as contradictory and hypocritical. In other words the respective solutions of these societies are rivals: they constitute alternative and competing answers to what is basically the same question. Each claims to do the job of regulating teenage sexuality *better* than it is done elsewhere.

One can imagine the view of H_2 being put forward in H_3 as a political proposal. Catholics, for example, or Christian fundamentalists may say: "If we want to effectively regulate teenage sexuality, we should prohibit unsupervised dating", and they may mention some traditional society like H_2 that actually does this. But putting forward such a proposal is not the same as claiming the right to practice it or put it into effect. Though the proposal may be based on sincerely held religious beliefs, it is put forward for social and political consideration, not as the basis of a claim that those who oppose unsupervised dating have a right to interfere with the practice. (A proponent of this view may of course limit the dating of his or her own children, but they are not entitled to put their convictions into effect as a social view. Analogously, an opponent of abortion may refrain from having an abortion herself, but she is not entitled to act on her view that abortion is murder, for example by breaking into clinics in defence of those she thinks are being murdered there, etc.)

Consider by contrast what happens when one of these rival solutions to the problem of regulating teenage sexuality is put forward, not as a social or political

---

[37] See "Lawyer Wants Iraqi Girl's Age Checked", *Omaha World-Herald*, 17 January 1997.

proposal, but as the content of a group right. We imagine a group or community, G_1, that exists within one of these larger societies—say, H_3—but which is in some sense an offshoot (say an emigrant community, or the rump of a colony, or a misplaced minority) of one of the other societies—say H_1—which takes a different view on the teenage-sexuality question. The culture and traditions of H_1 might form what I have called the *basis* of a self-determination claim by G_1, if G_1 were big enough or if its membership was not hopelessly intermingled with the rest of the membership of H_3. But since G_1 cannot claim self-determination, that basis will be used instead as the basis of group-rights claims, made in the context of the law and politics of H_3. Now, our example illustrates the point that the content of the alleged group right is usually a claim about how a whole society should be organised, not just a claim about how the members of G_1 should organise their own affairs. But it is not put forward as a political proposal, for the whole society to consider—in the way similar claims by (say) by defenders of the approach taken in H_2 are put forward in H_3. Instead it is put forward as something to be practised by the members of G_1 (for example, by fathers in G_1 controlling their teenage daughters) despite the fact that the issue is generally taken to be one on which *the whole society*, H_3, should settle a policy.

The problem here can be traced in part to the notion of *culture*, that often forms the basis of group rights claims.[38] Though the members of a group may insist that the group's culture forms part of their individual identity, we should remember that cultures are not like hairdressers, set up in order to furnish diverse and colourful identities for individual persons. In the sense in which the term is used in the politics of group rights, a *culture* is (something like) an enduring array of social practices, subsisting as a way of life for a whole people. Moreover, a culture is not like an array of clubs and hobbies; it represents the heritage of a particular people's attempts to address and come to terms with the problems of social life. A given culture will comprise a particular way of dealing, for example, with relations between the sexes, the rearing of children, the organisation of an economy, the transmission of knowledge, the punishment of offences, and in general the vicissitudes that affect all the stages of human life and relationship from conception to the disposition of corpses, and from the deepest love to the most vengeful antipathies. So when a person talks about her identity as a Maori, or a Sunni Muslim, or a Jew, or a Scot, she is relating herself not just to a set of dances, costumes, recipes and incantations, but to a distinct set of practices in which her people (the people she identifies with when she claims this as her identity) have historically addressed and settled upon solutions to the serious problems of human life. It may be the basis of life for a community that has always yearned for independence, or it may (as in the Iraqi case) be an off-shoot of a larger but monocultural community, which may have independence, but whose members or some of them are dispersed abroad.

---

[38] See also J Waldron, "Cultural Identity and Civic Responsibility" in W Kymlicka and W Norman (eds.), *Citizenship in Diverse Societies* (Oxford, Oxford University Press, 2000) 155.

Now group rights claims, I said, are characteristically made in the politics of a larger multi-cultural society. That larger society also has to deal with the ordinary problems of social life among its inhabitants. It too will be trying to set up practices and rules to govern relations between the sexes, the rearing of children, the organisation of an economy, the transmission of knowledge, the punishment of offences, etc. When it arrives at and tries to implement a set of solutions to these problems, those solutions will implicitly contradict some of the solutions arrived at as part of the heritage of the smaller cultures that make up the fabric of the larger society's multiculturalism. In this context, claims of right by particular groups within the larger society will tend to blur the line between proposals as to how the larger society (or any society) should organise itself, and claims about how individuals within the society should be permitted to order their own affairs. The blurring of this line is a standing danger for any polity in which group rights, on behalf of national or ethnic communities, have become part of standard political discourse. The danger may be worth bearing—that is, it may be worth putting up with some blurring of this line, in order to limit the hegemony of the mainstream culture over subordinate groups. But again, the matter is one of judgement, and the complexity of the considerations I have outlined counsels against any impulsive acceptance of group rights talk, born of sympathy perhaps for a marginalised group.

VI

Claims of right are always asserted in peremptory tones; that's part of the politics of rights. They do not invite discussion: they close it down, with claims of "self-evidence" and imputations of wickedness to those who question them. This has led some critics of group rights to suppose that one has to trip them up on logical grounds, or not at all. I have tried to argue in this paper, that the logical objections to group rights are mostly ill-founded. But the sentiments that prompt these objections are nevertheless worth considering as reasons for hesitation before admitting group rights to the prominent place in our political discourse that their proponents demand. Precisely because rights *are* peremptory, and tend to close down compromise and reconsideration, we ought to be very careful which rights we recognise, and be sure that we understand the nature and complexity of the issues that such rights-talk claims to settle.

12

Should Maori Group Rights be Part of a New Zealand Constitution?

ANDREW SHARP*

I

In New Zealand, no less than in other liberal democracies, special rights of tribal, ethnic and racial groups have been recognised in law and—as their recognition in law implies—in public morality. The logic of the morality of such recognition is this: for a group (as for an individual) to have special rights there must be something distinct about its history or present situation, in the absence of which its members would enjoy precisely and only those rights that the rest of the citizenry possess equally.[1] An individual can claim special rights to particular things only by virtue (say) of having been gifted that thing or having a contractually-based claim to it, or because for the moment he labours under some pressing need. On the same argument, if a group is to have special rights, it must inherit those rights as a consequence of some past fact or have a claim to them by virtue of some particular current condition. Often—in New Zealand as elsewhere—special group rights are the policy instruments of acknowledging and providing a remedy for the injustices and disadvantages of past and present wrongs, and of present suffering.[2] More to the point, if one is thinking about constitutions—which are more permanent than passing policies—special rights of groups are embraced as expressing some ideal of multiculturalism. Such multicultural ideals can either be positive and celebratory of "difference" and political "consociability"[3] across cultural divides, or

---

* The resources of the Marsden Fund, administered by the Royal Society of New Zealand, made the preparation of this piece possible.

[1] An extrapolation from H L A Hart, "Are There Any Natural Rights?" (1955) 64 *Philosophical Review* 175.

[2] A Sharp, "Civil rights, Amelioration, and Reparation in New Zealand" in M Brown and S Ganguly (eds.), *Government Policies and Ethnic Relations in Asia and the Pacific* (Cambridge, Mass., MIT Press, 1997) 421 has an account of the general civil rights available in New Zealand, and some of the special Maori rights.

[3] On difference, see I M Young, "Polity and Group Difference: A Critique of the Ideal of Universal Citizenship" (1989) 99 *Ethics* 250, and "Communication and the Other: Beyond Deliberative Democracy" in S Benhabib (ed.), *Democracy and Difference: Contesting the Boundaries of the Political* (Princeton, Princeton University Press, 1996) 120. On the constitutionalisation of difference see J Tully, *Strange Multiplicity: Constitutionalism in an Age of Diversity* (Cambridge, Cambridge University Press, 1996). On consociability, see A Lijphart, *Democracy in Plural Societies: A Comparative Exploration* (New Haven, Yale University Press, 1997).

they can be negative and concerned rather more simply with keeping the public peace.[4] Either way, they recognise it as a fact that people, irreducibly and over long time-spans, belong to differing cultures. They recognise that, as a consequence, members of different cultural groups ascribe and will ascribe differing meanings to their lives and activities; and because of that they have and will have systematically differing interests in pursuing differing ideals and needs under a constitution.

If, that is, some multicultural ideal is embraced, and if rights are understood as interests important enough to a political system to be protected and fostered by the imposition of duties on others, then groups living out a culture might well bear special rights. Such rights too—when they protect and foster long-term group interests—might be enshrined in constitutions.

The idea, then, of groups bearing rights is neither obviously incoherent nor obviously wrong, and it has been recognised in law. The insistence that "there is no such thing as group rights" is simply wrong as to the obvious facts of the matter; and it has not been too difficult for scholars to give accounts of what group (as contrasted with individual) rights are, or to specify the kinds of content they have and the purposes they exist to fulfil.[5] Nor have the architects of constitutions found it a bad idea to write group rights into constitutions: Canada, the United Kingdom, and Belgium come immediately to mind as distributing political authority along tribal, ethnic and national lines. Indeed, the very idea of a modern liberal democratic constitution entails taking group rights very seriously. And even if particular ethnic groups are not given any separate political authority, the constitution typically lays out the conditions in which a citizenry's *group* right to rule itself may be exercised, together with the limits of that rule—and limits not only as to individuals but as to special groups. Again, one might consider a constitution as being partly addressed to those abroad. Internally, the citizenry's right to rule itself is a general group right, inhering in all citizens without distinction as to their histories or the current claims each might have against each. This is one of the reasons for describing all citizens as equals. It is, however, a *special group right* considered over and against the rights of other states and other citizen bodies. There is, so to say, something special about this group of citizens—as opposed to other groups of people—that gives it a right to rule itself, and not be ruled by others. A prominent

---

[4] This is a theme recently developed by J T Levy in *The Multiculturalism of Fear* (Oxford, Oxford University Press, 2000).

[5] See eg, over a wide range of contexts and approaches: M Freeman, "Are There Collective Human Rights?" (1995) 43 *Political Studies* 25; P Jones, "Group Rights and Group Oppression" (1999) 7 *Journal of Political Philosophy* 353; E Kiss, "Democracy and the Politics of Recognition" in I Shapiro and C Hacker-Cordón (eds.), *Democracy's Edges* (Cambridge, Cambridge University Press, 1999) 193; W Kymlicka, *Liberalism, Community and Culture* (Oxford, Clarendon Press, 1989) chs. 7–12; W Kymlicka, *Multicultural Citizenship* (Oxford, Oxford University Press, 1995) ch. 3; W Kymlicka (ed.), *The Rights of Minority Cultures* (Oxford, Oxford University Press, 1995) *passim*; I Shapiro and W Kymlicka (eds.), *Nomos XXXIX: Ethnicity and Group Rights* (New York, New York University Press, 1997) *passim*, especially T Pogge, "Group Rights and Ethnicity" at 187 and J Levy, "Classifying Cultural Rights" at 22; A Sharp, "What if Value and Rights Lie Foundationally in Groups? The Maori Case" (1999) 2 *Critical Review of International Social and Political Philosophy* 1; M S Williams, "Memory, History and Membership: The Moral Claims of Marginalised Groups in Political Representation" in J Räikkä (ed.), *Do We Need Minority Rights? Conceptual Issues* (The Hague, Martinus Nijhoff, 1996) 85.

ideal of international, multilateral organisations, is that each state is equal and that none can be ruled by others.

Of course, to say that group rights make conceptual and moral sense, and play a prominent role in the practice of constitutionalism and in international relations, is not to answer questions about the possibility or desirability of any particular state's morally recognising, or legally instituting, any particular subordinate group's rights. There might be more important demands of individual rights to be met. Or the over-all good of the civic milieu (comprising the citizens and their civic culture) might count against particular group rights. These are matters of crucially important principle and detail, some of which Professor Waldron discusses here.[6] For my part, I wish to concentrate on a narrower but locally pressing question as to the coherence and justifiability of special Maori group rights to self-rule in a New Zealand constitution. I will not be directly concerned with current New Zealand law, with the rhetoric and practice of human rights and international law, or with the detail and language of current Maori claims. But I will be concerned with them peripherally, because those different modes of speaking appear to harbour certain assumptions and arguments for and against the proposition that certain Maori groups—perhaps Maori as a whole—ought to have rights to what is variously called "autonomy", "tino rangatiratanga", "Maori sovereignty", "mana motuhake", "mana tangata" and so on.[7] And my interest here will be in exploring a notion that I judge to underlie many of the words of the laws, customs, discourses and authorities commonly appealed to across quite a wide range of argument. The notion is that Maori as a whole, and/or various traditional Maori groupings, have *fundamental group rights* to self-rule by virtue of being what might be called *fundamental groups*.

I shall argue that claims to fundamental group rights are intellectually and therefore prescriptively incoherent, and should be resisted not only as incoherent but also as in practice foolish and damaging. Even, however, if I am right, and there is no place for the ideal of fundamental groups in an appropriately chastened political theory, this would not in itself mean that Maori should not have some kinds of autonomy rights enshrined (as lawyers put it) in a constitution. All rights of action,[8] after all—and not just the named rights to self-rule at issue in current argument—entail the freedom to act within the sphere they define. In a concluding series of remarks, which because of their brevity cannot be made in any way to add up to an argument, I try to suggest: (a) what kind of reasoning might lead one to endorse

---

[6] "Taking Group Rights Carefully", in this volume.

[7] A good introduction to the variety and discursive context of the claims is M Durie, "'Tino Rangatiratanga' Maori Self-Determination" (1995) 1(1) *He Pukenga Korero* 44–53 (more fully in his *Te Mana, Te Kawanatanga. The Politics of Maori Self-Determination* (Auckland, Oxford University Press, 1998). Another, enthusiastically messy one, is A Fleras and P Spoonley, *Recalling Aotearoa: Indigenous Politics and Ethnic Relations in New Zealand* (Auckland, Oxford University Press, 1999) chs. 1 and 2. Also A Sharp, *Justice and the Maori: The Philosophy and Practice of Maori Claims in New Zealand Since the 1970s*, 2nd enlarged edn. (Auckland, Oxford University Press, 1997) chs. 13–16 esp.

[8] The normal distinction is between "rights of action" (rights to do things or be something for oneself) and "rights of recipience" (rights to have or get something from others).

the notion of Maori autonomies (plural) and (b) what considerations might lead one to think that certain autonomies might be enshrined in a constitution. I shall not answer fully the question set in my title, though I hope I have disposed of some false claims and cleared the way a little for other attempts.

II

It is conventional liberal-democratic wisdom that what might justify (or condemn) the existence, activity, and rights of any group is that the group empowers the *individuals* who make it up to pursue their personal interests and life's ideals. Or if it does not empower them, at least it protects them in their pursuits. It is on individualistic grounds, too, that even the most communitarian of thinkers justify (for instance) the right of a group to have its language and traditional culture protected. Without a stable and powerful milieu of existence, the argument goes, no individual, constituted merely of unreliable, mortal flesh and blood, could be expected to flourish, let alone to develop the autonomous character devoted to choosing and shaping a life so valued by more straightforward liberals.[9] Such considerations provide good grounds on which the special rights of some of the minority groups in New Zealand—Maori rights included—might be defended. Such rights might include, for instance, exemptions from laws that penalise or burden certain cultural practices (exemption from employment laws regarding absenteeism for attendance at tangihanga, for example). They might also include rights designed to provide assistance for members of minority groups to do those things that members of the majority culture can do unassisted (rights to aid in sustaining the Maori language, for example, or rights for new immigrants to special English teaching). Rights might also be instituted that protect the integrity of a culture or a group from external attack and internal subversion; and there might be rights to political representation; and rights to a symbolic presence in the national life.[10] In my view, Maori may justifiably claim special group rights such as these, based on justifications that look to the good, or the interests or the rights of Maori individuals. And insofar as moral individualism has been the basis of their claims that New Zealand should become a bicultural society before it becomes a multicultural one, then the case has been made persuasively—if too unkindly to other minority groups, and too exclusively. When made persuasively the case has been no different in (individualistic) *kind* from those of other cultural groups; but it is one especially pressing on grounds of the greater numbers of Maori, and their greater (unchosen) suffering, social dislocation and loss of political power since the coming of the Pakeha.[11] Insofar too,

[9] The individualist case is summed up in Sharp and in Jones, above n. 5.

[10] I construct these examples with the aid of J T Levy, "Classifying Cultural Rights" in I Shapiro and W Kymlicka (eds.), *Nomos XXXIX*, above n. 5 at 22, also published as ch. 5 in Levy's *Multiculturalism of Fear*, above n. 4.

[11] A Sharp, "Why be Bicultural?" in M Wilson and A Yeatman (eds.), *Justice and Identity: Antipodean Practices* (Wellington, Bridget Williams Books, 1995) 116.

as New Zealanders remain concerned with minimising inequalities of social condition, then a great proportion of Maori—equalled only in proportion, though not
in numbers, by immigrants from the Pacific Islands—clearly find themselves in the
groups of those qualifying for the rights of the relatively-deprived and of the
absolutely needy.[12]

It is not, however, the value of the existence of such groups and the rights of
such groups that are my concern. They are not a problem to the conventional
wisdom that I have no desire to challenge at the moment.[13] From the liberal-
democratic perspective let us say that such groups are *derivative groups* and the rights
they enjoy are *derivative rights*. The groups and their rights derive their existence,
value and justification from individualistic, factual and value premises.[14] Whatever
the complicated facts about individual judgment of and choices about membership
of groups, it is the individual who is, so to say, the fundamental moral particle: the
basic element of ethical and thus legal life. It is the individual's good, rights and
interests that are foundational, even if the particular individuals in question have
not joined the group but were born into or thrown into it, or put there without
their knowledge or consent by outsiders who simply categorise them as members.
Even if the members of a group can imagine no other life than one according to
their group's culture; even when they are happy in such a life—especially when
they have never actually critically considered the lives the group and its culture
enables them to live—the liberal-democratic judgement of the matter is that the
group exists for them, and not they for the group. They should be free to leave.
Should they wish, they might do well to transform themselves in joining another
group and adopting another culture.[15] Of course, this is not to deny (indeed it is
precisely to acknowledge) that individuals often act in ways the significance of
which can adequately be captured only by an ineliminable reference to the collectivity in which they are acting. It is also to acknowledge that what the collectivity
does is distinct from anything that individuals can do, and that collective entities

---

[12] See A Sharp, "Civil Rights, Amelioration and Reparation" above n. 2, for the position in 1996.
For an official view on Maori deprivation and need see Te Puni Kokiri, *Progress Towards Closing Social
and Economic Gaps Between Maori and Non-Maori: A Report to the Minister of Maori Affairs* (Wellington, Te
Puni Kokiri, 1998 and 2000).

[13] See for this: G Sher, "Diversity" (1999) 28 *Philosophy & Public Affairs* 85; and C Offe,
"'Homogeneity' and Constitutional Democracy: Coping with Identity Conflicts Through Group
Rights" (1998) 6 *Journal of Political Philosophy* 113.

[14] On the kinds of individualistic premises see A Ingram, *A Political Theory of Rights* (Oxford, Oxford
University Press, 1994, reprinted 1998).

[15] For a clear voluntaristic critique of "associative political obligations" (a term of Ronald Dworkin's
in *Law's Empire* (Cambridge, Belknap Press, 1986) that stresses the non-voluntariness of much mutual
obligation), see J Simmons, "Associative Political Obligations" (1996) 106 *Ethics* 247. For a more complex defence of associative obligations, together with an introduction to the idea of obligations to a
"plural subject" (a group), see M Gilbert, "Reconsidering the "Actual Contract" Theory of Political
Obligation" (1999) 109 *Ethics* 236. For critiques of the very idea of being trapped in an ethnic identity,
see C Kukathas, *The Fraternal Conceit: Liberal vs Collectivist Ideas of Community* (Sydney, Centre for
Independent Studies, 1991), C Kukathas, "Cultural Toleration" in I Shapiro and W Kymlicka (eds.),
Nomos XXXIX, above n. 5 at 69, and C Kukathas, "Are There any Cultural Rights?" in W Kymlicka
(ed.), *The Rights of Minority Cultures*, above n. 5 at 228. See also J Waldron, "Minority Cultures and the
Cosmopolitan Alternative" in W Kymlicka (ed.), *The Rights of Minority Cultures*, ibid at 93.

can be perdurable, demonstrating a persistence through time that is relatively indifferent to the particular individuals who compose it at any particular moment.[16] Nor is an insistence on the derivative nature of groups to deny in a blanket way the possibility of the legitimacy of such a collectivity, or that it might have rights against its members and against non-members, and be entitled to expect (alternatively) their loyalty and respect.[17] It is only to say that all collectivities are *derivative* rather than fundamental: they derive their value from what they do for individuals. An individualist might well think that certain nation-states, considered as derivative collectivities rather than as indissoluble unions of blood and culture, are creations of great value and power. He need have no problem thinking that such a state may rightly demand sacrifices even to the death of its subjects in war, or at the hands of an executioner for crimes against it. On the other hand, however, the individualist will regard all folkstates as having rotten foundations even if they work well for individuals in practice.

But this individualist conception of groups and their rights does not properly capture the nature, value and rights of Maori groups on behalf of whom certain Maori (and Pakeha) claim autonomy. Nor do the judgements entailed in it match the judgements reached by a common Maori way of thinking, often endorsed, if not fully explained, by Pakeha.[18] The liberal-democratic way of seeing things, it is sometimes said, is too individualistic, too western, too monocultural. It is not "holistic", and breaks down into constituent parts that cannot be divided—the indivisible group. In this form of thinking so critical of individualism, Maori groups—sometimes said to be Maori as a whole, sometimes iwi, sometimes hapu—are to be regarded as *fundamental groups* and their rights are to be regarded as *fundamental group rights*. The political theory at stake here is one that insists that the group is the fundamental moral particle of social life, and that *its* good, *its* interests and *its* rights are foundational. The group has rights exclusive to itself and exercisable only by itself. Most important, (like the citizenry of a state) its members share in the right to self-rule. But where a citizenry might claim a merely derivative right to self-rule, from the perspective of the fundamental group, the group's right is primary and underived. It is "inherent". It is the group's property, and the group's to exercise in the light of its own judgement—in just the way

[16] A rendering of Professor Keith Graham (University of Bristol) in his account of the relationship of individuals to groups capable of agency: *Collective responsibility* (unpublished paper, 1998).

[17] The argument for the rangatiratanga of Te Whanau o Waipareira in Waitangi Tribunal, *Te Whanau o Waipareira Report (Wai 414)* (Wellington, GP Publications, 1998) is exactly of this sort. See my unpublished paper, "On the Meaning and Implications of the Waitangi Tribunal's Arguing that Rangatiratanga was Generated Among the Urban Maori of the Waipaireira Trust", delivered at Otago, Canterbury, Massey, and Victoria Universities in early 2000.

[18] Pakeha endorsements of fundamental Maori group rights come (so far as their reasoning is clear) from A Fleras and P Spoonley, *Recalling Aotearoa: Indigenous Politics and Ethnic Relations in New Zealand*, above n. 7, chs. 1 and 2; J Kelsey, *Rolling Back the State: Privatisation of Power in Aotearoa/New Zealand* (Wellington, Bridget Williams Books, 1993) Part 4, and J Kelsey "From Flagpoles to Pine Trees: Tino Rangatiratanga and Treaty Policy Today" in P Spoonley, D Pearson and C Macpherson (eds.), *Nga Patai: Racism and Ethnic Relations in Aotearoa/New Zealand* (Palmerston North, Dunmore Press, 1996) 177, esp 198–201.

that an individual is free to do what he wishes with his own property. Indeed, group autonomy is expressed precisely in the activity of governing what is the group's own. The group's judgement is its own—a product of its culture and the authority the group derives from that culture, the argument goes—to the exact degree an individualist might think that an individual's judgement is *his* own. Every individual organic human being within the group, and every human being or group outside the group, has authority and property only in so far as some formula relates those other individuals and groups to the existence, the authority and the good of the fundamental group. Thus, the rights of individuals are not and cannot be foundational or fundamental. They are always derived. Indeed, the individual has moral status only as part of the group. As Kakapaiwaho Kururangi Tibble of Ngati Porou put it in an affidavit in 1998:[20]

"When I was a child I recall meeting these kuia (my nannies) in the street or at a marae. They would reach out and begin wailing quietly and tears falling from their eyes and saying '*Ka kite atu i a koe ko o matua tonu*' 'seeing you is seeing your forbears.' I was taught that no Maori is an individual."

From the perspective of the fundamental group, the rights of other groups might on occasion be recognised as fundamental, in the same way as an individualist can recognise the fundamental individual rights of others; but even when they are recognised, they are limited by the inalienable rights of the fundamental group. The fundamental group retains the right to judge of its subjection or freedom from any outside control. On this view the Crown in New Zealand is to be regarded as the representative of a group (the Pakeha), and its existence and actions are always to be judged by the fundamental group in terms of its own culture. On this view too, the authority of Te Whakakotahitanga o nga iwi o Aotearoa (the Maori Congress) may not override the mana of its iwi constituents.[21] Ngai Tahu, for instance, may not be subject to, or co-operate with, other iwi, without its own continuing consent: and on this understanding of things it withdrew from te Whakakotahitanga after internal disagreements.

The relationships, then, of a fundamental group with other groups will always be those of what Thomas Hobbes called a "league": an association based on mutual covenant where each connected element is judge in its own cause, and where the connection remains only so long as there is "a similitude of wills and inclinations".[22]

---

[19] See eg, A Mahuika, "Whakapapa is the Heart" in K Coates, P McHugh et al (eds.), *Living Relationships/Kokiri Ngatahi. The Treaty of Waitangi in the New Millennium* (Wellington, Victoria University Press, 1998) 214, 219: "Whakapapa is the determinant of all mana rights to land, to marae, to membership of a whanau, hapu, and, collectively, the iwi whakapapa determines kinship roles and responsibilities to other kin, as well as one's place and status in society."

[20] *Te Runanga o Ngati Porou v. Treaty of Waitangi Fisheries Commission*: High Court of New Zealand, Auckland Registry, M734/95, 6–7. Cf T Reedy, Affidavit, *Te Runanga o Te Upoko o Te Ika Association v. Treaty of Waitangi Fisheries Commission* (1998) High Court of New Zealand, Auckland Registry, CP No 122/95, 19: "we are but the seeing eyes and speaking mouths of those who have passed on".

[21] L Cox, *Kotahitanga: The Search for Maori Political Unity* (Auckland, Oxford University Press, 1993) 147, 149–51, 157–8, 167–8, 184–6.

[22] T Hobbes, *Leviathan, or the Matter, Forme, and Power of a Commonwealth Ecclesiastical and Civil* (London, Andrew Crooke, 1651) part ii, ch. 22, p. 122.

Relations typical of those between states in an international system typify those between a fundamental group and all others.

Internally to itself the group proceeds by consensus—usually a consensus moulded by recognised leaders, but leaders with no independent power to decide for the whole. Their mana derives from the good they do the whole. Nor will the assent of a majority as such bind the members: for to make a group decision without the agreement of all the individuals is not to have made a *group* decision. The unity of will characteristic of the group in action means a congruence of individual wills. Is the group then, a league itself—a group only so long as unity of individual wills is attained? And does not the requirement of general agreement give a veto to the one or the few who disagree and thus reveal a political theory of derivative groups and a fundamental valuing of the individual? Not so. The group is bound by whakapapa, by ties of blood and continued group life. These insist that mutual discussion and negotiation continue until agreement is reached. There is no veto; no exit; only a time of waiting. Minority group members have no right that their dissent prevail any more than the majority have a right that their weightier will should prevail. Each side retains a duty to work towards agreement.

It might be questioned whether this political theory is in fact embraced by enough Maori to make it a serious political and constitutional question. And I admit to forcing into a pure ideal type what is a much more messy and formless thing on the ground.[23] Indeed, a leading expert on the international law of indigenous peoples, often quoted by what I would see as theorists of the fundamental group, derives their rights to autonomy from the consideration that group autonomy benefits the individual human beings who make up the groups.[24] But still—and in the face of serious arguments against group fundamentalism[25] (admittedly not often New Zealand ones)[26]—what is one otherwise to make of the normative substance (as opposed to the legal warrant) of recent findings of the Waitangi Tribunal?[27] It has declared that "autonomy is the inherent right of all peoples in their native countries" and that, "on the colonisation of inhabited countries, sovereignty, in the sense of absolute power, cannot be vested in only one of the parties"?[28] Its sayings do not, I think, simply add up to the factual claim that international law has come to recognise aboriginal autonomy, or that the *Draft*

---

[23] I have provided a fuller description of instances of the theory of fundamental groups among Maori in "What if Value and Rights Lie Foundationally in Groups? The Maori Case", above n. 5 at 1.

[24] S James Anaya, *Indigenous Peoples in International Law* (Oxford, Oxford University Press, 1996) 76, quoted by M Solomon, "The Context For Maori (II)" in A Quentin-Baxter (ed.), *Recognising the Rights of Indigenous Peoples* (Wellington, Institute of Policy Studies, 1998) 60, 64.

[25] See especially D L Horowitz, "Self-Determination: Politics, Philosophy, and Law" in I Shapiro and W Kymlicka (eds.) *Nomos XXXIX*, above n. 5 at 421, also published in M Moore (ed.), *National Self-Determination and Secession* (Oxford, Oxford University Press, 1998) 181. See also T Pogge, "Group Rights and Ethnicity" in I Shapiro and W Kymlicka (eds.), *Nomos XXXIX*, above n. 5 at 187.

[26] Though see D Graham, "The New Zealand Government's Policy" in A Quentin-Baxter (ed.), *Recognising the Rights of Indigenous Peoples*, above n. 24 at 3.

[27] Here I build on what I have said in *Justice and the Maori*, above n. 7 at 310–402, and "What if Value and Rights Lie Foundationally in Groups? The Maori Case", above n. 5.

[28] *The Taranaki Report Kaupapa Tuatahi (Wai 143)* (Wellington, GP Publications, 1996) 20, and see S. 2.1 generally.

Declaration of Rights of Indigenous Peoples proclaims rights of self-government for indigenous peoples.[29] Nor do they simply interpret what the "principles" of the Treaty of Waitangi might require in a way required and allowed by the statute on which the Tribunal's power is based. I think the Tribunal quite unequivocally endorses the claims as being plainly right: law or no law.[30] It is true that extra-legal reasoning is largely absent in the Tribunal's formulation of the autonomy claim— though at certain points it is argued that recognition of such rights would help ameliorate possible ethnic conflict, is not a bar to "national unity", and would not threaten the constitution or the peace.[31] Even so it may be hazarded that the Tribunal's view is that the group "Maori" had, and could not fully alienate (though it might alienate some of)[32] an "inherent" group right to self-government in 1840. Or else, building further on its other sayings, its view is that the various "peoples" who make up the Maori people—iwi and hapu are the "peoples" in question— have such rights to rule themselves, which are similarly inalienable, and which are a lien on the sovereignty of the Crown.[33] These rights might perhaps be exercised by others with the agreement of and for the benefit of the group or groups in question. But it remains the case that Maori as a whole, or else traditional Maori groups (or else both), retain the right to judge the exercise of their rights by others, if not the right to reassume their exercise for themselves.

It is as if Maori, or Maori groups, are like individual flesh-and-blood agents in bearing very important rights; but where individuals can alienate their rights, can subject themselves to the authority of a group and can make themselves incapable

[29] For principled scepticism on the *Draft Declaration*, see R Mulgan, "Should Indigenous Peoples Have Special Rights?" (1989) 33 *Orbis* 375.

[30] The Tribunal in *Te Whanau o Waipareira Tribunal (Wai 414)* above n. 16, § 8.2.3 at 215 speaks of human rights law as being a "counterpart" to Maori custom which asserts rights of self-government perfectly adequately for Maori purposes. See the similar but more energetic gloss on international and human rights law by C Wickliffe in "An Overview of Collective Human Rights Developments in the Pacific Region with an Emphasis on the Collective Right to Self-Determination" in N Tomas (ed.), *Collective Human Rights of Pacific Peoples* (Auckland, International Research Unit for Maori and Indigenous Education, University of Auckland, 1999) 151. Here the elements of "customary international law" that proclaim national self-determination and the rights of indigenous peoples are embraced, but not those that speak of territorial sovereignty or the need for stability. The criteria developed by the Decolonisation Committee are criticised thus: "I am saying that in the interests of equality there is really no reason why Maori or other Indigenous Peoples cannot claim the full right to self-determination. How they then cho[o]se to develop political options for manifesting that right will depend on the circumstances that prevail in their respective countries" (pp .161–2). The right of indigenous peoples to self-government is at one point said to be "inalienable"; at another it is said to be capable of being "ceded with informed consent" (pp. 159, 163).

[31] *The Taranaki Report Kaupapa Tuatahi (Wai 143)*, above n. 27, § 2.1.

[32] *Report of the Waitangi Tribunal on the Muriwhenua Fishing Claim (Wai 22)* (Wellington, Waitangi Tribunal, 1988) §11.3.4 (a).

[33] A Sharp, *Justice and the Maori*, above n. 7 at 302. *Report of the Waitangi Tribunal on the Motonui-Waitara Claim (Wai 6)* (Wellington, Waitangi Tribunal, 1983) § 10; *Report of the Waitangi Tribunal on the Orakei Claim (Wai 9)* (Wellington, Waitangi Tribunal, 1987) § 11.5; *Report of the Waitangi Tribunal on the Muriwhenua Fishing Claim (Wai 22)*, above n. 31, §§ 11.3.6 (c) and (d); 11.3.7 (p); *Fisheries Bill Claim (Wai 321)* (Wellington, GP Publications, 1992) §§ 6.2–6.9; *Ngai Tahu Land Report (Wai 27)* (Wellington, Brooker and Friend, 1991) §§ 4.6 and 4.7; *Mohaka River Report* (1992) § 5.5.2; *The Ngai Tahu Sea Fisheries Report, 1992 (Wai 27)* (Wellington, Brooker and Friend, 1992) §§ 4.2, 4.3, 11.1–11.5; *The Whanganui River Report (Wai 167)* (Wellington, GP Publications, 1999) xix §§ 2.3–2.5, 9.2.3–9.2.4.

of judging in their own cause, Maori groups cannot alienate their right to autonomy in every sphere they might happen to choose or their right to judge when that autonomy is being infringed upon. Where a liberal individualist finds himself having to agree that he should surrender private judgement for the good of a larger whole, no Maori group (when it is seen as a fundamental group) can do this.

Professor Mason Durie, author of the absorbing and informative book, *Te Mana, Te Kawanatanga: The Politics of Maori Self-Determination*,[34] appears to share some of these views. He quotes with approval the *Draft Declaration of Rights of Indigenous Peoples 1993*, together with those Maori who argue that because Hobbesian sovereignty incorporating Maori is not a Maori concept, "[t]he essential tasks are for Maori to reach agreement about decision-making within Maori society and for Maori and the Crown to agree on the most appropriate constitutional arrangements that will enhance the standing of both".[35] The various Maori groups must first negotiate their leagues with each other—there is no common judge among them— then the Maori league, now representing the power and judgement of Maori, should negotiate with the Crown, which, though it represents the rest of the citizenry (together perhaps with Maori in the aspect of citizens) has no right of final judgement. Professor Durie has an intimate knowledge of the workings of Maori society and carefully differentiates the different groupings, both fundamental and derived, from which a Maori league must be constructed. But he tends to take the factual as the normative (in particular, descriptions of the substance of Maori claims as statements of justified claims), and he often proceeds by the quotation of authorities rather than by argument. Thus, he continually endorses the assumptions of the theorists of fundamental groups, and works on the assumption that the Maori people as a whole are—whatever appears to the contrary by way of their actually being a Hobbesian league—*one fundamental group* with an inherent right to tino rangatiratanga, mana motuhake and self-government.

There is, it might be thought, a theoretical instability to group foundational claims, evident if the question is asked: just what *is* the fundamental Maori group that bears the right to self-rule? The instability was awkwardly evident in a 1997 conference paper by perhaps the most sophisticated living theorist on Maori autonomy, Professor Durie's brother, E T Durie, then Chief Judge of the Maori Land Court and Chairman of the Waitangi Tribunal. He began:[36]

> "In substance 'aboriginal autonomy', 'self-government', 'rangatiratanga' or 'mana motuhake', mean much the same. Each suggests that the indigenous people of a country have a right to determine their own policy, manage their own resources and control their own affairs, with only such interference from the state as may be necessary for the protection of legitimate national interests."

[34] Auckland, Oxford University Press, 1998.

[35] *Ibid*, 220.

[36] "Session on Aboriginal Autonomy", Conference "*The Treaty of Waitangi: Maori Political Representation*", Pipitea Marae, Wellington, 1 May 1997. Justice Durie is now a Member of the (normally 30–33 strong) High Court of New Zealand.

In sum, the paper argues for Maori autonomy within the New Zealand state. But, in the course of developing his case, Judge Durie shifts from speaking of the rights of the Maori "people", to the rights of Maori "peoples". He accords Maori a separate presence in a larger constitution, not as a single entity, but by virtue of their "particular constitutional status as the first peoples [plural]". It is not therefore clear just who the fundamental group is—just *whose* good, whose rights and whose interests are to be conceived of as shaping and justifying the actions of individuals: and if there is more than one fundamental group, it is not clear how the groups might relate each to the other, and how individuals (now belonging to more than one group) are to relate to each group of which they are members.

Indeed, and to speak more generally and critically as to the presence of assumptions proper to a theory of fundamental groups, a politics of fundamental groups and fundamental group rights often characterises relations between the group "Maori" and its constituent parts. This politics is to be observed in the difficulties of the Maori Congress, from which the constituent parts—iwi—retaining the right to secede, did just that. It is to be observed too in the internal Maori conflict that revolves around the respective claims of what the High Court, adjudicating on rights to Maori fisheries, has recently called "whakapapa" as opposed to "kaupapa"[37] iwi groups. When an iwi is a whakapapa group, it attains its membership only partly by choice: kinship through time is the necessary, involuntary qualification for an individual's choosing his or her allegiance among the groups available. A whakapapa group too, in its very nature inherits and transmits rights and obligations among the collectivity irrespective of the choice of any individual or generation; and it is a group that inherits a formula of internal authority that it must maintain in its unique kawa and tikanga, lest, changing the formula, it should lose its identity. By contrast, when an iwi is a kaupapa group—in the cases in point, a new, urban iwi—it is more like a seventeenth century English congregation, a gathered group sharing commitment to ideals and projects conceived in collective decision-making by its members, the formula for which decision-taking might perhaps be imitative of particular kawa or tikanga, but derives its moral force from the agreement of its members.[38] And proponents of the fundamental group are perfectly capable of denying such groups any legitimacy at all, or else expressing severe doubts as to the basis on which individual Maori might claim to be Maori if they are not members of fundamental groups. Thus, Sir Robert Mahuta of Waikato-Tainui: "I do not believe that urban Maaori groups have a rational basis for determining their membership and their needs."[39] Thus, Apirana Mahuika of Ngati Porou: "Without a whakapapa, you do not have inherited or whakapapa rights and mana. Such people are referred to as "rawaho" or outsiders! Indeed without a

---

[37] Terminology taken from the claimants in *Te Waka Hi Ika o Te Arawa* v. *Treaty of Waitangi Fisheries Commission* [2000] 1 NZLR 285, 330 (High Court), 336, 377 (CA).

[38] I have refined this view somewhat in my unpublished article: "On the Meaning and Implications of the Waitangi Tribunal's Arguing that Rangatiratanga was Generated Among the Urban Maori of the Waipareira Trust".

[39] Affidavit: *Te Runanga o Muriwhenua* v. *The Treaty of Waitangi Fisheries Commission* (1998) High Court of New Zealand, Auckland Registry, M 1514/94 31.

whakapapa, an individual would have difficulty establishing that they are Maori."[40] Thus, Hirini Moko Mead of Ngati Awa of those who claim to be an urban iwi: "they are strangers to each other".[41] On these understandings, perfectly illustrative of the political theory of fundamental groups sketched here, the politics of certain inter-and intra-iwi disputes are currently proceeding. An urban "iwi", could be a group well enough; but not a *fundamental* group:[42]

> "If the group is cultivating food . . . then that group would be called an ohu; if going to do battle, then a taua; if gathering for a tangihanga, then an ope; if travelling along the road, then a tira; if gathered in one place, a whakaminenga, a paenga, huihinga, rauhinga, rauikatanga, hunga or hanga; although however they are each of them gathered for a single purpose, none of them can be considered an iwi."

To give a concrete instance of dispute in conditions where the assumptions of fundamental group theory are present, the issue of Maori sharing of fisheries resources lies not just between fundamental and derivative iwi, but between iwi and hapu, each considered as fundamental groups. At which group "level", so to speak, does the right to the fishing lie? Is it the iwi (or federation) te Arawa, for instance, who bears the right to control its own fishing; or is it the hapu which lives at Maketu? Do, in general, hapu rather than iwi bear mana moana, the right to fish? And who will allow (and who has the right to allow) a non-member of the claimant group to judge?

Other examples abound,[43] generated in the process of other Treaty settlements, by the workings of the Resource Management Act which requires consultation with local Maori, and in land disputes taken to court. Where there is dispute *between* groups, no common judge will be recognised; where there is dispute *within* groups as to the formula by which the authority to represent it is distributed, not only is there no agreed formula, there is no judge as to what the formula should be. Moreover, there is no principle available to the theory of fundamental groups as to what the formula and who the judge might conceivably be. The principle is that the group must act for the good of the whole. But this does not help when there are conflicts between subgroups—what the English used to call "fractions" or "factions"[44]—of the whole: which faction is to judge? That is precisely the question. The group simply has no decision-procedure. It cannot act. It is, as James Harrington observed 350 years ago of a people without a constitution, a body

---

[40] Affidavit: *Te Runanga o Ngati Porou* v. *Treaty of Waitangi Fisheries Commission* (1998) High Court of New Zealand, Auckland Registry, M734/95, 8–9.

[41] Affidavit: *Te Runanga o Te Upoko o Te Ika Association (Inc)* v. *The Treaty of Waitangi Fisheries Commission* (1998) High Court of New Zealand, Auckland Registry, CP No 122/95, 29.

[42] Affidavit of Professor James te Wharehuia Milroy and Professor Timoti Samuel Karetu: *Te Runanga o Te Upoko o Te Ika Association (Inc)* v. *The Treaty of Waitangi Fisheries Commission* (1998) High Court of New Zealand, Auckland Registry, CP No 122/95, 7. Professor Sir Hugh Kawharu records tira, pahi, roopu, and taua. Affidavit: *loc cit*, 7.

[43] A Ward, *An Unsettled History: Treaty Claims in New Zealand Today* (Wellington, Bridget Williams Books, 1999) ch. 3 records some; also A Sharp, *Justice and the Maori*, above n. 7, ch. 16.

[44] See J A W Gunn, *Factions No More: Attitudes to Party in Government & Opposition in Eighteenth Century England* (London, Frank Cass, 1972) for suspicion of factions.

without a soul: "a living thing in pain and misery".[45] Such conflicts among Maori and groups of Maori, and Maori and the Crown, constitute of course what it has become fashionable to call the problem of "mandate". Who is to speak for, act for, and construct obligations for Maori? It will be clear that I think the problem is partly caused by the presence of beliefs, often unanalysed, which I have sketched as making up the theory of fundamental groups.

Now I do not wish to argue that conflict in general or arguments about mandate are bad things, or that the situation is as bad on the ground as it could be. As Apirana Mahuika found himself bound acidly to observe very recently:[46]

"Maori, or iwi, or both, have as much divine right as non-Maori or non-iwi to disagree on issues, as they are different as evidenced by dialect, interpretations of customs and traditions, ownership over specific resources and assets, and the like. This is no different from the Scots, Irish, and English who are notorious for their disagreements . . . in spite of the fact that they are on the same land mass."

Conflict makes for a healthy public life, and conflict may well include arguments about who should speak and act for whom. But political paralysis is not a good thing for those suffering from it, and in so far as conflict is generated by the theory of fundamental groups, it is an evil thing among those who must live together. For the theory yields the conclusion that where there is disagreement among or within fundamental groups then there is no judge or decision-maker, and so the conflicts in question are—whatever else they are—an inescapable *logical outcome* of disagreement in conditions of the theory of the fundamental group. They are the consequences of what Aristotle called a "practical syllogism",[47] according to which—given this axiom, and this fact—this *action* follows as a conclusion. So inasmuch as people think or argue on assumptions of fundamental group rights they are logically committed to the outcome of their theory: institutionally uninhibited conflict of competing authority—or mana, or rangatiratanga, or autonomies, or rights to self-determination or self-government. Of course, in place of the old weapons used among the iwi and hapu, there are new; and as Hirini Moko Mead said of the fisheries dispute, but which may properly be generalised: "perhaps the perverse irony is that this very dispute may ultimately be decided by five Pakeha peers sitting in London".[48] Intra-Maori conflict typically ends in court, in the appeal to an outside authority.[49]

Such conflict can have no conceivably good end for anyone in the real world in Aotearoa-New Zealand. Of course scarcely anyone—least of all most of those I have

---

[45] J Harrington, *A System of Politics* (c. 1661) in J G A Pocock (ed.), *The Political Works of James Harrington* (Cambridge, Cambridge University Press, 1977) 834, 838.

[46] "Whakapapa is the heart", 218.

[47] A McIntyre, "A Mistake about Causality in Social Science" in P Laslett and W G Runciman (eds.), *Philosophy, Politics and Society (Second Series)* (Oxford, Basil Blackwell, 1962) 48, 49–54.

[48] Affidavit: *Te Runanga o Te Upoko o Te Ika Association (Inc)* v. *The Treaty of Waitangi Fisheries Commission* (1998) High Court of New Zealand, Auckland Registry, CP No 122/95, 21.

[49] The Presbyterian Church, jealous of its autonomy, has found itself in fascinatingly similar circumstances in the course of internal disagreement. See D Réaume, "Common-Law Constructions of Group Autonomy: A Case Study" in *Nomos XXXIX*, above n. 5 at 257.

quoted as embracing the assumptions of the theory of fundamental groups—thinks in terms of the political theory of fundamental groups all the time. They are equally and rightly concerned to forge a kind of unity among very disparate groupings, mainly among Maori, but also between Maori and Pakeha. And in any case, the theory of fundamental groups will not work in Aotearoa/New Zealand. It is almost inconceivable in a polity of any territorial extent where peoples live promiscuously mixed that there should be universal agreement on all important matters between every group and among all the members of each group. Nor would one want agreement. Were the theory of fundamental groups to be exclusively embraced, there never could be tolerably lasting and principled settlements across equal groups, between "levels" of groups, and within groups. Loyalty and the surrender of private judgement except to one group among many would be almost unknown. If it were known—as where an individual might find himself faced with the claims on him of more than one fundamental group—surrender of private judgement would be accompanied by painful and irresolvable conflict of loyalties, or by recourse to that individual judgement, good, right and interest which is precisely denied by the theory of fundamental groups. Most of all, from a Maori point of view, a successful league of the Maori people under such a theory would be highly unlikely. And if no pan-Maori group capable of agency could be constructed, then, even though the group "Maori" might possess "passive" "rights of recipience" to benefits from others, practice and theory combine to suggest they could not exercise "active" "rights of agency" or, in sum, rights to autonomy. Rights of agency require—as matters both of conceptual coherence and practice—the actual capacity to exercise them.[50]

Of course, excesses of foundational individualism display analogous difficulties to the theory of foundational groups. As Jeremy Bentham rightly pointed out more than two hundred years ago, individual rights flatly contradict one another (liberty *and* property, *and* equality?) and in addition deny a justified basis to government (resistance to oppression?).[51] Even so, it is probably empirically true that foundational individualism is a better basis for the construction of groups that can *act* than group foundationalism, certainly in reasonably geographically extended societies. For group action requires at times—and certainly requires systematically—the surrender of private judgement. It requires that some be in authority over others, not because they are right or because everyone agrees with them but simply because a decision must be made and carried out.[52] And in these conditions individual

---

[50] As demonstrated by J Nickel, "Group Agency and Group Rights" in I Shapiro and W Kymlicka (eds.), *Nomos XXXIX*, above n. 5 at 235. I think this article should be compulsory reading for all those who wish to argue about group rights in a New Zealand constitution.

[51] J Bentham, "Anarchical Fallacies, being an Examination of the Declaration of Rights Issued During the French Revolution" in J Waldron (ed.), *Nonsense Upon Stilts: Bentham, Burke and Marx on the Rights of Man* (London, Methuen, 1987) 46.

[52] The best expression of this view is R B Freidman, "On the Concept of Authority in Political Philosophy" in R E Flathman (ed.), *Concepts in Social and Political Philosophy* (New York, MacMillan, 1973). For an application of its lessons to multicultural states (and a rejection of that application) see A Sharp, "What is the Constitution of "The Spirit of Haida Gwaii"? Reflections on James Tully's *Strange Multiplicity: Constitutionalism in an Age of Diversity* (1997) 10 *History and Anthropology*, 241, and Tully's reply immediately following.

foundationalism demands less of humanity than group foundationalism. It requires merely that from time to time an individual lays aside his personal view of what is right or what should be done and submits to the authority of the decision and those who make it. Group foundationalism on the other hand, requires that a *group* should submit. This can be a much harder thing than for an individual to submit, and not only because the *power* of groups makes it easier for them to resist than individuals. In addition, group *ideals*, and crucially the ideal of the fundamental group, make it hard for a particular group to submit to a superior group. If the group is the sole bearer of a self-sufficient "societal culture",[53] and rules itself internally, then its members might well think that to surrender group judgement to another country is to betray its culture. (Thus nationalism has problems with world government, and with the inroads of multinationals into settled ways of life.) Rather more to the point here, if the group is the sole bearer of a culture inside a state dominated by those of another culture, then it may well think that to surrender to the government is to betray its culture. For in such conditions, if the decisions of the government more often than not seem to such a group to go against their good, their interests and their rights, it will be hard to escape that conclusion.

Perhaps though, these cases do not prove anything about group *foundationalism*. Derivative groups might well think and react in precisely these unsubmissive ways—as national groups organised into states do even when they think of themselves and are thought of as collectivities justified by reference to individualist foundations. Take the USA; take Australia; take New Zealand indeed. Just so: "groupism"[54] may characterise derived as well as fundamental groups if they forget their individualist purposes. Maybe so: but the point on which I would conclude is that group foundationalism will severely hinder the creation of effective teams of action—citizenries or nations or (in the case of Maori) ethnic groups—in the first place. For if such a group is to be constructed from a series of groups bearing a culture, part of the content of which is a belief in group foundationalism, then each group will think that to surrender *its* judgement to those of its equals is to surrender the culture. The Maori case I think shows this. And so, whatever the abounding theoretical defects of foundational individualism, it most likely provides in contingent fact a better basis than group foundationalism for building and sustaining groups—both ruling and ruled—in territorial, multicultural societies.

III

For all that, one might equally assail the easy assumption that concentrating on individual rights will solve many problems. And one might further complain that

---

[53] Will Kymlicka's description of the kind of culture in which all things necessary for an individual's life choices may be found: named and discussed in *Multicultural Citizenship*, above n. 5, chs. 5–6; defended as important in *Liberalism, Community and Culture*, above n. 5, chs. 8–9.

[54] On "groupism" see R Brubaker, "Myths and Misconceptions in the Study of Nationalism" in M Moore (ed.), *National Self-Determination and Secession*, above n. 25, 233, 251–7.

any rights talk—whether of group or individual rights—tends to exacerbate conflict, treat as settled what is really up for negotiation, and accordingly diminish the place of political activity in building bases of co-operation.[55] It is highly likely, for instance, that the Maori theory of fundamental groups is to be explained as an invention called up by the (state) juridicalising of their relations each to each and with the Crown. Past and present facts of their group organisations suggest a very different and fluid Maori conception of groups.[56]

However this may be, the practice of individual rights is a fact, the practice of fundamental group rights is a fact, the juridicalising of difference between Maori and the Crown is a fact, and the question of a Maori place in a constitution is accordingly a live one. How might one think about this?

It would be wise in this legal-constitutional context to stop thinking of the Crown as a single entity representing any particular group, and as exercising the rights of sovereignty because it represents that group. This is pure Hobbesism, and in an important way mistaken, for it holds sovereignty and the representation of groups logically and normatively to precede tradition, habit and conventional norms. But in fact we have a constitution in which the powers of legal sovereignty—the highest legal powers of final determination on all matters internal to the state—are distributed by law and legally-recognised convention among a variety of organs of state and officials.[57] It is no more than a convenient (and obvious) fiction to pretend that sovereignty is located in the Crown if the Crown is conceived of as a single locus of the legal right to rule, let alone if the Crown is thought to be Queen Elizabeth II. The Crown must work within a set of conventions without which it would not *be* the Crown, and according to which a variety of official procedures are deemed to constitute (and limit) its acts. "The Crown" is a complex set of legal regulations and official relationships when passive; when active, it is officials acting according to the procedures which guide and limit their activity. For them to attempt to act otherwise is simply for them to fail to act as "the Crown", or it is for them to act without legal sanction.

It is less of an obvious fiction, but no less a fiction, that the locus of sovereignty lies in Parliament. For that assembly, by inherited English tradition and under the modern (highly conventionalised) principle of representation of the people, has the task of attending to the diffuse operations of state sovereignty and to regulating them and changing them as it judges wise. Even so—certainly as to moral and political

---

[55] R S Beiner, "National Self-determination: Some Cautionary Remarks Concerning the Rhetoric of Rights" in M Moore (ed.), *National Self-Determination and Secession*, above n. 25 at 158.

[56] A Ballara, *Iwi: The dynamics of Maori Tribal Organisation from c1769 to c1945* (Wellington, Victoria University Press, 1998); Affidavits on *Te Runanga o Te Upoko o Te Ika Association (Inc)* v. *Treaty of Waitangi Fisheries Commission* (1998), High Court of New Zealand, Auckland Registry, especially No CP122/95 Alan Ward, Whatarangi Winaiata, Angela Ballara.

[57] I leave aside the Privy Council. Besides that this account derives from H L A Hart, *The Concept of Law* (Oxford, Clarendon Press, 1961); the *Cabinet Office Manual* (Wellington: Cabinet Office, 1996); and P A Joseph, *Constitutional and Administrative Law in New Zealand* (Sydney, Law Book Company, 1993) ch. 9.

possibility and very possibly as to strict law[58]—Parliament cannot make all the decisions on all matters internal to the state. Sovereignty is here, as everywhere, diffused.[59] Leaving aside questions of physical competence (its members and delegates simply cannot do everything), it is itself the creature of convention. If it acts outside those conventions it either fails to act as a Parliament (its purported acts misfire), or (if it succeeds in overriding convention and popular expectation) risks losing its legitimacy with those it claims to rule. The sum of all this is that the citizenry's group right to rule itself, insofar as it issues in the legal sovereignty of the state, issues via law and convention in a wonderfully diverse and complex disposition of political authority and limits to that authority. The disposition is in the process of being discovered, taught, and disputed every day, and so the beliefs of the citizens themselves create and sustain those authorities and their limits as a matter both of morality and power. In brief, the New Zealand constitution (like the best working ones) is best seen as a set of conventional relationships, deeply informed by legal and popular principles and beliefs which are part of an inherited tradition. Were there no tradition—one might as well say were there no culture—there would be no constitution. If there were no constitution, there would be no sovereignty and no self-rule of any kind at all. The attempt to create a written constitution[60] uninformed by the actual traditions of a place is, therefore, an enterprise of the utmost folly.

But of course, Maori have been questioning the origins, traditions and culture of our constitution. This has been embarrassing. A modern liberal democratic state has difficulty in professing the obvious truth of itself and of probably all states in the world, that its origin as a persistent organisation of peoples in a territory lies in the enforcement of imperial will, and in blood and deception as much as agreement. Who would admit it? And further it is uncongenial to the plain private man or woman to think that the passage of time might redeem a tainted origin.[61] And so, since the 1980s, our politicians (both Maori and Pakeha) and our courts have created of the Treaty of Waitangi a consensual constitutional foundation. It is now widely, if often vaguely, said to be the "basis of our constitution". In this transformation, the Pakeha politicians and courts have quite simply, and openly, created a new tradition in place of an older one whereby the constitution took its origin from the will of the Crown and then came to find its legitimacy in consent. For their part, Maori have revived a tradition of the constitution's origin lying in the Treaty "covenant". The practice of government and subjection in Aotearoa, the tradition goes, is legitimate only in so far as it recognises the rights to self-determination set out—but not originating in—the Treaty. The Treaty tradition was nurtured among (only) certain groups, but it has been made a pan-Maori one.

---

[58] A point now conveniently stated in F M Brookfeld, *Waitangi and Indigenous Rights: Revolution, Law and Legitimation* (Auckland, Auckland University Press, 1999) 93–4.

[59] See M M Goldsmith, "Hobbes's 'Mortall God': Is There a Fallacy in Hobbes's Theory of Sovereignty?" (1980) 1 *History of Political Thought* 33.

[60] On the rather misleading distinction between written and unwritten constitutions, see Preston King, "Constitutionalism and the Despatch-Box Principle" (1999) 2 *Critical Review of Social and Political Philosophy* 29, esp 29–33.

[61] F M Brookfield, *Waitangi and Indigenous Rights*, above n. 58, makes this point.

And, as if that generalising Treaty turn were not enough, some are at the moment attempting to mount the claim (derived from a more exclusively Tai Tokerau tradition) that the Declaration of Independence (1835) signalled the origin of a pan-Maori nation among the hapu. This solves the problem of intra-Maori authority at the same time as it solves the Maori-Crown problem: for on this account Maori were constituted a nation state with a settled system of authority before Waitangi, and they at least residually retain the rights of a nation state.[62]

These narratives, compounded of fact and fiction, of logical and empirical possibility and impossibility, are all of them bent to explaining, whether to defend or attack, our present political and constitutional position.[63] They are now undeniably part of the principles and beliefs that our peoples inherit—or if not our peoples in general—then their leaders. So to subject such "juridical" histories to the cold scrutiny of reason or to re-impose a sense of historical complexity and anachronism is a practical impossibility and waste of time.[64] These simply *are* the narratives that guide our competing views as to what special rights Maori as a people, and as peoples, have. They specify what it is about them and their past which gives them rights different from other people. In an analogous way, particular iwi and hapu have developed and transmitted their own narratives of their sovereignty through time, as to why, for instance Waitaha or Kati Mamoe or Ngati Apa can never submit to government's settling their rights to reparation and autonomy on Ngai Tahu.[65]

My prescription, then, to any government is this. In general, respect the traditions of autonomy among groups that are older than you and have different aims in life. Try to imagine a world in which not all important activities are carried out by Crown entities or groups with Crown-delegated rights. Take Maori group rights seriously, both fundamental and derived, regarding them, like individual rights, as legal and quasi-legal fictions created for convenience. Entertain the thought that those Maori groups that can in fact act for themselves are actually

---

[62] The most accomplished example of this kind of constitutional history is I think M Solomon, "The Context For Maori (II)" in A Quentin-Baxter (ed.), *Recognising the Rights of Indigenous Peoples*, above n. 23 at 60. Among Pakeha, P McHugh, "Law, History and the Treaty of Waitangi" (1997) 31 *New Zealand Journal of History* 38, attempts a recasting of New Zealand constitutional history-writing to account for customary Maori rights.

[63] On some of the impossibilities, see W H Oliver, "Our Future Behind Us" in A Sharp and P G McHugh (eds.), *Histories, Power and Loss* (Bridget Williams Books, 2001 forthcoming). And see J G A Pocock, "Law, Sovereignty and History in a Divided Culture: The Case of New Zealand and the Treaty of Waitangi" (1998) 43 *McGill L J* 481, and "Waitangi as Mystery of State: Consequences of the Ascription of Federative Capacity to the Maori" in D Ivison, P Patton and W Sanders (eds.), *Political Theory and the Rights of Indigenous Peoples* (Melbourne, Cambridge University Press, 2000) 25 and "The Treaty Between Histories" in A Sharp and P G McHugh (eds.) *Histories, Power and Loss* (forthcoming).

[64] On the idea of "juridical history", see A Sharp, "History and Sovereignty: A Case of Juridical History in Aotearoa/New Zealand" in M Peters (ed.), *The Politics of Culture in the University* (Palmerston North, Dunmore Press, 1997) 159.

[65] See Submissions to the Maori Affairs Committee on the Ngai Tahu Claims Settlement Bill (1998): eg, NTS/ 1, 3, 4, 11, 11, 25, 36–55, 62–4, 75, 97, 152, 153A, 163W, 169W, 229. For Ngai Tahu problems with Ngai Tuhuru, see Waitangi Tribunal, *The Fisheries Settlement Report (Wai 307)* (Wellington: Waitangi Tribunal, 1992) §7.2. For the Ngai Tahu perspective see T O'Regan, "Old Myths and New Politics: Some Contemporary Uses of History" (1992) 26(1) *New Zealand Journal of History* 5.

already exercising a kind of self-rule, as many other groups and collectivities do. Entertain further the thought that as tradition and convention largely decree the workings of government and the constitution and ought not to be destroyed thoughtlessly, so do and ought traditions and conventions guide the actions of Maori groups. There is no general reason not to allow those traditions and conventions to continue. The principle of conservation that sustains governments in the English tradition should be applied equally to Maori and their traditions. I do not see, for instance, why Maori groups should be required to treat "public money" and other resources in exactly the way non-Maori groups are required to—why a kind of respectable and respected black box screening out inappropriate enquiry into methods of financial and management audit cannot be designed and put into place.[66] I do not see why the use to which iwi put reparatory payments should be any business of politicians and government officials. One may be reasonably assured that any malpractice, internal injustice or business incompetence will surface in the normal workings of the group itself and its surrounding critics. And my prescription for Maori groups would be this: enjoy "self-government at the Queen's command",[67] knowing that "the Queen's command" is no more—or less—than the outcome of debate over the whole of the political system in New Zealand, and that it is a system that already respects as a matter of settled custom many special Maori rights to autonomy, and is capable of respecting more without violation of its principles.[68]

I opposed an entrenched Bill of Rights when it was proposed sixteen years ago on grounds that it tried to simplify an inherited working complexity. I am inclined to think much the same as to whether special Maori rights should be further "enshrined" in a written constitution. Also, constitutions are for the long term, and one pertinent consideration is how long one would think that Maori in their

---

[66] This was written before the March–April 2000 parliamentary exchanges between John Tamihere (a new Labour Maori MP, ex-CEO of the urban "iwi", te Whanau o Waipareira) and Richard Prebble (leader of the ACT party). Accusations were made of Tamihere's and the Whanau's using funds irregularly. That should have been of no surprise to anyone, given the pressure of demands placed on the Whanau's resources, and its wide-ranging responsibilities. Questions might better have been asked about the good sense of the regulatory régime under which Mr Tamihere was required to operate.

[67] A well-known description of English government under Elizabeth I.

[68] Paul McHugh ("Aboriginal Identity and Relations in North America and Australasia" in *Living Relationships*, above n. 19 at 107, esp. 120–1, 170–9) notes, to condemn as unnecessary, the clash in international as well as New Zealand legal thinking between the "inherency" and state "delegation" views as to the source of aboriginal peoples' right to self-rule (either the right is inherent in the aboriginal group, or else it is delegated to them by the state). He suggests a "relational" approach between the parties, in which, each recognising the claims of the other, the two embark on a future of negotiation and compromise. This is a good enough political theory perhaps (though who decides if push comes to shove?); but it seems to me that the right direction for legal theory, also being developed by McHugh ("Law, History and the Treaty of Waitangi", above n. 62) is that both the state and aboriginal peoples derive their rights from the same complex of territorial constitutional custom. The point then would become that sovereignty and (for instance) tribal rights would be seen for what they are: diffused and rather unclear as to their scope and limits. It would still be a question as to who decided if push came to shove; but such exigencies would arise less often in such an ideal world, because the principle of the old quarrel—the proper basis of self-rule—would not be at issue: the answer would be in shared custom; thus there would be only concrete disagreements.

various groupings will have special interests that need to be protected and will suffer injustices that need to be redressed. Another consideration is as to how long Maori might persist as a people and as peoples. The answers are not clear. I would say, though, that it is as certain as anything can be that so long as Maori continue to be victims of marked relative deprivation they will continue not only to suffer in groups but to act in groups. So perhaps if a reasonable degree of equality of social well-being is not to emerge in New Zealand/Aotearoa, a constitutional settlement might be entered into as a substitute, and as a platform for their further action. Special group rights in a constitution could act as a defence against the majority and as a resource base from which to act. But, to end on a note that would have pleased Edmund Burke, having rights is never as good as having real advantages.

13

Constitutionalising Maori

JUSTICE EDDIE DURIE*

I INTRODUCTION

Some may recall a time in the 1950s when New Zealanders boasted of the best race relations in the world and the upset following the visit of an American, Dr Ausubel, claiming that the Maori voice had simply been forced underground. Since then the topic of race relations has so consumed discussion that today there is even discomfort when one uses the word "race".[1] In the debate two thoughts have been variously juxtaposed in ways that emphasise an inherent conflict—that we are all one people, and that we are of two races. Remarkably, proponents of either view can find support in the Treaty of Waitangi, but if one considers the approach of the missionaries, which influenced both Treaty parties considerably, the views would not be seen as mutually exclusive. The theology conveyed to Maori is that we are part of the one body and it is not unusual that the body should have more than one limb.

The view that colours my approach to the tension between individual and group rights is that they reflect different limbs of a single body that can be made to work in unison, or at least must be made to do so if the body is not to be dysfunctional. The point is that the division flows from different cultural realities which are unlikely to go away, and the only feasible option is to do our best, be it ever so imperfect, to harmonise them.

Maori tradition favours the view that the key to resolving difference lies first and foremost in the recognition of the mana, or status, of others and the development of ongoing relationships founded on mutual respect from which understanding then grows.[2] Support for the view that this is part of Maori tradition is found in the respect protocols still regularly acted out on marae. Further support is in the history of Maori and Pakeha relations before and after the Treaty of Waitangi. Historians have identified that for Maori, the central feature of the Treaty of Waitangi was its mutual recognition of two peoples. They consider the main cause

---

* I acknowledge the assistance of Dominic Wilson, a solicitor until recently with the Waitangi Tribunal, and Carwyn Jones, a law student of Ngai Te Apatu, Ngati Kahungunu. Ka nui te aroha ki a raua.

[1] Today's preferred word is "ethnicity", which is applauded for severing assumed inherited characteristics from the debate, but I suggest "race" is not without a proper place. While identity has become the major determiner of cultural persuasion or allegiance, the culture itself, while permitting of incorporation, derives primarily from concepts of ancestry, kinship and bloodlines.

[2] See Waitangi Tribunal, *Muriwhenua Land Report (Wai 45)* (Wellington, GP Publications, 1997).

of subsequent racial conflict, including the New Zealand Wars, was the failure to maintain that recognition.[3] The issue in the Wars was distinctly constitutional. It concerned the status of Maori in their own country. It is an issue that has not been resolved and continues to underlie modern claims to the Waitangi Tribunal[4] despite the substantial recognition now given to the Treaty of Waitangi.

This paper looks briefly at a small selection of national constitutions. This is mainly to show how distinct cultural or interest groups can be acknowledged and accommodated in the supreme instrument of a state, providing recognition and protection for indigenous and other political minorities while also acknowledging the interests of predominant groups and the rights common to all persons. The constitutions, at least on their face, assert the justness of societies founded on protocols of recognition, mutual respect and commitment to common good. In addition, enforcement mechanisms are provided. A similar constitution in New Zealand would provide a modern affirmation of the Treaty of Waitangi and a modern basis on which such claims as those for independent Maori rights or those alleging racial privilege can be tested. The question of whether such a constitution is politically feasible at this time is not addressed, though I consider that work to develop such a constitution should be encouraged.

The first part of the paper considers also the interplay of equal rights for indigenous and other minorities and any special rights that are considered to accrue. The paper looks secondly at the protection for Maori within the existing constitutional framework. It is mooted that even as matters stand, the interaction of international instruments and domestic law is such that the protection for Maori interests is larger than might generally be imagined. The third part touches on the "universalism v cultural relativity" and "individual v group rights" debates in the context of international instruments. While the debate represents a challenge to the realisation of indigenous peoples' rights, it is suggested that judicious application of the doctrine of cultural relativism, and working within the framework of each particular indigenous group, could alleviate most of the difficulties. Finally, consideration is given to the strengths within the common law for the judicial management of difference through the doctrine of aboriginal title, which is fundamentally about cultural relativism.

III STATE CONSTITUTIONS AND THE RECOGNITION OF PEOPLES

Matters have so advanced in Canada that in considering the acknowledgement given to aboriginal peoples and groups generally, mention should also be made of the practical application of general principles beginning with the rights of indigenous groups to equality. Section 15 (1) of the Charter of Rights and Freedoms provides:

---

[3] See Waitangi Tribunal, *Taranaki Report: Kaupapa Tuatahi (Wai 143)* (Wellington, GP Publications, 1996).

[4] See Waitangi Tribunal *Te Reo Maori Report* (Wellington, The Tribunal, 1986) and *Maori Electoral Option Report* (Wellington, Brooker's, 1994).

"Every individual is equal before and under the law and has the right to the equal protection and equal benefit of the law without discrimination and, in particular, without discrimination based on race, national or ethnic origin, colour, religion, sex, age or mental or physical disability."

Actual protection depends upon implementation and this is in turn affected by the interpretations of the courts. The traditional Diceyan view of equality as "equality of law", and the argument that if the law applies to everyone then there is equality, is claimed to have resulted in the judiciaries of common law-based countries applying "equitable principles without bringing about equality in result".[5] Early Charter cases showed a willingness to move from the Diceyan position in light of more awareness of its application in multi-cultural situations. In *Andrews* v. *Law Society of British Columbia*[6] the Supreme Court adopted a broad, purposive approach to the interpretation of section 15(1). The Court recognised "that the wording in s. 15 was deliberately chosen to overcome the shortcomings of the *Canadian Bill of Rights* and reflected [an] expanded concept of discrimination".[7] York reasons that if the process of litigating against discrimination through the Charter is not given effect then the Charter itself becomes meaningless.[8] Of course, the ebb and flow of judicial opinion generates a necessary discussion of principle and does not in itself diminish the value of judicial oversight.

Section 35 of the Canadian Constitution Act 1982 then provides specific recognition of and protection for aboriginal people. It specifically affirms their aboriginal, treaty, and other rights. Section 25 provides that nothing in the Constitution Act 1982 will abrogate those rights. In terms of practical application there have been both political and judicial initiatives. At a political level the Federal Government has been engaged in discussions with aboriginal groups on various treaty issues and is involved in self-government negotiations with over 350 first nations.[9]

At a judicial level, in *R* v. *Sparrow*[10] the Supreme Court attempted to give meaningful content to the constitutional recognition and affirmation of aboriginal rights, and to set out a framework for reconciling the competing interests affected by their recognition. The Court made it clear that rights had to be seen in light of the cultural life of the aboriginal people. The Court's view was very similar to that of the United Nations Human Rights Committee, which has suggested that[11]

---

[5] A York, "The Inequality of Emerging Charter Jurisprudence: Supreme Court Interpretations of Section 15(1)" (1996) 54 *U T Fac L Rev* 327, 330.

[6] [1989] 1 SCR 143.

[7] York, above n. 5 at 329.

[8] *Ibid*, 343.

[9] US Department of State, Canada: Country Report on Human Rights Practices for 1997. Released by the Bureau of Democracy, Human Rights, and Labor, 30 January 1998.

[10] [1990] 1 SCR 1075.

[11] UN General Comment 23, "The Rights of Minorities (Art 27)" para. 3.2, United Nations, *Compilation of General Comments and General Recommendations Adopted by Human Rights Treaty Bodies*, UN Doc HRI/GEN/1/Rev2, 1996.

"the rights of individuals . . . to enjoy a particular culture . . . may consist in a way of life which is closely associated with territory and use of its resources. This may particularly be true of members of indigenous communities. . .".

Thus, in *Sparrow* the Court was at pains not to conceptualise aboriginal rights through common law concepts, noting that:[12]

"[f]ishing rights are not traditional property rights. They are rights held by a collective and are in keeping with the culture and existence of that group. Courts must be careful, then, to avoid the application of traditional common law concepts of property as they develop their understanding of . . . the 'sui generis' nature of aboriginal rights."

Of course, this expressed nothing new in the judicial consideration of other cultures. The warning was given by the Privy Council in *Amodu Tijani* v. *Secretary, Southern Nigeria*[13] and *Oyekan* v. *Adele*.[14] In the first of these the Privy Council said:[15]

"In interpreting the native title to land, not only in Southern Nigeria, but other parts of the British Empire, much caution is essential. There is a tendency, operating at times unconsciously, to render that title conceptually in terms which are appropriate only to systems which have grown up under English law. But this tendency has to be held in check closely."

That the English common law is capable of understanding quite different and abstract cultural concepts was further demonstrated by the Privy Council in *Mullick* v. *Mullick*,[16] which concerned the legal status of a Hindu idol, and the English Court of Appeal in *Bumper Development Corp Ltd* v. *Commissioner of Police of the Metropolis*.[17] New Zealand courts have adopted the same position.[18]

It has then to be noted that while there is specific reference to the rights of aboriginal peoples, the Canadian Constitution also provides express recognition of the concept of unity within diversity. Section 27 of the Constitution Act 1982 provides that the Act itself will be interpreted consistently with the multicultural heritage of Canada.

The Constitution of the United States of America has given indirect protection for the indigenous peoples or "first nations" by reserving to the federal government the enforcement of treaties and the regulation of trade with the Native Americans through what is known as the Indian Commerce Clause. This states that "Congress shall have power . . . [t]o regulate commerce with foreign nations and among the several States, and with Indian tribes".[19] Judicial decisions depict tribal confederations

---

[12] [1990] 1 SCR 1075, 1112.
[13] [1921] 2 AC 399.
[14] [1957] 1 WLR 876.
[15] [1921] 2 AC 399, 402–3.
[16] (1925) LR 52, Ind App 245.
[17] [1991] 1 WLR 1362.
[18] See *Te Runanganui o Te Ika Whenua Inc Society* v. *Attorney-General* [1994] 2 NZLR 20, 26 (CA) and *Huakina Development Trust* v. *Waikato Valley Authority* [1987] 2 NZLR 188.
[19] The Constitution of the United States of America, Art. 1, s. 8.

as "dependent domestic nations", largely free and independent within their own territories.

Case law has confirmed the protections of Native American tribes. The Supreme Court held in *Antoine v. Washington*[20] that the state could not regulate Native American hunting rights as the rights were protected by a treaty with Congress. Treaties with Native American tribes are like any treaty of the federal government with a sovereign nation in that all states must comply.[21] This position was affirmed in *Washington v. Washington State Commercial Passenger Fishing Vessel Association*.[22] There the Supreme Court ordered that the Washington State Game and Fisheries Departments comply with a federal court's interpretation of the correct implementation of a treaty with the indigenous population and the federal jurisdiction to regulate treaties with first nations, overruling the state's general jurisdiction to regulate hunting and fishing. The Court stated that any "[s]tate-law prohibition against compliance with the District Court's decree cannot survive the command of the Supremacy Clause".[23]

The Constitution of South Africa 1996 recognises distinct cultural communities while acknowledging a collective national identity. Section 235 of the Constitution provides:

> "The right of the South African people as a whole to self-determination, as manifested in this Constitution, does not preclude, within the framework of this right, recognition of the notion of the right of self-determination of any community sharing a common cultural and language heritage, within a territorial entity in the Republic or in any other way, determined by national legislation."

Section 39(2) envisages a strong purposive approach for the effective protection rights affirmed by the constitutional documents. This requires that "every court . . . must promote the spirit, purport and objects of the Bill of Rights".

Part III of the Indian Constitution 1949 provides for rights of equality and non-discrimination. Articles 14 and 15, respectively, protect the rights to equality before the law and to freedom from discrimination on the grounds of religion, race, caste, sex, or place of birth. From early judgments the Indian Supreme Court has followed United States authority in recognising that the State must sometimes pass legislation which does distinguish on those grounds.[24] Accordingly, "to attract the operation of the clause, it is necessary to show that the selection or differentiation is unreasonable or arbitrary".[25] Articles 29 and 30 further protect the cultural interests of minority groups.

---

[20] 420 US 194 (1975).

[21] *Ibid*, 206–9.

[22] 443 US 658 (1979). As to the nature and extent of Native American fishing rights see *United States v. State of Washington* 384 F Supp 312 (W D Wash 1974) & 520 F 2d 676 (9th cir 1975) and 506 F Supp 187 (W D Wash 1980).

[23] 443 US 658, 695 (1979).

[24] P G Polyviou, *The Equal Protection of the Laws* (London, Gerald Duckworth & Co, 1980) 92.

[25] *Amcerunnissa Begun* v. *Mahboob Begun* (1953) SCR 404; AIR 1953, SC 91.

The Brazilian Constitution 1988 places positive obligations on the state to preserve the rights of the indigenous population to traditional lands and all the resources (including waters) within them, as well as languages, customs, traditions, and forms of social organisation. Art 231 provides:

> ". . .
>
> (2) The lands traditionally occupied by Indians are intended for their permanent possession, and they shall be entitled to exclusive use of the riches of the soil, rivers, and lakes existing thereon.
>
> (3) Hydric resources, including energy potential, may only be exploited and mineral riches in Indians lands may only be prospected and mined with the authorization of Congress, after hearing the communities involved, which shall be assured of participation in the mining results in accordance with the law.
>
> (4)The lands referred to in this article are inalienable and indisposable and the rights thereto are not subject to the statute of limitations.
> . . .."

Article 215(1) reflects the subsequent settlement of Brazil by diverse groups. The State

> "ensures a person full exercise of their cultural rights and access to sources of national culture and supports and encourages the appreciation and diffusion of cultural manifestations".

Article 216 indicates that the "Brazilian cultural heritage" is comprised of

> "assets of material and immaterial nature, considered either individually or as a whole, which bear reference to the identity, action, and memory of the various groups of Brazilian society . . .."

While national constitutions will obviously reflect unique local experiences, including preceding trauma, the impact of domestic history is especially self-evident in the Constitution of Fiji. The preamble to the 1997 Constitution acknowledges the local history of settlement and constitutional development. It specifically refers to "the indigenous Fijian and Rotuman people" and also the subsequent settlement by "Pacific Islanders, Europeans, Indians and Chinese". The Constitution recognises and affirms the cultural contributions of these various communities and notes that a rich variety of cultures make up modern Fijian society. Although "equitable sharing of political power amongst all communities in Fiji" is set down as a basic principle for the conduct of government (section 6(l)), so too is the protective principle that the interests of the indigenous Fijian community will not be subordinated to the interests of other communities (section 6(j)). The Constitution sets out to respect "the rights of all individuals, communities and groups" (section 6(a)). It also preserves "the ownership of Fijian land according to Fijian custom"(section 6(b)). Dealing with equality, section 38 provides:

> "(1)Every person has the right to equality before the law.
> . . .

(8) A law, or an administrative action taken under a law, may limit a right or freedom set out in this section for the purpose of:
(a) providing for the application of the custom of Fijians or Rotumans or of the Banaban community:
(i) to the holding, use or transmission of, or to the distribution of the produce of, land or fishing rights; or
(ii) to the entitlement of any person to any chiefly title or rank;
(b) imposing a restriction on the alienation of land or fishing rights held in accordance with Fijian or Rotuman custom or in accordance with Banaban custom; or
(c) permitting the temporary alienation of that land or those rights without the consent of the owners.

(9) To the extent permitted by subsection (10), a law, or an administrative action taken under a law, may limit a right or freedom set out in this section for the purpose of providing for the governance of Fijians or Rotumans or of the Banaban community and of other persons living as members of a Fijian, Rotuman or Banaban community.

(10) A limitation referred to in subsection (9) is valid only if it:
(a) accords to every person to whom it applies the right to equality before the law without discrimination other than on the ground of race or ethnic origin; and
(b) does not infringe a right or freedom set out in any other section of this Chapter."

The Philippines Constitution 1987 promotes "unity in diversity" as applied to cultural rights. A provision for land reform makes special mention of the traditional lands of indigenous communities, and the need to take account of the relationships of these communities to the land when considering agrarian development (Article XIII).

Belgium recognises linguistic minorities as well as those described as ideological and philosophical minorities.[26] The linguistic minorities have no special protection within the Belgian Constitution, although Articles 6 and 6*bis* prohibit discrimination on any grounds whatsoever. A special-majority law applies to the altering of the linguistic regime in some municipalities. The ideological minorities enjoy somewhat more constitutional protection with society divided into Catholic, Socialist, and Liberal groupings. Group adherence impacts on numerous aspects of an individual's life including such matters as primary, secondary, and tertiary education, hospital services, banking services and trade union membership.[27] Article 6*bis* includes an obligation for national and community legislators to guarantee the rights and liberties of ideological and philosophical minorities.[28] As a result of Articles 59*bis*.7 and 59*ter*.7, compelling the national legislature to make statutory provisions in order to prevent ideological discrimination, the Court of Arbitration is now entitled to annul laws that would violate Article 6*bis*. Further to the individual rights in the Constitution, Belgian law establishes group rights to participation in the elaboration of "cultural policies".[29]

---

[26] A Alen and G Van Haegendoren, "Constitutional Problems of Minorities" in A Alen (ed.), *Treatise on Belgian Constitutional Law* (Deventer, Kluwer, 1992) 210.

[27] *Ibid*, 211.

[28] *Ibid*, 220.

[29] *Ibid*, 221.

The Swedish Constitution contains several passages relevant to the cultural rights of minorities. Chapter 1 contains the basic principles that underlie the Constitution. It is stated that "the personal, economic and cultural welfare of the individual shall be fundamental aims of public activity" and, furthermore, that "[o]pportunities should be promoted for ethnic, linguistic and religious minorities to preserve and develop a cultural and social life of their own".[30] The Swedish Constitution also distinguishes between discrimination on the grounds of race, skin colour, or ethnic origin, and other forms of discrimination.[31]

Article 110a of the Constitution of the Kingdom of Norway 1814 provides:

> "It is the responsibility of the authorities of the State to create conditions enabling the Sami people to preserve and develop its language, culture and way of life."

Section 17 of the Constitution of Finland 1919 gives an interesting recognition of groups through language. It provides for Finnish and Swedish as the national languages and requires public authorities to provide for the educational, cultural and social needs of the Finnish-speaking and the Swedish-speaking populations. The Sami as an indigenous people as well as the Romanies and other groups have the right to maintain and develop their own languages and cultures.

The Australian Constitution is under review with the prospective recognition for the status of aboriginal people. It was assumed, when constitutional reform was proposed, that considerable public education would be needed and to this end the Constitutional Centenary Foundation was established.

New Zealand is unrepentant in maintaining its constitution in a substantially unwritten form, though the tradition for that derives from a comparatively homogenous society well beyond the Pacific. The New Zealand Constitutions of 1846 and 1852 made but passing reference to Maori, as with section 71 of the Constitution Act 1852, and made no mention of immigrant communities. The Constitution Act 1986 acknowledges only the Sovereign, the Executive, the Legislature, the Judiciary—and the Parliamentary Librarian. It does not inform of our autochthonous character or of the people of this country, their history and their values. It is not a useful prospectus for intending immigrants, though we expect that they should buy into our social contract.

Again, the brevity of the New Zealand Constitution is not because there is and never has been the need for something more. Apart from the fact that an indigenous population exists as part of the family of peoples in the Pacific, when it is argued that constitutions usually derive from some national trauma, there is a tendency to forget that New Zealand has had one. The wars are not forgotten by those who suffered the consequences. They were primarily about the constitutional status of Maori.

On the eve of the New Zealand wars and the invasions of Taranaki and Waikato, the desired constitutional position was posited by the Kingitanga in characteristic

---

[30] Constitution of Sweden adopted on 1 January 1975, ch.1, Arts. 2(2) and 2(4).
[31] *Ibid*, Arts. 15 and 16.

imagery, proposing that there should be the Maori King on one side, the English Queen on the other, God over both and love uniting them together. Symbols are important in oral cultures and here the image found some expression in the subsequent promulgation of the current Coat of Arms; but Maori have long maintained that the Coat of Arms is not reflected in legal reality. The question is whether the Constitution should provide for Maori rights, though it may be borne in mind that at the time of the wars the Maori talk was not of being armed with rights but of being clothed with the dignity of recognition.

In considering the prospect of constitutional reform, or to borrow a term from Paul McHugh, the "indigenisation" of the New Zealand Constitution,[32] other national constitutions serve to remind of the issues of equality, protection from discrimination, recognition of indigenous status and the compatibility of unity and diversity. We should be conscious of the conceptualisation of equality as affirmed by the judiciary. The examples of Canada, the United States of America and South Africa suggest that the courts must aim to protect substantive equality of outcomes if the protections in the constitutions are to be effective and meaningful. There are also issues surrounding the determination of what aboriginal rights actually are. The decision of the Canadian Supreme Court in *Sparrow* provides a useful approach. Another approach is to protect those rights guaranteed in treaties. As applied in Canada and the United States of America, this approach can be seen as complementary to (rather than exclusive of) the approach in *Sparrow*.

In assessing rights according to the perceptions of aboriginal people, care must be taken not to diminish them by fossilising custom. The customs of aboriginals are no less dynamic than those of other peoples, and the right of peoples to develop themselves and their resources must also be respected. It might then be seen that in defining rights by reference to territory or traditional user, one is defining the origin of the right and not necessarily its appropriate application in a modern situation. There appears to be no proper logical base for using territory or traditional user to restrict the right of indigenous groups. This seems especially so when the rights of others have been allowed to travel with them, even upon historic, territorial invasions, and when the rights of others to develop resources have never been constrained.

III CURRENT PROTECTION FOR INDIGENOUS NEW ZEALANDERS

Although there is room for constitutional reform to recognise New Zealand Maori, there is also potential for protection for Maori within the existing structure through the combined effects of the Treaty of Waitangi, the New Zealand Bill of Rights Act 1990 and international obligations.

---

[32] See P G McHugh, "From Sovereignty to Settlement Time: The Constitutional Setting of Maori Claims in the 1990s" in P Havemann (ed.), *Indigenous Peoples' Rights in Australia, Canada, and New Zealand* (Auckland, Oxford University Press, 1999) 447, 456.

As Hunt and Bedggood have noted, "the distinction between international and domestic human rights protection is increasingly blurred",[33] and international human rights jurisprudence can impact on New Zealand domestic law in various ways. Alexander Blades has maximised the potential for Maori cultural rights by synthesising New Zealand's commitment to the International Covenant on Civil and Political Rights ("ICCPR"), its Bill of Rights, and growing international opinion on obligations under the former.[34] He argues that Article 27 of the ICCPR imposes positive obligations and duties on states and that in New Zealand that would include the implementation of the Treaty of Waitangi. He then contends that section 20 of the New Zealand Bill of Rights Act 1990 must be interpreted consistently with Article 27 of the ICCPR. The following remarks draw on his arguments.

That Article 27 of the ICCPR requires positive measures from States parties is asserted in a flow of literature from the United Nations and in opinions of the Human Rights Committee and its members. Thus, from the Committee:[35]

> "States parties have also undertaken to ensure the enjoyment of these rights to all individuals under their jurisdiction. This aspect calls for specific activities by the States parties to enable individuals to enjoy their rights. This is obvious in a number of articles . . . but in principle this undertaking relates to all rights set forth in the Covenant."

In considering States parties reports, Mr Ndiaye of the Committee said "it was not enough for a State not to restrict minority rights; it must actively foster them through positive discriminatory measures in favour of minorities".[36] Others have commented similarly.[37] Communications under the Optional Protocol have also indicated that the article imposes positive obligations.[38] Periodic reports of States parties to the Covenant show increasing support for this position and arguably a majority of States at least implicitly accept it.[39]

The Human Rights Committee is said also to take the view that if there is a treaty relationship between a State party and an indigenous population, that treaty will act as a foundation for the implementation of Article 27.[40] Accordingly, in *Lubicon Lake Band* v. *Canada*[41] Canada was found to have breached the Article by

---

[33] P Hunt and M Bedggood, "The International Law Dimension of Human Rights in New Zealand" in G Huscroft and P Rishworth (eds), *Rights and Freedoms* (Wellington, Brookers, 1995) 37.

[34] A B Blades, "Article 27 of the International Covenant on Civil and Political Rights: A Case Study on Implementation in New Zealand" [1994] 1 *Canadian Native Law Reporter* 1.

[35] UN Doc CCPR/C/21/Rev 1 (1989) 3, para. 1.

[36] *Summary Record of the Human Rights Committee*, 35th Session, UN Doc CCPR/C/SR 879, p. 6, para. 29 (1989).

[37] *Ibid*, 8–13.

[38] *Lovelace* v. *Canada*, Comm No. R 6/24 (29 Dec 1977), GAOR, 36th Sess, UN Doc Supp No 40 (A/36/40) at 166 (1981); *Lubicon Lake Band* v. *Canada*, Comm No 167/1984 (26 March 1990), GAOR, 45th Sess, UN Doc Supp No 40 (A/45/40) at 1 (1990); *Kitok* v. *Sweden*, Comm No 197/1985 27 July 1988), GAOR, 43rd Sess Supp No 40, UN Doc A/43/40 at 221 (1988).

[39] *Summary Record*, above n. 36 at 16–23.

[40] *Summary Record*, above n. 36 at 24.

[41] Comm No 167/1984 (26 March 1990), GAOR, 45th Sess, UN Doc Supp No 40 (A/45/40) at 1 (1990).

not fulfilling a treaty with the Lubicon Lake Band. The Treaty of Waitangi is argued to be no exception to this development. In reporting on local measures to effectuate Article 27, New Zealand representatives have focused almost exclusively on the Treaty of Waitangi.[42] During the discussion of New Zealand's report in the Thirty-fifth Session,[43] one member of the Human Rights Committee "firmly located the Treaty's implementation, whether in law or otherwise, in the sphere of New Zealand's obligations under the Covenant".[44]

Blades considers the concept of using the Treaty of Waitangi as a basis for implementing Article 27 is particularly significant when considered with paragraph 3.2 of General Comment 23 adopted by the Human Rights Committee. This states:[45]

"The enjoyment of the rights to which article 27 relates does not prejudice the sovereignty and territorial integrity of a State party. At the same time, one or other aspect of the rights of individuals protected under that article—for example, to enjoy a particular culture—may consist in a way of life which is closely associated with territory and use of its resources. This may particularly be true of members of indigenous communities constituting a minority."

Closely linked to the ICCPR is the New Zealand Bill of Rights Act 1990.[46] The long title declares that at least part of the purpose is to "affirm New Zealand's commitment to the International Covenant on Civil and Political Rights". The Court of Appeal has thus considered that the Act should be interpreted consistently with the Covenant and related jurisprudence.[47] In *Ministry of Transport* v. *Noort*,[48] Cooke P considered that "[i]n approaching the Bill of Rights Act it must be of cardinal importance to bear in mind the antecedents". There has also been a rights-centred perspective and a purposive approach to interpretation. As noted by Richardson J in *R* v. *Te Kira*, the Court of Appeal in *R* v. *Goodwin*[49] considered that "the premise underlying the Bill is that the courts will affirmatively protect those fundamental rights and freedoms by recourse to appropriate remedies within their jurisdiction".[50] It is accepted that the protection of these fundamental rights requires positive obligations. It would equally follow, in Blade's argument, that section 20 of the Bill of Rights Act must be given an interpretation consistent with the application of Article 27 of the Covenant.

The relationship between the ICCPR and the New Zealand Bill of Rights Act 1990 and comments of the Human Rights Committee and its members[51] suggests

---

[42] *Summary Record*, above n. 36 at 25–7.

[43] *Summary Record of the Human Rights Committee*, 35th Session, U.N. Doc. CCPR/C/SR 888, p. 9, para. 41.

[44] *Summary Record*, above n. 36 at 27.

[45] *Compilation of General Comments*, above n. 11 at 39.

[46] *A Bill of Rights for New Zealand: A White Paper*, New Zealand Parliament, House of Representatives, 1985, AJHR A6, 30–1.

[47] *Ministry of Transport* v. *Noort*; *Police* v. *Curran* [1992] 3 NZLR 260 (CA); *R* v. *Goodwin (No. 2)* [1993] 2 NZLR 390 (CA); *Flickinger* v. *Crown Colony of Hong Kong* [1991] 1 NZLR 439 (CA).

[48] [1992] 3 NZLR 260, 270.

[49] *R* v. *Goodwin* (No. 2) [1993] 2 NZLR 390.

[50] *R* v. *Te Kira* [1993] 3 NZLR 257, 265–6.

[51] *Summary Record*, above n. 36 at 8–28.

to Blades a legal argument for Treaty rights to be enforced at a domestic level. Thus, the opinion in *Hoani Te Heuheu Tukino* v. *Aotea District Maori Land Board*[52] that the Treaty is unenforceable in domestic law unless expressly incorporated into statute, may yet fall to a developing international position. Arguably there is already a convention not to legislate contrary to the Treaty of Waitangi. Following a route through the New Zealand Bill of Rights Act 1990 the Treaty too could be "affirmed as part of the fabric of New Zealand law".[53]

There may be guidance too from the decision in *Department of Labour* v. *Latailakepa*[54] that international treaties may aid statutory interpretation because domestic legislation is presumed to be consistent with international obligations, and *Huakina Development Trust* v. *Waikato Valley Authority*,[55] where the Treaty assisted statutory interpretation, although it was not mentioned in the legislation. *Te Runanga O Wharekauri Rekohu Inc* v. *Attorney-General*[56] raises further possibilities. In addition, if through Article 27 of the Covenant section 20 of the New Zealand Bill of Rights Act incorporates the Treaty, and as section 6 prefers the interpretation of statutes consistently with the Bill of Rights, there may be a mandate for the judicial and administrative interpretation of the statutes consistently with the Treaty. However, the protection of Maori rights remains limited by the fact that the New Zealand Bill of Rights is not "higher law", and cannot be invoked to override inconsistent enactments.

IV INDIGENOUS RIGHTS AND INTERNATIONAL INSTRUMENTS

An obstacle to implementing universal standards of human rights is the argument that there is no such thing as a *universal* standard. As Joyner and Dettling put it, "different cultures put different normative weight on the place of individual human rights in their societies".[57] It is argued that generally the declarations that make up the International Bill of Rights are constructed around the rights of individuals, reflecting an individualistic conception of rights.[58] The International Bill of Rights is seen to have been promulgated by a United Nations dominated by the West, so that the so-called universal rights are posited as rights as seen by the West. The debate is described under the heading of "*universalism v cultural relativity*".

While western orientation is said to lean towards individual rights, other societies emphasise the rights of the group and the individual's responsibilities to it. Thus the matter is also characterised as the "*individual rights v group rights*" debate.

---

[52] [1941] AC 308.

[53] *Simpson* v. *Attorney-General [Baigent's Case]*[1994] 3 NZLR 667, 676 (CA).

[54] [1982] 1 NZLR 632 (CA).

[55] [1987] 2 NZLR 188.

[56] [1993] 2 NZLR 301, 305 (CA).

[57] C C Joyner and J C Dettling, "Bridging the Cultural Chasm: Cultural Relativism and the Future of International Law" (1990) 20 *Cal W Int'l LJ* 275, 288.

[58] P Hunt, *Reflections on International Human Rights Law and Cultural Rights*, Waikato University, New Zealand, UNESCO/CNZJ Cultural Rights Workshop, October 1998.

The debate has significance for indigenous peoples who live or lived a tribal life in districts occupied by small but autonomous and competitive bands, clans or hapu without allegiance to a central regime. Their survival depended on group integrity and individual loyalty so that their perspective on rights is different. The significance for indigenous people is twofold. First, as they now generally exist as units within (or overlapping) national states, as a people they have not subscribed to United Nations covenants and, until recently, have not participated in their formulation. The states have decided for them. The second is that the interests of the state are often distinct. In illustration, Maori suffered the enforced individualisation of their tribal lands because it suited the state. It did not suit them, though, and the tenure reform weakened their corporate identity. The consequences have continued to the present, making Maori land unmanageable, exposing it to alienation, and denying the group a corporate asset.

Despite the suffering of Maori through the imposition of inappropriate norms, it is another matter to say that cultural difference invalidates the search for universal standards. Thus one would think that the oppressively cruel treatment of an offender cannot be justified in today's world simply because that treatment is normal in that offender's society. Today's societies no longer exist in isolation but as part of a global community and, for personal fulfilment and world peace, it remains necessary to promote global standards that societies should aspire to. What needs to be held in check is the tendency, sometimes unwitting, to impose foreign norms that are not appropriate. The task is to ensure the judicious application of norms having regard to the circumstances of the case, a task requiring a sensitive approach rather than a strict bureaucracy.

It may then be found that cultures can undertake considerable change, voluntarily, without detriment to their basic underlying values. No culture is static and most are receptive to change, but cultures may tend to fossilise if threatened. Consider for example the enormous changes in Maori society at a time when Maori reigned freely before the Treaty of Waitangi of 1840 and when there was only the moral influence of a small number of missionaries. During that time Maori totally or substantially jettisoned endemic practices of cannibalism, infanticide, sorcery, slavery and to a lesser extent, warfare. These were major reforms with economic consequences, at least with regard to slavery, but there was no lasting impact on the Maori value system. Nor should it be forgotten that cultural rights have both an individual and collective aspect to them. I suggest that some modern reluctance to give full vent to women's rights in some Maori practices reflects the fact that with the dominance of western norms Maori society is now threatened. The answer appears to lie not in enforcing change but in actually encouraging the current trend of the state to take positive steps to assist cultural survival.

In short, there is a workable compromise between these two extremes of universalism and cultural relativity that could allow the development of a framework that recognises cultural diversity while encouraging a high level of human rights protection. It requires working within the underlying value system of each culture.

Indigenous peoples' rights may be seen to derive from their own cultural norms, from concepts of the common law, from treaty agreements and from other intercultural negotiations. Many of these are now given expression in international instruments. Here the concern is with the conceptual basis for these and the difficulties of implementation that such a conceptual framework presents. This calls for a brief analysis of the rights protected in the ICCPR, the International Covenant on Economic, Social and Cultural Rights ("ICESCR"), the International Labour Organisation's Convention on Indigenous and Tribal Peoples in Independent States ("ILO 169"), and the Draft Declaration on the Rights of Indigenous People.

Article 27(1) of the Universal Declaration of Human Rights reflects an individualistic conception of cultural rights—"[e]veryone has the right to freely participate in the cultural life of the community". A number of States sought provision for the cultural rights of groups during the drafting stage, but this view did not prevail. Article 22 provides:

> "Everyone, as a member of society, has the right to social security and is entitled to realization, through national effort and international cooperation and in accordance with the organization and resources of each State, of the economic, social and cultural rights indispensable for his dignity and the free development of his personality."

Article 15 of the ICESCR, formulated some 18 years later, gave a more binding character to cultural rights though still formulated as the rights of individuals. Thus, "The States Parties to the present Covenant recognize the right of everyone . . . to take part in cultural life . . ." (Article 15(1)(a)).

In comparison to the ICESCR, the ICCPR does not contain many protections for cultural rights that are vital for indigenous peoples. However, it recognises minority cultures, and unlike the ICESCR there is attached to the ICCPR, in the form of the Optional Protocol, a process for hearing complaints against states. Article 27 of the ICCPR states:

> "In those States in which ethnic, religious or linguistic minorities exist, persons belonging to such minorities shall not be denied the right, in community with the other members of their group, to enjoy their own culture, to profess and practise their own religion, or to use their own language."

This expresses what may be described as norms of "cultural integrity".[59] As already seen, General Comment 23 of the United Nations Human Rights Committee elaborates on the components.[60] Article 27 is "directed towards ensuring the survival and continued development of the cultural, religious and social identity of the minorities concerned".[61] Thus permission to speak the language is not enough and instead there is a duty to actively ensure language survival. General Comment 23 also makes it clear that Article 27 does not prejudice the sovereignty and integrity of any State party, and that the rights protected are individual rights, not group

---

[59] S J Anaya, *Indigenous Peoples in International Law* (New York, Oxford University Press, 1996) 99.
[60] UN General Comment 23, *Compilation of General Comments*, above n. 11 at 39.
[61] *Ibid*, cl. 9.

rights. However, as has been noted, effective enjoyment of cultural rights might be closely associated with use of a particular resource or territory, and these individual rights will depend on the ability of the group as a whole to maintain its culture.[62] The fundamental premise underlying norms of cultural integrity is that of "securing the survival and flourishing of indigenous cultures through mechanisms devised in accordance with the preferences of the indigenous peoples concerned".[63]

Equality of rights and non-discrimination are further core concepts of many human rights instruments.[64] The United Nations Declaration on the Rights of Minorities in this regard goes further than the ICCPR. Article 4(2) of the Declaration on the Rights of Minorities provides:[65]

"States shall take measures to create favourable conditions to enable persons belonging to minorities to express their characteristics and to develop their culture, language, religion, traditions and customs."

The International Labour Organisation Convention concerning Indigenous and Tribal Peoples in Independent Countries requires that States take action, including measures:[66]

"(a) ensuring that members of these peoples benefit on an equal footing from the rights and opportunities which national laws and regulations grant to other members of the population;

(b) promoting the full realisation of the social, economic and cultural rights of these peoples with respect for their social and cultural identity, their customs and traditions, and their institutions;

(c) assisting the members of the peoples concerned to eliminate socio-economic gaps that may exist between indigenous and other members of the national community, in a manner compatible with their aspirations and ways of life."

The Draft Declaration on the Rights of Indigenous Peoples provides a landmark within the United Nations system. In its present form the Draft Declaration could provide comprehensive protection for the rights of indigenous peoples. Perhaps the most significant provision in the Draft Declaration is the recognition that indigenous peoples have the right to self-determination.[67] One commentator has described this as "a right to 'rights'" and "pivotal" to the "objective of raising human rights standards for indigenous peoples".[68] Commentators have also

---

[62] *Ibid*, cl. 3.2, cl. 6.

[63] S J Anaya, above n. 59 at 104.

[64] A Bloch, "Minorities and Indigenous Peoples" in A Eide, C Krause and A Rosas (eds.), *Economic, Social and Cultural Rights: A Text Book* (Dordrecht, Martinus Nijhoff Publishers, 1995) 309.

[65] United Nations Declaration on the Rights of Persons Belonging to National or Ethnic, Religious and Linguistic Minorities, Art. 4(2).

[66] International Labour Organisation Convention Concerning Indigenous and Tribal Peoples in Independent Countries, Art. 2(2)(a).

[67] Draft Declaration on the Rights of Indigenous Peoples, Art. 3.

[68] M E Turpel, "Commentary" [1994] 1 *Canadian Native Law Reporter* 50, 51.

pointed to the drafting process as being significant in itself for allowing indigenous people speaking rights along with government representatives.[69]

Realising the rights expressed in these documents provides a number of challenges. It has been argued that for the better protection of indigenous peoples' rights by the international community some form of monitoring mechanism is necessary. Real problems can focus issues in a way that abstract discussions cannot, and a monitoring body or system could provide a framework for inquiry. Further, a complaints procedure encourages groups to organise and articulate their positions.[70] Muntarbhorn has advocated using treaties and national pacts to express the social rights of indigenous people in a concrete form.[71] It matters not whether such pacts are legally binding, for what is important is recognition at a concrete rather than abstract level.[72] Muntarbhorn also advocates "a national forum where compromises may be worked out between the diversity of interests, governmental and non-governmental, indigenous and non-indigenous",[73] balancing national opinion with the doctrine of cultural relativism. Of course, we have already seen this in practice in New Zealand.

The basic premise of the doctrine of cultural relativism is that "[c]ultures operate according to different but equally valid patterns of social logic [and] . . . none can be considered more valid and authentic than any other".[74] Imposing the standards of one cultural group upon another has been shown to be largely ineffective in improving human rights standards.[75] However, as already indicated, recognising the principles of cultural relativism does not render useless the instruments and organs of the United Nations, or any other international organisation. Tempering ideals of universal standards of human rights with the doctrine of cultural relativism can provide effective protection of human rights for people of all cultures in a culturally appropriate manner. "Diversity is not, in itself, contrary to unity, any more than uniformity itself produces the desired unity."[76] Joyner and Dettling argue that the natural social structures of a cultural group should not be disturbed or disrupted by external groups unless there is "a legal and moral justification [which is] subject to a constitutional due process consistent with international law".[77]

Although it is argued that cultural rights are not justiciable in the same way that other human rights are because they lack clear definition, in essence human rights are interrelated and indivisible even though they might be separated into workable categories on paper.[78]

---

[69] D Sanders, "A Text and a New Process", and Turpel, "Commentary" [1994] 1 *Canadian Native Law Reporter* 48 and 50.

[70] H Niec, *Cultural Rights at the End of the World Decade for Cultural Development* (Stockholm, Intergovernmental Conference on Cultural Policies for Development, 1998).

[71] V Muntarbhorn, "Realizing Indigenous Social Rights" (1990) 2(2) *Without Prejudice* 7.

[72] *Ibid*, 20.

[73] *Ibid*, 22.

[74] Joyner and Dettling, above n. at 57 at 277–8.

[75] K Miller, "Human Rights of Women in Iran: The Universalist Approach and the Relativist Response" (1996) 10 *Emory Int'l L Rev* 775.

[76] Muntarbhorn, above n. 71 at 24.

[77] Joyner and Dettling, above n. 57 at 290.

[78] Niec, above n. 70.

It may also be considered that law, whether it be international conventions or domestic law, cannot be effective if it does not recognise the cultural values of the society within which it operates. The Australian Law Reform Commission has recently argued for recognition of Aboriginal customary law so that the Australian legal system operates more effectively for both the Aboriginal and non-Aboriginal populations.[79] There is a strong feeling that matters which are "purely internal" to the Aboriginal community should be dealt with under Aboriginal customary law. Garkawe argues that "purely internal" matters could be identified either by designated Aboriginal community areas or by establishing that the situation at issue is one where both the offender and the victim have similar perceptions of what customary law entails.[80]

At an international level, attempts to implement "universal" concepts of human rights in Iran have so far failed. Women in Iran are still discriminated against ostensibly because of the cultural values of Islamic law. However, Kristin Miller has illustrated that finding a middle approach between the two extremes of universalism and cultural relativism can encourage recognition of the human rights of women without imposing Western values, which ultimately destroys cultural diversity.[81] Miller notes that there is effective recognition of the rights of women in Tunisia, a country which, like Iran, is governed by Islamic law. This suggests that it is not the fundamental values of Islamic culture that are limiting the rights of women in Iran.

It is argued that the applicable concept is that of retaining the ideal of a single set of human rights standards while valuing the rights of groups to self-determination and to live according to their own values and practices. Miller argues that the role of the international community is not that of police officer or paternal teacher, but rather that of an educative facilitator. The international community can help by raising awareness among individuals within the community in question. "Universalist ideals will gain legitimacy by working within the culture, rather than against it."[82] The approach to protecting human rights that is advocated by Garkawe, Miller, Joyner and Dettling and others is to work within the underlying values of cultural groups. Therefore, there needs to be an element of flexibility within the structural framework of international human rights. Guiding principles rather than concrete entitlements are suggested.[83] For example, it might be valuable to interpret all words, phrases and expressions used in international instruments in a culturally sensitive manner.[84] This approach would require working with indigenous groups and understanding and accepting the social structures and cultural framework within which they are operating.

---

[79] Australian Law Reform Commission, *The Recognition of Aboriginal Customary Laws* (ALRC 31) (Canberra, Government Printer, 1986).

[80] S Garkawe, "The Impact of the Doctrine of Cultural Relativism on the Australian Legal System" (1995) 2(1) *E-Law*, Murdoch University School of Law.

[81] Miller, above n. 75.

[82] *Ibid*, 829.

[83] Niec, above n. 70.

[84] Muntarbhorn, above n. 71.

I thus pass to consider how some of the conflicts between individual rights and the rights of indigenous peoples could be resolved using the above approach. In New Zealand this requires some exploration of the Maori value system and identifying structural aspects which could be recognised by New Zealand's legal framework if it is to effectively protect the rights of Maori as indigenous people.

Maori conduct is governed by a set of fundamental principles that have been described as conceptual regulators.[85] As the description suggests, these were concepts that regulated behaviour within traditional Maori society. A common feature of Maori law was that it was based around relationships between people.[86] However, while maintenance of personal relationships required observance of protocol, Maori law is values based, not rules oriented.[87] The Maori value system has been described as agent-centred rather than act centred, so conduct is governed not by a set of rules but by the overwhelming desire to behave in a manner consistent with those who have great mana.[88] This model has parallels with the model of ethics described by Aristotle as virtue ethics.[89] It is suggested that Maori sociopolitical organisation can be derived from the basis of a virtue ethics model. Virtue centred morality requires a moral community which conceives of its life as a shared project,[90] which the Maori value system certainly provides. The concept of whanaungatanga encourages collective rather than individual responsibility. It has been suggested that the "desire or necessity to unite individuals with one another and strengthen the kinship ties is a basic cultural value so strong that whanaungatanga must be seen by members [of the kinship group] for it to operate effectively".[91] The idea of collective responsibility that is integral to whanaungatanga means that it is impossible for a clear distinction to be made in the Maori world between egoism and altruism, because acting for the group is acting for oneself.[92]

The conceptual basis of whanaungatanga can be illustrated in the operation of muru. Muru is a mechanism that was used to restore balance. It is a form of utu which aims to contain retribution from escalating to harmful levels within close kin groups. The operation emphasises the fact that the entire kin group is accountable for the actions of individuals within the group. Furthermore, examples of muru show that when there is a conflict of tikanga (proper principle), there is a balancing process to determine which tikanga will prevail in the circumstances. This shows that there is great flexibility in applying tikanga. As discussed earlier, this flexibility of practices can be significant for increasing protection of individual rights without disturbing fundamental cultural values.[93]

---

[85] E T J Durie, "Custom Law" (Wellington, Waitangi Tribunal, 1994) 104.
[86] *Ibid.*
[87] *Ibid.*
[88] J Patterson, *Exploring Maori Values* (Palmerston North, Dunmore Press, 1992).
[89] *Ibid*, 103.
[90] *Ibid*, 109.
[91] M Henare, "Nga Tikanga me nga Ritenga o Te Ao Maori", in *Report of the Royal Commission on Social Policy* (Wellington, Royal Commission on Social Policy, 1988) 7.
[92] Patterson, above n. 88.
[93] Joyner and Dettling, above n. 57.

Maori customary law has conceptual regulators that have remained important for many Maori. The way that these conceptual regulators are expressed in today's society is not identical to the way that they were expressed before the Treaty of Waitangi, at the time of the Treaty of Waitangi over 160 years ago, or as they will be expressed in 160 years from now. Change has occurred within Maori society to produce a different set of standards that are acceptable, but the underlying values remain the same. Tikanga Maori has always been very flexible, but the values that the tikanga is based on are not altered. One of the values that may now form part of the Maori value system is that of equality, which may have precedence over other values at times. It thus seems to me entirely evident that Maori cultural practices can change to accommodate, for example, gender non-discrimination rights, without breaching the rights of Maori as indigenous people or attacking the fundamental values of Maori society.

In summary, while the international law framework has served to prevent breaches of many of the rights of indigenous people, the framework could be improved by the addition of a body that can adequately monitor economic, social and cultural rights. It is still important that international documents such as the ICCPR, the ICESCR, ILO 169 and the Draft Declaration on the Rights of Indigenous People, should seek to encapsulate indigenous peoples' rights, though additional approaches appear necessary.

One such additional approach is to overlay the international law framework with the doctrine of cultural relativism, not to deny the validity of fundamental human rights but to perfect their application in diverse situations. Using the ideals of international law and cultural relativism together, it is possible to arrive at culturally appropriate standards of human rights provided the approach is to work within the cultural framework of the society in question. Thus Maori society exists within a framework of conceptual regulators within the bounds of which there is flexibility to allow the cultural practices to adapt to changing circumstances. However,[94]

> "[i]n determining the psychic, cultural, and legal borders of 'differences', serious attention must be paid to normative and institutional frameworks in order to manage border crossings and border disputes, and to draw the appropriate borders".

V INDIGENOUS PROPERTY RIGHTS AND ABORIGINAL TITLE

The doctrine of aboriginal title illustrates the management of cultural relativity by the courts. The underlying principles are useful to consider when developing structures to accommodate rights from more than one legal system.

The legal principles were expressed in *The Case of Tanistry*,[95] which considered the status of Irish customary law subsequent to English conquest. It was considered

---

[94] P Havemann, "Colonisation, Criminalisation, and Indigenous Peoples' Rights" in P Havemann (ed.), *Indigenous Peoples' Rights in Australia, Canada, and New Zealand* (Auckland, Oxford University Press, 1999) 278, 281–2.

[95] (1608) Davies 28, 80 ER 516 (KB).

that the indigenous laws of a country survived British sovereignty so long as they met the requirements of reasonableness, certainty, immemorial usage and compatibility with the prerogative (sovereignty) of the Crown.[96] Despite an early distinction between the laws of "infidel" nations and those of Christian peoples, *Campbell* v. *Hall*[97] clarified that any laws, Christian or otherwise, that met the qualifications in *Tanistry* were presumed to continue. A distinction developed, however, between "conquered or ceded" colonies where the common law did not automatically hold sway, and "settled" colonies where it did. By the end of the eighteenth century new colonies with a non-Christian, indigenous population were often treated as settled colonies but this constitutional categorisation did not effect the legal system of the indigenous population as such. Rather, it "explained the legal position of the settlers and defined the way in which the Crown's constituent power would be exercised".[98] By the mid-nineteenth century it was clear that local circumstances limit the introduction of English law. "English law is introduced to a new colony only to the extent that local circumstances allow."[99] That principle had and continues to have statutory reinforcement in New Zealand.

The doctrine of aboriginal title is essentially the application to indigenous property rights of the common law principles outlined above. The Crown acquired the radical title to the territory and the indigenous population in possession of the land was said to possess the aboriginal title as a burden on the title of the Crown.[100] The legal principles were scrutinised in the authoritative judgments of the Supreme Court of the United States of America under Chief Justice Marshall. The judgments in *Johnson* v. *M'Intosh*,[101] *Worcester* v. *Georgia*,[102] and *Mitchel* v. *US*[103] were of significant influence in Anglo-American jurisdictions.

New Zealand law was strongly influenced by Marshall's judgments. *R* v. *Symonds*[104] relied upon those principles in holding that Maori retained a legal right to use and occupy their traditional land although British sovereignty placed limits on its alienability. The "'legal doctrine as to the exclusive right of the Queen to extinguish the native title' did not affect the tribal law of tenure".[105] As in the United States, this approach was entirely consistent with the practice of the colonial authorities. It appears to have been adopted in *Re The Lundon and Whitaker Claims Act, 1871*,[106] where the Court of Appeal stated that the Crown was "bound, both by the common law of England and by its own solemn engagements, to a full recognition of Native proprietary right", and that "[w]hatever the extent

---

[96] P G McHugh, *The Maori Magna Carta: New Zealand Law and the Treaty of Waitangi* (Auckland, Oxford University Press, 1991) 87.
[97] (1774) 1 Cowp 204; 98 ER 1045.
[98] McHugh, above n. 96 at 89.
[99] *Ibid*, 93.
[100] *Ibid*, 104.
[101] *Johnson* v. *M'Intosh* 21 US (8 Wheat) 543 (1823).
[102] *Worcester* v. *Georgia* 31 US (6 Pet) 515 (1832).
[103] *Mitchel* v. *US* 34 US (9 Pet) 711 (1835).
[104] *R* v. *Symonds* (1847) NZPCC 387 (SC).
[105] McHugh, above n. 96 at 110.
[106] (1872) 2 NZCA 41.

of that right by established Native custom appears to be, the Crown is bound to respect it".[107] The Privy Council also approved of it in cases such as *St Catherine's Milling and Lumber Company* v. *The Queen*,[108] *Nireaha Tamaki* v. *Baker*[109] and *Wallis* v. *Solicitor-General for New Zealand*.[110]

There was a move from this position in *Wi Parata* v. *The Bishop of Wellington*.[111] There the denial of claims based on aboriginal title flowed from two strands of reasoning. The first was that insofar as the Treaty of Waitangi purported to cede sovereignty it was a simple nullity, and "Maori customary law being uncivilized, any property rights created by it were unenforceable in the courts".[112] The second strand of reasoning was that in dealing with tribal societies the Crown is the "sole arbiter of its own justice" and transactions with Maori "for the cession of their title to the Crown are thus to be regarded as acts of State, and therefore are not examinable by any Court".[113] Essentially the approach adopted by Prendergast was that "all property rights derived from a grant by a sovereign. If a society lacked an original sovereignty, it therefore lacked any property rights upon the acquisition of its territory by the Crown".[114] However, whatever the status of Maori society in sociological terms, the doctrine of aboriginal title was not based on the level of "civilisation" of indigenous societies or on whether property rights in such societies are derived from a sovereign:[115]

"The common law doctrine of aboriginal title sidestepped any such theorizing in so far as it located the title in the fact of the tribal occupation of their land under a customary if 'barbaric' system of tenure."

Wi Parata was followed in subsequent New Zealand decisions,[116] though the original position has since been restored.

After a legislative change in 1909 the New Zealand courts adopted the approach of accepting Maori traditional rights only when they were recognised in legislation. In *Tamihana Korokai* v. *Solicitor-General* it was held that[117]

"the Supreme Court could take no cognizance of treaty rights not embodied in a statute, and that Native customary title was a kind of tenure that the Court could not deal with".

Waipapakura v. *Hempton*[118] also followed this approach. McHugh suggests that the approach adopted by the local courts was, at least in part, due to the nature of the arguments put by counsel.[119] Maori litigants tended to base their claims on the

---

[107] *Ibid*, 49.
[108] (1888) 14 App Cas 46 (PC).
[109] [1901] AC 561 (PC).
[110] [1903] AC 173 (PC).
[111] *Wi Parata* v. *Bishop of Wellington* (1878) 3 NZ Jur (NS) SC 72.
[112] McHugh, above n. 96 at 114.
[113] (1878) 3 NZ Jur (NS) SC 72, 77.
[114] McHugh, above n. 96 at 115.
[115] *Ibid*, 117.
[116] See *Hohepa Wi Neera* v. *Bishop of Wellington* (1902) 21 NZLR 655 (CA).
[117] *Tamihana Korokai* v. *Solicitor-General* (1912) 32 NZLR 321, 344 (CA).
[118] (1914) 33 NZLR 1065.
[119] McHugh, above n. 96 at 122.

Treaty of Waitangi rather than in the common law doctrine of aboriginal rights, but the Privy Council has tended to dismiss claims based on rights derived from treaties of cession,[120] while recognising rights that pre-date them.[121]

The restrictive doctrine of statutory derived rights stood until the case of *Te Weehi* v. *Regional Fisheries Officer*.[122] In finding that Tom Te Weehi continued to possess a customary right to collect paua (according to Maori customary rules), Williamson J resurrected the *Symonds* approach to aboriginal title.

Te Weehi was consistent with modern developments of the doctrine of aboriginal title in commonwealth jurisdictions. These were set in motion by the Canadian case of *Calder* v. *Attorney-General of British Columbia*.[123] In *Calder* the Court found that at common law the Nishga tribe of British Columbia held an aboriginal title over their ancestral lands at the time of British sovereignty. Hall J went on to suggest that the presumption of continuity expressed in *Campbell* v. *Hall* should be applied with even stronger force over a "settled" colony, confirming that this categorisation of colonies does not have any great effect on the relationship between the legal system of the tribe and the legal system of the Crown.[124] *Calder*, like *Te Weehi*, recognised the continued existence of customary rights and in effect forced negotiation of claims to aboriginal title with indigenous groups.

The concepts underlying aboriginal title continued to be developed throughout the 1980s and 1990s. In *Guerin* v. *The Queen* the Canadian Supreme Court reaffirmed that "Indians have a legal right to occupy and possess certain lands, the ultimate title to which is in the Crown".[125] *Guerin* also developed the idea that the Crown has a fiduciary duty in respect of aboriginal title. McHugh summarises the reasoning for finding such a duty:[126]

> "So far as an aboriginal title is concerned, it has been seen that an important reason for the Crown's taking feudal title in territory occupied by tribal societies was to prevent land-jobbing and to establish an orderly tenure system for the settlers. In placing itself in this position and adopting a protective role over the tribal societies, the Crown thus assumed a fiduciary duty."

R v. *Sparrow*[127] affirmed the unique nature of the property right of aboriginal title, and also the fact that it was this *sui generis* status that was the source of the fiduciary obligation on the Crown. The judgment in *Sparrow* also examines the distinction between extinguishment of aboriginal title and the regulation of aboriginal title that had previously been raised in *R* v. *Kruger & Manuel*[128] and *R* v. *Agawa*.[129] It was held that regulation or partial extinguishment could take place without necessarily

[120] See *Vajesingji Joravasingji* v. *Secretary of State for India in Council* (1924) LR 51 Ind App 357 (PC).
[121] See *Amodu Tijani* v. *Secretary, Southern Rhodesia* [1921] 2 AC 399 (PC).
[122] [1986] 1 NZLR 680.
[123] [1973] SCR 313.
[124] McHugh, above n. 96 at 127.
[125] *Guerin* v. *The Queen* [1984] 2 SCR 355, 339.
[126] McHugh, above n. 96 at 129.
[127] [1990] 1 SCR 1075, 1108.
[128] [1978] 1 SCR 104.
[129] (1988) 53 DLR (4th) 101.

extinguishing all rights flowing from aboriginal title over a particular area.[130] This approach has also been adopted in New Zealand.[131]

In recent years there have been significant developments particularly in the Canadian courts. In 1996 the Supreme Court of Canada found that aboriginal rights are not necessarily dependent on title to land in a case which was very similar to *Te Weehi*.[132] Also in 1996, *R* v. *Van der Peet*[133] reaffirmed the principle laid down in *Johnson* v. *M'Intosh* that aboriginal title should be compromised only to the extent necessary to give effect to Crown sovereignty.

However, the most important recent decision is *Delgamuukw* v. *British Colombia*.[134] The claimants sought a declaration of aboriginal title and self-government over the disputed lands. They argued that the aboriginal title was tantamount to a fee simple, which confers on aboriginal peoples the right to use those lands as they choose and that this had been given constitutional force by section 35(1) of the Constitution Act 1982. The respondents argued that aboriginal title was "no more than a 'bundle of rights to engage in activities which are themselves aboriginal rights' and that aboriginal title 'encompasses the right to exclusive use and occupation of land in order to engage in those activities which are aboriginal rights themselves'".[135] The Court effectively enlarged the scope of aboriginal title from that previously recognised in cases such as *Baker Lake* v. *Minister of Indian Affairs & Northern Development*,[136] but the decision can also be seen to restrict aboriginal title severely. It was held that, if the land is used in a manner that interferes with its traditional use, the "special bond" between aboriginal communities and the land that gives rise to the aboriginal title will be broken.[137] This would prohibit many modern forms of land development and utilisation. The Court found that aboriginal title was *sui generis* and that there was broad judicial power to regulate the development of aboriginal lands.[138]

The basis for placing unique restrictions on aboriginal title in that case seems somewhat flawed, the better position appearing to be that any restrictions a court adopts must have their sources in the aboriginal systems of law.[139] In New Zealand there has been some limited provision for the evolution of aboriginal customary law as indicated in *Te Runanganui o Te Ika Whenua Inc Soc* v. *Attorney-General*.[140] Nevertheless, this still falls well short of the "exclusive use and enjoyment" that principles of equality could require.[141]

---

[130] *R* v. *Sparrow* [1990] 1 SCR 1075, 1111–12.

[131] See *Te Runanga O Muriwhenua* v. *Attorney-General* [1990] 2 NZLR 641 (CA).

[132] *R* v. *Adams* [1996] 3 SCR 101.

[133] [1996] 2 SCR 507.

[134] [1997] 3 SCR 1010.

[135] W F Flanagan, "Piercing the Veil of Real Property Law: *Delgamuukw* v. *British Columbia*" (1998) 24 *Queen's LJ* 279, 287.

[136] [1980] 1 FC 518.

[137] *Delgamuukw* v. *The Queen* [1997] 3 SCR 1010, 1089.

[138] Flanagan, above n. 135 at 283–4.

[139] *Ibid*, 300–22.

[140] [1994] 2 NZLR 20, 24 (CA).

[141] R Bartlett, "The Content of Aboriginal Title and Equality Before the Law" (1998) 61 *Sask L Rev* 377

There are thus several approaches that may be taken to aboriginal title. It can be approached strictly as English common law, as entirely determined by indigenous customary law, or somewhere in between as a kind of "bicultural jurisprudence". The first assumes the superiority of English common law and does not take into account the history of relations between first nations and Europeans.[142] The second, which would place no reliance on English legal principles, may not in fact achieve indigenous people's goals. If indigenous groups seek to fit their laws into the constitutional framework of their country then there must be certain aspects of those laws that can be described in terms compatible with the dominant legal system if only to specify how the rights will interact with general law.[143] However, aboriginal title can be viewed as[144]

> "an over-arching body of law, bridging the gap between aboriginal land systems on the one hand and English . . . land systems on the other. Neither side is subordinate to the other; each operates within its own sphere of influence. The status of each system and their interrelations are regulated by this higher level of law, which owes its origins to the interactions of British and First Nations over a long period of time, and draws on the legal conceptions and interest of both sides."

Viewed this way, the concepts that form the basis of aboriginal title fit with the model for international cultural relativism discussed earlier. I suggest that this ancient doctrine provides the guidelines required for the interaction of indigenous and non-indigenous cultures and the legal system.

---

[142] Slattery, "The Legal Basis of Aboriginal Title" in F Cassidy (ed.), *Aboriginal Title in British Columbia: Delgamuukw v. The Queen* (Victoria, Oolichan Books and The Institute for Research on Public Policy, 1992) 113–14.

[143] *Ibid*, 115.

[144] *Ibid*, 120.

PART IV

Internationalism

14

The Rule of International Law?

PAUL RISHWORTH

I INTRODUCTION

Common lawyers know that legislation is to be read on the assumption that it was intended to be consistent with fundamental principles underlying the legal order, especially those concerning the rights of persons. Happily, that assumption is safe to make, most of the time. It is important to stress this at the outset, because otherwise an essay about how human rights should be accommodated by judges within a country's constitutional arrangements might suggest, contrary to fact, that legislators are not concerned with human rights. In fact, litigation about rights and statutory interpretation usually arises out of competing conceptions—as between courts and legislature—of the scope and impact of a right in a specific context, or from a lack of awareness on the part of the legislature that rights are implicated by the detail of its legislation. In neither of these cases is there likely to be a desire on the part of the legislature to override rights. The first scenario arises only if courts take a different view as to the substance of a right,[1] and in the second scenario it is probable, though admittedly not inevitable, that accommodating fundamental rights within a broad legislative scheme is entirely consistent with the legislature's overall objective.

For a long time the judicial role of making statutes conform, where possible, to fundamental rights was premised on the legislature's presumed intention. That seemed a satisfactory explanation of most cases, albeit *ex post facto* and often fictional. It was really a matter of deemed legislative intent, for the presumption might ascribe to legislatures a somewhat unrealistic concern for detail. But recent developments in common law method reflect a quite separate rationale: direct allegiance by judges to the fundamental principles themselves. The principles are now brought to bear on legislation because of their intrinsic moral suasion, and are not mediated through the device of presumptions about legislative intent. It is not so much that legislators must have intended to conform to fundamental principles; the new view is that, *whether or not they so intended*, those principles must be accommodated. Indeed, in the area of fundamental rights, a "manner and form" limitation

---

[1] This explains *R v. Pora* [2001] 2 NZLR 37, where the Court of Appeal agreed that legislation offended the principle against retrospective legislation by increasing the minimum non-parole period attached to life sentences (though divided over what the implications of that conclusion were). But, for its part, Parliament seems to have considered that alterations to parole periods within a life sentence did not implicate the principle at all.

has evolved: unless express words of abrogation are used, or abrogation is necessarily implicit in the chosen words, fundamental rights will prevail. The search for legislative intent has been turned on its head: it is now a search to see if a legislature intended to *oust* fundamental rights.[2]

That second conception of direct allegiance is plainly in the ascendant.[3] But, in any event, it has been expressly enacted as law in the UK and NZ. In those countries, the respective parliaments have affirmed a set of fundamental rights and required that judges interpret all legislation so as to give effect to them. The rights (in the Human Rights Act 1998 and New Zealand Bill of Rights Act 1990 respectively) are a domestic enactment of internationally-sourced rights, the European Convention on Human Rights (ECHR) in the case of the UK and the International Covenant on Civil and Political Rights (ICCPR) in the case of NZ. The consequence of statutory affirmations of rights has been a more assiduous judicial inquiry into their meaning and impact, akin to the type of inquiry already made by courts enforcing constitutions. These developments lead to the questions that are pursued at the end of this essay. If (1) judges are the ultimate guardians of rights, (2) those rights are themselves an affirmation of corresponding rights in an international treaty, and (3) an international body is empowered by that treaty to hear cases brought by way of further "appeal" from a state's highest domestic court, then (4) where does final authority lie to determine the meaning and effect of rights? In the context of the ICCPR, for example, does final authority lie with the Human Rights Committee, or with domestic courts and legislatures, in whatever balance a particular country strikes between these two institutions? I argue that ultimate authority should remain in the domestic and not international sphere; the Views of the Human Rights Committee should be regarded as persuasive, but not binding. This is the status quo, albeit a somewhat unexamined one, and there are good reasons why it should be maintained.

II THE FUNDAMENTAL RIGHTS PRINCIPLES AND JUDGES AS THEIR GUARDIANS

By "fundamental principles of the legal order" I mean those principles that express, in general terms, the rights of persons within that order, along with those that

---

[2] *R* v. *Pora*, [2001] 2 NZLR 37, 50.

[3] The path to direct allegiance can be tracked through successive "Bangalore Principles", ten years apart. In the first set, declared by a group of judges after a meeting in Bangalore in 1988, the role of international human rights treaties was said to lie in resolving interpretive issues where domestic law was uncertain or incomplete. In the revised and restated set of principles, dating from December 1998, it was said:

"3. It is the vital duty of an independent, impartial and well-qualified judiciary . . . to interpret and apply national constitutions and ordinary legislation in harmony with international human rights codes and customary international law, and to develop the common law in the light of the values and principles enshrined in international human rights law."

The requirement of ambiguity, and as a corollary, the issue of deemed legislative intention, has been dropped. The judicial duty is simply to interpret domestic legislation in accordance with international human rights principles. The revised set of principles may be seen in the article by Lord Lester of Herne Hill, "The Challenge of Bangalore: Making Human Rights a Practical Reality" [1999] *EHRLR* 273, 288.

determine its basic structure.[4] For present purposes I am concerned with human rights principles. These map out a *prima facie* boundary of legitimate state power. It is "prima facie" in the sense that the principles are generally understood to exhaust themselves in the interpretation process. They operate only until such time as they are unambiguously contradicted by contrary legislation, at which point they retreat. Whether that retreat ought to be accompanied by a declaration that fundamental principles have apparently been abrogated is an intriguing question. As we shall see, the idea of judicial declarations of inconsistency with rights is the centrepiece of the United Kingdom's new Human Rights Act, and is also a possibility under the New Zealand Bill of Rights.[5] The present point is simply that the idea of judicial declarations was always implicit in common law method as well.

In the past, various factors restrained judges from making statements about inconsistency with rights. One was a conception of the separation of powers—that assessments about the value and impact of competing rights are best made in legislatures.[6] Another reason was that the fundamental rights, as traditionally conceived, operated only as highly abstracted and vague generalisations. When conceived in this way, it was often possible to conclude both that they were ousted by legislation, and that this was probably not a matter of great moment. For example, if a statute imposed restrictions on expression in, say, the censorship context, it would be very easy for judges to conclude that freedom of expression was simply overridden in its entirety to the extent necessary to make the statute work. They were unlikely to be receptive to detailed argument about the degree of restriction imposed, nor to seek to accommodate within the statute such aspects of expression as might have been protected by a constitutional right, if one existed.[7] The truth was that common law rights did not function in the same way as constitutional rights, nor in the same way as rights protected under the ECHR. Fundamental rights at common law were blunt instruments, capable of deflecting a court from settling on an iniquitous possible meaning in favour of a benign possible alternative, but only when a court was satisfied it was confronted with ambiguity.

Even so, it required no legislation or constitution to alter the way in which fundamental principles might operate in the UK and NZ—only a change of judicial approach, and that began to happen in the 1990s. In the UK, under the influence of European human rights law and the looming advent of the Human Rights Act 1998, judicial inquiry into the nature of fundamental rights became more rigorous

---

[4] By structural principles I mean those principles that are not about the rights of persons but concern the nature of institutions, especially the separation of powers.

[5] See the contributions of Huscroft, Butler and Leigh in this volume.

[6] Even in the early Bill of Rights years this view was taken, albeit not whole-heartedly, by Cooke P in *Temese v. Police* (1992) 9 CRNZ 425. But this reticence gave way in *Moonen v. Board of Film and Literature Review* [2000] 2 NZLR 9 (CA).

[7] Cf *R v. Sharpe* [2001] 1 SCR 45, in which the Supreme Court of Canada "read in" specific exceptions so as to protect, in the child pornography context, two categories of speech that they regarded as constitutionally protected.

and nuanced than it once was.[8] In 1998, in *R* v. *Home Secretary ex parte Pierson*,[9] Lord Steyn spoke of the "principle of legality" that undergirded English law, requiring that law must be taken to affirm "minimum standards of fairness, both substantive and procedural".[10] This approach had two important ramifications, the first of which was exemplified by the result of the particular case. First, a careful scrutiny of rights claims might compel judges to a conclusion that a reasonably limited form of the right at stake could and must be accommodated within the statutory words, in which case there was some compromise between the rights claim and the aims of the legislature. Second, if the conclusion were that the right could not be accommodated due to its being ousted by clear words to that effect, then this was likely to have been reached after careful argument, and expressed in a reasoned judgment. Judges were more likely, after that process, to wish to state and defend a conclusion that rights have been unreasonably abrogated by legislation.

The English developments were followed by New Zealand judges who saw them, rightly, as replicated in section 6 of New Zealand's Bill of Rights, which was taken to implement the "principle of legality".[11] If the principle was inherent in the nature of law (and in any event mandated by statute in New Zealand), it was not simply a question whether the legislature intended to act in accordance with it. Rather, it meant, as Lord Hoffmann put it in *R* v. *Secretary of State ex parte Simms*[12] in 1999, "that [in departing from fundamental rights,] Parliament must squarely confront what it is doing and accept the political cost". The ultimate question therefore became whether Parliament had evinced an intention to *depart* from fundamental principles, and a clear intention was demanded.[13]

---

[8] In *Pierson* v. *Secretary of State for the Home Department* [1998] AC 539 the question was whether a statutory provision, authorising the Home Secretary to adopt a policy on non-parole terms for prisoners, allowed the *increase* of a prisoner's non-parole period once set. That appeared to infringe a principle against retroactive increase of punishments, for non-parole periods were accepted to be part of the sentence. The House of Lords held that, as put by Lord Browne-Wilkinson, "basic rights are not to be overridden by the general words of a statute since the presumption is against the impairment of such basic rights" (p 575). This included, the majority agreed, a right against retroactive increase of penalty. It followed that the statutory power could not be read to authorise increases.

[9] *Ibid*, 587–8.

[10] *Ibid*, 591.

[11] See Elias CJ in *Ngati Apa Ki Te Waipounamu Trust* v. *The Queen* [2000] 2 NZLR 659, 675 (para 82) and Elias CJ and Tipping J (Thomas J concurring) in *R* v. *Pora* [2001] 2 NZLR 37, 50.

[12] [2000] 2 AC 115, 131.

[13] In this sentence the word "clear" carries a lot of weight. In *R* v. *Pora* [2001] 2 NZLR 37, for example, the offending statutory provision (s 2(4) of the Criminal Justice Amendment (No 2) Act) provided:

"(4) Section 80 of the principal Act (as amended by this section [to increase minimum non-parole period for murder]) applies in respect of the making of any order under that section on or after the date of commencement of this section, *even if the offence concerned was committed before that date* (emphasis added)."

Three judges held this to be not clear enough to oust the principle against retrospectivity that was also affirmed by a provision in the same enactment, though enacted at an earlier time. If one asks how clarity could have been attained one thinks of phrases such as "and this means that it has retrospective effect" or "the principle of legality is hereby abrogated to the extent required".

It is possible that judicial declarations as to the inconsistency of statutes with fundamental principle might have evolved even within the common law method. But matters were put beyond doubt when the UK Human Rights Act imposed a statutory direction that judges make declarations of incompatibility (as between a UK enactment and the ECHR) when appropriate. Around the same time, the New Zealand Court of Appeal inferred a similar power and duty to make declarations of incompatibility under the New Zealand Bill of Rights. In these ways, courts in the UK and New Zealand came to acquire or assert a mandate to assess the rights implications of legislation and to declare their findings.

III THE IMPACT OF WRITING RIGHTS DOWN

Consider these two quotations:

> "It is emphatically the province and duty of the judicial department to say what the law is. . . . If courts then are to regard the constitution; and the constitution is superior to any ordinary act of the legislature; the constitution, and not such ordinary act, must govern the case to which they both apply."

> "The purpose of [the Bill of Rights] necessarily involves the court having the power, and on occasions the duty, to indicate that although a statutory provision must be enforced according to its proper meaning, it is inconsistent with the Bill of Rights, in that it constitutes an unreasonable limitation on the relevant right or freedom which cannot be justified in a free and democratic society."

The first will be recognised as Chief Justice Marshall's famous assertion of the US Supreme Court's judicial review authority in *Marbury* v. *Madison* in 1803.[14] The second is the work of Tipping J, writing for the unanimous New Zealand Court of Appeal in *Moonen* v. *Film and Literature Board of Review*,[15] a case about the importance of reading a censorship statute in light of freedom of expression and establishing judicial declarations of inconsistency as a Bill of Rights remedy in New Zealand.

While it has long been traditional to note the differences between the US and (latterly) the Canadian positions on the one hand, and New Zealand and the United Kingdom on the other, now it is the increasing similarities that deserve attention. Each jurisdiction requires judicial allegiance to a set of rights against which the reasonableness of laws is to be judged. In the US and Canada the potential end point is a declaration of unconstitutionality, which is in practice a refusal, for constitutional reasons, to enforce an enactment. In NZ and the UK an enactment that has been construed as unreasonably limiting rights may prompt the same type of declaration, without the ability to refuse to enforce the enactment. But there are reasons for thinking that the interpretation process will result in relatively few cases where the courts are pressed into such declarations. In any event, the

---

[14] (1803) US 1 Cranch 137, 138.
[15] [2000] 2 NZLR 9, 17 (CA).

political pressure for a legislative response to a judicial declaration is likely to be strong in most cases.

Each development—*Moonen* in New Zealand as much as *Marbury* in nineteenth-century America—was more or less inevitable once rights were written down in a document binding the branches of government. When rights are enshrined in a document devoted to limiting the power of government or instructing judges on interpretative method, they become something concrete and "out there", waiting to be appealed to. They must be reckoned with in the litigation context, and this will usually involve a careful scrutiny of their claims. It was otherwise with vague and shadowy fundamental principles about rights. They were often too general to do much specific good. But it always seemed unattractive that a court might say, of the New Zealand Bill of Rights for example, that merely because of the nature of the instrument in which rights are affirmed, those rights are intrinsically weaker and less consequential than their analogues in constitutions around the world.

Ironically, in the case of New Zealand's Bill of Rights Act, the nature of the instrument turned out—no doubt unintentionally so—to validate the idea of judicial declarations of inconsistency. Section 4 was added at a late stage to make it clear that judges could not strike down statutes on the grounds of inconsistency. Indeed, section 4 is a smorgasbord of things that judges are *not* to do if an enactment is inconsistent with the Bill of Rights: they must not hold the enactment to be impliedly repealed, revoked, invalid, ineffective in any way, nor decline to apply it. But all this, of course, assumed that a prior determination of inconsistency had been made. And a power to make *declarations* of consistency, something not precluded by section 4, was therefore inferred by the Court of Appeal in terms that suggested the inference was not even controversial. And so a rights jurisprudence was generated even within the confines of an explicit parliamentary supremacy.[16]

The reduction of rights to writing therefore draws us into discerning their meaning and effect. Rights have a power that can end up transcending the limitations of the document in which they appear. That is proving to be the New Zealand experience. Members of the Opposition were prescient in claiming, at the time of its enactment, that the Bill of Rights was a Trojan Horse.[17]

IV IS THE ALLEGIANCE, ULTIMATELY, TO INTERNATIONAL RIGHTS?

The UK's Human Rights Act and New Zealand's Bill of Rights are each expressly linked to international instruments. The purpose of the UK Act is to make the European Convention on Human Rights the benchmark for legislation and state

---

[16] [2000] 2 NZLR 9, 17 (CA). The seeds of this case lay in *Quilter* v. *Attorney-General* [1998] 1 NZLR 523. For commentary see P Rishworth, "Reflections on the Bill of Rights after *Quilter* v. *Attorney-General*" [1998] *NZ Law Review* 683 and A S Butler, "Judicial Indications of Inconsistency— A New Weapon in the Bill of Rights Armoury?" [2000] *NZ Law Review* 43. See also the judgment of Thomas J in *R* v. *Poumako* [2000] 2 NZLR 695.

[17] See P Rishworth, "The Birth and Rebirth of the Bill of Rights" in G Huscroft and P Rishworth (eds.), *Rights and Freedoms* (Wellington, Brookers, 1995) ch. 1.

conduct in the UK. In New Zealand, the link is to the ICCPR, and although its text is not directly reproduced in full, it is plainly reflected in most of the individual sections affirming rights. In addition, of course, the Preamble to the New Zealand Bill of Rights expressly states that it is intended to "to affirm, protect, and promote human rights and fundamental freedoms in New Zealand", and to affirm New Zealand's commitment to the ICCPR.

Does this mean that the "principle of legality"—that law involves adherence to fundamental substantive and procedural principles discerned by judges—can be equated with the rights in these international instruments? It is not self-evident that this is so, but there must at least be a significant overlap. In the UK it has been observed that those fundamental common law principles are "reflected in" the ECHR, whose drafting history owed much to English lawyers. And it is significant that, as ultimate recourse to the European Court of Human Rights became more common in English litigation, the House of Lords repeatedly emphasised the basic commonality between English common law and the ECHR, at least in the freedom of expression area.[18]

In any event, it is not critical for present purposes to decide the precise relationship between the principle of legality and the standards of the ECHR. The position is simply this: whatever residual work the principle of legality may be called upon to do in the UK, the primary task of UK courts is now to reconcile UK enactments to the ECHR, and to make declarations of incompatibility where that cannot be done. It is likely that this task is substantially the same as if the principle of legality, and not the ECHR, were the standard. Whether or not that is so, the important point for the purposes of this essay is that the assessment of ECHR standards made by UK courts is open for further review on an application brought before the ECtHR in Strasbourg. For the first time, national and international tribunals will be directly addressing the same issue: the impact of ECHR rights.

The position in New Zealand is basically similar, but in relation to the ICCPR. The Bill of Rights implements the ICCPR, whose Optional Protocol permits recourse to the Human Rights Committee by individuals complaining that their Covenant rights have been breached. In both the UK and NZ, therefore, domestic law requires domestic courts to consider rights issues in the same language and in the same framework as the international tribunals to whom the litigants might have ultimate recourse. Note, also, that this fulfils the broad aims of international law in this area. Accession to the ICCPR necessarily involves the implementation of its rights domestically, and the OP involves submission (at least to an extent we shall explore in a moment) to the views of the Human Rights Committee as to the state's performance in observing those rights. But that scrutiny is contingent on exhausting domestic remedies. The logic of the system is that, ideally, domestic courts hearing rights cases will address the same substantive issues as might be brought ultimately before the international tribunal. Indeed, this logic supported adoption of the Human Rights Act in the UK, for it made little sense that UK cases

---

[18] See *Derbyshire County Council* v. *Times Newspapers Ltd* [1993] AC 534, 551.

could end in Strasbourg without UK courts first having the opportunity to implement the ECHR in their decisions.[19]

And so one reaches the set of questions posed at the beginning of this essay. If there are to be competing conceptions of what rights mean and the impact they are to have in particular fields of public or private life, then whose conception prevails? To the extent it is for courts at all, then is it the national or the international body that decides what rights mean? Who has ultimate authority in rights adjudication?

V   ULTIMATE AUTHORITY IN RIGHTS INTERPRETATION

In what follows I will confine myself mainly to the position of NZ, and similarly situated countries, in relation to the ICCPR and decisions of the Human Rights Committee. The question is whether and in what sense New Zealand courts are bound, when searching for the meaning and effect of rights, to follow decisions of the Human Rights Committee.

When reckoning with the ICCPR in the course of deciding Bill of Rights cases, New Zealand judges have four primary sources of potential influence. The first is the ICCPR text itself. There are Bill of Rights cases where direct recourse to text forms part of the reasoning process in determining the meaning and impact of a Bill of Rights right. Sometimes it assists in the reasoning process of determining what rights mean and how they apply;[20] other times the point of referring to the ICCPR text is to note that the particular right in question does not follow the Covenant wording and that this is significant.[21] The other three sources of influence are, first, the Committee's comments made in the course of Country Reports under Article 40; second, its General Comments;[22] and third, its "views" adopted in individual communications under the OP. It is the final source—"views"—with which we are concerned here.[23]

It now assists to separate out two possible ways in which one might say that the Human Rights Committee's "views" in a particular case are, or should be treated as, "binding".

---

[19] In New Zealand somewhat similar reasoning prompted Cooke P to hold in *Tavita* v. *Minister of Immigration* [1994] 2 NZLR 257, 266 (CA) that the ICCPR and the CRC could be treated as incorporated into law as *implied* mandatory relevant considerations in appropriate cases, since otherwise the state's performance might be the subject of adverse comment before the relevant Committee when its own courts had not had a chance to address those same issues.

[20] *Re J (An Infant): B and B* v. *Director-General of Social Welfare* [1996] 2 NZLR134 (CA).

[21] *R* v. *Goodwin* [1993] 2 NZLR 153; *R* v. *Barlow* (1995) 2 HRNZ 635 (CA).

[22] In theory there might be interpretations of ICCPR provisions made in the course of state against state complaints, but since there have not been any of those this source can be discounted.

[23] I am not aware of any suggestion that the interpretations adopted or assumed in Country Reports should be binding or even regarded as persuasive authority in relation to other countries. Even so, on particular issues, it is not unknown for persons to research the interpretative position apparently taken or assumed by the Committee and individual states parties across a range of country reports. They at least serve as indications of the position the Committee may take in Views.

First, there is the question of whether a state party must accede, when a determination has been made against it in a particular case, to the Committee's "views" that there has been a violation, and perhaps as to the required action to resolve it. This is the question that Scott Davidson addresses in the next essay, noting the views of some Committee members that the "views" are binding because the Covenant obligation to provide a remedy is triggered by a Committee determination that a remedy is required. Davidson expresses reservations about that view, albeit suggesting that New Zealand should act as if it were correct. Happily this is not yet a practical issue for New Zealand; the eight communications brought against it since accession to the OP in 1989 having all been held inadmissible or dismissed on the merits.[24]

Second, there is the very different question of whether, as a general matter, domestic courts are bound, when interpreting the ICCPR or domestic provisions implementing it, to follow the jurisprudence of the Human Rights Committee as to what a particular right means. It might be said that a state party is so bound, whether the relevant decisions of the Committee originate from that state or from any other party.

Currently, the status quo in New Zealand is that courts do not regard themselves as bound by Committee decisions on rights and this is also the position in Canada, where allegiance is plainly to the Canadian Charter of Rights and Freedoms.[25] This approach has been affirmed at least twice by the New Zealand Court of Appeal, and is not particularly controversial, although on each occasion there is the suggestion that a revisiting of the issue is possible. In *R* v. *Goodwin (No 2)* Cooke P noted that, in any event, Committee decisions were of considerable persuasive authority.[26] In *Nicholls* v. *Registrar of the Court of Appeal*[27] Eichelbaum CJ observed that it was "unnecessary to consider" whether it was open to a New Zealand court to reach a different conclusion from the Human Rights Committee, but repeated that such decisions were of "considerable persuasive authority" and that "given the strength and logic of the international jurisprudence"—that is, in relation to the particular provision at issue there—"it would be untenable for New Zealand to be seen as striking out in the opposite direction".[28]

In contrast, Elizabeth Evatt, a former member of the United Nations Human Rights Committee, expresses the following opinion as to the authority of the Committee's "views" in her essay in this part:

"The view put forward [that is, by her], based on the nature of the Covenant as an international instrument, on the Committee's work and on the legal status of the Committee's views is that those views should be considered highly influential, if not authoritative."

---

[24] These are noted in Davidson's contribution in this volume.

[25] The most recent illustrative case is *United States* v. *Burns* [2001] 1 SCR 283 in which s. 7 of the Canadian Charter was interpreted to preclude the extradition of two accused persons to the USA unless assurances were given that they would not face the death penalty. In this decision the Charter secured a level of protection that the ICCPR did not guarantee.

[26] [1993] 2 NZLR 390, 393.

[27] [1998] 2 NZLR 385.

[28] *Ibid*, 404.

That proposition is advanced as a "view" to be "put forward", accepting that it is not the current position and no doubt accepting also that the Committee is not in a position to force acceptance of the position. Even so, it prompts me to defend the status quo, wherein the Committee's "views" are appropriately regarded as influential but not binding.

First, and most obviously, there are concerns about the selection of Committee members and about Committee processes, including its workload. But I do not base my concerns on these, since even if the system were reformed to the extent that it is reasonable to expect it might, my concerns would remain. And there are issues about the Committee's minimalist reasoning style, which is given to lengthy recitations of the opposing arguments followed by somewhat brief and conclusory reasons for the actual result reached, and which may throw no light on general principles that would resolve cases on different facts. But this may change too, and there are already some signs that it is changing.

Next, I am not oblivious to the fact that the practical significance of treating the Committee's decisions as binding might be small given the likelihood that points of distinction will usually be available to courts unwilling to adopt the Committee's approach on particular issues—a feature that Ian Leigh notes in his review of the early UK experience with the Human Rights Act 1998.

Nor am I oblivious to the fact that few people are presently pressing the conception that the Human Rights Committee's "views" are binding in the sense I am now discussing. It seems to me, nonetheless, that it is worth briefly exploring, as a matter of principle, whether it is desirable that they be so. I am not persuaded that it is.

The real problem is the danger in a single body having a monopoly on the meaning of rights. To say that rights are universal does not commit one to a sole universal adjudicator. It leads more naturally to the proposition that a concern for human rights arises out of all societies in some form or another. While there will be disagreements about rights, and an internal if not an external means for resolving those disagreements is required, it still does not follow that ultimate authority must reside at the international level. The ICCPR reflects the commitment of many states to a set of fundamental rights, but (to take up the point made by Grant Huscroft in relation to bills of rights) that is not the same thing as a commitment to the "views" of the 18 members of the Human Rights Committee interpreting those rights. It is true that this approach will lead, as Elizabeth Evatt notes, to some states defending, as culturally appropriate, conduct that appears to offend Covenant rights. But it is a mistake to regard this problem as being resolved simply by the conception that the Committee's "views" are authoritative. Even if we grant that the Committee were likely to be right on the merits in all these cases, and even if, contrary to fact, there were an enforcement mechanism, the fact would remain that cultures cannot be changed though coercion of this kind. The most that can be expected is a long-term transformation of a cultural practice or world view through the exchange or perhaps even the one-way impartation of ideas. The ICCPR and its procedures, and the human rights treaties generally, form a part of this process, but coercion is not a component. For the ICCPR is more about community than it is about a coercive hierarchy, as an examination of its procedures for the so-far-unused state versus state complaint will reveal.[29]

The suggested "top down" approach in which the Committee's "views" are authoritative strikes me as the opposite of what is now needed for the renewal of civil society in a time of disengagement by citizens and declining regard for national politicians. There is a growing resentment of matters of local import being settled in far away places by unknown people.[30] There is also a justified perception that the enthusiasm of people for recourse to international tribunals turns ultimately on their views about the prospects of success in relitigating domestic battles in those forums. This is human nature and understandable, but it does show how quickly the tables might turn. If the Committee were, for example, to declare that a foetus had a right to life with which States must reckon in abortion law, one can see the realignment that would rapidly take place about the weight to be given to its decisions and its place in the scheme of things. And the Committee will soon have to reckon with same-sex marriage, and the way it does this will have important ramifications both for its future as well as in determining the constituency of advocates for and against its being regarded as the ultimate authority on rights issues.

There is also a proper concern about human rights being surrendered to "experts" in the first place. While human rights *law* is undoubtedly a specialist field requiring expertise, human rights themselves are and ought to be the concern of everyone. A respect for them grows first and foremost out of family and community and a nation's own important values. In this regard I believe the majority of the Supreme Court of Canada got it right when in *Baker v. Minister for Immigration and Ethnic Affairs*[31] it steered a steady course through the well-known arguments that unincorporated treaty obligations (making the interests of a child paramount in decisions affecting it) are a mandatory component of a lawful deportation decision, or at least a "legitimate expectation" of the potential deportee. In similar cases the New Zealand Court of Appeal held, in obiter but considered dicta, that a relevant but unincorporated treaty was a mandatory relevant consideration in this field,[32] while the High Court of Australia reached the same end point by focusing on the deportee's legitimate expectation that the treaty obligations would be considered.[33] The insight of the Canadian Court, however, was that a concern for the interests of children who are dependent on a potential deportee arises out of the values underlying *Canadian* law, and could be seen as a part of the legal requirements of a valid deportation decision on that basis alone. True, that feature of Canadian

---

[29] See Arts. 41 and 42. The emphasis throughout is on mediation and conciliation.

[30] Trade treaties and the popular movement in opposition to them exemplifies this. As Forrest McDonald puts it (*States' Rights and The Union: Imperium in Imperio, 1776 – 1876* (Lawrence, University Press of Kansas, 2000), quoted in *Atlantic Monthly*, March 2001, p. 82): "Programmed into the human soul is a preference for the near and familiar and a suspicion of the remote and abstract . . .".

[31] [1999] 2 SCR 817. See K Knop, "Here and There: International Law in Domestic Courts" (2000) 32 *NYU J Int'l Law & Pol* 501 for valuable commentary.

[32] *Tavita* v. *Minister of Immigration* [1994] 2 NZLR 257 (CA).

[33] *Minister of State for Immigration and Ethnic Affairs* v. *Teoh* (1995) 183 CLR 273.

policy was underscored and affirmed by the ICCPR, but that was not its principal source.[34] That seems right to me: one needs no international obligation to hold that regard should, in appropriate circumstances, be had to the interests of children and that this is what a statute might envisage. For the same reasons we ought not to need international obligations to tell us that persons have rights to life, expression, religion and so on. While some have criticised the Canadian approach for not putting international obligation at the forefront of its reasoning, in my view it was correct to regard the international obligation as a mere affirmation of that which resided in Canadian values. The international obligations are there as part of the appropriate checks and balances devised by the world community in 1948, but they are not the *source* of the principles they affirm and nor ought they be made the starting point in rights cases.

And finally, there is the question of who protects us from the human rights protectors. At bottom, it should not be forgotten that courts and commissions enforcing human rights statutes, and international bodies opining on international human rights standards, are, respectively, arms of the state and the international order. The history of rights adjudication in the western common law world reveals that courts may sometimes disappoint (*Liversidge* v. *Anderson*;[35] *Plessy* v. *Ferguson*;[36] *Hertzberg* v. *Finland*[37]), and may sometimes even be perverse (*Scott* v. *Sandford*;[38] and, as a significant number of Americans would see it, *Roe* v. *Wade*[39]). This is not a reason for abandoning high expectations of courts and tribunals, but it does remind us that judicial decisions are a product of time and culture, and that in the long term it is the vitality of that culture and its regard for human rights that is most important. In maintaining that vitality and regard, we would do well to continue to keep in mind Judge Learned Hand's advice: liberty (and if he were speaking now I suspect he would say "human rights" as well) lies in the hearts of men and women, and must be nurtured there if courts are to be able to do their job.[40] The renewed *international* emphasis on human rights is itself helpful in keeping human rights in our vision. But it ought to be seen as a "backstop", there for the cases in which a nation's own standards do not supply the answers to the questions that human rights raise, and where the articulation of an alternative vision is helpful as a check. My point has simply been that an international committee's vision of human rights is not the only vision, and that the courts of states parties (and litigants before them)

---

[34] Some years ago at a competitive moot in the Auckland Law School a student submitted to the judge that the "right to marry and found a family was affirmed in the international instruments". The presiding High Court judge, married with children and grandchildren and from a legal background in which the only international instruments to cross his desk would have been extradition and mutual assistance treaties, raised his eyebrows and with a palpable cynicism responded "Really? Oh, good". Well, you had to be there.

[35] [1942] AC 206.

[36] 163 US 537 (1896).

[37] Comm No 61/1979, 2 April 1982.

[38] 60 US 393 (1856).

[39] 410 US 113 (1973).

[40] L Hand, "The Spirit of Liberty" in I Dillard (ed.), *The Spirit of Liberty: Papers and Addresses by Learned Hand* (New York, Knopf, 1953) 189, 190.

must be free to advance competing visions without it being suggested that the matter has already been resolved by the Human Rights Committee whose decision is binding.

So let us think hard before concluding that the views of the Human Rights Committee should have more than a persuasive authority. Indeed, the position is that persuasive authority in human rights cases now abounds in the jurisprudence of appellate courts around the world. As the logic of international human rights law requires, increasingly human rights issues are confronted in the domestic courts of States parties that have implemented those rights. In this state of affairs, the Human Rights Committee also has much to learn from—but is equally not bound by—the way in which the highest domestic courts of States parties have resolved rights issues. That may or may not be the status quo—one suspects that Committee members already have regard to these sources—but it is a sound way forward. In a secular age, where human rights standards serve as a new secular moral code, a degree of humility in declaring human rights standards is still appropriate. For, in contentious cases, all parties are likely to be claiming that, if not God, then the spirit of human rights is on their side.

15

The Impact of International
Human Rights on Domestic Law

ELIZABETH EVATT

I INTRODUCTION: ADDING AN INTERNATIONAL DIMENSION

The viewpoint presented by this paper is that of a practitioner in international human rights law, and in particular that of a member of the United Nations Human Rights Committee, the body which monitors compliance by States with their obligations under the International Covenant on Civil and Political Rights ("the Covenant").[1]

International human rights law began a period of rapid expansion in the post-World War II era. Until that time, with few exceptions, the rights of individuals were a matter of purely domestic concern, within the sovereign jurisdiction of each State. Although the United Nations Charter recognised the principle of non-interference in domestic affairs,[2] it introduced a new dimension which was to have far reaching consequences. It required member States to undertake to promote universal respect for and observance of the human rights of everyone, everywhere.[3] Machinery was established to define these rights in a series of instruments, including the Universal Declaration of Human Rights and the two Covenants, which collectively are termed the International Bill of Human Rights.[4]

States have undertaken internationally to advance and respect human rights. But for rights to be effective for individuals these undertakings have to be matched by action taken by States at the domestic level.[5] In the past fifty years much effort has been spent on the problem of how to ensure that States make rights a reality for people through their domestic legal systems. This paper focuses on one aspect of this problem, namely, how the Human Rights Committee monitors compliance by States with their obligation to implement the rights recognised by the Covenant.

---

[1] Adopted by the General Assembly on 16 December 1966; entered into force 23 March 1976.

[2] Art. 2(7).

[3] Arts. 55 and 56.

[4] Arts. 62(2) and 68 provide for the Commission on Human Rights. The Universal Declaration of Human Rights was adopted by the General Assembly on 10 December 1948. The International Covenant on Economic, Social and Cultural Rights was adopted by the General Assembly on 19 December 1966 and entered into force on 3 January 1976.

[5] R Higgins, *Problems and Process: International Law and How We Use It* (Oxford, Clarendon Press, 1994) 96: "International human-rights law is the source of the obligation, albeit that the obligation is reflected in the content of the domestic law."

II THE COMMITTEE AND ITS ROLE

The Human Rights Committee ("the Committee") is an independent expert body established by the Covenant.[6] The 18 members of the Committee are elected by the States parties but serve in their personal capacities. Their expertise is drawn from academia, from judicial practice and from human rights practice and activism. States parties are required to submit reports to the Committee within a year of becoming a party and at intervals thereafter set by the Committee.[7] The Committee engages in dialogue with the representatives of each State on the basis of the State's written report. Committee members make comments and ask questions. After the dialogue the Committee draws up its concluding observations, pointing to any weaknesses or gaps in the law or practice of the State which may leave rights without adequate protection and making recommendations.

The Committee is competent to receive and consider communications from individuals who complain that their rights under the Covenant have been violated; this applies only where the relevant State has ratified the Optional Protocol to the Covenant. Ninety-two States, out of 145 States parties have done so.[8] The Committee also drafts General Comments, setting out its views on the scope of particular provisions of the Covenant.[9] These Comments draw on the Committee's experience in reviewing State reports, and in communications.

To understand the Committee's thinking about the interpretation and application of the Covenant, consideration should be given to its concluding observations on State reports, its views in individual communications and its General Comments. All three sources are drawn on in this paper.

III HOW DOMESTIC LAW SHOULD GIVE EFFECT TO HUMAN RIGHTS:
THE OBLIGATIONS

A Primary Obligations under the Covenant

When the Covenant was being drafted, it was debated whether States should be required to make the Covenant itself a part of domestic law, and whether States would have to bring their legal systems into line with the Covenant before

---

[6] ICCPR, Art. 28.

[7] ICCPR, Art. 40. The current practice of the Committee is to set the date for the next report after its consideration of the report from each State.

[8] The annual reports of the Committee include lists of States parties.

[9] *Compilation of General Comments and General Recommendations Adopted by Human Rights Treaty Bodies* HRI/GEN/1/Rev.3, 15 Aug 1997. General Comments can also be found in the Committee's Annual Reports to the General Assembly, and on the web site: www.unhchr.ch/tbs/doc.nsf.

ratification or within a reasonable or specified time thereafter.[10] In the outcome, there is no express requirement to incorporate the Covenant in domestic legal systems.[11] It is left to States parties to determine how to implement their obligations.[12] On the other hand, the drafters rejected progressive implementation in favour of an immediate obligation by States parties to respect and ensure Covenant rights immediately from the time of ratification.[13] A State may limit its obligations by means of reservations; reservations which are incompatible with the object and purpose of the Covenant are not permitted.[14]

In practice, this paper suggests, the Committee leans strongly to the view that implementation of the Covenant is not likely to be effective unless States include Covenant rights and freedoms within their domestic legal systems.

B Making Rights Effective

Article 2 of the Covenant sets out what States must do to make rights effective. Paragraph (1) provides that States parties are to respect and to ensure Covenant rights to everyone without distinction of any kind. Equality and non-discrimination are fundamental principles underlying the Covenant. Paragraph (2) of Article 2 requires States to take steps, in accordance with their constitutional processes and with the Covenant, to adopt such legislative or other measures as may be necessary to give effect to Covenant rights where these are not already in place. Paragraphs (1) and (2) give rise to specific obligations on the part of the State. As a minimum, the State should review relevant laws; often it will need to enact implementing legislation.

Most Covenant rights need to be protected by specific legislative measures. For example, States must ensure that legal measures dealing with arrest and detention comply with Article 9. The prohibition of torture under Article 7, of slavery under Article 8, protection of the right to life under Article 6 and of privacy under Article 17 all require legal sanctions of general application. The Committee considers that States should enact laws in respect of violence against women, including domestic

---

[10] M Bossuyt, *Guide to the Travaux Préparatoires of the International Covenant on Civil and Political Rights* (Dordrecht; Boston, M Nijhoff, 1987) 57–62.

[11] M Nowak, *UN Covenant on Civil and Political Rights: CCPR Commentary* (Kehl, Engel, 1993) 54; Bossuyt, above n. 10 at 62.

[12] General Comment No 3, Art. 2: Implementation at the National Level (13th session, 1981): "1. The Committee notes that art 2 of the Covenant generally leaves it to the States parties concerned to choose their method of implementation in their territories . . ." *Compilation of General Comments*, above n. 9 at 4.

[13] Nowak, above n. 11 at 56, 58ff; D McGoldrick, *The Human Rights Committee: Its Role in the Development of the International Covenant on Civil and Political Rights* (Oxford, Clarendon Press, 1991) 273–4. Note, however, that States are asked to report on "progress . . . in the enjoyment of rights" under Art. 40.

[14] Vienna Convention on the Law of Treaties, signed at Vienna, 23 May 1969, entry into force 27 January 1980, Art. 19(3). This paper does not discuss the implications of reservations. See the Committee's General Comment No 24 on Issues Relating to Reservations (52nd session, 1994) *Compilation of General Comments*, above n. 9 at 42.

violence and rape, which threaten the right to life and to security of person.[15] Laws should also prohibit discrimination on the grounds specified in Article 26 in public and private contexts. Preferential treatment may be necessary to bring a disadvantaged group into a position equal to that of the rest of the population.[16] Where the Covenant permits rights and freedoms to be restricted by law, as in the case of freedom of expression and the right to peaceful assembly, the relevant laws must comply strictly with the Covenant.[17]

In addition to legislative measures, States will usually need to adopt "other measures" of a non-legislative kind to make Covenant rights effective.[18] For example, States should ensure that those who exercise public power, such as government officials, judges, police and security forces, are trained to understand and respect fully the rights of individuals. This calls for revision of operating procedures, and for training and education programmes.[19] Specific policies and programmes are needed to meet the obligation under Article 10 to ensure that prison conditions meet minimum standards.[20] Measures of protection for children, required by Article 24, include programmes and services as well as legal measures.

In some contexts positive measures may be needed to protect rights from violation by private parties. For example, in its general comment on Article 27, the Committee stressed the obligation of States to protect the rights of members of minorities through positive measures against acts of the State party or acts of third persons.[21] To comply with Article 26, States may need to take positive steps to overcome discrimination and discriminatory attitudes, whether by government agencies or private parties.[22]

C Effective Remedies

Paragraph (3) of Article 2 recognises that rights without remedies have little value. It requires States to ensure that effective and enforceable remedies are available to

---

[15] See eg, the Committee's concluding observations in October 1998 on Japan, para. 30 and Austria, para. 16; and in July 1999 on Poland, para. 14, Mexico, para. 16, Cambodia, para. 17, and Romania, para. 8. These all appear in the Annual Report of the Committee for 1999 (A/54/40) at paras. 172, 194, 347, 328, 309, and 367 respectively.

[16] General Comment No 18 on Non-discrimination (37th session, 1989) *Compilation of General Comments*, above n. 9 at 26, para. 10.

[17] Examples are Art. 12(3), 18(3), 19(3) and 22.

[18] General Comment No 3 on Art. 2: Implementation at the National Level (13th session, 1981) *Compilation of General Comments*, above n. 9 at 4, para. 1: "to ensure the enjoyment of these rights to all individuals under their jurisdiction . . . calls for specific activities by the States parties".

[19] General Comment No 20 on Art. 7 (44th session, 1992) *Compilation of General Comments*, above n. 9 at 31, para. 10.

[20] General Comment No 21 on Art. 10 (44th session, 1992) *Compilation of General Comments*, above n. 9 at 33.

[21] General Comment No 23, The Rights of Minorities (50th session, 1994) *Compilation of General Comments*, above n. 9 at 39, para. 6.1.

[22] General Comment No 18 on Non-discrimination (37th session, 1989) *Compilation of General Comments*, above n. 9 at 26, para. 10.

individuals in case of violation of rights. The right to claim a remedy is to be determined by competent judicial, administrative or legislative authorities or by other competent authorities of the State party. States have an express obligation to develop the possibility of judicial remedies.[23]

The Covenant does not, in general, prescribe what kinds of remedies are to be provided in respect of particular rights.[24] However, to be "effective", a remedy must end the violation, overcome or compensate for its effects and ensure that no further violations will occur. The existence of remedies is a necessary aspect of preventing and deterring future violations. The most common remedy is compensation. The Committee proposes compensation for many violations, including inhuman treatment and discrimination.[25] Domestic legal systems should provide for the award of compensation or other forms of reparation or restitution to individuals whose rights have been violated, determined ideally by an independent court or tribunal.

Where a violation or abuse is continuing or may occur again, measures must be taken to end the abuse and to avoid further abuses of a similar kind.[26] For example, laws which cannot operate compatibly with the Covenant should be set aside, modified or reviewed to avoid any further violation of rights.[27] Unless domestic courts have constitutional power to override or limit the application of such laws, legislation may be necessary.

The Committee has held in several cases that while private individuals may seek remedies, such as compensation or reparation for violation of their rights, they have no right under the Covenant to demand that the State criminally prosecute another person as part of their remedy.[28] But the State's obligations to make Covenant rights effective require that it investigate abuses and take appropriate action against alleged perpetrators. Where human rights violations are widespread and endemic, such as where extra-judicial executions, disappearances, torture or arbitrary detentions are

---

[23] For history of the provision, see Nowak, above n. 11 at 60; Bossuyt, above n. 10 at 64ff.

[24] The Covenant imposes a specific obligation to provide compensation in two cases, Arts. 9(5) and 14(6).

[25] For example, *Adam* v. *Czech Republic* 586/1994, 23 July 1996, HRC Annual Report 1996 (A/51/40) vol II p. 165 (discrimination); *Antonio Viana Acosta* v. *Uruguay* 110/1981 29 March 1984, *Selected Decisions of the Human Rights Committee under the Optional Protocol* vol II (CCPR/C/OP/2) (New York, United Nations, 1990) 148 (serious beatings); *Young* v. *Jamaica* 615/1995, 4 November 1997, HRC Annual Report 1998 (A/53/40) vol II p. 69 (violations of Arts. 7 and 10.1); *Sterling* v. *Jamaica* 598/1994, 22 July 1996, HRC Annual Report 1996 (A/51/40) vol II p. 214; *Williams* v. *Jamaica* 609/1995, 4 November 1997, HRC Annual Report 1998 (A/53/40) vol II p. 63 (medical treatment proposed).

[26] *Antonio Viana Acosta* v. *Uruguay* 110/1981, 29 March 84, *Selected Decisions*, vol II, above n. 25 at 148; *Young* v. *Jamaica* 615/1995, 4 November 97, HRC Annual Report 1998 (A/53/40) vol II p. 69; *Daniel Larrosa* 88/1981, 29 March 1983, *Selected Decisions*, vol II, above n. 25 at 118; *Matthews* v. *Trinidad and Tobago* 569/1993, 31 March 1998, HRC Annual Report 1998 (A/53/40) vol II p. 30.

[27] *Toonen* v. *Australia* 488/1992, 31 March 1994, HRC Annual Report 1994 (A/49/40) vol II p. 226. *Adam* v. *Czech Republic* 586/1994, 23 July 1996, HRC Annual Report 1996 (A/51/40) vol II p. 165.

[28] *HCMA* v. *Netherlands* 213/1986, 30 March 1989, HRC Annual Report 1989 (A/44/40) p. 267; *SE* v. *Argentina* 275/1988, 26 March 1990, HRC Annual Report 1990 (A/45/40) vol II p. 159 at 164; *RA et al* v. *Argentina* 343–5/1988, 26 March 1990, HRC Annual Report 1990 (A/45/40) vol II p. 191.

alleged to have been committed by police or security forces, the State must commit itself to investigating the circumstances, bringing perpetrators to justice and taking positive steps to avoid further abuses, as well as providing compensation to victims.[29]

D Access to Rights and Remedies

The Committee expects States to publish the Covenant in local languages and to ensure that the community is fully informed about rights and how to claim them.[30] The Committee encourages States to ensure that individuals have access to courts and tribunals to seek remedies, and that legal aid is provided where necessary.[31] In other situations it may recommend that States establish independent agencies, such as an Ombudsman or a human rights commission, to receive individual complaints, to monitor implementation of rights and to report to government on any deficiencies in that regard.[32] If provision is made for conciliation or mediation as a means of negotiating a remedy, for example, where it is claimed that rights have been violated by private parties, this should not exclude the possibility of recourse to a court or tribunal if the process fails.

IV STATE PRACTICE

Although States can, in principle, choose how to implement the wide-ranging obligations imposed by Article 2, they must perform those obligations in good faith, and they may not use their domestic law as an excuse for not doing so.[33] The Committee's task in the reporting process is to ascertain whether each State

---

[29] *Chaparro* v. *Colombia* 612/1995, 29 July 1997, HRC Annual Report 1997 (A/52/40) vol II p. 173; *Celis Laureano* v. *Peru* 540/1993, 25 March 1996, HRC Annual Report 1996 (A/51/40) vol II p. 108. See concluding observations on Colombia, HRC Annual Report 1997 (A/52/40) vol I pp. 44ff; *Bautista* v. *Colombia* 563/1993, 27 October 1995, HRC Annual Report 1996 (A/51/40) vol II p. 132, para. 8.6; *McTaggart* v. *Jamaica* 749/1997, 31 March 1998, HRC Annual Report 1998 (A/53/40) vol II p. 221. In regard to amnesty laws see: *Rodriguez* v. *Uruguay* 322/1988, 19 July 1994, HRC Annual Report 1994 (A/49/40) vol II p. 5. General Comment No 20 on Art. 7 (44th session, 1992) *Compilation of General Comments*, above n. 9 at 31, paras. 14–15 stresses the duty to investigate human rights violations, to guarantee freedom from such violations within its jurisdiction and to ensure that similar violations do not occur in the future.

[30] General Comment No 3 on Art. 2: Implementation at the National Level (13th session, 1981) *Compilation of General Comments*, above n. 9 at 4, para. 2.

[31] Where a condemned prisoner has no means to meet the costs of legal representation in order to pursue a constitutional remedy, and where the interests of justice so require, legal aid should be made available by the State party. *Desmond Taylor* v. *Jamaica* 705/1996, 2 April 1998, HRC Annual Report 1998 (A/53/40) vol II p. 174, para. 7.3 (dissenting views at 182).

[32] The establishment or strengthening of national institutions has been recommended. See Concluding Observations on: Ukraine, HRC Annual Report 1995 (A/50/40) vol I para. 324; Mexico, HRC Annual Report 1994 (A/49/40) vol I paras. 166ff, 178; Italy, HRC Annual Report 1994 (A/49/40) vol I paras. 271ff, 284; Tunisia, HRC Annual Report 1995 (A/50/40) vol I para. 92.

[33] Vienna Convention, above n. 14, Arts. 26, 27. See Higgins, above n. 5 at 205, referring to the *SS Wimbledon* 1923 PCIJ Ser. A No 1.

has effectively implemented its obligations. In doing so, it has to grapple with 145 different legal systems and as many variations on the theme of implementation.

States can be grouped loosely into categories: those which incorporate the Covenant into domestic law, those which protect rights through the Constitution or other entrenched law, and those which rely on legislative or other solutions. It should not be implied from this discussion that the level of protection of human rights depends solely on whether the Covenant has been incorporated into domestic law, or on the formal legal framework for the protection of rights. The inquiry is about the optimum means of complying with the Covenant and this involves aspects other than the formal legal system. Many examples could be provided of States which do incorporate Covenant rights into their laws, or which have extensive constitutional protection of rights, but where rights are not respected or are violated with impunity. By contrast, States which have a high level of respect for the rule of law and for rights of the individual may provide a reasonable level of protection, even if they have not incorporated the Covenant into their laws or provided specific remedies for every kind of violation. The discussion that follows is confined to States which do have basic respect for the rule of law, and focuses on the different ways that States without entrenched protection of rights have implemented their obligations under the Covenant.

A Incorporation of Covenant Rights

In some States ratification of the Covenant (which may require legislative approval) incorporates it into domestic law, often with a status superior to ordinary national law. In these States, national courts can enforce Covenant rights directly, and the effect can be to invalidate or render inapplicable national laws which are incompatible with Covenant rights. Sometimes, however, incorporation of the Covenant into domestic law gives its provisions only the status of ordinary laws. Although Covenant rights are enforceable in the courts, they can be overridden by later domestic legislation.[34]

In States such as France,[35] the Netherlands,[36] Switzerland[37] and Argentina,[38] where the Covenant has been made part of domestic law with special status, and

---

[34] The Committee regretted that Peru recently changed its Constitutional provisions to reduce the status of the Covenant to that of ordinary laws; Concluding Observation, HRC Annual Report 1997 (A/52/40) vol I para. 152.

[35] Constitution Art. 55. The Covenant is accorded priority over simple laws. See *Faurisson* v. *France* 550/1993, 8 November 1996, HRC Annual Report 1997 (A/52/40) vol II Annex VI I p. 84; *Hopu* v. *France* 549/1993, 29 July 1997, HRC Annual Report 1997 (A/52/40) vol II Annex VI H p. 70.

[36] Constitution Arts. 93, 94. Treaty provisions override inconsistent legislation, if they are self-executing. See Annual Report of the HRC 1989 (A/44/40) paras. 192–4. The State representatives referred to numerous cases applying the Covenant.

[37] Annual Report 1997 (A/52/40) vol I para. 89: The Covenant forms an integral part of the legal system with a status higher than domestic law, its provisions may be directly invoked by private individuals before the courts and Swiss courts have on numerous occasions referred to the provisions of the Covenant and to the Committee's general comments.

[38] Constitution, Arts. 31 and 75(22), HRC Annual Report 1995 (A/50/40) vol I para. 147.

where there is a respect for the rule of law and human rights, there should be a high level of compliance with the Covenant. If violations occur, individuals are able to seek remedies. Because of the status of the Covenant there are likely to be references to its provisions and to the jurisprudence of the Committee in court decisions.[39] Problems of implementation may arise from differing interpretations of rights or lack of clarity as to how inconsistencies between the Constitution and the Covenant are resolved, or whether Covenant rights would prevail over incompatible domestic laws.[40]

The full incorporation of Covenant rights into domestic law is commended and encouraged by the Committee,[41] especially where national courts have regard to the jurisprudence of the Committee in interpreting and applying Covenant principles.

B Entrenched Protection, Canada and the United States

In States which do not incorporate treaties into domestic law, Covenant rights may nevertheless be guaranteed by constitutional provisions or by entrenched legislation which overrides laws incompatible with their protection. If the rights so protected are expressed in terms similar to the Covenant, the Courts may draw on the jurisprudence of the Committee or other international human rights bodies. But in some cases the domestic provisions differ materially from the Covenant. The United States and Canada are in this group.

Ratification of the Covenant by Canada does not give it direct legal effect. However, the Canadian Charter of Rights and Freedoms[42] provides entrenched protection of rights which are similar in substance to those of the Covenant, though not expressed in exactly the same language. That protection is not absolute. Federal or provincial legislatures may exclude the operation of the Charter on a particular Act or provision for up to five years.[43] Furthermore, Charter rights may be subject to such reasonable limits as prescribed by law as can be demonstrably justified in a free and democratic society.[44] The Canadian courts often refer to the decisions of international human rights bodies in interpreting the Charter. Canada

---

[39] See Committee's Concluding Observations on Switzerland, HRC Annual Report 1997 (A/52/40) vol I para. 89ff.

[40] See Committee's Concluding Observations: Tanzania, HRC Annual Report 1993 (A/48/40) vol I para. 179ff, 184; Japan, HRC Annual Report 1994 (A/49/40) vol I para. 98 and HRC Annual Report 1999 (A/54/40) vol I para. 150; Malta, HRC Annual Report 1994 (A/49/40) vol I para. 117ff; Jordan, HRC Annual Report 1994 (A/49/40) vol I para. 227ff; Nepal, HRC Annual Report 1995 (A/50/40) vol I para. 65; Estonia, HRC Annual Report 1996 (A/51/40) vol I para. 108.

[41] For example, in regard to Finland the Committee noted with appreciation "the reform of the Finnish Constitution in 1995 to incorporate the provisions of the Covenant and other human rights instruments into the Constitution . . ." (Concluding Observations of the Human Rights Committee: Finland, 8 April 1998, CCPR/C/79/Add 91, para. 3).

[42] Constitution Act, 1982, Sched. B, Part I, Canadian Charter of Rights and Freedoms.

[43] Canadian Charter of Rights and Freedoms, s. 33: the "notwithstanding" provision.

[44] Under s. 1 of the Charter, the rights and freedoms are guaranteed "subject only to such reasonable limits prescribed by law as can be demonstrably justified in a free and democratic society".

is also a party to the Optional Protocol and has been the source of communications, dealing with such matters as minority and indigenous rights, discrimination, extradition, deportation, freedom of expression, religion and association.

While acknowledging that Canada's human rights record is good, the Committee has found it to be in violation of Covenant rights in a few instances, as a result of differing interpretations[45] or because the Charter did not apply.[46] When considering Canada's report under Article 40 of the Covenant, the Committee drew attention to gaps in the level of protection under the Charter.[47]

The United States Bill of Rights protects certain rights and freedoms and can be applied by the courts to strike down incompatible laws. It does not cover all rights and freedoms set out in the Covenant, which the US ratified in 1992.[48] Although the US Constitution provides for treaties duly made by the US to be enforceable in the courts as supreme law,[49] the US made a number of Reservations, Declarations and Understandings in respect of the Covenant,[50] one effect of these being to exclude the Covenant from incorporation as a self-executing treaty. The application of certain provisions of the Covenant was excluded, and it was made clear that the US considers certain Covenant rights to have the same meaning as rights included in the Bill of Rights. In effect, the US insulated itself from any actual effect of ratification.

The Committee was critical of the US for ratifying the Covenant without any intention of modifying either federal or state law or practice, and for its significant reservations to rights, including those prohibiting the capital punishment of minors. It asked the United States to withdraw its reservations and to consider ratification of the Optional Protocol.[51]

---

[45] For example, *Bernard Ominayak, Chief of the Lubicon Lake Band* v. *Canada* 167/1984, 26 March 1990, HRC Annual Report 1990 (A/45/40) vol II p. 1 (Art. 27); *Ng* v. *Canada*, 469/1991, 5 November 1993, HRC Annual Report 1994 (A/49/40) vol II p. 189 (Art. 7).

[46] *Lovelace* v. *Canada* 24/1977, 30 July 1981, *Selected Decisions of the Human Rights Committee under the Optional Protocol* (CCPR/C/OP/1) 83 (Art. 27); *Ballantyne, Davidson and McIntyre* v. *Canada* 385/1989 and 359/1989, 31 March 1993 HRC Annual Report 1993 (A/48/40) vol II p. 91 (use of "notwithstanding" clause; expression); *Singer* v. *Canada* 455/1991, 26 July 1994, HRC Annual Report 1994 (A/49/40) vol II p. 155; *Gauthier* v. *Canada* 633/1995, 7 April 1999, HRC Annual Report 1999 (A/52/40) vol II p. 93.

[47] Concluding Observations on Canada's Fourth Periodic Report, April 1999, to appear in Annual Report 1999 (A/54/40 at paras. 231 and 232); the Committee's concerns related, inter alia, to Arts. 2, 3 and 26 of the Covenant.

[48] 8 June 1992, with effect from 8 September 1992.

[49] US Constitution, Art. 6(2).

[50] For discussion, see L Lijnzaad, *Reservations to UN-Human Rights Treaties: Ratify and Ruin*, (Dordrecht, Boston: M Nijhoff, 1995) 185ff; D Stewart, "United States Ratification of the Covenant on Civil and Political Rights: The Significance of the Reservations, Understandings, and Declarations" (1993) 42 *DePaul L Rev* 1183.

[51] Human Rights Committee, Concluding Observations on the Initial Report of the United States, HRC Annual Report 1995 (A/50/40) paras. 278, 279, 292. The Committee was particularly concerned at reservations to Art. 6, para. 5, and Art. 7 of the Covenant, which it believed to be incompatible with the object and purpose of the Covenant.

C Legislative Protection of Rights: United Kingdom, New Zealand and Australia

States which do not incorporate the Covenant into domestic law and which do not have constitutional or entrenched protection of rights, may recognise and protect rights by legislation which is modelled to a greater or lesser extent on the Covenant or other international instruments. In these mainly common law countries, some rights may be protected under common law (for example the right to a fair trial). The courts may try to ensure that as far as possible statutory interpretation, the development of the common law and administrative decisions accord with the international obligations undertaken by the State.[52] But unless Covenant rights are part of the common law or are covered by legislation they cannot be enforced directly.[53] Even if Covenant rights and freedoms are enjoyed on a *de facto* basis, the absence of entrenched protection leaves them vulnerable to restriction and erosion by legislation. The United Kingdom, Australia and New Zealand are all within this group.

The United Kingdom implements rights by a combination of common law and legislation, including anti-discrimination laws. But this protection has been far from comprehensive, at least until recently. The UK has been the unsuccessful defendant in many claims taken to the European Court and Commission on Human Rights under the European Convention.[54] In 1995, the Human Rights Committee noted the absence of effective remedies under UK domestic law for many violations of Covenant rights, and observed that implementation of the Covenant in that country was impeded by the combined effects of the non-incorporation of the Covenant into domestic law, the failure to accede to the first Optional Protocol and the absence of a constitutional Bill of Rights.[55]

The situation in the UK changed dramatically with the coming into force of the Human Rights Act 1998. This Act gives legislative effect to rights and freedoms guaranteed under the European Convention on Human Rights,[56] and provides for

---

[52] See eg, *Derbyshire City Council* v. *Times Newspapers Ltd* [1992] 1 QB 770 (CA); *Ministry of Transport* v. *Noort* [1992] 3 NZLR 260 (CA); *Tavita* v. *Minister of Immigration* [1994] 2 NZLR 257 (CA); *Mabo* v. *Queensland (No 2)* (1992) 175 CLR 1; *Minister for Immigration and Ethnic Affairs* v. *Teoh* (1995) 183 CLR 273. See *Developing Human Rights Jurisprudence: The Domestic Application of International Human Rights Norms*, Judicial Colloquium in Bangalore, 24–6 February 1988 (London, Human Rights Unit, Commonwealth Secretariat, 1988). The Bangalore Principles encourage the judiciary to interpret and apply national constitutions and law in the light of universal human rights. See also the Victoria Falls Declaration, *Promotion of the Human Rights of Women and the Girl Child through the Judiciary: Commonwealth Declarations and Strategies for Action* (London, Commonwealth Secretariat, 1997).

[53] *R* v. *Home Secretary, ex parte Brind* [1991] 1 AC 696 (HL); *Minister for Immigration and Ethnic Affairs* v. *Teoh* (1995) 183 CLR 273, 286–7, per Mason CJ and Deane J.

[54] In 1965 the UK accepted the jurisdiction of the European Court of Human Rights, whose decisions are binding. Among the cases in which it was found to be in violation of the Convention were those of *Campbell and Cosans* v. *UK* (1982) 4 EHRR 293 (birching in school); *Dudgeon* v. *UK* (1982) 4 EHRR 149 (privacy, homosexual); and *Brogan* v. *UK* (1989) 11 EHRR 117 and (1991) 13 EHRR 439 (arbitrary detention under anti-terrorism laws).

[55] HRC Annual Report 1995 (A/50/40) vol I paras. 416ff.

[56] Not all rights are covered, s. 1(1)(a).

judicial remedies in case of violation of those rights.[57] Decisions made under the European Convention are to be considered by the courts where relevant.[58] The Act requires both primary and subordinate legislation to be interpreted compatibly with Convention rights if possible, and empowers the courts to make judicial declarations where legislation is found to be incompatible with those rights.[59] However, the incompatible legislation is not thereby overruled or invalidated. Instead, the Minister has power to make remedial orders, subject to Parliamentary approval, to effect necessary amendments to laws.[60]

The Human Rights Committee would probably take the view that the new UK Act, which is based on the European Convention, is not an adequate implementation of the Covenant, because the European Convention does not cover all rights protected by the Covenant.[61] It is likely to press the United Kingdom to give similar treatment to Covenant rights,[62] and to ratify the Optional Protocol.

The New Zealand Bill of Rights Act 1990 is based on the Covenant. Its purpose is to affirm and promote human rights and New Zealand's commitment to the International Covenant on Civil and Political Rights (ICCPR).[63] It enacts, though not fully, the provisions of the Covenant. Limitations similar to those of the Canadian Charter may be imposed in respect of rights and freedoms.[64] Wherever an enactment can be given a meaning that is consistent with the rights and freedoms contained in the Bill of Rights, that meaning is to be preferred to any other meaning.[65] Rights are not entrenched against the effect of later legislation which, in effect displaces the Bill of Rights.[66] However, the attention of Parliament has to be drawn to aspects of draft legislation which may raise questions of compatibility with the Bill of Rights Act.[67] The Act makes no express provision for remedies.

Despite its objectives, the Act omits certain Covenant rights. An example is privacy. In *R v. Gardiner*,[68] where the New Zealand Court of Appeal was considering

---

[57] S. 8 makes specific provision for damages or other appropriate remedies to be awarded by courts to victims of an unlawful act constituting a breach of Convention rights.

[58] S. 2; "decisions" include those of the European Court and Commission of Human Rights and the Committee of Ministers.

[59] Ss. 3 and 4.

[60] S. 10 and Sched. 2.

[61] There is no equivalent to Arts. 26 or 27 of the Covenant. The anti-discrimination provision, Art. 14 of the European Convention on Human Rights, applies only to Convention rights.

[62] The Committee has proposed this to many European States which have incorporated the European Convention. See Concluding Observations: Iceland, HRC Annual Report 1994 (A/49/40) vol I para. 69ff, 80, and HRC Annual Report 1999 (A/54/40) vol I para. 61; Malta, HRC Annual Report 1994 (A/49/40) vol I para. 117ff, 123; Denmark, HRC Annual Report 1997 (A/52/40) vol I para. 65; Austria, HRC Annual Report 1999 (A/54/40) vol I para. 184.

[63] Long title to the New Zealand Bill of Rights Act 1990.

[64] S. 5 provides that the rights and freedoms contained in the Bill of Rights may be subject only to such reasonable limits prescribed by law as can be demonstrably justified in a free and democratic society; cf Canadian Charter Art. 1; European Convention on Human Rights Arts. 6, 8, 9, 10, 11; ICCPR Arts. 21 and 22(2).

[65] S. 6.

[66] S. 4.

[67] The Attorney-General is to bring to the attention of the Parliament any possible inconsistency with rights and freedoms in Bills, s. 7.

[68] (1997) 15 CRNZ 131.

issues relating to the validity of search and seizure under the Bill of Rights, it could not apply the Covenant provisions relating to privacy and could not consider whether the surveillance at issue should be considered arbitrary.

Despite the gaps and differences between its provisions and those of the Covenant, the Bill of Rights Act gives the courts a statutory basis for interpreting and applying many Covenant rights. The Act has opened the way for the courts to refer to decisions of international bodies, and of other national courts applying similar human rights principles.[69] The New Zealand courts have implied a power to give effective remedies where rights are violated.[70] New Zealand is a party to the Optional Protocol, but there have been few decisions and no violation has been found;[71] some cases are pending.

The Human Rights Committee welcomed the New Zealand Bill of Rights Act.[72] The Committee regretted, however, that it did not go far enough, and:[73]

> "that the provisions of the Covenant have not been fully incorporated into domestic law and given an overriding status in the legal system. Article 2, paragraph 2, of the Covenant requires States parties to take such legislative or other measures which may be necessary to give effect to the rights recognized in the Covenant. In this regard the Committee regrets that certain rights guaranteed under the Covenant are not reflected in the Bill of Rights, and that it does not repeal earlier inconsistent legislation and has no higher status than ordinary legislation. The Committee notes that it is expressly possible, under the terms of the Bill of Rights, to enact legislation contrary to its provisions and regrets that this appears to have been done in a few cases."

The Committee recommended the incorporation of all Covenant rights into New Zealand's domestic law, that remedies be provided and that the courts have power to strike down, or decline to give effect to legislation on the ground of inconsistency with Covenant rights.

Australia's implementation of human rights instruments has been affected by its federal system and by the reluctance of the Commonwealth government to encroach upon areas of State responsibility (for example in criminal law), despite

---

[69] For example in Re *"Penthouse (US)" Vol 19, No. 5* [1991] NZAR 289, the Tribunal relied on the decision of the European Court in *Handyside* v. *UK* (1976) 1 EHRR 737 in deciding that sexually explicit material had the protection of freedom of expression; *The Sunday Times* v. *UK (No 1)* (1979) 2 EHRR 245 was considered in *Auckland Area Health Board* v. *Television New Zealand* [1992] 3 NZLR 406 (CA): clear and compelling reasons were required to issue an injunction against a broadcast which an Area Health Board considered defamatory. See also per *Ministry of Transport* v. *Noort, Police* v. *Curran* [1992] 3 NZLR 260 and *Tavita* v. *Minister of Immigration* [1994] 2 NZLR 257 (CA).

[70] *Simpson* v. *AG (Baigent's* case) [1994] 3 NZLR 667 (CA): The BOR implies that effective remedies be available for its breach. Casey J (691–2): "By its accession to the First Optional Protocol . . . New Zealand accepted individual access by its citizens to the United Nations Human Rights Committee . . . and it would be a strange thing if Parliament which passed [the Act] one year later, must be taken as contemplating that New Zealand citizens could go to the United Nations Committee in New York for appropriate redress, but could not obtain it from our own courts".

[71] *Drake* v. *New Zealand* 601/1994, 3 April 1997, inadmissible, HRC Annual Report 1997 (A/52/40) vol II p. 273.

[72] Concluding Observations on 3rd Report of New Zealand, April 1995, HRC Annual Report 1995 (A/50/40) paras. 166, 170ff.

[73] *Ibid*, para. 176.

its recognised power to legislate to implement international treaties and to override inconsistent State laws.[74] The Covenant is annexed to the Commonwealth Human Rights and Equal Opportunity Act, 1986 (Cth), but while this may entail limited recognition of human rights it does not give the Covenant legal force, or allow it to be directly enforced by the courts.[75] A small number of rights are protected under the Constitution[76] and others are covered by federal and State anti-discrimination laws, by other legislation, by administrative review and by common law. But most Covenant rights and freedoms have no guarantee against legislative encroachment by either State or Federal Parliaments.

Justices of the High Court of Australia have recognised the importance of developing the law consistently with international human rights principles where possible. They drew upon international jurisprudence in the landmark decision to recognise native title.[77] The High Court has found in the Constitution an implied protection of freedom of communication in regard to public affairs and political discussion.[78] It has also determined that ratification of the Convention on the Rights of the Child gave rise to a legitimate expectation that decision-makers would exercise their discretion in matters affecting children in conformity with the terms of the Convention, even though the Convention has not been given legal effect.[79] But there are limits to this judicial creativity.

Australia is a party to the Optional Protocol, and has been found to have violated the Covenant in two instances.[80] In neither case did the Australian courts have the opportunity or the power to consider whether the relevant law or practice was compatible with Covenant rights. Some members of the High Court commented in another context that it is:[81]

> "curious that the Executive Government has seen fit to expose Australia to the potential censure of the HRC without endeavouring to ensure that the rights enshrined in the ICCPR are incorporated into domestic law."

The Committee's finding of violation in one case led to the enactment of federal legislation which provides a specific remedy for arbitrary interference with the privacy of sexual conduct between consenting adults, in violation of Article 17 of the Covenant.[82] This is the only Covenant right for which a specific remedy has been enacted.

---

[74] Constitution of the Commonwealth of Australia, ss. 51(xxix) and 109.

[75] For example, *Chu Kheng Lim* v. *Minister for Immigration* (1992) 176 CLR 1, 38, 51–2, 74–5; *Minister for Immigration and Ethnic Affairs* v. *Teoh* (1995) 183 CLR 273, 286–7, per Mason CJ and Deane J.

[76] Constitutional protection of rights in Australia extends to jury trial for indictable offences, religious freedom (from Commonwealth interference), democratic participation and just compensation for acquisition of property. The High Court has implied a right to freedom of expression on political matters.

[77] *Mabo* v. *Queensland (No 2)* (1992) 175 CLR 1.

[78] *Australian Capital Television Pty Ltd* v. *The Commonwealth* (1992) 177 CLR 106.

[79] *Minister for Immigration and Ethnic Affairs* v. *Teoh* (1995) 183 CLR 273.

[80] *Toonen* v. *Australia* 488/1992, 31 March 1994, HRC Annual Report 1994 (A/49/40) vol II p. 226; *A* v. *Australia* 560/1993, 3 April 1997, HRC Annual Report 1997 (A/52/40) vol II p. 125.

[81] *Dietrich* v. *the Queen* (1992) 177 CLR 292, 305.

[82] The Human Rights (Sexual Conduct) Act 1994 (Commonwealth).

Australia's compliance with the Covenant was reviewed by the Committee in 1988.[83] Australia's poor record in submitting reports meant that the Committee did not have an opportunity to draw up a further comprehensive concluding observation on its situation until 2000.

V COMMITTEE'S PREFERENCE IS FOR INCORPORATION OF RIGHTS

In general, implementation of Covenant rights other than by full incorporation into domestic law will leave gaps in the protection of rights. The rights protected by domestic constitutions or laws may not be expressed in the same way as Covenant rights, or the domestic law may permit limitations and restrictions on rights which are more extensive than those permitted under the Covenant. The view taken of particular rights by national courts may differ from that of the Committee.[84] Rights may be protected under domestic law only in respect of actions by government or public authorities,[85] whereas the Covenant requires protection against certain violations of rights by private agencies as well as by public authorities.[86]

Unless domestic law protects all Covenant rights, individuals will be deprived of remedies in case of violation of rights, contrary to the requirements of Article 2(3).[87] Individuals may be able to take their cases to the Human Rights Committee under the Optional Protocol. But there will have been no previous consideration of the issues by national courts.

A more serious problem is that unless the domestic laws which protect rights are given entrenched status, they may be overridden by later, incompatible legislation. This leaves the protection of rights in the hands of political forces rather than those of an independent judiciary, despite the fact that many threats to rights come from the exercise of legislative powers.

Bearing in mind that the rights protected by the Covenant have a universal character, it is of concern that individuals in many States parties cannot seek effective remedies for violations of Covenant rights and that they may not even be able to approach the Committee under the Optional Protocol. While, in theory, it may be up to States to decide how to implement the Covenant and while there is no express obligation on States to incorporate Covenant rights into domestic law, unless those rights are made part of domestic law and are enforceable in the courts, then States will have fallen short of fulfilling their obligations under Article 2.[88]

---

[83] HRC Annual Reports 1988 (A/53/40) para. 413ff and 2000 (A/55/40) para. 498ff.

[84] In *Lansman* v. *Finland* 511/1992, 26 October 1994, HRC Annual Report 1995 (A/50/40) vol II para. 2.7 p. 67, Art. 27 had been invoked in the Supreme Administrative Court, but it was not addressed there (2.7).

[85] As in the United States and under the Canadian Charter, s. 32.

[86] For example Arts. 7, 8, 17, 19, 20 and 27.

[87] In *A* v. *Australia* 560/1993, HRC Annual Report 1997 (A/52/40) vol II p. 125, the Committee found a violation of Art. 2(3) in addition to Arts. 9(1) and (4).

[88] See, eg, Concluding Observations on the 3rd report of Mauritius, HRC Annual Report 1996 (A/51/40) vol I para. 148: "The Committee is concerned that the non-incorporation into domestic law of all the rights guaranteed in the Covenant and the existence of non-permissible limitations affect the

Ideally, rights should not only be made part of domestic law, but also given an entrenched status. Entrenchment of rights is the path preferred by the Committee to guarantee that the requirements of Article 2 will be met. The Committee frequently recommends to States that they incorporate Covenant rights into the legal system with a superior status to ordinary laws, and ensure that those rights can be invoked in the courts.[89] The UK Human Rights Act offers an alternative model which falls short of entrenchment. Its effectiveness has not yet been tested and will depend on whether the executive and Parliament will play their part in implementing remedies when necessary. One cannot say how big an "IF" those provisos involve.

In order to ensure that remedies will be provided in every case of violation, the Committee frequently recommends that States adhere to the Optional Protocol. The Optional Protocol itself emphasises the importance of the obligation under Article 2, paragraph 3, to provide effective remedies by requiring that domestic remedies be exhausted before the Committee can consider a claim.[90]

VI INTERPRETATION AND APPLICATION OF COVENANT RIGHTS BY THE COMMITTEE

If States fulfilled their obligations to give effect to Covenant rights in their domestic legal systems, national courts would have a significant role in the interpretation and application of Covenant rights. This section of the paper considers the approach which national courts and authorities should take towards the views and interpretations of the Committee in interpreting and applying Covenant rights. The view put forward, based on the nature of the Covenant as an international instrument, on the Committee's work and on the legal status of the Committee's views, is that those views should be considered highly influential, if not authoritative.

---

full implementation of the Covenant in Mauritius and that, accordingly, the legal system of Mauritius does not ensure effective remedies in all cases of violations of rights guaranteed in the Covenant."

[89] Concluding Observations: Mongolia, HRC Annual Report 1992 (A/47/40) vol I para. 602; Ireland, HRC Annual Report 1993 (A/48/40) vol I paras. 593ff, para. 610; Hungary, HRC Annual Report 1993 (A/48/40) vol I para. 665; Iceland, HRC Annual Report 1994 (A/49/40) vol I para. 69ff, para. 79; Malta, HRC Annual Report 1994 (A/49/40) vol I para. 117ff, para. 128; Jordan, HRC Annual Report 1994 (A/49/40) vol I paras. 227ff, para. 237; El Salvador, HRC Annual Report 1994 (A/49/40) vol I para. 209ff, para. 214; Cameroon, HRC Annual Report 1994 (A/49/40) vol I paras. 183ff, 199; Norway, HRC Annual Report 1994 (A/49/40) vol I para. 84ff, para. 91; Morocco, 3rd report, HRC Annual Report 1995 (A/50/40) vol I para. 105; Nepal HRC Annual Report 1995 (A/50/40) vol I para. 12; Latvia, initial report, HRC Annual Report 1995 (A/50/40) vol I para. 351; Sweden, 4th report, HRC Annual Report 1996 (A/51/40) vol I para. 82, 91; Denmark, HRC Annual Report 1997 (A/52/40) vol I paras. 65, 71; India HRC Annual Report 1997 (A/52/40) vol I para. 428; Zimbabwe, HRC Annual Report 1998 (A/53/40) vol I para 211; Israel, HRC Annual Report 1998 (A/53/40) vol I para. 305; Tanzania, HRC Annual Report 1998 (A/53/40) vol I para. 394.

[90] Optional Protocol to the International Covenant on Civil and Political Rights, Arts. 2 and 5(2)(b).

A Interpretation of the Covenant

The international principles applicable to the interpretation of the Covenant are those codified in the Vienna Convention on the Law of Treaties. Under those principles, a treaty is to be interpreted[91]

> "in good faith in accordance with the ordinary meaning to be given to the terms of the treaty in their context and in the light of its object and purpose".

Certain provisions in the Covenant refer expressly to its interpretation.[92] Supplementary material, including the preparatory work may be referred to in case of ambiguity or obscurity.[93]

Although the provisions of the Covenant have to be interpreted and applied in the context of a particular legal system, their meaning cannot be derived from the legal concepts of any particular legal system.[94] Members of the Committee have to turn from the familiar meanings of words and phrases which appear to be similar to those of their own legal system and take a broad, international, approach to the potential meaning of Covenant provisions, for example, "penalty" under Article 15 and "rights and obligations in a suit at law", under Article 14(1).[95]

The Committee's approach to interpretation is that each Covenant right must be given its full scope in accordance with its ordinary meaning, and should not be cut down by reference to any other right, whether in the Covenant or another instrument.[96] Restrictions or limitations on rights, on the other hand, are to be strictly construed; they are exceptions which must not put in jeopardy the right itself.[97]

In the Optional Protocol procedure, the Committee sometimes refers to the debates of the Commission on Human Rights and the Third Committee on the draft of the Covenant to discover what was intended.[98] Unfortunately, the political

[91] Vienna Convention, Art. 31(1). Nowak, above n. 11 at XXIII. For application of these provisions, see *JB et al* v. *Canada (Alberta Union Case)* 118/1982, 18.7.86, *Selected Decisions*, vol II, above n. 25 at 34 para. 6.3; *S W M Broeks* v. *The Netherlands*, 172/1984, 9 April 1987 *Selected Decisions*, vol II, ibid, 196, and *F H Zwaan-de Vries* v. *the Netherlands*, 182/1984, 9 April 1987, *Selected Decisions*, vol II, ibid, 209 para. 12.3.

[92] Arts. 5, 46, 47.

[93] Vienna Convention, Art. 32.

[94] *Gordon van Duzen* v. *Canada*, 50/1979, 7 April 1982, *Selected Decisions*, above n. 46 at 118 para. 10.2: "its interpretation . . . has to be based on the principle that the terms and concepts of the Covenant are independent of any particular national system of law and of all dictionary definitions".

[95] Nowak, above n. 11 at 277, 241–2; *Gordon van Duzen* v. *Canada*, 50/1979, 7 April 1982, *Selected Decisions*, above n. 46. Each of the five official languages of the Covenant is equally authentic: ICCPR, Art. 53.

[96] *S W M Broeks* v. *The Netherlands*, 172/1984, 9 April 1987, *Selected Decisions*, vol II, above n. 25 at 196, and *F H Zwaan-de Vries* v. *the Netherlands*, 182/1984, 9 April 1987, *Selected Decisions*, vol II, above n. 25 at 209 para. 12.1: despite overlap with other instruments, it is necessary for the Committee to apply fully the terms of the ICCPR.

[97] General Comment No 10 on Art. 19 (19th session, 1983) *Compilation of General Comments*, above n. 9 at 11.

[98] See, eg, *JB et al* v. *Canada (Alberta Union case)* 118/1982, 18 July 1986, *Selected Decisions*, vol II, above n. 25 at 34 para. 6.3, the Committee examined the discussions of the CHR on the scope of freedom of association and the right to strike (there was a dissenting view); *S W M Broeks* v. *The Netherlands*,

compromises involved in the drafting of the instrument often make resort to the *travaux* a disappointing exercise and it is not always possible to discover why a particular term was used, or with what meaning.[99] Furthermore, the Covenant has now been in force more than twenty years. Changes in the international climate since 1976 have opened the way for broader interpretations, bearing in mind the need to respect consistency of principle in light of the Covenant's objectives.

B Relevance of National Laws

The application of domestic law is a matter for domestic courts. For example, the question whether detention is lawful under domestic law is not a matter for the Committee, but for the courts or other competent authorities of the State party, unless it is established that they acted in bad faith or committed an abuse of power.[100]

In some cases, however, when the Covenant refers to the "lawfulness" or "unlawfulness" of acts, this brings into question compliance with both domestic law and the Covenant. For example, the question under Article 12 (or Article 13) whether a person is "lawfully within the territory of a State" is primarily a question of domestic law, as interpreted by domestic courts. But the domestic laws relevant to the entry of aliens must themselves be in compliance with the State's international obligations, including those under the Covenant; for example, they must be non-discriminatory.[101] Similarly, when Article 13 provides that the expulsion of an alien must be "in accordance with law", the Committee has asserted that the provisions of domestic law relating to expulsion must in themselves be compatible with the provisions of the Covenant.[102] Further, in two cases, the Committee has found that detention, though lawful in accordance with domestic law, was nevertheless arbitrary and therefore in violation of Article 9(1) of the Covenant, which prohibits arbitrary arrest and deprivation of liberty other than in accordance with law.[103]

172/1984, 9 April 1987, *Selected Decisions,* vol II, above n. 25, and *F H Zwaan-de Vries v. the Netherlands,* 182/1984, 9 April 1987, *Selected Decisions,* vol II, above n. 25; *Kindler v. Canada* 470/1991, 30 July 1993, HRC Annual Report 1993 (A/48/40) vol II, p. 138, para. 6.6 (reference to the *travaux preparatoires* in regard to extradition arrangements).

[99] See, eg, *Stewart v. Canada* 538/1993, 1.11.96, HRC Annual Report 1997 (A/52/40) vol II Annex VI G p. 47. On the disputed value of *travaux,* see Nowak, above n. 11 at XXIV.

[100] *Maroufidou v. Sweden* 58/1979, 9 April 1981, *Selected Decisions,* above n. 46 at 80. *Jakes v. Czech Republic* 724/1996, 26 July 1999, HRC Annual Report 1999 (A/54/40) p. 330; *Sánchez v. Spain* 698/1996, 29 July 1997, HRC Annual Report 1997 (A/52/40) vol II p. 337, law interpreted or applied arbitrarily in violation of Art. 26; Nowak, above n. 11 at 656.

[101] See General Comment No 15 on the Position of Aliens (27th session, 1986) vol I para. 5: in certain circumstances an alien may enjoy the protection of the Covenant even in relation to entry or residence, for example, when considerations of non-discrimination, prohibition of inhuman treatment and respect for family life arise.

[102] *Maroufidou v. Sweden* 58/1979, 9 April 1981, *Selected Decisions,* above n. 46 at para. 9.3.

[103] *van Alphen v. the Netherlands* 305/1988, 23 July 1990, HRC Annual Report 1990 (A/45/40) vol II p. 108: his detention, though lawful, was arbitrary, because in the circumstances it was not reasonable and necessary; *A v. Australia* 560/1993, 3 April 97, HRC Annual Report 1997 (A/52/40) vol II Annex VI L p. 125.

VII UNIVERSAL STANDARDS AND DOMESTIC EVALUATIONS

There is potential for the Committee to take a completely different view from that of domestic courts as to how Covenant rights should be applied in particular situations. Sometimes these differences arise as a result of particular cultural or religious values. The Committee on the whole takes a universalist approach to the interpretation and application of Covenant rights, on the basis that those rights do not owe their existence to any particular legal system but reside in all human beings and that the Covenant is a global international instrument, establishing minimum universal standards equally applicable to all countries and all cultures.[104] For example, in regard to women's rights, the Committee has not accepted the argument that local conditions, customs or religious tenets are reasons for denying the equal enjoyment of rights by women.[105] Some States which have made reservations to the Women's Convention[106] on the ground that it must take effect subject to the Islamic Shari'a have not made any similar reservation to the Covenant, and are therefore bound to implement the provisions on equality in enjoyment of rights by men and women and equality of rights in marriage.[107] Regrettably, this obligation is not always respected in practice.

One context in which differences may arise between the Committee and domestic authorities concerns the limitations or restrictions which the Covenant permits to be imposed on certain rights, such as freedom of movement and expression. In general, such restrictions must be imposed by law and must be necessary for the purpose of protecting, inter alia, public morals, national security or public order.[108] The validity of any restrictions imposed by the State depends on an assessment of what is necessary in the circumstances of the case. Such an assessment will generally be made by national courts or authorities in deciding whether certain restrictions were necessary. How far should the Committee have regard to such assessments?

The European Court of Human Rights has recognised that national courts or other domestic authorities have a "margin of appreciation" in deciding, for example, whether restrictions on certain freedoms are necessary in a democratic society.[109] Restrictions are permissible only if they are in pursuit of a legitimate aim,

---

[104] *Vienna Declaration and Program of Action,* World Conference on Human Rights, Vienna, 14–25 June 1993, A/CONF.157/24, 12 July 1993, para. 5; *Copenhagen Declaration on Social Development,* Adopted by the World Summit for Social Development, Copenhagen 6–12 March 1995 para. 28, commitment 1(n).

[105] Concluding Observations on Senegal, HRC Annual Report 1993 (A/48/40) vol I, para. 108ff, 111–12.

[106] Convention on the Elimination of All Forms of Discrimination Against Women ("CEDAW"), Adopted by the General Assembly on 18 December 1979, came into force 3 September 1981. Morocco and Libya have made reservations of the kind mentioned.

[107] ICCPR, Arts. 3 and 23.

[108] For example Arts. 12, 18, 19, 21 and 22. Restrictions must be necessary "in a democratic society" in the case of Arts. 21 and 22.

[109] European Convention on Human Rights, Arts. 8–11.

and proportionate to that aim.[110] If these conditions are met, the European Court may give weight to the assessment of domestic authorities concerning the need for the restrictions. For example, in one case the Court found that in the absence of a common European standard of morality considerable weight could be given to the finding by state authorities that restrictions were necessary to protect morals.[111] The extent to which the Court will defer to the views of national authorities depends on the actual issues at stake; the Court must satisfy itself as to the necessity of the restriction.[112] Nevertheless, the tendency to give weight to the views of national courts could impose a burden on complainants to show that the State exceeded the proper ambit of its discretion in balancing individual rights against community purposes.

In one of its early decisions, the Human Rights Committee took an approach similar to that of the European Court, in recognising that State authorities might have a margin of discretion in deciding whether it was necessary to restrict freedom of expression in order to protect public morals.[113] The Committee noted that there was no universally applicable common standard of public morals, and that a certain margin of discretion must be accorded to the responsible national authorities. It could not question the decision of the national authorities that national broadcasting is not an appropriate forum to discuss the issue of homosexuality. There was a dissenting opinion,[114] and the decision has been criticised, because the Committee did not itself consider whether the restriction was necessary, in terms of Article 19(3).[115]

In recent years, however, the Committee has reserved to itself the decision whether there were circumstances which justified a restriction of rights, without deferring to the opinion of national authorities. The questions asked by the Committee are whether the purpose of the restriction is legitimate, whether the restriction is proportionate to the purpose, and whether the restriction is the minimum necessary to achieve that purpose, bearing in mind that exceptions from rights are to be strictly construed.[116]

---

[110] *The Sunday Times* v. *UK (No 1)* (1979) 2 EHRR 245; *Jersild* v. *Denmark* (1994) 19 EHRR 1.

[111] *Handyside* v. *UK* (1976) 1 EHRR 737, "The Little Red School Book case". See also *Otto-Preminger Institute* v. *Austria* (1995) 19 EHRR 34 (seizure of allegedly blasphemous film upheld); *Chorherr* v. *Austria* (1994) 17 EHRR 358 (arrest of a person handing out leaflets, allegedly in pursuit of public order, upheld). Restrictions should correspond to a pressing social need.

[112] *The Sunday Times* v. *UK (No 2) (Spycatcher)* (1992) 14 EHRR 229.

[113] *Hertzberg* v. *Finland* 61/1979, 2 April 1982, *Selected Decisions*, above n. 46 at 124: the authors claimed that their freedom of expression had been violated by the application of provisions in the Penal code which prohibit the encouragement of indecent behaviour.

[114] An individual opinion pointed out that since the concept of public morals is relative, freedom of expression should not be restricted in such a way as to perpetuate prejudice or promote intolerance. See also Nowak, above n. 11 at 358.

[115] See criticisms in McGoldrick, above n. 13 at 467–8, and references.

[116] The interference must be proportionate to the legitimate aim pursued: *Pietraroia Zapala* v. *Uruguay* 44/1979, 27.3.81, *Selected Decisions*, above n. 46 at 76. The principle of proportionality required specific justification for a measure depriving a person of all political rights for a period of 15 years, but none had been advanced. See also General Comment No 22 on Art. 18 (48th session, 1993) vol I para. 8. In *Toonen* v. *Australia* 488/1992, 31 March 1994, HRC Annual Report 1994 (A/49/40) vol II p 226, para. 8.3: "any interference with privacy must be proportional to the end sought and be necessary in the circumstances of any given case".

This approach has been applied by the Committee to find that freedom of expression was violated by the Korean National Security Laws, despite the claim of the State that its own views as to the existence of a threat to public security should be respected.[117] The Committee also held that the right to privacy was violated by Australian laws criminalising homosexual conduct between consenting adults, rejecting the argument that moral issues were a matter of domestic concern.[118] In another case, the Committee rejected the argument of the State that a certain margin of discretion must be allowed to national authorities in the application of Article 27, and that "in many cases, . . . the national judge is in a better position than the international judge to make a decision".[119]

VIII   BINDING EFFECT OF OP VIEWS

When the Committee finds that a State has violated rights under the Covenant, it also expresses its views as to the appropriate remedy, and reminds the State of its obligation under Article 2(3) to provide effective remedies.[120]

Neither the Covenant nor the Optional Protocol provide that the views of the Committee on violations or remedies are legally binding on States parties. They do, however, carry the moral authority of an independent expert body whose primary task is to interpret and apply the Covenant and to consider whether States parties have fully implemented their obligations.[121] As the monitoring body established by the Covenant, the Committee considers that its interpretation of rights and freedoms should be considered authoritative. Furthermore, the Committee's views are not without legal effect. A State party which has ratified the Optional Protocol has recognised the competence of the Committee to receive and consider communications from individuals and to express its views as to whether there has been a violation of rights.[122] The Committee is, in practice, the only international body with the competence to form the view that there has been a violation of the Covenant. If it reaches this view, then under Article 2(3) of the Covenant the State has undertaken to ensure that the person whose rights were violated has an effective and

---

[117] *Jong-Kyu Sohn* v. *Korea* 518/1992, 19 July 1995, HRC Annual Report 1995 (A/47/40) vol II p. 98, para. 10.4; *Kim* v. *Republic of Korea* 574/1994, 3 November 1998, HRC Annual Report 1999 (A/54/40) vol II Annex XI A 1; *Tae Hoon Park* v. *Republic of Korea* 628/1995, 20 October 1998, HRC Annual Report 1999 (A/54/40) vol II Annex XI K 85.

[118] *Toonen* v. *Australia* 488/1992, 31 March 1994, HRC Annual Report 1994 (A/49/40) vol II p. 226. The European Court of Human Rights also concluded that laws prohibiting homosexual conduct were not necessary to protect morals: *Dudgeon* v. *UK* (1982) 4 EHRR 149; *Norris* v. *Ireland* (1991) 13 EHRR 186.

[119] *Ilmari Länsman* v. *Finland*, 511/1992, 26 October 1994, HRC Annual Report 1995 (A/50/40) vol II p. 74.

[120] E Klein, "Individual Reparation Claims under the ICCPR: the Practice of the Human Rights Committee" in A Randelzhofer and C Tomuschat (eds.), *State Responsibility and the Individual: Reparation in Instances of Grave Violations of Human Rights* (Dordrecht, Martinus Nijhoff, 1999) 27–41, discusses the Committee's jurisdictional competence and the substantive legal basis for remedies.

[121] See Nowak, above n. 11 at 649–50, 710.

[122] Optional Protocol, Arts. 1 and 5.

enforceable remedy. The Committee's competence to determine whether a remedy is effective is expressly recognised in the Optional Protocol itself.[123] Failure to take action in respect of the Committee's views will leave the State in violation of its obligations under Article 2(3), regardless of the status of the Committee's views.

When the Committee finds that a State has violated Covenant rights, it reinforces its views by calling on the State to respond within ninety days with information about the measures taken to give effect to the Committee's views.[124] A follow-up procedure has been established to ensure that States do respond. States which do not respond, or whose responses are not satisfactory, are invited to participate in discussions with representatives of the Committee.[125] When the State later presents a report to the Committee, it will be asked further questions about the action it has taken to provide the victims of any violation with a remedy. The Committee may also recommend that States establish mechanisms to give effect to its views.[126]

Some States have accepted and implemented the Committee's views,[127] while others have not, and yet others have adopted a selective approach. Action taken by States to comply with the Committee's views confirms the State's recognition of the Committee's role in interpreting and applying the Covenant in individual cases. Although one cannot ignore the cases where States have not accepted or implemented the Committee's views, the Committee itself is not willing to let these matters go unnoticed, and continues to insist that States must respect the obligations they have undertaken. The Committee expects that its views may also influence the interpretation and application of Covenant rights at national level, in legislation, or in decisions of courts.

IX OBSERVATIONS AND CONCLUSIONS

This brief survey of the interaction between the Covenant and national laws protecting rights suggests that in many States Covenant rights need to be better integrated into national legal systems. The significance of the Covenant as an international

---

[123] Under Art. 4(2) of the Optional Protocol the Committee may establish whether the alleged violation has been effectively remedied.

[124] A standard paragraph is appended to each determination:

"Bearing in mind that, by becoming a State party to the Optional Protocol, the State party has recognised the competence of the Committee to determine whether there has been a violation of the Covenant or not and that, pursuant to Art. 2 of the Covenant, the State party has undertaken to ensure to all individuals within its territory and subject to its jurisdiction the rights recognised in the Covenant to provide an effective and enforceable remedy in case a violation has been established, the Committee wishes to receive from the State party, within ninety days information about the measures taken to give effect to its views".

[125] The details of the Committee's follow up procedures are set out in its Annual Reports to the General Assembly.

[126] For example, Concluding Observations: Sweden, HRC Annual Report 1996 (A/51/40) vol I para. 84, 92; France, HRC Annual Report 1997 (A/52/40) vol I para. 397; Austria, HRC Annual Report 1999 (A/54/40) at para. 185.

[127] *Jorge Villacnés Ortega* v. *Ecuador* 481/1991, 8 April 1997, HRC Annual Report 1997 (A/52/40) vol II Annex VI. Just recently Ecuador informed the Committee that it had reached agreement to pay compensation for torture and degrading treatment.

human rights instrument, and the role of the Committee in monitoring compliance, suggest that States should do more to make the Covenant and the work of the Committee better known. While it is encouraging to note that in some States Covenant rights are part of domestic law, and that national courts have interpreted and applied those rights, regrettably, there may be little knowledge of or reference to the jurisprudence of the Human Rights Committee. The provisions and application of domestic laws do not always match the requirements of the Covenant. A further problem is that States do not always take action to implement the Committee's views under the Optional Protocol or its Concluding Observations in respect of State Reports. The result is that the Committee is continually confronted with State reports which reveal serious deficiencies in the implementation of Covenant rights, and failure to take action in respect of the Committee's specific recommendations for change.

If a comparison were made between the implementation of the Covenant and that of the European Convention, which protects similar (though not identical) rights, it could be observed that there are significant differences in the legal framework and the institutional mechanisms. The European Court of Human Rights has ample resources. Its decisions are legally binding and are largely respected. The Council of Europe works actively with States aspiring to membership to encourage those reforms which are needed to bring their laws and practices into line. Some European countries examined recently by the Human Rights Committee have shown improvements in human rights which were attributable at least in part to their adherence to the European Convention.

Regrettably, the United Nations' human rights system, while it has produced very fine standards, including the Universal Declaration and the two Covenants, has fallen short in regard to implementation and enforcement mechanisms. The Human Rights Committee has made the most of its mandate, by calling on States parties to take part in a dialogue with members of the Committee, and by making specific recommendations to States to bring their laws and practice into line with their Covenant obligations. It has insisted that States respond to its views in the communications procedure, and has followed up on this to make it clear that States must take seriously their obligations. But its views are not expressly binding, and the resources to fulfil the Committee's mandate are pitiful in comparison with those available to the European Court.

There is, in addition, a lack of reciprocity in the United Nations human rights system—there are no incentives or pressures which would encourage States to comply or make it uncomfortable for them not to comply. States do not generally find that any aspect of their self-interest is threatened should they fail to co-operate with the Committee. No outside pressures are brought to bear on those who fall short of standards as assessed by the Committee. The Commission on Human Rights is highly politicised and is not impartial and objective in regard to the human rights records of particular States.

Does this matter? Some may think that the task of enforcing human rights is best done by national courts, working within the framework of their own constitutions and legal systems, developing and applying principles in response to the circumstances that arise. On this view, the words of the Covenant and the interpretations developed by the Committee are of limited interest; no more than a source of ideas.

My own view is that it matters a great deal whether States respect and implement the binding legal obligations they have undertaken, and whether they respect the interpretations and views of the Committee which the Covenant has established as its monitoring body. The rights and freedoms of the Covenant are universal minimum standards, which should have the same meaning for everyone throughout the world. To yield to relativism or to "margins of discretion" would put at risk the rights of individuals in countries which are only too willing to interpret Covenant rights as they see fit.

I believe that it matters now, and it will matter more in the century to come, that ways are found to ensure universal respect for the international rule of law, including the principles of the Universal Declaration and the Covenants. My point can be illustrated by reference to the recently established war crimes tribunals for the former Yugoslavia and Rwanda, to the indictment of Karadjic and Milosevic, to the extradition proceedings against Pinochet and to the new international criminal court. All these procedures and mechanisms draw upon the principles of international human rights. But Yugoslavia and Rwanda were parties to the International Covenant on Human Rights before the massive violations which have appalled us all. Chile signed the Covenant before the handover of power by Pinochet.

In States which do not have the basic conditions of democracy and the rule of law, it is unlikely either that respect for rights can be ensured, or that individuals will be able to secure or enforce effective remedies, whatever the status of the Covenant on paper. The Committee has great difficulties in dealing with States such as Afghanistan, North Korea, Sierra Leone, Angola and Yugoslavia, all of which are parties and some of which have reports pending. The Committee's usual procedures seem totally inadequate where the State party appears unable or unwilling to respect the basic requirements of the Covenant.

Better ways must be found to ensure respect for international obligations, to promote the international rule of law and to prevent further violations. States which are committed to human rights should show leadership in this, by implementing the Covenant fully, by respecting the views and interpretations of the Committee, by supporting the Committee's work, and by ensuring the quality of its membership and the adequacy of its resources. They should be willing to respect fully human rights standards, especially those of the Covenant, which have been developed as statements of the ideal at international level, and ensure that they are given a primary role in the reform and development of national law. Domestic courts should be empowered to make greater use of the Covenant and the jurisprudence of the Committee, so that the principles of the Covenant hold their central meaning wherever applied. States parties which are confident that they have met their own obligations under the Covenant can be a model for other States and can be active in persuading those others to follow their example.

16

Intention and Effect:
The Legal Status of the Final Views
of the Human Rights Committee

SCOTT DAVIDSON

I INTRODUCTION

Like the majority of states within the Western Europe and Others Group of the United Nations human rights system, New Zealand has become party to a significant number of international human rights instruments in recent years.[1] In so doing, it has demonstrated a commitment to the cause of human rights on the international level and has reinforced the protection of human rights at the domestic level.[2] Nowhere has this been more apparent than in New Zealand's accession to the International Covenant on Civil and Political Rights (ICCPR) and its first Optional Protocol (OP).[3]

A state that is party to the ICCPR's OP recognises the competence of the eighteen person Human Rights Committee (HRC) to receive communications from individuals subject to its jurisdiction who claim to be victims of a violation of any of the rights set forth in the Covenant.[4] For New Zealand this is of particular significance, since it grants individuals a procedural right to vindicate substantive human rights violations before an independent and impartial international body which is not a constituent part of the New Zealand state. It is, perhaps, of even greater significance that this body derives its competence not from a legislative act of the New Zealand Parliament, but from an executive act of the Crown. This has

---

[1] New Zealand is party to the following major human rights instruments: International Covenant on Civil and Political Rights 1966; Optional Protocol to the International Covenant on Civil and Political Rights 1966; Second Optional Protocol International Covenant on Civil and Political Rights 1989; International Covenant on Economic Social and Cultural Rights 1966; International Convention on the Elimination of All Forms of Racial Discrimination 1966; Convention on the Elimination of All Forms of Discrimination Against Women 1981; Convention Against Torture and Other Cruel, Inhuman or Degrading Treatment or Punishment 1984; Convention on the Rights of the Child 1989.

[2] For an overview of New Zealand's activities in the field of human rights see Ministry of Foreign Affairs and Trade, *New Zealand Handbook on International Human Rights* (Wellington, Ministry of Foreign Affairs and Trade, 1998). See also S Upton, "New Zealand's International Human Rights Policy: Bridging the Gap Between Ideals and Practice", paper delivered at the 1998 Otago Foreign Policy School, 3 July 1998.

[3] New Zealand became party to the ICCPR on 28 December 1978 and to its OP on 26 May 1989.

[4] Art. 1 OP.

been something of a quiet constitutional revolution, so quiet indeed, that in most areas of society it has gone virtually unnoticed.[5] Despite this, it behoves us to examine carefully the powers of the HRC under the ICCPR OP in order to determine what the implications might be for New Zealand.

While there have been few individual communications from New Zealand in the last decade and no adverse findings against this country to date, it cannot be assumed with any degree of certainty that this position will continue to obtain indefinitely.[6] It is more probable than not that at some stage New Zealand will have to deal with a finding that it has breached its obligations under the ICCPR. This begs a crucial and fundamental question: what exactly is the legal status of the views of the HRC? From this basic inquiry flow a number of other questions. If the views of the HRC are not legally binding, are States parties obliged to comply with them and any remedy that might be indicated by the Committee? What sanctions can be invoked if a State party fails to comply with the HRC's views? If the views are, in a State party's opinion, manifestly in error, can they be challenged?

II FINAL VIEWS: THE TRADITIONAL VIEW

The individual communication procedure under the OP is a matter of last resort, since it may only be engaged if a respondent State fails to provide an appropriate remedy to an individual who alleges a violation of one or more of the rights

---

[5] On New Zealand's accession to the OP see J Elkind, "The Optional Protocol: A Bill of Rights for New Zealand" [1990] *NZLJ* 96.

[6] The HRC has dealt with eight complaints against New Zealand since 1990.

(1) *SB* v. *NZ*, Comm 475/1991; 4 April 1994 (complaint about pension entitlements; held inadmissible).

(2) *Julian and Drake* v. *NZ*, Comm 601/1994; 3 April 1997 (complaint as to non-compensation of New Zealand prisoners of war under 1952 Peace Treaty between Allies and Japan; held inadmissible).

(3) *Potter* v. *NZ*, 632/1995; 18 August 1997 (arbitrary detention, fair trial, treatment in prison, discrimination by Parole Board; inadmissible on grounds of being unsubstantiated and failure to exhaust domestic remedies).

(4) *A* v. *NZ*, Comm, 754/1997; 3 August 1999 (mental health, whether detention arbitrary; no breach found but minority opinion would have found that the delays (on the facts) in judicial review of A's detention violated Art. 9(4)).

(5) *Tamihere* v. *NZ*, Comm 891/1999; 18 April 2000 (fair trial; held inadmissible on grounds that complainant sought only to have factual findings of trial court reviewed)

(6) *Mahuika* v. *NZ (the "Sealords Case")*, Comm 547/1993; 15 November 2000 (whether global settlement of Maori commercial fishing claims violated Art. 27 right to culture for dissenting Maori tribes; no violation found)

(7) *Buckle* v. *NZ*, Comm 858/1999; 16 November 2000 (removal of guardianship rights by state contested by complainant; no violation found).

(8) *Toala* v. *NZ*, Comm 675/1995, 22 November 2000 (whether legislated removal of New Zealand citizenship from 100,000 Western Samoans in Western Samoa, in response to 1982 Privy Council decision holding, unexpectedly, that they were New Zealand citizens under a 1928 enactment, violated, in relation to complainants, Arts. 12 and 26. Complaints held partly inadmissible and those remaining admissible dismissed on merits.

See D MacKay, "The UN Covenants and the Human Rights Committee" (1999) 29 *VUWLR* 11, 15.

protected by the ICCPR.[7] Only when the formal requirements for admissibility have been met is the HRC competent to deal with the merits of a communication.[8] This is done by considering written submissions in closed session.[9] The process of the HRC is normally concluded when its "views", more typically known as "final views", are forwarded to the State party and the aggrieved individual.[10] Where a breach is found, the HRC will usually indicate the remedial action to be taken by the delinquent State.[11]

A starting point in analysing the legal status of the HRC's final views is to examine the term itself. During debate on the OP in the Third Committee of the United Nations General Assembly, the term "views" was adopted in preference to either "recommendations" or "suggestions".[12] While Schwelb suggests that the OP's use of the French term "constatations" is stronger in meaning than the word "views", it nonetheless connotes a determination of the issues that is short of a legally binding obligation.[13] This position is supported not only by the drafting work of the Third Committee and initial statements by the HRC itself; it is also a view shared by a number of commentators. Nisuke Ando, a present member of the Committee, has written:[14]

> "Everyone is aware that the HRC is not a court of law. It can only adopt 'views' which are not binding on States parties concerned and they have the discretion to implement the views or not."

Manfred Nowak is also of the opinion that while decisions of the HRC have great moral authority, they are not binding under international law.[15]

II AN EXPANSIVE APPROACH?

Despite this widely received opinion, it is clear that the HRC has, since the pronouncement of its very first "views" in *Massera* v. *Uruguay*,[16] adopted a much more

---

[7] On the individual communication procedure under the OP see D McGoldrick, *The Human Rights Committee: Its Role in the Development of the International Covenant on Civil and Political Rights* (Oxford, Clarendon Press, 1991); P R Ghandhi, *The Human Rights Committee and the Right of Individual Communication: Law and Practice* (Aldershot, Hants, England; Brookfield, Vt, Ashgate, Dartmouth, 1998); and S Davidson, "Individual Communications to the United Nations Human Rights Committee: A New Zealand Perspective" [1997] *NZ Law Review* 375.

[8] The formal requirements for admissibility are set down in Arts. 2, 3 and 5(2) Optional Protocol. These have been developed by the HRC's jurisprudence. See Davidson, above n. 7 at 380–5.

[9] Arts. 5(1) and (3) Optional Protocol. On the confidentiality of the procedure see M Nowak, *UN Covenant on Civil and Political Rights: CCPR Commentary* (Kehl, N P Engel, 1993) 707–8.

[10] Art. 5(4) OP.

[11] There is no explicit provision permitting the HRC to indicate remedies, but it seems to have inferred this power from its understanding of state obligations under Art. 2(3) ICCPR.

[12] See Nowak, above n. 9 at 708; Ghandhi, above n. 7 at 329–35.

[13] E Schwelb, "Civil and Political Rights: The International Measures of Implementation"(1968) 62 AJIL 827, 858 and 867–8.

[14] N Ando, "The Future of Monitoring Bodies—Limitations and Possibilities of the Human Rights Committee" (1991–1992) *Canadian Human Rights Yearbook* 169, 171–2.

[15] Nowak, above n. 9 at 710–11.

[16] Comm No R 1/15, 15 February 1977, UN Doc Supp No 40 (A/34/40) at 124 (15 August 1979).

expansive approach to the question of their legal significance. This approach can be discerned from the very process and format employed in the delivery by the HRC of its "final views". In the words of former HRC member Christian Tomuschat:[17]

"None of the decisions hitherto handed down reads like a diplomatic communiqué. Obviously, they have all been drafted on the pattern of a judicial decision. After an accurate description of the facts of the case and of the proceedings before the HRC, legal reasons are set out. In a final operative part a precise enunciation of the violations having occurred is given, coupled with the invitation to the Government concerned to take immediate steps in favour of the victims."

McGoldrick puts it rather more succinctly:[18]

The HRC's views follow a judicial pattern and are effectively decisions on the merits.

Form, however, is not necessarily indicative of substance, nor of legal status, and even Tomuschat acknowledges that the HRC's "views" have simply become an efficient "tool of evaluation" under the ICCPR.[19] Despite this, the HRC has always indicated the remedial action required of a State party in order to comply with its obligations under the Convention, and as Ando has pointed out, some States have complied with this aspect of the HRC's "views" and some have not.[20]

IV   A NEW APPROACH?

Despite the HRC's expansive approach to the formulation of its "final views", even it was aware at the outset that they lacked legal solidity. In its second volume of collected decisions it acknowledged that the "Committee is neither a court nor a body with a quasi-judicial mandate" but that it applied the Covenant and the OP in a "judicial spirit".[21] More to the point, it noted that it had "no power to hand down binding decisions".[22] It seems, however, that the dogmatic position that the "final views" of the HRC are not legally binding cannot now be accepted without further investigation. According to former HRC member Professor Fausto Pocar, a close examination of the relationship between Article 2(3) of the ICCPR and the OP suggests that the "final views" of the HRC might have some indirect legally binding force.[23] He argues that Article 2(3) ICCPR provides that where a violation of an individual right under the ICCPR takes place, the State is under a legal

---

[17] C Tomuschat, "Evolving Procedural Rules: The United Nations Human Rights Committee's First Two Years of Dealing with Individual Communications"(1980) 1 *HRLJ* 249, 255. See also Nowak, above n. 9 at 708–9.

[18] McGoldrick, above n. 7 at 151.

[19] Tomuschat, above n. 17 at 255.

[20] Ando, above n. 14 at 172.

[21] *Selected Decisions under the Optional Protocol, Vol II* (New York, United Nations, 1982–1988) 1–2.

[22] *Ibid.*

[23] F Pocar, "Legal Value of the Human Rights Committee's Views" (1991–1992) *Canadian Yearbook of Human Rights* 119.

obligation to provide an effective and enforceable remedy. The OP provides the machinery to establish whether such a violation has occurred. Where a violation is found by the HRC, therefore, the State is under a legal obligation to provide a remedy. He says:[24]

> "The decision concluding the procedure under the Optional Protocol contains the finding of a violation. Although the decision is not binding as such, it makes the provision of article 2 applicable in the particular case."

He further argues that Article 2(3)(b) ICCPR makes it clear that a person claiming a remedy for the violation of a right is to have that remedy determined by a competent legal authority of the State. This, in his opinion, supports the view that States intend to "accept the determination of the victim's right made by the Committee, even if it is contained in a formally non-binding decision".[25] Pocar finds additional support for this contention in the Preamble to the OP, in which that instrument is described as being a means of implementing the ICCPR. Because of this, he argues, it may be assumed that States parties are under an obligation to cooperate with the Committee when a violation is brought before the HRC. He says:[26]

> "Such cooperation cannot be considered as confined to the procedure leading to the adoption of the views of the Committee, but must logically include the views themselves."

Pocar's conclusion, therefore, is that although the HRC's "views" are not of themselves immediately binding, "they provide a basis and reference for the appreciation of a State's compliance with two international obligations: the obligation to remedy a violation that has been identified and determined, and the obligation to cooperate with the Committee".[27] Despite this, even Pocar admits that States may "under particular circumstances" adopt a different view.[28] He does not say what these "particular circumstances" might be, but the fact that he envisages situations in which a State might come to a different conclusion to the HRC suggests that even on his analysis the HRC's "final views" cannot be regarded as binding *stricto iure*.

V ARE "FINAL VIEWS" LEGALLY BINDING?

The current position adopted by the HRC on this matter seems to be rather more robust than that suggested by Pocar in his essay. In recent "final views", the HRC itself has clearly linked a State party's obligations under Article 2 ICCPR with the

---

[24] *Ibid*, 120.
[25] *Ibid*.
[26] *Ibid*.
[27] *Ibid*.
[28] *Ibid*.

competence of the HRC to determine whether or not there has been a breach and to indicate a remedy. The typical formula now used by the HRC is as follows:[29]

> "Bearing in mind that, by becoming a party to the Optional Protocol, the State party has recognized the competence of the Committee to determine whether there has been a violation of the Covenant or not and that, pursuant to article 2 of the Covenant, the State party has undertaken to ensure to all individuals within its territory and subject to its juris-diction the rights recognized in the Covenant and to provide an effective and enforce-able remedy in cases where a violation has been established, the Committee wishes to receive from the State party, within 90 days, information about the measures taken to give effect to the Committee's Views."

There would seem to be little doubt that in this oft-repeated formula, the HRC is claiming legal competence to make an authoritative determination of whether a violation has occurred. In two earlier cases, *Bradshaw* v. *Barbados*[30] and *Roberts* v. *Barbados*,[31] the HRC had declared that, in light of the fact that Barbados had recog-nised the competence of the HRC to receive and consider individual commun-ications under the OP, "it is an obligation for the State Party to adopt appropriate measures to give legal effect to the views of the Committee as to the interpretation and application of the Covenant in particular cases arising under the Optional Protocol".[32] Ghandhi has suggested that while this statement might lead one to believe that the HRC was claiming legal effect for its "final views", it only endorses "the approach for arguing that a State Party has an obligation to render the provi-sions of the Covenant "effective" under article 2(3)(a)".[33] This is also the view adopted by Elizabeth Evatt, a former member of the HRC, who has written:[34]

> "The Committee . . . is the only international body with the competence to form the view that there has been a violation of the Covenant. If it reaches this view, then under article 2(3) of the Covenant the State has undertaken to ensure that the person whose rights were violated has an effective and enforceable remedy. The Committee's com-petence to determine whether a remedy is effective is expressly recognised in the Optional Protocol itself. Failure to take action in respect of respect the Committee's views will leave the State in violation of its obligations under article 2(3)."

With respect to Pocar, Ghandhi and Evatt, it seems that they are straining the lan-guage of the law in order to avoid a pronouncement that the "views" of the HRC are legally binding *in toto*. By focusing on the end result of a finding of breach by

---

[29] See, for instance, the Committee's Views in cases Nos. 532/1993, *Thomas* v. *Jamaica*; 555/1993, *La Vende* v. *Trinidad and Tobago*; 569/1993, *Matthews* v. *Trinidad and Tobago*; 577/1994, *Polay Campos* v. *Peru*; 585/1994, *Jones* v. *Jamaica*; 609/1995, *Williams* v. *Jamaica*; 615/1995, *Young* v. *Jamaica*; 623/1995, *Domukhovsky* v. *Georgia*; 624/1995, *Tsikhlauri* v. *Georgia*; 626/1995, *Gelbakhiani* v. *Georgia*; 627/1995, *Dokvadze* v. *Georgia*; 672/1995, *Smart* v. *Trinidad and Tobago*; and 676/1996, *Yasseen and Thomas* v. *Guyana*.

[30] *Bradshaw* v. *Barbados* Comm No 489/1992, UN Doc CCPR/C/51/D/489/1992 (1994).

[31] *Roberts* v. *Barbados* Comm No 504/1992, UN Doc CCPR/C/51/D/504/1992 (1994).

[32] *Bradshaw*, above n. 30 at para. 5.3; *Roberts*, above n. 31 at para. 6.3.

[33] Ghandhi, above n. 7 at 333.

[34] E Evatt, "The Impact of International Human Rights on Domestic Law" (internal footote omit-ted), ch. 15, pp. 300–301 in this volume.

the HRC rather than examining the nature and legal consequences of the breach itself, they provide only a partial juridical picture of the process which results in the adoption of the HRC's "final views". If one starts with the conclusion that a State party to the ICCPR is obliged to provide an effective remedy in cases of breach, such an obligation can only arise if there has been a prior determination by the HRC that a substantive right protected by the Covenant has been breached. If there has been no such prior determination of breach, then, by definition the obligation to provide an effective remedy cannot arise. Such a breach cannot exist in the abstract, for if it did, any remedy would also exist in the abstract and that would be a legal absurdity. There must be an actual breach of legal obligation which gives rise to an obligation to provide a legal remedy: the two cannot be separated. If, then, the determination by the HRC of a breach of the ICCPR by a State party is a statement which carries only moral weight and lacks legal substance, as suggested by Evatt,[35] Nowak[36] and de Zayas,[37] there can be no legal obligation upon a State to provide a remedy. In other words, the only way in which a legal obligation to provide a remedy can arise is if the determination of a breach of the ICCPR by the HRC is itself of legal significance, that is, legally binding. To suggest that there is an obligation to provide a remedy under the ICCPR which is independent of any legally binding determination of a breach is extremely troublesome, to say the least. Furthermore, even if one leaves aside the HRC's strong pronouncements in *Bradshaw* v. *Barbados* and *Roberts* v. *Barbados*, there is certainly sufficient evidence in the current formulation of the HRC's "final views" to imply that its pronouncements on breach are legally binding. When the Committee says that "the State party has recognized the competence of the Committee to determine whether there has been a violation of the Covenant or not", does this refer to moral or legal competence? For the reasons suggested above, it must mean legal competence, otherwise it would be difficult to require states fulfil their legal obligations on what would otherwise simply be a moral determination of the issues. Besides, the term "competence" is well understood in law, especially Civil law, as meaning legal power or legal capacity to perform certain acts or functions. It surely cannot be accidental that the members of the HRC have decided to use a term which is loaded with such legal significance. The impression the HRC gives in the formulation of its "final views" is that it is staking a strong claim that these "views" should be treated as legally binding in their entirety. Such an impression not only coincides with the language used, but also with the clear expectation of compliance which the HRC's "views" and follow-up procedure evince.

This suggestion finds some support from Don MacKay, the former Deputy Secretary of the New Zealand Ministry of Foreign Affairs and Trade, who argues that:[38]

---

[35] *Ibid.*

[36] Nowak, above n. 9 at 710.

[37] A de Zayas, "The Follow-Up Procedure of the UN Human Rights Committee" (1991) 47 *Review of the International Commission of Jurists* 28.

[38] MacKay, above n. 6 at 16.

"[w]hile it has been well established that the Committee issues 'views' not 'decisions', and that its 'views' are not binding . . . recent developments could be taken to imply that some judicial or quasi-judicial status should be attached to them".

MacKay's subsequent observations on this point indicate that he is not in favour of such a development. He says:[39]

"Whether this is a good thing or a bad thing is obviously a matter for debate, and I do not propose embarking on that here. But it does raise another question, whether it is appropriate for an international body to have such a judicial or quasi-judicial role in cases which may have huge significance for states—more significance perhaps than some of the cases before the International Court of Justice or the WTO Disputes Settlement Body— if it does not have robust procedures and resources to match."

Simon Upton, the former Associate Minister of Foreign Affairs and Trade concurs, in a rather more succinct fashion, with this assessment. He says:[40]

"The willingness of the Human Rights Committee to consider complaints by groups has considerably broadened the scope of matters before the Committee beyond those for which it was designed. It has also taken steps to elevate the status of its 'views' and 'decisions' to those of a judicial body. Yet the Committee is simply not equipped for this kind of task."

If it is correct to suggest that the HRC has taken a deliberate step to increase the legal authority of its "views", and the existing formula which it employs seems to indicate that it has, then I would argue that the HRC is seeking to build a substantial legal edifice on weak foundations. From the point of view of legal certainty, it would be better if, as suggested in the HRC's own submission to the World Conference on Human Rights in Vienna in 1993, steps were taken to ensure that states accepted the "views" of the HRC as legally binding.[41] McGoldrick has also argued that "the HRC's views would obviously carry greater authority if they were legally binding".[42] Whether it is desirable that it do so, however, is a matter of policy to be determined consciously by the States parties, and not something to be introduced by juridical sleight of hand.

If States parties wished the views of the HRC to be binding *stricto iure*, it would be necessary to amend the OP according to the procedure contained in Article 11 OP. This requires one third of the States parties to the OP to agree to the calling of a conference under the auspices of the United Nations to consider amendment. Any such amendment must be adopted by a majority of the States parties present and voting. Amendments will only enter into force, however, when they have been approved by the General Assembly of the United Nations and accepted by a two-thirds majority of the Statees parties to the OP. This is clearly a lengthy and complex procedure, and it is probably the case that States are not yet ready to

---

[39] MacKay, above n. 6 at 16.
[40] Upton, above n. 2 at 12.
[41] See A/CONF 157/PC/62/Add 15, 8.
[42] McGoldrick, above n. 7 at 151.

confer direct legally binding status on the "final views" of the HRC. This is certainly the view of Professor Ando. He says:[43]

> "Does the possibility exist to authorize the HRC to render binding decisions as in the case of the European or the Inter-American Court of Human Rights? As I see it, the competence of those courts to render binding decisions is based on the strong conviction shared by all the States parties to the respective conventions which establish them. This conviction has been nurtured by a long tradition of common history, religion, culture and human values. Where there is no such conviction and tradition, it is perhaps premature to expect that States parties are ready to authorize any monitoring body to render binding decisions."

Despite this persuasive observation by Professor Ando, the HRC does, as we have seen above, seem to have taken quite a long stride down the road of declaring its views to be legally binding. This inevitably begs the question of why the HRC has done this, seemingly in the absence of any formal consent by the States parties. There are two possible explanations: either the HRC, as a body, has increased in confidence and feels able to assert both its moral and presumed legal authority to secure compliance by States parties, or it might be that given the disparity in the levels of compliance among States parties, the HRC considers that it has needed to become more assertive. Given the development of the HRC's follow-up procedure it would seem that the second of these explanations is the more likely.

VI FOLLOW-UP PROCEDURE

During its thirty-ninth session, in July 1990, the Committee established a procedure by which it monitors the follow-up to its "views" by States parties under Article 5(4) OP, and it created the mandate of a Special Rapporteur for the Follow-Up on Views.[44] The mandate of the Special Rapporteur is set out in rule 95 of the Committee's rules of procedure. The Special Rapporteur began to request follow-up information from States parties in 1991. Since then, follow-up information has systematically been requested in respect of all "views" with a finding of a violation of the Covenant. In particular, the Special Rapporteur seeks information on the measures which have been taken to give effect to the HRC's "views" and the remedies indicated therein. Certain States have not been particularly cooperative in this regard. In the HRC's 1998 Annual Report it stated that by the beginning of its sixty-third session, roughly 30 per cent of the replies received in response to follow-up action could be considered satisfactory in that they demonstrated the

---

[43] Ando, above n. 14 at 172

[44] At the Committee's fifty-ninth session, Mr Prafullachandra Natwarlal Bhagwati assumed the duties of Special Rapporteur for the Follow-Up on Views. See *Report of the Human Rights Committee, Volume I*, 1998, GAOR, 53rd Sess, Supp No 40, A/53/40, para. 481. On the follow-up procedure see A de Zayas, above n. 37; Nowak, above n. 9 at 711–12; Ghandhi, above n. 7 at 335–53; and D Harris and S Joseph, *The International Covenant on Civil and Political Rights and United Kingdom Law* (Oxford, Clarendon Press, 1995) 38–9.

State party's willingness to implement the Committee's views or to offer the applicant an appropriate remedy.[45] In the remaining 70 per cent of cases, replies from States parties explicitly challenged the Committee's findings, on either factual or legal grounds; constituted tardy submissions on the merits of the case; promised an investigation of the matter considered by the Committee or indicated that the State party would not, for one reason or another, give effect to the Committee's recommendations.[46] The measures which can be taken by the HRC in the absence of compliance are limited to sending the Special Rapporteur to conduct an on-site fact finding visit with the permission of the State party in question and to include a State's response to follow-up in its annual report which is submitted to the General Assembly via the UN Secretary-General. Despite the HRC's statement that the lack of explicit enforcement machinery is available under the OP is "a major shortcoming in the implementation machinery established by the Covenant",[47] continuous dialogue and adverse publicity seem to be the only sanctions which are available in the case of a recalcitrant State.

VII THE HUMAN RIGHTS COMMITTEE: FORM AND FUNCTION

Even if the nature and experience of the follow-up procedure is itself not conclusive of the legal status of the HRC's "final views", does the character of the HRC and the quality of its reasoning contribute anything towards the debate?

The HRC is the body established by the ICCPR to supervise its implementation and to deal with individual applications under the OP. As Tomuschat, Ando and the HRC itself have noted, the HRC is neither a court nor a quasi-judicial institution.[48] This view has also recently been endorsed by the European Court of Justice in *Grant* v. *South-West Trains Ltd*,[49] in which it said that the HRC "is not a judicial institution"[50] and that its "findings have no binding force in law".[51] It seems then that the character of the HRC is more in the nature of the former European Commission on Human Rights[52] and the current Inter-American Commission on Human Rights, save that it cannot, at present, engage in the process of conciliation in individual communications.[53] On this view, therefore, it might be argued that the "final views" of the HRC have a character similar to the decisions of the European and American Commissions.

---

[45] See *Report of the Human Rights Committee, Volume I*, 1998, above n. 44 at para. 486.

[46] *Ibid.*

[47] *Ibid.*

[48] For other observations on the status of the HRC see McGoldrick, above n. 7 at 53–4; Ghandhi, above n. 7 at 41; and Nowak, above n. 9 at 506–7.

[49] Case C–249/96 of 17 February 1998.

[50] *Ibid*, para. 46.

[51] *Ibid.*

[52] Following the entry into force of Protocol 11 to the European Convention on Human Rights and Fundamental Freedoms 1950, the European Court of Human Rights has taken over the functions of the former Commission which is now no longer in existence.

[53] The position is different in the optional inter-state complaint procedure contained in Arts. 41–45.

The composition of the HRC may also be of some significance. The main qualifications for election to membership of the HRC are possession of "high moral character" and "recognized competence in the field of human rights".[54] While legal expertise is not required of HRC members, Article 28 ICCPR provides that some consideration should be "given to the usefulness of the participation of some persons having legal experience".[55] MacKay appears to take a rather sceptical view of the composition of the Committee saying that:[56]

"As a body of the United Nations, voting on candidates is inevitably subject to political considerations and extraneous influences such as vote-swapping for other bodies."

He fails to note, however, that Committee members serve in a personal capacity[57] and must take a solemn oath to discharge their obligations impartially and conscientiously.[58] Furthermore, a perusal of the present composition of the HRC reveals that it numbers among its members persons of some eminence in the law.[59] There are, however, some members who, being diplomats and former politicians, do not have direct legal experience. While such persons are in a minority, Ando nonetheless thinks this is desirable "considering the global character and current competence of the HRC". He goes on to say:[60]

"[I]f the international community is not ready to grant the HRC a court-like competence, then maintaining professional judges alone on a permanent basis may not be a practical solution. In fact, such a solution would eliminate a wide range of competent persons from candidacy to membership on the HRC and make the Committee's work needlessly legislative."

This broad membership of the HRC has not, however, found approval with everyone. In a 1996 report for the Committee on International Human Rights Law and Practice of the ILA, Professor Anne Bayefsky wrote:[61]

"There is . . . sufficient divergence of opinion among the members of the Committee to impede the development of a common and sophisticated jurisprudence."

In fairness, Bayefsky's critique might have more to do with the HRC's modus operandi than with the composition of the Committee. Among the present members

---

[54] Art. 28(2) ICCPR.
[55] *Ibid.*
[56] MacKay, above n. 6 at 16.
[57] Art. 28(3) ICCPR.
[58] Art. 38. The text of the oath is contained in Art. 16 Rules of Procedure of the Human Rights Committee, CCPR/C/Rev.5, 11 August 1997.
[59] The Committee's 18 expert members are: Abdelfattah Amor (Tunisia); Nisuke Ando (Japan); Prafullachandra Natwarlal Bhagwati (India); Christine Chanet (France); Maurice Glele-Ahanhanzo (Benin); Louis Henkin (United States of America); Eckart Klein (Germany); David Kretzmer (Israel); Rajsoomer Lallah (Mauritius); Cecilia Medina Quiroga (Chile); Rafael Rivas Posada (Colombia); Nigel Rodley (United Kingdom); Martin Scheinin (Finland); Ivan Shearer (Australia); Hipolito Solari Yrigoyen (Argentina); Ahmed Twafik Khalil (Egypt); Patrick Vella (Malta); and Maxwell Yalden (Canada).
[60] Ando, above n. 14 at 172.
[61] International Law Association, *Report of the Sixty Seventh Conference: Held at Helsinki, Finland, 12 to 17 August 1996* (London, International Law Association, 1996) 346.

are individuals with excellent credentials in the law, but they are bound to operate by way of consensus.[62] As anyone who has examined a judgment of the European Court of Justice will be aware, there are occasions on which a consensus among those with divergent views produces a judgment which is either oracular or anodyne or both. As McGoldrick observes, "[t]he necessity for consensus inevitably reduces clarity and precision".[63] The reliance upon written procedure alone further dilutes the authority of the HRC's proceedings, since they are unable to call, hear and cross examine witnesses. Given the backlog in the HRC's consideration of individual communications,[64] the Secretariat has taken to providing summaries of communications for the Committee. Few HRC members actually see the entire file. Furthermore, the HRC is under-resourced and overworked given that it has only three six week sessions to devote to its tasks. Since most (approximately two-thirds) of these sessions are taken up by consideration of periodic reports, the Committee has little time to devote to individual applications. All this may lead to a less than rigorous review of the issues. MacKay notes:[65]

> "This may suggest a need for caution in any elevation of the Human Rights Committee as part of our quasi domestic legal structure, and the status to be accorded its views. The Committee should not be seen as a substitute for domestic processes, nor is it there to function as a final Court of Appeal in assessing whether a particular decision is right or wrong."

In this comment MacKay seems to be obliquely criticising certain judicial statements in New Zealand which have described the HRC as "in substance a judicial body of high standing"[66] and "in a sense part of this country's judicial structure".[67] It should be noted, however, that the majority of the Court of Appeal in *Wellington District Legal Services Committee* v. *Tangiora*[68] held that the HRC was not a "judicial authority" for the purposes of s 19(1)(e)(v) of the Legal Services Act 1991. This finding was confirmed by the Privy Council.[69] Among the reasons for the Court of Appeal adopting this position was the fact that the "final views" of the HRC were not, in the majority's opinion, binding.[70]

---

[62] Individuals may, however, append their opinions to the Committee's views: Rule 94 of the Rules of Procedure of the Human Rights Committee.

[63] McGoldrick, above n. 7 at 199.

[64] Harris, above n. 44 at 38, notes that the average length of time taken to determine a communication is four years and one month, with some cases being decided as speedily as within one year and ten months and others taking in excess of five years.

[65] MacKay, above n. 6 at 17.

[66] [1994] 2 NZLR 257, 260 per Cooke P.

[67] *Ibid*, 266 per Cooke P. This view has been cited with apparent approval by Williams J in *Lawson* v. *Housing New Zealand* [1997] 2 NZLR 474, 497 and in *Elika* v. *Minister of Immigration* [1996] 1 NZLR 741, 744; by Cartwright J in *Northern Regional Health Authority* v. *Human Rights Commission* [1998] 2 NZLR 218, 236; and by Tipping J in *Quilter* v. *Attorney-General* [1998] 1 NZLR 523, 577.

[68] [1998] 1 NZLR 129. Thomas J partly dissenting on the ground that because the HRC was competent to make a definitive ruling on the question of breach of the ICCPR, it was clothed "with the mantle of judicial authority".

[69] [2000] 1 NZLR 17.

[70] [1998] 1 NZLR 129, 136, Keith J giving judgment for the majority.

VIII JURISPRUDENTIAL QUALITY OF "FINAL VIEWS"

In the light of these rather critical observations, what can be said about the quality of the legal reasoning of the Committee in its "final views"? The Bayefsky report suggests that the HRC[71]

"has not handled more subtle human rights issues, such as those raising questions of discriminatory benefits from facially neutral rules, as well as it has gross violations of human rights, like infringements of the right to life . . .."

There should, however, be no surprise about the mixed performance of the HRC in this regard. Individual communications originate from a broad array of States with quite diverse political and social cultures. In some States, respect for the rule of law and human rights is barely established, if at all, while in others all the impedimenta of sophisticated civil society are firmly emplaced. Paradoxically, the HRC is better equipped to deal with the former circumstances where the issues are typically fact driven, rather than the latter where the issues involved usually require detailed analysis of substantive human rights law at the most refined level.[72] It is apparent that the HRC has neither the resources, the organisation, nor the procedures to allow it to undertake extended jurisprudential analysis similar to that of the European or Inter-American Court of Human Rights. Despite this, scrutiny of the HRC's follow-up procedure demonstrates that it is States in which human rights violations might be said to be on the margins of contestability, in the sense that the issues generally involve very fine interpretation of the law, rather than those in which violations are flagrant, which are most compliant in giving effect to the HRC's final views.[73] Perhaps Tomuschat's observations are pertinent here:[74]

"Legally, the views formulated by the Human Rights Committee are not binding on the State party concerned which remains free to criticize them. Nonetheless, any State party will find it hard to reject such findings in so far as they are based on orderly proceedings during which the defendant party had ample opportunity to present its submissions. The

---

[71] International Law Association, above n. 61 at 346.

[72] See, for instance, a number of communications involving Art. 26. Although the HRC has declared Art. 26 to be an autonomous right which extends to substantive rights not covered by the ICCPR, such as the right to be free from discriminatory treatment in the area of economic, social and cultural rights, its approach has been criticised for not giving sufficient weight to the fact that such rights are to be implemented programatically and progressively. Indeed, the German Government entered a reservation to the ICCPR largely as a result of the HRC's approach in this area. See M Schmidt, "The Complementarity of the Covenant and the European Convention on Human Rights: Recent Developments" in Harris, above n. 44 at 629. See also See Communication Nos 212/1986, *PPC* v. *The Netherlands*, CCPR/C/OP/1 at 70; 218/1986, *Vos* v. *The Netherlands*, CCPR/C/44/D/218/1990; 395/1990 *Sprenger* v. *The Netherlands*, CCPR/C/44/D/395/1990; 415/1990, *Pauger* v. *Austria*, CCPR/C/47/D/415/1990; 418/1990, *Araujo-Jongen* v. *The Netherlands*, CCPR/C/49/D/418/1990; 406 and 426/1990, *Oulajin and Kais* v. *The Netherlands*, CCPR/C/46/D/406/1990; 478/1991, *APLvdM* v. *The Netherlands*, CCPR/C/48/D/4781991; 477/1991, *JAMB-R* v. *The Netherlands*, CCPR/C/50/D/477/1991; and 425/1990, *Lanooij Neefs* v. *The Netherlands*, CCPR/C/51/D/425/1990.

[73] See Part VIII of the *Report of the Human Rights Committee, Volume I*, above n. 44.

[74] Tomuschat, above n. 17 at 255.

views of the Human Rights Committee gain their authority from their inner qualities of impartiality, objectiveness and soberness. If such requirements are met, the views of the Human Rights Committee can have a far-reaching impact, at least vis-à-vis such Governments which have not outrightly broken with the international community and ceased to care anymore for concern expressed by international bodies. If such a situation arose, however, even a legally binding decision would not be likely to be respected."

IX RECONSIDERATION OF "FINAL VIEWS"

Both Ando[75] and Tomuschat[76] suggest that since the HRC's "views" are not legally binding, they can be challenged or criticised. While this might be true in a general sense, the HRC has since 1984 had in place a mechanism for reconsidering its "views". There was some debate about whether the HRC had the necessary legal competence to do this.[77] A minority of members took the view that since the HRC was a *sui generis* body with no judicial powers, the implementation of its "views" depended on the good will of the State party concerned, and there was no useful progress to be made "in trying to press States to do what they were not obliged to do".[78] The majority, however, rejected this approach based, it would seem, largely on the need to render the OP effective. It said that "the Committee could not let its work under the Optional Protocol degenerate into an exercise of futility" and that "due consideration had to be paid to the letter and the spirit" of the ICCPR.[79] Thus, where the HRC reasonably believed that certain action was open to it, and where it was not expressly prohibited, such action could be taken. The process adopted by the HRC for reviewing its views is, however, limited in nature and restricted to a review of the facts rather than law:[80]

"Its [the HRC's] role in the examination of any given case comes to an end by the adoption of views or by the adoption of another decision of a final nature. Only in exceptional circumstances may the Committee agree to reconsider an earlier final decision. Basically, this would only occur when the Committee is satisfied that new facts are placed before it by a party claiming that these facts were not available to it at the time of the consideration of the case and that these facts would have altered the decision of the Committee."

The reconsideration procedure has not, in fact, been utilised, and has been largely overtaken by the development of the more sophisticated follow-up procedure referred to above.

---

[75] Ando, above n. 14 at 171–2.
[76] Tomuschat, above n. 17 at 255.
[77] *Report of the Human Rights Committee*, GAOR, 38th Sess, Supp No 40, A/38/40, 93–4.
[78] *Ibid.*
[79] *Ibid.*
[80] *Report of the Human Rights Committee*, GAOR, 39th Sess, Supp No 40, A/39/40, 126.

X CONCLUSIONS

In the beginning it was accepted by states parties to the OP and the HRC itself that the Committee's final views were not legally binding. This position has undoubtedly changed, with the Committee explicitly asserting a greater legal status for its "views". As if to reflect this enhanced status, the word "views" has now acquired an upper case "V" in the HRC's documents. It is, in fact, my contention that the Committee has, in recent "views", taken the explicit step of declaring them to be legally binding. As indicated above, the rationale for this is a matter of speculation, but it does seem to represent a conscious policy on the part of the HRC. As also indicated above, I have reservations about this step since it is unlikely to command the support of all States parties to the ICCPR given the Committee's current composition, procedures and resource base. While there is no official sanction for the failure of States to implement the "views" of the HRC, the development of a fairly rigorous (yet substantially underfunded) follow-up procedure seems to indicate a more robust approach by the Committee to the question of non-compliance.

Where does this leave a State like New Zealand? As a general proposition, the issue of the legal status of the "final views" of the HRC to New Zealand is, at present, a matter of theoretical interest alone. The level of applications from New Zealand to the Committee has been low and, as yet, no adverse finding has been made against this country. This seems to be consistent with the position of other States in the Western European and Others group. As Bayefsky pointed out in her report for the ILA, while 40 per cent of the case load of the HRC comes from Western European and Others group, only 12 per cent of the total violations found by the HRC originate from States within that group.[81] MacKay makes a similar point:[82]

"Amongst the top five countries against which most complaints were made, were Canada, France and the Netherlands. In a world which has recently witnessed genocide, and where torture, arbitrary executions, imprisonment, and disappearances are commonplace, we must ask whether Canada, France and the Netherlands are really at the cutting edge of international human rights violations?"

Despite this highly pertinent observation, even these States, which have sound reputations in the field of human rights, have been found, on occasion, to be in breach of their obligations under the ICCPR. Where this has occurred the reaction has been significant. In the vast majority of cases, they have made the necessary modifications to their laws and have paid compensation to victims. There has been no attempt to contest the HRC's views on the grounds of their legal validity. This seems to suggest that there is a reasonably high level of trust between most Western States and the HRC. This is probably buttressed by the fact that Western States also have a weather eye on their international reputations and the fact that these

---

[81] International Law Association, above n. 61 at 346.
[82] MacKay, above n. 6 at 14. The same point is made by Upton, above n. 2 at 11.

reputations would not be enhanced by a visibly hostile attitude towards the Committee. A further reason for the more sanguine approach by Western States perhaps, is that the number of complaints which are able to overcome the procedural hurdle of the exhaustion of domestic remedies is very low indeed, thus indicating the general efficacy of domestic human rights protection and, perhaps, a willingness by the HRC to allow such States a degree of latitude in the fulfilment of their obligations. It might also be noted that most Western States are party to regional human rights supervisory systems which bear the characteristics of supranational constitutional courts and which have competence to hand down legally binding decisions and to award compensation. A litigant who truly believes that his or her rights have been violated is more likely to seek vindication through regional institutions, especially the European Convention system, rather than the HRC whose procedures are unduly protracted and whose views and remedies may or may not have legally binding force.

Applications by individuals under international procedures for the vindication of human rights violations are always a matter of last resort in the sense that these procedures may only be engaged when all domestic remedies have been exhausted. In New Zealand the political and legal traditions which are underpinned by the doctrines of the rule of law, the separation of powers, the principle of legality, and, more recently, by a burgeoning corpus of distinct human rights law, ensures that the domestic system of human rights protection at the individual level is, for the most part, sufficiently robust to withstand the scrutiny of an international body such as the HRC. As Sir Geoffrey Palmer has pointed out, however, all is not perfect, and it is the role of international human rights bodies to indicate such imperfections.[83] Although New Zealand has not yet been the subject of an adverse ruling by the HRC, it would, in my opinion, be unreasonably sanguine to take the view that this is a practical impossibility. There may well come a time, perhaps in the not too distant future, when the New Zealand Government will have to grapple with an adverse ruling by the HRC which has far-reaching implications for social policy.[84] At that stage, New Zealand will be compelled to address the issue of its obligations under the ICCPR and its OP. Like many States before it, it might not like or even disagree with the Committee's final views, but unless the HRC is manifestly in error in the formulation of its views or, and this would seem highly unlikely, acting in bad faith, it would seem to be politically unwise to argue that such views are not technically legally binding on the State, especially since the State is able to muster all of its legal resources to contest any communication. If, as

---

[83] Sir G Palmer, "Human Rights and the New Zealand Government's Treaty Obligations" (1999) 29 *VUWLR* 57.

[84] This is a fear which is articulated by MacKay, above n. 6 at 14–15. He cites Communication No 488/1992, *Toonen* v. *Australia*, CCPR/C/50/D/488/1992 as an illustration of the far-reaching implications which a decision of the HRC might have for the social policy of States. The then current litigation against New Zealand concerning the 1992 Sealords Fisheries Settlement may also have prompted this type of concern, though ultimately no violation was found: see *Mahuika* v. *New Zealand*, ablove, n. 6.

MacKay seems to suggest,[85] New Zealand has reservations about the composition, modus operandi and resourcing of the HRC and that deficiencies in these areas reflect adversely upon the quality of the Committee's jurisprudence, then there are a number of possible solutions. New Zealand could continue to work actively for reform of the UN system;[86] it could agitate for a trans-Tasman or regional Pacific human rights system; but the most obvious and least costly solution is to promote vigorous debate about human rights within New Zealand, and for every area of government, especially the Executive, to take its human rights responsibilities seriously. As in most areas of human endeavour, an ounce of prevention is worth a pound of cure.

---

[85] MacKay, above n. 6 at 16.

[86] This appears to have been the former New Zealand Government's preferred option. See Upton, above n. 2 at 13.

17

The UK's Human Rights Act 1998: An Early Assessment

IAN LEIGH

I INTRODUCTION

In a single week in October 2000 two very different revolutions occurred. One, on the streets of Belgrade, toppled a dictator—and replaced him with a Professor of Constitutional Law. The second took place peaceably in every court in the United Kingdom, from the local magistrates' and county courts to the House of Lords, when the Human Rights Act 1998 (HRA) came into force.[1] The Home Secretary's pre-publicity had trailed this as the biggest legal reform since the Bill of Rights 1689.[2] The change was accompanied by extensive preparations. All four thousand of Her Majesty's Judges were trained in the largest ever programme run by the Judicial Studies Board at a cost of nearly £5 million. Civil servants had spent two years anxiously scouring legislation and policies which could be at risk in the courts. Commentary upon the Act from academics and practitioners has been voluminous. The long period of preparation allowed many arguments to be devised which have formed early test cases, and perhaps explains the large number of cases under the Act from the outset.

In this paper an attempt will be made to assess a selection of the earliest cases arising under the Act (those in the first seven months). This is a very short time in the life of a major piece of constitutional legislation intended to operate for decades. Nevertheless, the volume and complexity of case law is sufficient for some trends to be tentatively identified. There are too many decisions for a comprehensive survey. Instead, the account here concentrates on three issues: the use made by judges of the European Convention on Human Rights (ECHR) and its case law; the effect in public law; and the arguments raised in civil litigation (the so-called horizontality issue). First a brief outline of the main features of the Act.

Revolutionary the Act may be but it is not a Bill of Rights—the courts cannot use it to override statutes. Instead, there is the duty of the courts to read legislation to conform to the ECHR, in the words of section 3, "[s]o far as it is possible to do

---

[1] In some respects the Act was in force in Scotland from summer 1999 as a consequence of devolution: under the Scotland Act 1998 both the Scottish Parliament and the Scottish Executive enjoy limited powers. Neither can act to violate a person's Convention rights unless the violation is clearly required under Westminster legislation.

[2] White Paper, *Rights Brought Home: The Human Rights Bill*, Cm 3782 (1997).

so". This carefully crafted provision strengthens the influence of the Convention in at least two ways. Previously the courts required legislation to be ambiguous before they would refer to the Convention to settle differences of meaning, on the assumption (which could be displaced) that Parliament intended to legislate in accordance with the Crown's international treaty obligations. Section 3 no longer requires there to be a statutory ambiguity before the threshold can be crossed. The Convention must be considered in all cases by all courts and tribunals and even where to adopt a Convention-friendly reading might seem unnatural—provided it is *possible*.

The prospect that it may be impossible to read some statutes to conform is the escape-hatch that has been left for Parliamentary sovereignty. In these cases the superior courts may issue a curious order—a declaration of incompatibility.[3] For litigants this is a form of booby prize since the Act states clearly that incompatible legislation remains valid and effective.[4] The practical effect of the declaration is to signal to Parliament that there is a problem and to allow Ministers to expedite changes in the law[5]—if they choose. Controversy rages over how far this shifts the balance between Parliament and the courts.

In the first seven months' operation of the Act three declarations of incompatibility were given.[6] The first threw the system of land planning into disarray when the High Court held that where the relevant government minister acted in a dual capacity—in determining a planning appeal which had been called in from the local planning authority and applying his own policy guidelines—there was a breach of Article 6.[7] That Article requires that a person's civil rights and obligations be determined by an independent and impartial tribunal. The decision was, however, overturned on appeal by the House of Lords.[8] It held that on a correct understanding there was safeguard in judicial review of the minister's decision (and so no incompatibility with Article 6). In the second case the system of appeals for prisoners detained on mental health grounds was found to breach Article 5.[9] The applicant had been convicted of manslaughter and detained in a mental hospital. He applied unsuccessfully to the Mental Health Review Tribunal for his release. The Court of Appeal found that section 73 of the Mental Health Act breached Article 5 of the Convention (protecting liberty of the person) since it effectively reversed the

---

[3] Human Rights Act 1998 ("HRA"), s. 4. The declaration may be issued by the High Court, Court of Appeal, House of Lords or the Judicial Committee of the Privy Council.

[4] HRA, s. 4(6).

[5] HRA, s. 10 and sched. 2.

[6] A fourth case has raised, as yet undetermined, incompatibility issues. In *R* v. *Y (Sexual offence: Complainant's sexual history)*, *The Times*, 13 February 2001, the Court of Appeal apparently would have considered making a declaration of incompatibility but did not since the issue was raised on an interlocutory application and the Secretary of State was not represented. The House of Lords is considering the appeal (including whether s. 41 of Youth Justice and Criminal Evidence Act 1999 is incompatible with Art. 6): see *R* v. *A* [2001] 1 WLR 789.

[7] *R* v. *SSE, ex parte Holding and Barnes plc*, *The Times*, 24 January 2001.

[8] *R* v. *SSE, ex parte Holding and Barnes plc* [2001] 2 WLR 1389 (HL).

[9] *R (on the application of H)* v. *Mental Health Review Tribunal, North and East London Region* [2001] 3 WLR 512 (CA).

burden of proof against the detained person. In the third case the Court of Appeal found that a statutory bar on the enforcement of security under section 127(3) of the Consumer Credit Act 1974 unless certain conditions were complied with was incompatible with Article 6 or Article 1 of the First Protocol to the Convention (the right to peaceful enjoyment of one's possessions).[10] The Court of Appeal was unable either to read the provision to comply with the Convention or to find an adequate explanation (either from the Parliamentary material or otherwise) for why such a draconian provision had been enacted. Accordingly, it found that the section did not fall within what it otherwise recognised would have been a wide discretionary area of legislative judgment to be respected in matters of social policy.[11]

These last two cases shed light on the approach to the interpretive obligation under section 3. In the consumer credit case the court stated that it was required to look for "some other legitimate interpretation":[12]

"The court is required to go as far as, but not beyond, what is legally possible. The court is not required, or entitled, to give to words a meaning which they cannot bear; although it is required to give to words a meaning which they can bear, if that will avoid incompatibility, notwithstanding that that is not the meaning which they would be given in a 'non-Convention' interpretation."

This is illustrated by the words of Lord Phillips of Worth Maltravers MR in the Mental Health Act case. He stated that section 3:[13]

"did not permit the court to interpret a requirement that a tribunal had to act if satisfied that a state of affairs did not exist as meaning that it had to act if not satisfied that a state of affairs did exist. The two were patently not the same."

Overall, it is hard to find many cases in which the duty of the courts under section 3 has made an appreciable difference to the outcome.

Only two instances stand out. The first involved a reading of the Sex Discrimination Act 1975 by the Employment Appeal Tribunal, which on the strength of the Human Rights Act ventured where courts have previously feared to tread in holding that sex discrimination also encompassed discrimination on grounds of sexual orientation.[14] In the second, if anything bolder, decision the Court of Appeal reinterpreted previous authority on the imposition of automatic life sentences where an offender committed a second serious offence because it felt compelled to do so under the Act.[15] Previously the courts had given a highly

---

[10] *Wilson v. First County Trust Ltd* [2001] 3 WLR 42 (CA) argument had earlier been adjourned to allow argument on the incompatibility point: *Wilson v. First County Trust* [2001] 2 WLR 302 (CA).

[11] *Ibid*, paras. 33–40.

[12] *Ibid*, para. 42.

[13] Above n. 9. Under the Act the tribunal was to direct his release if satisfied: "(i) that he is not then suffering from mental illness, psychopathic disorder, severe mental impairment or mental impairment or from any of those forms of disorder of a nature or degree which makes it appropriate for him to be liable to be detained in a hospital for medical treatment; or (ii) that it is not necessary for the health or safety of the patient or for the protection of other persons that he should receive such treatment . . .".

[14] *MacDonald v. Ministry of Defence* [2001] 1 All ER 620 (EAT).

[15] *R v. Offen* [2001] 1 WLR 253.

restricted reading to the judge's discretion not to impose such a sentence in "exceptional circumstances" under section 2 of the Crime (Sentences) Act 1997.[16] The Court of Appeal held that this interpretation could lead to the section operating in a disproportionate manner inconsistent with Articles 3 and 5 of the Convention. Accordingly, the section would henceforth be interpreted so that offenders were not sentenced to life imprisonment where they did not constitute a significant risk to the public. The sentencing provision in question was one that several senior judges had publicly opposed when it was before Parliament, on the basis that it interfered with the proper discretion of the courts in sentencing matters. Striking as these two decisions may be, however, they are exceptional.

The second main extension under section 3 of the courts' duty is that legislation *in all fields* is to be read in a convention-friendly way. This applies as much in the private sphere, for example, to landlord and tenant and family legislation, where there is on the face of it no clash between the individual and the state. This is one of several ways in which the Act may apply "horizontally"—a topic explored below.

More briefly, the second major effect of the Act is to impose a new duty on all public authorities not to act incompatibly with a person's Convention rights. Parliament is exempted, but ministers, their officials, local authorities, the police, and "quangos" are included. The boundaries of the public sector here are unclear since "hybrid" public authorities are envisaged, whose "public" functions will fall under the Act but whose "private" ones will not.[17] However, courts and tribunals are named explicitly in section 6 as public authorities. Controversy ranges over the full implications. In particular, two possible effects of section 6 are discussed below. The first is the consequences for private litigation. On the one side there are some who appear to treat this subsection as the key to the entire Act, requiring courts to uphold Convention rights in all cases whatever the previous law says. On the other side is the more modest position that its effect is limited to discretionary decisions, procedural and evidential matters, and the scope of orders and remedies granted. This is a controversy to which we return in Part III below. The second contentious question is the effect of section 6 on the standard of review in public law cases: this is discussed in Part II.

Having given a preliminary outline of the main features of the Act, let me turn now to some of the most important early trends and developments.

A brief comment is required to explain why I have chosen not to focus on criminal cases. After all, the experience in countries such as Canada and New Zealand, which have adopted domestic Bills of Rights in recent decades, has been that the greatest use of these protections occurs in criminal trials. This is unsurprising: individuals are most at risk of state coercion and abuse from the penal law and those who enforce it. There has been no shortage of arguments raised in criminal cases in Britain either, but, with one or two short-lived exceptions, they have nearly all

---

[16] R v. *Kelly (Edward)* [2000] 1 QB 198.
[17] HRA, ss. 6(3)(b) and (5).

failed. To explain why would require an article in its own right. Several factors can be briefly mentioned, however. The courts have been unwilling to reconsider the long-established non-exclusionary rule.[18] Moreover, the Court of Appeal has held that its power to cure trial defects can put right breaches of the right to a fair trial by a lower court.[19] This is a restrictive reading of the duty of the lower court as a public authority under section 6 of the HRA. Without a basis for excluding evidence obtained in violation of the Convention, the possible effect of the Act is limited to procedural matters[20] and to rare situations in which an offence or type of sentence or court order is said to violate rights. The courts have, for example, dismissed several arguments that statutory provisions reversing the onus of proof violate the Convention,[21] including those relating to confiscation of assets.[22] A restrictive reading has been given to the concept of a "criminal charge" so as to minimise the field of application of the fair trial right under Article 6.[23] In criminal law, therefore, the Act has yet to make much impact.

II THE USE OF CONVENTION JURISPRUDENCE

One significant difference marks out the development of law under the UK Human Rights Act from the earlier experiences in Canada, New Zealand and South Africa with the adoption of Bills of Rights. In Britain's case the exercise was not merely one of incorporating into domestic law an established international treaty. With the treaty text comes also a significant body of jurisprudence from the European Court of Human Rights and the European Commission.[24] This case law has been developed over forty years (the Court gave its first decision in 1959) and in cases from a steadily increasing number of member States (over forty countries are now signatories to the Convention). As a legal text the Convention is now in its mid-life, with most traits of its personality and character firmly established. Consequently, very many questions of interpretation have already been settled and judges in the United Kingdom have come on the scene relatively late in the day.

This is not to say, however, that there is no scope for judicial creativity. The use of the Convention in a domestic setting is a different kind of exercise from its use at an international level. As an international supervisory court, Strasbourg has often been restrained from intervening by what it describes as "the margin of appreciation"

---

[18] *AG's Reference (No. 3 of 1999)* [2001] 2 WLR 56, 64 (Lord Steyn) and 65 (Lord Cooke of Thorndon); *R v. P* [2001] 2 WLR 463, 471–5 (Lord Hobhouse).

[19] *R v. Craven, The Times*, 2 February 2001 (CA).

[20] Delay in trial has been a favourite target of defence advocates, but largely unsuccessfully.

[21] For example, *R v. Lambert* [2001] 2 WLR 211; *Re K* [2001] 1 Cr App R 493 (CA).

[22] *McIntosh v. Lord Advocate* [2001] 3 WLR 107 (PC); *R v. Benjafield* [2001] 3 WLR 75 (CA).

[23] The following have been held not to be criminal charges: Sex offenders orders (*B v. Chief Constable of Avon and Somerset Constabulary* [2001] 1 WLR 340 (DC)); an anti-social behaviour order (*R (McCann) v. Crown Court at Manchester* [2001] 1 WLR 358 (DC)); prison disciplinary proceedings (*Greenfield v. Secretary of State for the Home Department* [2001] EWHC Admin 129).

[24] The latter was abolished under the 11th Protocol to the Convention.

that domestic authorities have under the Convention. This is a recognition that human rights protection operates internationally as a floor of rights and that on many issues there is no common European standard to which States must conform in every respect. Use of the margin has been particularly developed where the Court has considered whether permissible restrictions under Articles 8–12 are "necessary in a democratic society" for one of the permitted reasons. Following incorporation one significant area of uncertainty was the extent to which UK courts would apply or mirror the margin of appreciation to give latitude to the legislature or the executive.

On the one hand, there are strong arguments that the margin of appreciation should have no domestic equivalent since its whole rationale lies in the limits of the Strasbourg court and in the recognition of domestic legal differences throughout Europe. This approach would incidentally enlarge the scope for creative judicial interpretation since, with the margin of appreciation discarded, domestic judges would have a freer hand to determine for themselves the meaning of the limitations on Convention rights in a uniquely British context. On the other hand, deference to Parliament and respect for the executive are quintessential features of the UK legal system that have shaped the role of judges since the Glorious Revolution in the seventeenth century, and it seemed unlikely that this tradition would be transformed overnight. Commentators therefore argued that some equivalent domestic "proportionality" test or "margin of deference" would emerge.

The courts have declared that the margin of appreciation does not apply. In *Kebilene* Lord Hope stated that:[25]

> "This technique is not available to the national courts when they are considering Convention issues arising within their own countries. But in the hands of the national courts also the Convention should be seen as an expression of fundamental principles rather than as a set of mere rules. The questions which the courts will have to decide in the application of these principles will involve questions of balance between competing interests and issues of proportionality."

Likewise, in *Brown* v. *Stott* Lord Bingham stated:[26]

> "While a national court does not accord the margin of appreciation . . . it will give weight to the decisions of a representative legislature and a democratic government within the discretionary area of judgment accorded to those bodies."

In that case the Judicial Committee of the Privy Council found in an appeal from Scotland that the use of compulsorily obtained statements from the driver of

---

[25]   *R* v. *DPP, ex parte Kebilene* [2000] 2 AC 326, 380–1 (HL).

[26]   [2001] 2 WLR 817, 835 (PC). In *Wilson* v. *First County Trust Ltd* [2001] 3 WLR 42 the Court of Appeal accepted the need for deference to the legislature in matters of social policy but continued (para. 33):

> "[U]nless deference is to be equated with unquestioning acceptance, the argument . . . recognises . . . the need for the court to identify the particular issue of social policy which the legislature or the executive thought it necessary to address, and the thinking which led to that issue being dealt with in the way that it was. It is one thing to accept the need to defer to an opinion which can be seen to be the product of reasoned consideration based on policy; it is quite another thing to be required to accept, without question, an opinion for which no reason of policy is advanced".

a vehicle under the Road Traffic Act 1998 did not violate Article 6 since it was not a disproportionate legislative response to problems of road safety.[27]

The logical implication of holding the margin to be inapplicable is that UK laws which have already been upheld or would be upheld at Strasbourg because of the margin should, nevertheless, be open to be given a more rights-friendly reading at the domestic level. However, the courts appear reluctant to take up the challenge. As we have seen in the criminal sphere, where the margin is wide because of differences across Europe in criminal procedure and evidence, judges have been content to refer to restrictive Strasbourg precedents and have used the *outcome* to show that the HRA makes no difference, ignoring the fact that the margin which Strasbourg applied in these decisions need not constrain them.

A second limiting device should be mentioned—discouraging the citation of Convention jurisprudence. A minority of judges clearly think that the Convention has little to add to the domestic law and have tried to dissuade counsel from even citing relevant cases. This phenomenon predates the Human Rights Act. In the area of freedom of expression the House of Lords declared itself satisfied that the common law was identical to Article 10 of the Convention,[28] so there was little point in engaging seriously with the (extensive) Strasbourg case law. Even rulings from Strasbourg pointing out where common law doctrines had failed to meet the standard of the Convention[29] have apparently done little to shake this breezy self-confidence. Fresh variations on the theme have emerged after the Act.

In some cases counsel have been told the domestic legislation already fully takes into account the Convention so that it is unnecessary to cite relevant jurisprudence. Mr Justice Wall was unreceptive in the family law appeal of *Re F (care: termination of contact)*,[30] decided before the Act came into force. The mother of children in care (aged 3 and 5) appealed against a justices' order giving the council leave to terminate contact with her. She argued that the making the order was premature and would be an infringement of her rights under Articles 6.1 and 8 of the European Convention. Wall J said that while the Children Act 1989 had to be read and given effect in a way that was compatible with the Convention rights, it was for the English courts applying what he called "English criteria of fairness and justice" to decide whether those rights had been breached. He would be:[31]

> "disappointed if the European Convention on Human Rights were to be routinely paraded in cases of this nature as make-weight grounds of appeal, or if there were in every case to be extensive citation of authorities from the European Court of Human Rights, particularly where reliance was placed on cases pre-dating the 1989 Act".

[27] See especially the judgments of Lord Steyn (*ibid*, 841–3) and Lord Hope of Craighead (*ibid*, 853–5).

[28] *Attorney-General v. Guardian Newspapers (No. 2)* [1990] 1 AC 109, 284–5 per Lord Goff; *Derbyshire CC v. Times Newspapers Ltd* [1993] AC 534, 550–1 per Lord Keith of Kinkel; and *R v. Secretary of State for the Home Department, ex parte Simms* [2000] AC 115, 123–4 per Lord Steyn.

[29] *Sunday Times v. UK* (1979) 2 EHRR 245; *Observer & Guardian v. UK* (1991) 14 EHRR 153; and *Tolstoy Miloslavsky v. UK* (1995) 20 EHRR 442.

[30] *The Times*, 22 June 2000 (Family Div).

[31] *Ibid.*

These comments suggest an unwilling judicial embrace of the Strasbourg jurisprudence, coupled with a dangerous complacency over homegrown standards of justice, with a dash of mild Europhobia thrown in for good measure. The assumption that legislation already complies with the ECHR, so that courts need not look beyond it, has too often in the past proved to be unfounded (the UK has been found to be in breach of the Convention on more than fifty occasions). Moreover, if this approach were to be followed it would contradict section 2 of the HRA, which stipulates that a court "must" take Strasbourg decisions into account, although it goes on to add "so far as, in the opinion of the court or tribunal, it is relevant to the proceedings". The attempt to restrict citation of Strasbourg case law to post-1989 cases (that is, those post-dating the Children Act) flies in the face of the duty to take account of such jurisprudence "whenever made or given". Indeed it is doubtful if judges can refuse to hear ECHR arguments, however confident they may be in domestic law, in view of the wording of section 2. On the contrary, far from discouraging advocates from raising Convention points, one plausible interpretation of this provision is that it requires the judge to take the *initiative* and consider Convention arguments, whether or not the parties or their legal advisers do so.

A restricted reading was given to section 2 when the Court of Appeal reviewed the infamous "M25 murder" case.[32] The Court of Human Rights had earlier held that the defendants' rights under Article 6 had been breached because of the failure to disclose at the trial that a key prosecution witness was a paid police informant.[33] The issue for the Court of Appeal was whether the conviction was unsafe.[34] Lord Justice Mantell stressed that the duty under the HRA to "take account" of the Strasbourg decision did not mean that the English court had "to adopt" or "to apply" it. He obviously had in mind that the UK courts might on some future occasion treat as safe a conviction obtained in a trial which had been found to be unfair, although here the court found that the conviction was unsafe in any event.[35]

Another understandable, but nevertheless questionable, approach has been to treat the previous pronouncements of UK courts as binding where they have considered Convention case law, even where it is arguable that the earlier courts have misunderstood it. In a decision shortly before the Act came into force, the Divisional Court was faced with a Convention challenge to orders requiring the Guardian and Observer newspapers to hand over to the police letters received from the former MI5 officer David Shayler, concerning his allegations of a British plot to assassinate Colonel Gaddaffi.[36] It was argued that to force one of the journalists to do so would amount to a violation of his right not incriminate himself, since he

---

[32] *R* v. *Davis, The Times*, 25 July 2000.

[33] *Rowe and Davis* v. *UK* (2000) 30 EHRR 1.

[34] Criminal Appeal Act 1968, s. 2 (as amended by Criminal Appeal Act 1995).

[35] In a second case, however, the Lord Chief Justice stated that it was "almost inevitable" that unfairness at the trial would make the conviction unsafe and that it would be "most unfortunate" if the approach of the European Court and the English courts differed unless it was a requirement of legislation: *R* v. *Togher, The Times*, 21 November 2000.

[36] *R (Bright)* v. *Central Criminal Court* [2001] 1 WLR 662.

was under investigation for a possible offence under the Official Secrets Act. Notwithstanding the 1997 European Court decision of *Saunders* v. *UK*,[37] the Divisional Court regarded itself bound by decisions of the English courts on the meaning of the rule against self-incrimination, together with their interpretation of whether Article 6 was satisfied. Judge LJ said:[38]

> "[W]here such a decision or group of decisions has been examined by the House of Lords or Court of Appeal, this court is bound by the reasoning of the superior courts in our jurisdiction. We are not permitted to re-examine decisions of the European Court in order to ascertain whether the conclusion of the House of Lords or Court of Appeal may be inconsistent with those decisions, or susceptible to a continuing gloss."

In related fashion some judges have sought to limit the application of Strasbourg precedents in contentious areas by making somewhat unconvincing attempts to "distinguish" them. This is a technique that is rarely appropriate since the Strasbourg court does not regard itself as engaging in fact-finding. In *Ashworth Hospital* v. *MGN Ltd*[39] the Court of Appeal cited again the discredited formula that there is no difference in principle between English law and Article 10 of the Convention. It then went on to distinguish a decision of the European Court in which it been held that an order to disclose the identity of a whistle-blower violated Article 10[40] before proceeding to make a similar order—in this instance that a newspaper should identify the source of stories concerning the health of the convicted murderer, Ian Brady.[41] Similarly, a ground-breaking Strasbourg ruling with potentially wide application for undercover policing, *Teixeira de Castro* v. *Portugal*,[42] has been distinguished by two different benches, apparently fearful that it would introduce a defence of entrapment into English law.[43]

In a sense the invocation of the doctrine of precedent and attempts to distinguish Strasbourg case law are reassuring, as they indicate just how quickly most judges appear to have adjusted to the influx of a substantial new source of law into the legal system. Most Human Rights Act judgments are marked by engagement with the Strasbourg decisions at a detailed and sometimes extensive level. This remarkable transformation of opinion writing in such a short period is no doubt due in large part to the training programme within the judiciary and to the presence on the bench of former advocates who have argued cases in Strasbourg.

---

[37] (1997) 23 EHRR 313.

[38] Above n. 36 at 682. These strictures only apply where the appellate courts have *considered* the Strasbourg jurisprudence in question. The door may be open, then, for lower courts to revisit earlier decisions of higher courts where either the Strasbourg case law was not considered before or where it has developed significantly in the interim.

[39] [2001] 1 WLR 515.

[40] *Goodwin* v. *UK* (1996) 22 EHRR 123.

[41] *Ashworth Hospital* v. *MGN Ltd* [2001] 1 WLR 515, 534–7 (per Lord Phillips of Worth Maltravers MR).

[42] (1998) 28 EHRR 101.

[43] *Nottingham City Council* v. *Amin* [2000] 1 WLR 1071, 1080–1 (per Lord Bingham) (CA); *R* v. *Shannon* [2001] 1 WLR 51, 69–70 (per Potter LJ) (CA).

Overt negative reactions from the judiciary have been rare but one example stands out. Outright hostility bordering on xenophobia was manifested by one senior Scottish judge, Lord McCluskey, when he wrote that the Act would be "field day for crackpots, a pain in the neck for judges and legislators and a goldmine for lawyers".[44] The article went on specifically to discuss surveillance against drugs dealers and Article 8—the very issue at stake in a case that he had heard only days before. The High Court of Justiciary held that his remarks would raise in an informed observer a reasonable apprehension of bias against the Convention and ordered that the appeal be heard by a different bench.[45]

Equally, at the other extreme one can find examples of an enthusiastic embrace of the new learning. Indeed, on occasion some courts have not been prepared to stop at Strasbourg in their quest for comparative material. Most remarkable were the Scottish decisions on the independence of temporary sheriffs[46] and on the use of compelled road traffic evidence[47] which, quite apart from sophisticated engagement with the ECHR jurisprudence, went on an extensive comparative survey, reminiscent of the Canadian Supreme Court. Indeed, when the Privy Council considered the appeal in the latter case Lord Hope of Craighead sought to set some parameters to forays into comparative law. He pointed out that the court's use of Canadian precedents was unhelpful in view of differences in the law being interpreted by the Canadian courts, whereas a check against practices in other European states was more instructive.[48] Nevertheless, in another Privy Council appeal from Scotland under the Act, Lord Hope used not just the Convention but also Canadian, Australian and Irish material.[49]

We move next to consider the extent of the change in the second area to be examined, judicial review.

III THE STANDARD OF REVIEW IN PUBLIC LAW

English administrative law has, on the whole, failed to offer effective protection for Human Rights against incursions by public officials and authorities because of a long tradition of judicial deference to the executive. Nevertheless, it can be argued that the greater self-confidence that the judges have displayed in developing the grounds and reach of judicial review over the past three decades has brought incidental benefits, if somewhat belatedly, in protection of individual liberty.

Judicial attitudes to the European Convention have played no small part. Only a decade ago the House of Lords ruled that the Home Secretary was not legally

---

[44] *Scotland on Sunday*, 6 February 2000.

[45] *Hoekstra, van Rijs et al v. HM Advocate (No. 2)* 2000 SLT 605. Lord McCluskey has been a long-term public opponent of incorporation, since at least since his 1986 Reith Lectures: J H McCluskey, *Law, Justice and Democracy* (London, Sweet & Maxwell, 1987).

[46] *Starrs v. Ruxton* (2000) SLT 42.

[47] *Stott v. Brown* (2000) SLT 379.

[48] *Brown v. Stott* [2001] 2 WLR 817, 853–6 (PC).

[49] *Montgomery v. HM Advocate* [2001] 2 WLR 779, 810 (PC).

obliged to consider the Convention right of freedom of expression when imposing restrictions on television and radio interviews with people connected with a
terrorist organisation.[50] Their Lordships considered that to hold otherwise would
amount to what they described as "back door" incorporation of the Convention
and that they should not rush in where (at that time) Parliament had chosen not to.

Despite this retrograde ruling, other judicial techniques have been developed to
encourage a greater official solicitude for rights. Where the decision-maker claimed
to have considered the Convention the courts were prepared to examine whether
he or she had done so correctly.[51] The *Wednesbury*[52] test was modified in all but
name by the requirement that courts subject administrative decisions involving
human rights implications to what was described as "anxious scrutiny".[53] Later
cases in which gay and lesbian service personnel challenged the reasonableness of
their discharges from the armed forces have confirmed that the greater the human
rights dimensions of a case, the closer the attention the courts will give to the legality of the official decision.[54] Some judgments speak of the need for a "substantial
objective justification".[55] Hence, *Wednesbury* has become in effect a variable
standard: the more fundamental the right interfered with the greater the need for
justification. Nevertheless, as the "gays in the army" case shows, the judges
regarded themselves (if reluctantly) to be restricted to secondary review of administrative discretion. It was left to the Strasbourg Court to vindicate human-rights in
that case.[56]

An additional complicating factor is the recent judicial discovery within the common law of a jurisprudence of fundamental rights irrespective of the Convention,
which will only be taken to be over-ridden by the clearest of statutory words.[57] So
far these fundamental rights are limited; they are centred on the right of access to a
court (and, related, to a journalist to raise a miscarriage of justice) and, perhaps, the
entitlement of asylum seekers to social benefits.[58] How far this fundamental rights
jurisdiction overlaps with the Human Rights Act is a difficult question—in some
respects it mirrors the interpretive obligation now contained in section 3.

[50] *R v. Secretary of State for the Home Department, ex parte Brind* [1991] 1 AC 696 (HL).
[51] *R v. Secretary of State for the Home Department, ex parte Launder* [1997] 1 WLR 839, 867 per Lord
Hope of Craighead.
[52] *Associated Provincial Picture Houses Ltd v. Wednesbury Corporation* [1948] 1 KB 223, 229.
[53] *Bugdaycay v. Secretary of State for the Home Department* [1987] AC 514, 531 per Lord Bridge.
[54] *Ministry of Defence, ex parte Smith* [1996] QB 517; *R v. Secretary of State for Home Department, ex
parte Leech* [1994] QB 198.
[55] *R v. Lord Saville of Newdigate, ex parte A* [2000] 1 WLR 1855, 1866–7; and *R v. Secretary of State
for the Home Department, ex parte Launder* [1997] 1 WLR 839, 867; cf *Ministry of Defence, ex parte Smith*
[1996] QB 517, 554 .
[56] *Smith and Grady v. UK* (1999) 29 EHRR 493.
[57] See *R v. Lord Chancellor, ex parte Witham* [1998] QB 575, where Laws J struck down an order by
the Lord Chancellor substantially increasing court fees (including those for litigants in person) because
it infringed the fundamental right of access to a court. In *R v. Secretary of State for the Home Department,
ex parte Simms* [2000] AC 115 the House of Lords held that a prisoner's rights of access to journalists
could not be taken away under Prison Rules because of the fundamental importance of their role in
exposing miscarriages of justice: see especially Lord Steyn, pp. 129–30 and Lord Hoffmann, pp. 131–2.
[58] *R v. Secretary of State for Social Security ex parte Joint Council for the Welfare of Immigrants* [1997] 1
WLR 275 (CA); *R v. Home Secretary ex parte Jammeh, The Times*, 11 September 1997.

Despite these developments, even in the period immediately prior to the Human Rights Act entering into force there was a reluctance to develop administrative law doctrine to fill the rights gap. In *Kebilene* the High Court declined to develop the doctrine of legitimate expectation so as to impose on a prosecutor a duty to exercise the discretion to bring a prosecution in a prospective defendant's favour where a violation of Convention rights might result if there was a conviction.[59]

Ironically, while judicial review has become more rights-conscious the European Court of Human Rights has shifted in precisely the opposite direction in its understanding of the inadequacy of judicial review as an effective remedy for human rights breaches. Whereas in 1988 in *Soering* v. *UK*[60] it ruled that judicial review was an adequate remedy, in 2000 it distinguished this and concluded in *Smith and Grady* v. *UK*[61] that the domestic availability of judicial review had not satisfied Article 13. The Court of Appeal had found that the armed services' policy of discharging homosexuals was not irrational, despite its human rights implications. The Court of Human Rights concluded that it was clear that the domestic threshold in judicial review cases was set at such a high level that it effectively excluded any consideration by the domestic courts of whether the interference with the applicant's art 8 (respect for private life) rights answered a pressing social need or was proportionate to a legitimate aim. A further blow was struck in *Kingsley* v. *UK*,[62] where the Strasbourg court held that the applicant's rights under Article 6 of the Convention had been violated by the process under which the Gaming Board had denied him a licence following an order of the High Court quashing an initial determination by the Board and remitting it to them to re-determine. This aspect of the procedure is a routine feature of administrative law and follows from the fact that the court is a forum for review not of appeal. Nevertheless, the European Court held that Kingsley was denied a fair hearing by an impartial tribunal since the body to which his case was returned was identical in composition to the one which had already found against him. Plainly, the implications of both these judgments could be profound and require a substantial intensification of judicial review.

Prior to the coming into force of the Act there was some debate as to whether it would cause a shift in the standard of review with abandonment of judicial deference to the executive.[63] One surprising feature of the drafting of the Act was the strong wording of section 6. This appears to make breach of Convention rights by a public authority a distinct new ground of illegality, with the consequence that the

---

[59] *R* v. *DPP, ex parte Kebilene* [2000] 2 AC 326, 339 per Lord Bingham CJ; contrast *Minister for Immigration and Ethnic Affairs* v. *Teoh* (1995) 128 ALR 353, 365 (HCA). In *Kebilene* the legitimate expectation point was dropped on appeal.

[60] (1989) 11 EHRR 439; see also *Vilvarajah* v. *UK* (1991) 14 EHRR 205.

[61] (1999) 29 EHRR 493, 543–4.

[62] *Kingsley* v. *UK*, *The Times*, 9 January 2001 (ECtHR).

[63] Lord Irvine of Laire, "The Development of Human Rights in Britain under an Incorporated Convention on Human Rights" [1998] *PL* 221, 232ff; D Pannick, "Comment: Principles of Interpretation of Convention Rights under the Human Rights Act and the Discretionary Area of Judgment" [1998] *PL* 545; The Hon Sir John Laws, "The Limitations of Human Rights" [1998] *PL* 254.

courts would become concerned with the merits and effects of the decision, rather than the process by which it was reached. Judicial deference to the executive could only be maintained so far as the Convention permitted limitations to rights under the so-called proportionality doctrine. Debate in the academic journals on this issue has, predictably, spilled over into the courts in the early public law decisions.

Broadly, there are two contrasting positions. The conservative approach sees review under section 6 as a continuation of the existing approaches to judicial review: there must be due deference to the executive acting within law. This approach was asserted by Schiemann LJ in a deportation case, in holding that the Human Rights Act did not allow the court to substitute its view for that of the executive.[64] In immigration cases concerning the right to family life it was, he said, appropriate for the judiciary to recognise that was an area of judgment where they would defer to the opinion of the elected body or person whose decision was said to be incompatible. Continuity with *Wednesbury* can also be maintained by treating human rights matters as mandatory relevant considerations for the decision-maker (in effect a reversal of *Brind*).[65] One of the judges most associated with the view that the common law can develop effective rights protections of its own, Sir John Laws,[66] has taken this view, both on and off the bench.[67]

The alternative is to see the Act as bringing about a fundamental shift towards substantive review, as has been suggested by some academic commentators.[68] Writing before the first decisions were delivered under the Act, Professor Jeffrey Jowell argued that while the Act would not bring about merits review as such, it nevertheless (together with common law decisions on fundamental rights) pointed towards the development of "constitutional review", by which he meant that judges would need to justify their decisions in terms of the necessary qualities of a democratic society.[69]

Both views can be seen in operation in another deportation decision, *Mahmood*.[70] Lord Phillips MR held that the "substantial justification" approach required adaptation in the new environment: interference with human rights could only be justified to the extent permitted by the Convention itself.[71] In the same case, however, Laws LJ claimed that the Human Rights Act did not authorise the court to stand in the shoes of the decision-maker and there had to be a "principled

---

[64] *R v. Secretary of State for the Home Department, ex parte Isiko* [2001] Imm AR 291 (CA).

[65] *R v. Secretary of State for the Home Department, ex parte Brind* [1991] 1 AC 696 (HL).

[66] The Hon Sir John Laws, "Is the High Court the Guardian of Fundamental Constitutional Rights?" [1993] PL 59; *R v. Lord Chancellor, ex parte Witham* [1998] QB 575.

[67] The Hon Sir John Laws, "The Limitations of Human Rights" [1998] PL 254; see his judgment in *R (Mahmood) v. Secretary of State for the Home Department*, [2001] 1 WLR 840 (CA).

[68] M Taggart, "Tugging on Superman's Cape: Lessons from Experience with the New Zealand Bill of Rights Act 1990" in The University of Cambridge Centre for Public Law, *Constitutional Reform in the United Kingdom: Practice and Principles* (Oxford, Hart Publishing, 1998) 85, 92; I Leigh and L Lustgarten, "Making Rights Real: the Courts, Remedies, and the Human Rights Act" (1999) 58 *CLJ* 509.

[69] J Jowell, "Beyond the Rule of Law: Towards Constitutional Judicial Review" [2000] PL 671, 682.

[70] *R (Mahmood) v. Secretary of State for the Home Department* [2001] 1 WLR 840 (CA).

[71] *Ibid*, 857.

distance" between the court's adjudication and the Secretary of State's decision based on his analysis of the case.[72] In the event both approaches led on the facts to the same outcome.

A fundamentally different approach was taken in a further deportation case, where the judge was prepared to review evidence considered by the Secretary of State and concluded that the minister must have fallen into error in deciding that Pakistan was generally a safe country to which to return asylum seekers.[73] Rose J concluded that despite the historical reluctance to do so in judicial review cases, an effective remedy under the HRA required reconsideration of the evidence before the minister. The judge's scrutiny established that women and religious minorities were liable to face persecution in Pakistani society, and that the Secretary of State's decision to include Pakistan in a designated list of safe countries approved by Parliamentary order could only have been reached on an erroneous view of law or the facts, or both. In blunt language which cut through the circumspection normally followed in administrative law he stated: "the Home Secretary was plainly wrong".[74] Accordingly, he issued a declaration that the minister had erred in law.

An unresolved struggle between two different standards in judicial review following the Act is plainly underway. If the revisionist view prevails this last decision may well be seen in retrospect as the one in which the Human Rights Act was used to cross the rubicon into substantive review.

III   HORIZONTAL RIGHTS

The possible "horizontal effect" of the Human Rights Act has resulted in a burgeoning academic literature,[75] mainly because of the complex variety of routes by which the Act can apply in civil litigation and some enigmatic comments by ministers in the course of the Parliamentary debates.[76]

---

[72] *R (Mahmood)* v. *Secretary of State for the Home Department* [2001] 1 WLR 855 (CA).

[73] *R* v. *Secretary of State for the Home Department, ex parte Javed; R* v. *Secretary of State for the Home Department, ex parte Zulfiqar Ali; R* v. *Secretary of State for the Home Department, ex parte Abid Ali* [2001] 3 WLR 323 (CA); see also *R* v. *Secretary of State for the Home Department, ex parte Turgut* [2001] 1 All ER 719 and *B* v. *Secretary of State for the Home Department* [2000] Imm AR 478.

[74] *R* v. *Secretary of State for the Home Department, ex parte Javed, ibid.*

[75] M Hunt, in this volume, and at [1998] *PL* 423; I Leigh, "Horizontal Rights, the Human Rights Act and Privacy: Lessons from the Commonwealth?" (1999) 48 *ICLQ* 57; B Markesinis, "Privacy, Freedom of Expression and the Human Rights Bill: Lessons from Germany" (1999) 115 *LQR* 47; G Phillipson, "The Human Rights Act, 'Horizontal Effect' and the Common Law: a Bang or a Whimper?" (1999) 62 *MLR* 824; G Phillipson and H Fenwick, "Breach of Confidence as a Privacy Remedy in the Human Rights Act Era" (2000) 63 *MLR* 660; Sir Richard Buxton, "The Human Rights Act and Private Law" (2000) 116 *LQR* 48, Sir William Wade, "Horizons of Horizontality" (2000) 116 *LQR* 217; A Lester and D Pannick, "The Impact of the Human Rights Act on Private Law: the Knight's Move" (2000) 116 *LQR* 380; N Bamforth, "The Application of the Human Rights Act 1998 to Public Authorities and Private Bodies" (1999) 58 *CLJ* 159; N Bamforth, "The True Horizontal Effect of the Human Rights Act 1998" (2001) 107 *LQR* 34.

[76] Initially the Lord Chancellor, Lord Irvine of Lairg, specifically stated during the Second Reading debate on the Bill in the House of Lords that it was not intended to apply between private individuals: HL Debs, 3 November 1997, col 1231–2. In a later debate, however, he indicated that the courts would

The controversy is too complex to recount more than a thumbnail sketch here. At one extreme is Sir William Wade, who argues for comprehensive horizontal application of the Convention rights under the Act. At the other extreme is Sir Richard Buxton, who argues that it has no application to private litigation. For Wade the decisive provision is section 6(3), which treats all courts and tribunals as public authorities and so requires them to uphold Convention rights wherever they are claimed. This argument has difficulty in explaining why the Act carefully refers to public authorities, which on Wade's thesis would be unnecessary, and to the interpretation of statutory provisions but not to the common law. Buxton, on the other hand, stresses that the ECHR is a treaty regarding the rights of individuals against the state and it retains that character when incorporated into domestic law. This approach, however, must face the fact that in limited spheres the Convention organs themselves have recognised a positive obligation on the state[77] (including its courts) to protect individuals from incursion of their rights by other private individuals and, moreover, that the Act gives domestic courts freedom to develop rights in ways not limited by the ECHR jurisprudence provided they do not contradict it.

Despite these views at the outer ranges of the spectrum of possible opinions, a broad measure of agreement has emerged that there are differing degrees of horizontal effect, which are for the most part uncontroversial. At least six possible types of horizontal effect can be identified under the Act.[78]

First, statutes applying between private individuals are subject to the interpretative duty to give effect wherever possible to Convention rights (*"direct statutory horizontality"*). This is uncontroversial: it follows from the plain wording of section 3. For example, claims invoking the Convention in family law legislation were inevitable, given the Strasbourg court's jurisprudence on the application of Article 8 to family proceedings. They have duly materialised.[79] In a different context, an unsuccessful argument for statutory horizontality was mounted in *Ashdown v. Telegraph Group Ltd*,[80] where an attempt was made to use Article 10 to read limitations into the Copyright, Designs and Patents Act 1988 over and above the express exceptions. Sir Andrew Morritt, VC held that the balance between freedom of expression and the owner of the copyright[81] had been struck by the legislation, in particular a rule preventing the enforcement of copyright on the ground of public interest.

---

be able to refer to the Convention as a source of inspiration in developing the common law principles applicable between private individuals: HL Debs, 24 November 1997, col 783; and see the statement of Mr Mike O'Brien (a Home Office minister): HC Debs, vol 315, col 561 (2 July 1998).

[77] See eg, *X and Y v. Netherlands* (1986) 8 EHRR 235, 239–40.

[78] See further Leigh, above n. 75.

[79] For example, *In re H (a Child)(Adoption: Disclosure); In re G (a Child)(Adoption: Disclosure), The Times*, 5 January 2001 (Fam D); *Payne v. Payne* [2001] 2 WLR 1826 (CA); *In Re B (Minor: Adoption order), The Times*, 23 March 2000.

[80] [2001] 2 WLR 967.

[81] The document was politically sensitive: a minute of a meeting with the Prime Minister written by Paddy Ashdown, former leader of the Liberal Democrat party.

Similarly (and secondly), an extended application of the Convention may arise if bodies or persons for which the state would not be liable under the Convention machinery were to be treated as public authorities for the purpose of the Act (*"public liability horizontality"*). Controversy in the parliamentary debates over the possible application of the Act to churches and religious charities centred around this issue.[82] One difficulty with using the Convention as a source of novel rights against non-state bodies is that in many instances *both* parties will have potential Convention rights to consider. This is well illustrated in a case involving the well-known charity the Royal Society for Prevention of Cruelty to Animals, in which the High Court was asked to give a declaration on the legality of a proposed change in the membership rules. It held that Article 11 of the ECHR (the right to freedom of association) included the right of the Society to refuse membership to potential applicants who the society thought might damage its objectives (including those seeking to reverse its stance against hunting with dogs). The applicants had no countervailing right of freedom of expression which demanded admittance. For other reasons, however, the declaration was refused.[83] The decision can be read as a denial of horizontal rights (of freedom of expression)[84] but equally, in a different sense, it affirms that the right of freedom of association extends to relations between private associations and individuals, at least by way of defence.

A third type of horizontality (*"intermediate horizontality"*) is where a public authority stands between (as an intermediary) two private parties. The authority may have powers to protect one person against infringements of their Convention rights emanating from another private person: the effect of section 6 may be to compel the public authority to intervene where it has such powers. The position of press regulators may raise such issues in future.[85]

The remaining three possible types of horizontal application focus on the role of the courts. Judges exercising discretionary powers in private litigation must do so in conformity with Convention rights, since courts are counted as public authorities under section 6(3)(a) (*"remedial horizontality"*). It is clear also, irrespective of the Act, that the Convention should be influential in the general development of the common law as it applies between private parties (*"indirect horizontality"*). Finally,

---

[82] HL Debs, 5 Feb 1998, cols 805*ff*; HC Debs, vol 312, 20 May 1998, cols 1014ff; for analysis: I Leigh, "Towards a Christian Approach to Religious Liberty" in P Beaumont, *Christian Perspectives on Human Rights and Legal Philosophy* (Carlisle, Paternoster, 1998) 83–99.

[83] *Royal Society for the Prevention of Cruelty to Animals* v. *Attorney-General* [2001] 3 All ER 530 (Ch), Lightman J. However, for other reasons relating to the arbitrary nature of the process, the proposed change in membership rules could not be implemented.

[84] See, however, the comments of Sedley LJ (in *Hello!* v. *Douglas* [2001] 2 WLR 992 (CA)).

[85] At the time of writing there are reportedly several actions pending against the Press Complaints Commission. Cf *R* v. *Broadcasting Standards Council, ex parte BBC* [2000] 3 WLR 1327, in which the Court of Appeal had to determine in the context of an application for judicial review whether the BSC had applied the correct understanding of "privacy" (used in the Broadcasting Act 1996). The high street electrical retailer, Dixons, complained of secret filming in one of its shops by BBC journalists for a consumer affairs programme. The case was decided before the coming into force of the HRA. However, had it come later the BSC would have been regarded as a public authority (although the BBC probably would have as well). A case brought against the Commission involving a similar complaint against a commercial broadcaster would raise intermediary issues.

and more controversially, it could be argued that the inclusion of courts as public authorities requires effect to be given to Convention rights in all private common law litigation, whether or not the pre-incorporation law was uncertain by the creation of wholly new causes of action (*"full"* or *"direct"* *horizontality*). It is these three possible court-centred types of horizontality that the remainder of the account here concentrates upon.

The position of the court may lead to ingenious attempts to smuggle Convention arguments into otherwise routine civil actions. For instance, an unsuccessful attempt was made by residents living near to Biggin Hill airport to have their Convention arguments raised in the construction of a lease in an action between the landlord (Bromley LBC) and the airport operator (the tenant).[86] They argued that their Convention rights were engaged because, as a public authority, the court was involved in the construction of the lease after the coming into force of the HRA (although the lease had been entered into in 1994). On this foundation the residents argued that the court had a duty to construe the lease compatibly with their Convention rights and so to respect their private lives and homes by prohibiting scheduled air services from the airport.[87] Moreover, it was suggested that since any declaration that the court made would affect the residents' rights as victims (under section 7(1) of the HRA), they were entitled to intervene as third parties. The residents' action was opportunist in the sense that had the landlord and tenant litigation not been before the court (so opening the "court as public authority" argument), the bar on retroactive use of the HRA as a sword[88] would have been fatal to any attempt to sue the council directly.

One of the undoubted dangers of importing human rights standards into contractual relations is that of undermining the certainty and intentions of the parties. The judge pointed out that although section 3(1) of the HRA required Convention-friendly interpretation of statutes, including those preceding the Act, there was no corresponding provision for contracts and leases. To the contrary, there was consistent authority that a contract was to be construed according to the factual context at the time that it was entered into, which, in this case, did not include consideration by the council of the Convention.[89] The judge argued that

---

[86] *Biggin Hill Airport v. Bromley London Borough Council, The Times,* 9 January 2001.

[87] Alternatively, an implied term prohibiting Bromley from interfering with their Convention rights should be read into the lease or the user clause should be read down after the coming into force of HRA in so far as it interfered with Convention rights. These arguments were presumably premised on the fact that the landlord was itself a public authority.

[88] HRA 1998, s. 22(4).

[89] The same reasoning disposed of the implied term argument. This reasoning is not wholly persuasive since it could be argued that the duty of the court under s. 6 required a fresh approach. (Contrast the position of a consumer contract where statutory horizontality can be invoked: *Wilson v. First County Trust Ltd* [2001] 3 WLR 42 (CA), discussed above.)

Whether this principle can apply in the same way to decisions of public authorities post-HRA must be debatable and would depend on whether making a contract was taken to be in the nature of a private function: s. 6(5). Recognition that a public authority must act compatibly with other peoples' Convention rights even when acting as landlord would be a natural development of jurisprudence requiring the property rights of public landowners to be constrained on other public law grounds: *R v. Somerset County Council, ex parte Fewings* [1995] 1 WLR 1037 (CA); *Wheeler v. Leicester City Council* [1985] AC 1054.

if the court found in favour of the tenant on the user clause point this would not affect the residents' Convention rights and nor would any declaration that the court granted. He therefore declined to allow the residents to be joined in the proceedings. In any event it is plain that the judge was of the opinion that overt consideration of Article 8 would have made no material difference, since the council had not in his view failed to prohibit, through its powers as landlord, any interference with the residents' Convention rights.

The case clearly shows that victims may be tempted to invoke the duties of the court as a public authority when direct attack on one of the principal actors is barred.[90] If this route is open it will of course be available also where both the plaintiff and defendant are private sector actors, both as regards their own Convention rights and, perhaps, where a third party attempts to intervene.

The position of the court as public authority proved decisive in the next case to be considered, which concerned injunctions to protect the child murderers of the toddler Jamie Bulger.[91] In an unprecedented ruling, Butler-Sloss J granted an injunction *contra mundum* to prevent their whereabouts after release from custody or their new identities from being revealed. In two respects the decision breaks new ground. Previously, and quite exceptionally, injunctions have been issued to protect convicted notorious child criminals from further intrusive publicity until they reach adulthood under the wardship jurisdiction. This had been done in the case of Thomson and Venables, but since they had reached majority[92] the wardship approach could no longer apply. The Court found the basis for further restriction in the law of confidence. Secondly, the court order was directed at people who were not parties to the action—contrary to the well-known dictum of Lord Eldon in *Iveson* v. *Harris*[93] that an injunction cannot be granted except against a party to the suit. In the words of the judge:[94]

> "we are entering a new era, and the requirement that the courts act in a way that is compatible with the Convention, and have regard to European jurisprudence, adds a new dimension to those principles".

Butler-Sloss J's decision extends the positive duty of the state to protect individuals from threats to their lives. The judge equated the statements of the European Court of Human Rights about the *state's* duties with the duty of the *court* as a public authority under section 6. This is something of a stretch from the most similar Convention decision, *Osman* v. *UK*,[95] where it was the *police* that had failed to

---

[90] It can be safely predicted that it will be attempted, for example, to circumvent the three month time limit on judicial review.

[91] *Venables* v. *News Group Newspapers* [2001] 1 All ER 908 (Fam D).

[92] An earlier notorious child murderer, Mary Bell, had been protected into adulthood, but by then she had a daughter of her own who the court was keen to shield from intrusive journalists; see: *Re X (a minor) (wardship: injunction)* [1984] 1 WLR 1422.

[93] (1802) 7 Ves 251, 32 ER 102)

[94] *Venables* v. *News Group Newspapers* [2001] 1 All ER 908, 939 (Fam D).

[95] (1998) 29 EHRR 245. The controversial equation by the European Court of Human Rights of the public policy exception in domestic tort law with a denial of a "right to court" under Art. 6 has attracted criticism: *Barrett* v. *Enfield BC* [1999] 3 WLR 79, 84 per Lord Browne-Wilkinson. For a sustained academic critique see C Gearty, "Unravelling *Osman*" (2001) 64 *MLR* 159.

provide adequate protection for the victim of crime, following repeated threats. It might be argued that the court's role is more diffuse and its responsibility less obviously engaged than a branch of the executive. Judges do not act operationally and depend on others to bring knowledge of pressing threats before them and to enforce their orders. A second decision of the Strasbourg court, however, directly concerns judicial responsibility. In *A* v. *UK* the Court found that the UK had violated Article 3 in failing to protect a victim of physical abuse by his stepfather.[96] The stepfather had been tried for assault but acquitted by a jury applying the parental "reasonable chastisement" exception. The state was liable for the failure of the judicial process to secure a conviction in circumstances where it was judged that exceptionally important Convention rights of the victim were at stake. The separation of powers is no shield to Convention liability and it can be argued that section 6 of the HRA has similar domestic effect. It is clear from Butler-Sloss J's judgment that responsibility for preventing harm to Thomson and Venables weighed heavily upon her once she was satisfied of the reality of the danger. After citing *Osman* she stated:[97]

> "In the present case, the authority is this court. I know of the existence of a real risk, which may become immediate if confidentiality is breached."

The inventiveness of the court faced with a claim that its actions as a public authority could lead to a breach of Convention rights contrasts starkly with the Biggin Hill airport case.

The decision lends little support, however, to the campaign to create a right of privacy by virtue of the "horizontal" application of Article 8 (the right to respect for one's private life). The judge specifically stated that the Human Rights Act was engaged because of the court's role as a public authority,[98] and doubted that it created a free-standing cause of action based directly on the Convention.[99] Moreover, she suggested that had there been no credible threat to the physical well being of Thomson and Venables so that Articles 2 and 3 were not in consideration, the case might not have justified issuing an injunction under Article 8 alone. The mode of reasoning and the outcome support the approach of several commentators that it is permissible to use the Convention both to broaden the existing common law (here on confidentiality) and to develop (or inhibit) remedies, in this instance relating to injunctions.

---

[96] *A* v. *UK* (1998) 27 EHRR 611. Nevertheless, there are important differences: in *A* the assault had occurred whereas in *Thomson* it was not merely anticipated but also dependent on a set of hypothetical circumstances. Secondly, there is the indirect nature of the threats and responsibility for them. The threat to Thomson and Venables came not from the newspapers, but from people who might act on information that they might publish. The court was no more responsible for the newspapers' actions than the newspapers would be for the actions of their readers. The experience of a recent campaign run by *The News of the World* was, however, fresh in the minds of all concerned (the judge referred to it [2001] 1 All ER 908, 936): that newspaper had run a campaign in which it published photographs of convicted paedophiles, leading to an outbreak of vigilante-style violence, harassment and forcible eviction.

[97] *Venables* v. *News Group Newspapers* [2001] 1 All ER 908, 934.

[98] *Ibid*, 917–18.

[99] *Ibid*, 918.

The courts came nearer to the long-expected creation of a right of privacy in a second breach of confidence case, this time an action brought by the actors Michael Douglas and Catherine Zeta-Jones to prevent *Hello!* magazine from publishing unauthorised photographs of their wedding.[100] The couple had an exclusive commercial agreement for publication of photos with a rival magazine, *OK!*, who were also joined to the action. The Court of Appeal declined to grant an injunction to restrain publication of the photographs because the balance of convenience (the test to be applied in the case of an interim injunction) favoured publication, although at least two of the three judges believed that an action for breach of confidence was likely to succeed at trial. Lord Justice Sedley described the plaintiffs as having a "powerfully arguable case" that they had a right to privacy which English law would recognise and in appropriate circumstances, protect. He argued that this need no longer be grounded, as in the past, in an artificially constructed relationship of confidentiality between the intruder and the victim but could now stand on its own feet as a legal principle drawn from the "fundamental value of personal autonomy".[101] In the same way Keene LJ argued that the difference between recognition of privacy per se and confidentiality was now merely semantic.

Sedley LJ used the court's duty to consider the probability of success at trial as an opportunity to elaborate, obiter, on the possible recognition of a right of privacy. He took section 12(4) of the Human Rights Act (which requires the court to have "particular regard" to the importance of freedom of expression) as evidence that Article 10 at least could apply horizontally between private individuals. Moreover, to the extent that "the rights of others" were a recognised limitation under Article 10(2), the court would then be bound to consider Article 8 also. The reasoning is ingenious and may suffice to insulate section 12 from the charge that in preferring freedom of expression to respect for private life Parliament unwittingly violated the ECHR.[102] Its limitations should be also noted, however. It only goes so far as to show that Article 8 is relevant in decisions over whether to restrain publication; it does not establish that Article 8 should be recognised to the extent of conferring an action in damages. In Hohfeldian terms, section 12 of the HRA may require Article 8 to be treated as a liberty but it does not require it to be treated as a claim-right. Whether the Human Rights Act finally tips the balance towards recognition of privacy will await another day, but there are clear hints in that direction in these judgments.[103]

---

[100] *Douglas v. Hello! Ltd* [2001] 2 WLR 992 (CA).

[101] *Ibid*, 1025.

[102] Both Sedley and Keene LJJ found that internal consistency required s. 12 to be interpreted in the light of the earlier duty under s. 3, to interpret legislation (including the HRA itself) to give effect so far as is possible to Convention rights: *ibid*, 1028 and 1031–2, respectively.

[103] *Ibid*, 1026 per Sedley LJ, arguing that if confidentiality does not already comply with the Convention then the innovation "is precisely the kind of incremental change for which the Act is designed"; and 1036 per Keene LJ. For the argument that the Convention would be the pretext for rather than the cause of any such development see Leigh, above n. 75.

V CONCLUSION

If the Human Rights Act is the catalyst for the recognition of a general right of privacy or the introduction of substantive judicial review plainly it will be seen as of major and lasting constitutional significance. Some of these developments might have come about in the long run without the Act, but at the very least the process has been accelerated. Ultimately the changed judicial climate and creativity that it has ushered in may be more important than the lack of formal powers for the courts to strike down legislation. And there can be little doubt that the climate has changed dramatically. The courts are now entertaining inventive Convention arguments on a daily basis as they grapple to graft into UK law a substantial body of Convention jurisprudence. Although for the most part settled principles have been re-affirmed on Convention grounds, there has been the occasional surprise.

By far the biggest to date was the Scottish "temporary sheriffs" case.[104] There the system of appointing lower level judges for one year at a time and the power to recall (that is, dismiss) them were found to potentially compromise their independence and to constitute a violation of Article 6 (which requires a fair and public hearing before an independent and impartial tribunal). The ruling was quickly heeded south of the border by the Lord Chancellor and the conditions on which deputy recorders were employed was speedily changed. The case sent shockwaves reverberating around the judicial system in part for reasons of self-interest but also because it demonstrates that even the most established constitutional principles may be open to reconsideration in the light of Convention jurisprudence.

Elsewhere the turmoil predicted by some critics as a result of the Act has failed to materialise. The Conservative Shadow Home Secretary, Ann Widdicombe, welcomed the new Act with apocalyptic visions of the courts being paralysed with reckless and unsustainable Convention rights claims brought by "cranks and busybodies". As has been noted, however, if anything the showing in criminal cases has been disappointing especially since, above all else, the Convention is intended to protect individuals from the state. A few judges perhaps share these misgivings and Lord McCluskey's lack of enthusiasm. If so they have kept their own counsel and resorted instead to more technical means of limiting the impact of the Convention.

Overall it can be said that the reception of Convention case law has been considerable. Not surprisingly, some individual judges appear more enthusiastic in their recourse to Strasbourg material than others and a variety of techniques in the use of these cases (some constraining and some empowering) is emerging. In short, a cluster of lawyer-like skills is developing around a new source of law. There is every sign that the common law will take the incorporation of the Convention in its stride.

---

[104] *Starrs* v. *Ruxton* (2000) SLT 42.

Index

USA (*cont.*):
  Constitution (*cont.*):
    First Amendment, 11, 35, 92, 94–5, 151,
      154–5, 157, 160, 162, 165–6, 169, 171,
      207
    originalist approach to, 20–2, 26, 43
    viewed as living organism, 22–3, 26–7
    constitutional straight jacket, 104–6
    Native American tribes, 244–5
    Supreme Court, 11, 20–7, 94, 150, 153, 161,
      165–6, 168, 210, 245, 260, 271–2
    and constitutional questions, 12–13
    evolutionary constitionalism of, 22–3, 26–7
    isolationist stance, 152
  utilitarian approach, 9, 16, 30–1, 33, 45–6, 205

Van Haegendoren, 247
viewpoint-neutrality principle, 11, 154–5, 161–2
virtue ethics, 258
vision of society, 92–100, 102–3, 109, 135, 207,
    278–9
Volokh, 158
Volpp, 216

Wade, 68–9, 78–9, 81, 336–7
Waldron, 5, 8–9, 14, 30–1, 37, 40–1, 190, 191,
    193–5, 198–200, 202–3, 205–9, 219,
    223, 225, 234
Wales, 210
Walker, 149–50, 169
Wall, 329
Walsh, 157
Waluchow, 200–2
Warbrick, 11
Ward, 232
Warren, 22, 168
Wash, 245
Wednesbury test, 333, 335

Weiler, 66
Weinstein, 11
Weisbrod, 217
Wellman, 208
Wennergren, 144
West, 36
Whanaungatanga, 258
Whyte, G, 45, 54
Whyte, 66
Wickliffe, 229
Widdicombe, 343
Wight, 212
Wilberforce, 3, 9
Williams, B, 197
Williams, M, 211, 222
Williams, W, 145
Wilson, 112, 115–16
Wilson, M, 224
Wilson, W, 137
Winter, 180
women, 166–7
  rights of, 160, 168, 170, 175–8, 253, 257,
      283–4, 298
Wong, 197
Wood, 43
Wyman,152

Yeatman, 224
Yilmaz-Dogan, 145
York, 243
Young, A, 51
Young, I, 146–7, 211, 221
Yrigoyen, 142
Yugoslavia, 303
Yun, 154

Zimbabwe, 295
Zola, 172

Printed in the United Kingdom
by Lightning Source UK Ltd.
106079UKS00001B/112